Hindustani Music

A Tradition in Transition

New Vistas in Indian Performing Arts

No. 1 Hindustānī Music and the Aesthetic Concept of Form by Anjali Mittal (ISBN 81-246-0134-8)

No. 2 Hindustani Sangeet and a Philosopher of Art — Music, Rhythm and Kathak Dance — *vis-à-vis* — Aesthetics of Susanne K. Langer by S.K. Saxena (ISBN 81-246-0180-1)

No. 3 Speaking of Dance — The Indian Critique by Mandakranta Bose (ISBN 81-246-0172-0)

No. 4 Performing Artistes in Ancient India by Iravati (ISBN 81-246-0207-7)

No. 5 Ritual as Ideology : Text and Context in Teyyam by T.V. Chandran (ISBN 81-246-0275-1)

No. 6 Tantra — Mantra — Yantra in Dance : An Exposition of Kathaka (ISBN 81-246-0268-9)

New Vistas in Indian Performing Arts, no. 7

Hindustani Music

A Tradition in Transition

by
Deepak S. Raja

Foreword by
Pandit Shivkumar Sharma

Introduction by
Lyle Wachovsky

D.K.Printworld (P) Ltd.
New Delhi

Cataloging in Publication Data — DK
[Courtesy: D.K. Agencies (P) Ltd. <docinfo@dkagencies.com>]

Raja, Deepak S., 1948 -
Hindustani music : a tradition in transition /
by Deepak S. Raja: foreword by Shivkumar
Sharma ; introduction by Lyle Wachovsky.
p. cm. (New vistas in Indian performing arts, no. 7)
Includes bibliographical references (p.)
Includes index.
ISBN 8124603200 (Hbk.)
ISBN 8124603219 (Pbk.)

1. Hindustani music — Theory. 2. Music — India.
I. Title. II. Series : New vistas in Indian performing arts, no. 7

DDC 780.954 21

ISBN 81-246-0320-0 (Hbk)
ISBN 81-246-0321-9 (Pbk)
First Published in India in 2005

Published and printed by:
D.K. Printworld (P) Ltd.
Regd. office : *'Sri Kunj'*, F-52, Bali Nagar
New Delhi - 110 015
Phones : (011) 2545-3975; 2546-6019; *Fax* : (011) 2546-5926
E-mail: dkprintworld@vsnl.net
Web: www.dkprintworld.com

To
my mother
Smt. Kamlini Raja
who gave me my love of music
and of literature
and so much else!

FOREWORD

Change is the only permanent reality in music. Even the music of the same *gharānā* changes from generation to generation. No musician can be a perfect xerox of his *guru*. This is the way it has been, this is the way it will remain, and this is the way it should be. It is this process that allows new styles to emerge, and new genres of music to be created. If classical music does not change constantly, it will stagnate, and become irrelevant to society.

Along with accepting the permanence of change, we have to acknowledge that, in music, as in other fields, each generation is attuned to certain values based on the environment in which it has been brought up. Because of their conditioning, a majority of people tend to develop firm notions about what is good and what is bad, or what is right and what is wrong, and find change difficult to accept. Their initial response to anything new is often rejection, and even condemnation. It is only gradually that society begins to discover the elements of truth in the newer manifestations of human endeavour, and concedes legitimacy to them.

To develop an intelligent approach to change and diversity in music, we have to recognize that classical music, like any other art form, evolves in society in response to the changing socio-economic realities, and sustains itself by fulfilling the cultural needs of society. Its evolution is the result of an interaction between musicians and their audiences and reflects the quality of the relationship they wish to forge between them.

In our own era, say a little before that, performances of classical music were confined to the courts of the Mahārājās and Nawābs. Outside this circle, concerts took place primarily in private gatherings. They were either "Jumme-kā-takiyā" (Friday evening gatherings) or special occasions where either a musician's son was getting married, or some musician was hosting a commemorative concert for a deceased father or relative. Sometimes, a local aristocrat hosted these concerts. In most cases, the organizers and the audiences were either musicians, or close friends and relatives of musicians — in short, people of considerable discernment in matters of classical music. The event had virtually no financial implications for anyone. This was the chamber-music stage of evolution of our tradition. Considering the context of these gatherings, the music of the era was naturally of a very high standard, very intellectual, very competitive, and perhaps even intimidating.

In the second quarter of the twentieth century, music came out of the chamber music context into the public arena. These were also the sunset years of British rule and the era of Mahārājās and Nawābs as patrons of music. That was the time when scholars like Pandit V.N. Bhatkhande, and enthusiastic patrons like Jeevanlal Mattoo in Lahore and Lala Babu in Calcutta started organizing music conferences. At that stage, musicians were still poorly paid; and audiences were not large — maybe 500 or 700 people at the most. But, musicians got an opportunity to acquire a following, and create a market for their music. Around the same time, the radio and the gramophone record also started taking music all over the country. So, there was an opportunity as well as an attraction for reaching out to audiences — of shaping a career in music.

From this stage onwards, the receptivity of audiences became an important determinant of the quality of music that was performed.

I am sure that, out of audiences 500 or 700 strong in that era, 100 per cent of the listeners were not knowledgeable about the intricacies of music. The proportion of audiences who understood, for instance, the nuances of the *gāndhāra* of Darbārī was probably not much higher than it is today. From that stage to present times, audiences have become larger, their profile has changed, their expectations from music have changed, and the media for exposure to music have grown in number and reach. But, as a percentage of the total population, I doubt if classical music audiences are much larger today than they were 50 years ago. I also doubt if the ratio of the discerning to the rest is very much smaller today.

I am driving at two points here. Firstly, that music has changed much more because society has changed, and not as much because the discerning audiences have been reduced to a small minority. Secondly, despite dramatic changes in the quality of music, which some regard as signs of decay, the musicians who enjoy stature along with popularity today exhibit the same values as those of the early twentieth century, whom we mention with reverence. And this quality is what I call the "Musician's Truth."

The "Musician's Truth" touches the mind, heart, and soul of audiences irrespective of their level of discernment. This truth goes beyond *rāga* grammar, and aspects of music theory. People relate to music in a million different ways, and it is futile for a musician to think that he can tailor his music to specific audience profiles and needs. The only thing he can rely on is a steadfast commitment to the "Musician's Truth," and help his audiences to become receptive to it. He may not accomplish this in a year, or five years, or even ten years. But, abandoning it is no solution to his relevance as a musician. If this element of "Truth" is missing from a musician's art, even the undiscerning listener will be uneasy, though he may not be able to tell you why he is uneasy. If it is present, even the total ignoramus will go home happy, and will return for more. In the short run, a musician may be able to create a niche for himself without the "Musician's Truth." But, he will find it impossible to retain that position without a secure grip over it.

The foundation of the "Musician's Truth" is sincerity and seriousness of purpose. This is reflected in several facets of music, which have remained, and will remain, fundamental to our music. A musician's intonation should be perfect. Whatever his interpretation of a *rāga*, his exposition of it should be consistent and coherent. He should organize his musical material neatly and logically. There should be a reasonable balance between the melodic and rhythmic elements in his music. While a degree of partiality to either melodic or rhythmic elements is acceptable in our tradition, an obsession with either of them at the cost of the other deprives the music of its aesthetic value. These qualities qualify as good music by any yardstick of value.

The "Musician's Truth" has exhibited amazing resilience for over a century now, and I have no doubt that it will continue to attract musicians in sufficient numbers for the tradition to survive. However, I am concerned about the threats that have emerged in the last decades of the twentieth century. The threat comes from two recent developments — the tidal wave of consumerism, and the "commoditization" of music.

It takes 10 or 15 years of rigorous training to groom a classical musician, and another 10 to 12 years of concert experience for him to reach his peak level in the profession. A life in classical music requires the musician to defer his economic aspirations until he is about 40. This is asking for a lot of self-denial from a musician who sees a successful pop singer achieve a glamorous lifestyle at the age of 20 or 25.

This reality may, or may not, shrink the inflow of top class talent into classical music. But, it will certainly encourage classical musicians to think in terms of a "strategy," in which the "Musician's Truth" becomes the first casualty. With the growing impatience of musicians to live well, and an environment that offers ample opportunities for exposure, we now find a large number of talented musicians struggling — somehow, and even anyhow — to create a comfortable niche for themselves. This tendency is crowding the music market with a lot of dishonest classical music.

However, there is no reason to be pessimistic about the future of Hindustani music. I believe so because a few of the musicians struggling in the "somehow-anyhow" circuit might stumble upon the "Musician's Truth," even if inadvertently. Moreover there will always be musicians outside this circuit who have the *junūna* (passion/commitment) to pursue the "Musician's Truth" irrespective of the financial consequences. The number of such musicians has always been small, and will remain small.

The task before the community of musicians and music-lovers is to make the world of Hindustani music more receptive to the "Musician's Truth," which will continue to shine forth, though almost certainly in less homogeneous and more unfamiliar manifestations. This requires us to rise above our conditioning, and open our minds to change and variety. It also requires us to drop the arrogance of the classical music world, and appreciate the manifestations of the "Musician's Truth" in other forms of music — semi-classical, folk and even popular.

It is in this context, that I commend Deepak Raja's book "Hindustani Music: A Tradition in Transition" as a panoramic, and serious, review of the Hindustani music tradition in the post-Independence era. Deepak is an author with a keen analytical mind, imbued with a scientific approach. His chapters on *rāga* grammar, *rāga* authenticity, *rāga* chemistry, and his introductory essays on Dhrupad, Khayāl, Ṭhumarī and Ṭappā can be of immense value to music students and scholars. His essay on the time-theory of *rāga*s is a thought-provoking piece of writing, which deserves the attention of the music fraternity in view of the changing context of music performance and enjoyment. I may not personally agree with all his views on the current trends in Hindustani music. However, I acknowledge them as representing those of his generation of hard-core *rasika*s, who find themselves in a minority today.

I sincerely hope that this book will be widely read, and will encourage serious discussion and debate on different facets of Hindustani music. I wish Deepak success in his endeavours as a student of Hindustani music and as an author.

May 16, 2004
Mumbai

Shivkumar Sharma

PREFACE

This book is a collection of essays written between 1996 and 2003. Some of them have appeared in *Sruti*, the performing arts monthly published from Chennai; some are papers published in other journals or read at seminars; and the rest are backgrounders forming part of my commentaries on recordings produced by India Archive Music Ltd. (IAM) New York.

The moment this book was envisaged, the sub-title, "A tradition in transition" acquired a degree of inevitability. This meta-theme pervades the essays featured in this book, and has been central to my efforts at interpreting the Hindustani musical tradition. The theme also reflects the very essence of Indian culture, with its infinite propensity for change without losing its intrinsic character.

The book begins with a Prologue, which sets out the perspectives that have guided my writings on music up to this stage. The main body of the book is divided into six parts.

Part I deals with some important societal, cultural, economic and technological drivers of Hindustani music in the contemporary context. These facets of our musical culture have received some attention from Western musicologists. Although I have no quarrel with alien perspectives, the emergence of an Indian viewpoint on them is, I hope, helped by my consideration of the issues.

Part II deals with musical forms and structures. In this part, I have dealt with issues pertaining to architectural and sculptural, rather than stylistic aspects of Hindustani music, and some presentation formats. The limited choice of subjects for this part could reflect merely the urgency with which the Hindustani music community, I feel, needed to take cognisance of present-day tendencies.

Part III deals with the world of *rāga*s. The papers in this part attempt to give the reader a feel for the notion of *rāga*-ness, understood intuitively by cultivated Indian listeners, but an enigma for uninitiated, though enquiring, audiences. However, the number of connoisseurs who found these essays informative has surprised me.

Part IV presents backgrounders on the four major genres of Hindustani vocal music — Dhrupad, Khayāl, Ṭhumarī, and Ṭappā. They attempt to outline the historical, structural as well as aesthetic aspects of these genres.

Part V consists of backgrounders on the major solo melodic instruments of the Hindustani tradition. The specific recordings for which they were originally written have determined the thrust of these backgrounders. For this reason, they might appear to lack the uniformity of format and coverage evident in the backgrounders on the vocal genres. However, they do uniformly highlight the essential as well as the little-known facets of the instruments, and have been appreciated widely by lovers of Hindustani music.

Part VI presents a glossary of words in italics, a list of suggested readings, and an index. The list of suggested readings includes sources I have relied on, but is intended, in general, for the relative beginner and the cognoscenti of music, rather than for scholars.

This book makes no claims to scholarship. Nor is it a journalistic endeavour. It is writing that has secured the support of the most demanding Editors outside academia and deserved the attention of some astute lovers of Hindustani music in several parts of the world. Explicitly, it addresses music lovers of above-average familiarity with Hindustani music, and curiosity about its inner workings. Incidentally, it may also prove useful to other writers on music, and to scholars.

Whatever its merits, this book would have almost certainly not been in your hands, but for the Foreword written by Pandit Shivkumar Sharma, amongst our most learned, popular, and respected musicians. I have no words to thank him for helping me to reach you.

Baroda, Dec. 10, 2004 **Deepak S Raja**

CONTENTS

PART V
The Major Instruments

ACKNOWLEDGMENTS

I acknowledge the blessings of, Śrī Vighneśvara who permits this endeavour to reach fruition, and Śrī Naṭarāja and Mātā Sarasvatī who allow me access to knowledge of music.

My lifelong quest for knowledge of music has been guided by outstanding *gurus*, to all of whom I express my deepest gratitude (in chronological order): Shri Chandrakant Pandit (Gandharva), Shri Usman Khan Abdul Kareem Khan, late Shri Pulin Behari Deb Burman, Pandit Arvind Parikh, and Pandita Dhondutai Kulkarni.

In the mid-1960s, my Professor of Philosophy at Hindu College, Delhi, Dr. S.K. Saxena, offered to oversee my grooming as an aesthetician. His aspirations for me have remained unfulfilled. However, when I was ready with the manuscript of this book, he introduced me to Shri Sushil Mittal of D.K. Printworld, and made this book possible. I cannot thank him enough for his inspiration, kindness and affection.

In the 1970s, well before I became a professional journalist, three friends allowed me to test my abilities as a writer on music: Vinod Mehta as Editor of Debonair magazine, Umaima Mulla-Phiroze, as Managing Editor of the Taj Magazine, and M.J. Akbar, as Editor of Sunday magazine. I seek the compassion of the above-named for the juvenility of my responses to the glimpse they gave me of destiny.

For launching me as a writer on music with negligible proof of competence, I acknowledge my debt to Lyle Wachovsky, Managing Director of India Archive Music Ltd., New York. Since March 1996, he has kept me fully involved in his missionary task with rewarding work, unmatched friendship, and great depth of understanding. He has also given me a *carte blanche* for including any part of my work done for him in this book, and waived all copyright claims in my favour. For all his support, I remain most grateful.

My intensive and extensive exposure to recordings of India Archive Music Ltd. triggered off perspectives on several aspects of modern and contemporary music. In converting these into readable text, I have received invaluable encouragement from Kishor Merchant, Publisher of the *Mumbai Rasika*, and the late Dr. N Pattabhiraman, Editor of *Sruti*. Almost half of this book is a direct result of their encouragement and the access they gave me to their columns.

My attempts at interpreting Hindustani music have drawn immeasurable inspiration from the writings of the late Shri Vamanrao Deshpande, whom I acknowledge, in all humility, as my intellectual guide.

As a writer, my search for superior wisdom has led me repeatedly, and always fruitfully, to three mentors (in order of seniority): My Guru, Pandit Arvind Parikh, the renowned musicologist, Prof. Ashok Ranade, and my learned friend, Dr. Suvarnalata Rao. For their magnanimity and affection, I am deeply indebted to them.

In addition to these, I express my heartfelt thanks to all the musicians whom gave me interviews while I was attempting to interpret the music they have recorded for India Archive Music Ltd. Their contribution to my understanding of music, and to the writing of this book, is considerable, even if it is not identifiable.

My evolution as a writer has benefited greatly from the encouragement of a few friends, many of whom I have never met and will, perhaps, never meet. Because of their friendship, I have the satisfaction of having real people to address when I write. Else, I would have been vulnerable to the writer's risk of addressing an assumed audience, the like of which may not exist anywhere on earth.

Amongst these, I owe a special debt of gratitude to Ailsa Mathiesen and Alessandro Dozio for previewing the manuscript of this book, and to Eric Landen for a nuts-and-bolts surgery on it. Each of them has brought a different perspective to the scrutiny of this work, and enriched the final product.

"An introduction to Dhrupad" in this book is reproduced, though in edited form, from the 1999 issue of the Journal of the Indian Musicological Society, with the kind consent of the Secretary General of the Society. The paper titled "Architecture in modern Hindustani music" is reproduced from Sangeet Natak, journal of the Sangeet Natak Akademi with permission. The paper titled "An introduction to Thumree" relies substantially on the work of Prof. Peter Manuel of the City University of New York. I acknowledge, with gratitude, the prior consent of each of these authors/publishers for their waiver of copyright claims in my favour.

In preparing the manuscript of this book for acceptance by a publisher, I have received immensely valuable and affectionate help from my friend and graphic designer, Smt. Malti Gaekwad, and her associate, Shri Chetan Boda of Datasafe, Baroda. Without their inputs, this book might still have been waiting for a publisher.

The most fruitful contribution to this book has been that of Shri Susheel Kumar Mittal of D.K. Printworld, and his team. Without their professionalism, this book would not have been in your hands. I am deeply indebted to them for the trust they have reposed in my capabilities and for what they have contributed to my acceptability to a discerning audience.

I admit, without hesitation, that your willingness to open this book could have been influenced decisively by Pandit Shivkumar Sharma's Foreword, and the Introduction contributed by Lyle Wachovsky. Without their endorsement, this book could have remained largely unsold and unread.

My journey to this point would have been inconceivable without the support of my wife, Meena. She married a business executive, but ended up with a writer on music for a husband. I remain indebted to her for accepting the unpleasant surprises of life most gracefully.

For all those — named or otherwise — who have made this book possible, I wish the satisfaction of having supported a worthy beneficiary.

Deepak S. Raja

KEY TO TRANSLITERATION

अ *a* (but)	आ *ā* (palm)	इ *i* (it)
ई *ī* (beet)	उ *u* (put)	ऊ *ū* (pool)
ऋ *ṛ* (rhythm)	ए *e* (play)	ऐ *ai* (air)
ओ *o* (toe)	औ *au* (loud)	ळ* ḷ
क *ka* (skate)[1]	ख* *kha* (blockhead)[1]	ग *ga* (gate)[1]
घ *gha* (ghost)[1]	ङ *ṅa* (sing)[1]	
च *ca* (chunk)[2]	छ* *cha* (catch him)[2]	ज *ja* (john)[2]
झ *jha* (hedgehog)[2]	ञ *ña* (bunch)[2]	
ट *ṭa* (start)[3]	ठ* *ṭha* (anthill)[3]	ड *ḍa* (dart)[3]
ढ* *ḍha* (godhead)[3]	ण* *ṇa* (under)[3]	
त *ta* (path)[4]	थ *tha* (thunder)[4]	द *da* (that)[4]
ध* *dha* (breathe)[4]	न *na* (numb)[4]	
प *pa* (spin)[5]	फ* *pha* (philosophy)[5]	ब *ba* (bin)[5]
भ *bha* (abhor)[5]	म *ma* (much)[5]	
य *ya* (young)	र *ra* (drama)	ल *la* (luck)
व *va* (vile)	श *śa* (shove)	ष *ṣa* (bushel)
स *sa* (so)	ह *ha* (hum)	क्ष *kṣa* (*kṣatriya*)
त्र *tra* (*trishūl*)	ज्ञ *jña* (*jñāni*)	

अं (ं)*ṁ* (*saṁskṛti*) *ṁ anusvāra* (nasalisation of preceding vowel)

अः *ḥ* (*prātaḥ*) *ḥ visarga* (aspiration of preceding vowel)

* No exact English equivalents for these letters.

[1] guttural [2] palatal [3] lingual [4] dental [5] labial

PROLOGUE

This prologue was an afterthought. It was conceived as an Epilogue, but finds itself at the beginning of the book because referees of superior wisdom wanted it so. They felt that the book, although a collection of essays, has a uniformity of perspective — perhaps even a world-view — running through it, and that this needs to be crystallized, up-front, for the benefit of readers. They wanted me to be explicit about whom I am addressing, and what I hoped to achieve by this enterprise. This was a fair demand, and deserving of compliance.

By a conspiracy of circumstance, my writing on music has come to address cultivated listeners of Hindustani music — the connoisseurs. My endeavour has been to enhance their insights into the inner workings of modern and contemporary music. For this purpose, it is hardly necessary to distinguish between different categories of connoisseurs. For, irrespective of their level of discernment, and almost by definition, they seek to achieve a better understanding of what they hear, and of the forces that shape their musical experience.

These tasks are worthy of attention because understanding is an important pathway to enjoyment. Higher levels of understanding and enjoyment also bestow upon connoisseurs higher status and influence in the community of musicians and music lovers. And, by virtue of the status and influence that connoisseurs acquire, they fortify the cultural mechanism — nebulous though it might be — which ensures that art-music retains the features that distinguish it from other forms of music, especially entertainment.

Our society has been starved of periodical media to serve the special needs of connoisseurs. Academic journals, which might partially address these needs, are largely beyond their physical as well as conceptual reach. At the other extreme, we have the lay media, which are habitually oriented towards personalities and events, and do not serve the connoisseur's purpose either. The Internet has begun to serve the connoisseur in recent years. But, its use, especially in India, is not yet widespread. It is primarily the writers of books who have performed the task of strengthening the forces of discernment. Not surprisingly, after working through a few other media, and rejecting untested options, I have gravitated to the same medium — the book — for making this contribution to the cultural process.

Not by Accident Alone

Although I apparently became a writer on music by accident rather than deliberate design, it seems as if destiny had prepared me for this from childhood. Nature gave me the basic equipment for involvement with music. Thereafter, destiny took charge. It took me through several decades of training in music with outstanding *gurus*, representing the most respected lineages of Hindustani music. This training even enabled me to enjoy a short stint as a performing musician. It encouraged me to build up a sizeable library of significant recordings and books, and to invest a large part of my leisure in its study. It brought to me several friends amongst archivists, who generously shared their resources. It gave me several assignments in journalism, which matured my skills as a communicator in print. It allowed me a formal education and a professional trajectory, which honed an analytical ability, and enabled my observations to be made with a degree of confidence. This combination of influences has equipped me to decipher some facets of the Hindustani music tradition with a reasonable degree of satisfaction.

The ability to share this understanding with fellow connoisseurs was tested and cultivated on the job. In March 1996, when Lyle Wachovsky of India Archive Music Ltd. [IAM], New York, asked me to write a commentary [sleeve notes] for a CD he had produced, I had a reasonable reputation as a writer on media, marketing, and finance, but virtually no experience as a writer on music. He liked what I wrote, and that turned out to be a turning point in my life. It gave me my fourth profession. Between then and now [July, 2004], I have studied over 100 *rāga*s recorded for him by over 45 musicians, representing eight instruments, and all the genres of vocal music. Based on my understanding of this music, I have written commentaries of 8,000 to 18,000 words on each of them, with the total wordage now approaching a million.

For these commentaries, I interviewed as many of the musicians as was possible, and developed valuable insights into the relationship between the artist and the art. To acquire a perspective on their styles, I located recordings of their *guru*s, and attempted to identify elements of continuity as well as change between two consecutive generations. In order to understand the *rāga*s they performed, I studied authoritative texts as well as several recordings of the same *rāga*s by other contemporary and recent musicians. As this activity grew into a full-time occupation, the focused efforts, originally aimed at understanding and explaining *rāga*s, genres, lineages, and musicians, began to yield a bigger picture of what Hindustani music is, and where it is heading.

The Bigger Picture

It was this bigger picture, which triggered off my column for

Sruti, the monthly magazine on music and dance, published from Madras. When I sent the first essay for publication in 1998, I hesitantly asked the Editor if he would consider more contributions from me. I got a telegraphic reply: "Keep sending." And, that is what I did. The result was a series of essays published in *Sruti* many of which have found a place in the present book.

My writings for *Sruti* owe their content, character and inspiration to several sources. The first, of course, was my reading of what was happening to the world of Hindustani music, and the different forces shaping it. The second was the editorial environment of *Sruti*, with its bias in favour of Carnatic music. Because of this, I felt the need to deal with several issues in Hindustani music, which could help widen the appreciation of Hindustani music amongst audiences not greatly cultivated in the tradition. The third source was the set of ideas that had arisen from my involvement as a repertoire analyst for IAM. The fourth source was the thinking stimulated by the occasional papers I wrote for seminars and academic journals on music.

The *Sruti* and IAM associations have worked beautifully together. Although their audiences are different, and so is the context in which I address them, each has gained immensely from the other. Both would have been poorer in the absence of the other in my literary life. Considering that I started late in this profession, their simultaneous presence has enabled me to grow faster than I might otherwise have done.

Amongst the audiences of these media, I have acquired a few friends in several countries, all of whom are exceptionally astute musical minds. They established contact with me after reading my work, and thought it worthwhile to develop a regular correspondence on musical matters. I now habitually check out my writings with several of them — in addition to my referees closer to home — before I publish them. Their views and concerns have now become an important trigger for enlarging, deepening, and sharpening my understanding of music, and guided my writing in terms of content as well as style.

The Language Issue

It is also because of these two involvements that my work on music came to be written in English, rather than Hindi, the only language with which I am equally comfortable. My mentors amongst scholars have, in fact, pointed out that because my writings have forced me to think in English, I might have done less than justice to some Indian musicological concepts, which do not lend themselves to effective communication in English. They have even suggested that I should do all my writing first in Hindi, and then translate it into English.

I accept these comments as embarrassingly valid. Despite my comfort with English, I have struggled often to communicate certain concepts effectively. However, I have reason to believe that the outcome of my struggle has benefited my readers, though probably not in a manner that my scholarly friends would approve. In many cases, I have had to invent an expression in English to represent a complex idea, originally expressed in Sanskrit. This "invention" has often redefined the original in a contemporary conceptual framework. And, to the extent that the expression is consistent with my analytical approach, without being necessarily discordant to the original idea, it probably makes a small contribution towards making its logic accessible to audiences outside India, and even Indian audiences who think in English. I record this possibility with the support of several scholarly readers abroad, who have valued the access I have given them, for the first time, to certain concepts in Indian musicology.

I cannot, however, be satisfied with making a virtue out of an obvious weakness. My writings must move towards a more accurate expression of Indian musicological ideas in English. To this end, I must expose myself more extensively and intensively to significant writing in the Indian languages. Until then, the readers of my writings in English will have to bear with approximations, which might occasionally represent a conceptual refinement.

Predictably, along with admiration, my writings have also brought me my share of criticism. And, it seems proper that I deal with the issues that have exposed me to it.

Issues of Objectivity

In my efforts at understanding and interpreting Hindustani music, I have encountered, and dealt with, two basic phenomena — the unity within diversity, and the continuity within change. As cultural phenomena, the two are inseparable because diversity at any given point in time carries within itself the germ of change over a period of time. Both are expressions of the pluralistic and dynamic culture of a vibrant, multi-racial, multi-lingual nation.

I have sought to do justice to these features of our culture by adopting a descriptive-analytical stance, as free from a judgemental tendency as is possible. In this spirit, I have treated every piece of music, every genre, every lineage and every trend, as legitimate, as long as it claims an audience. My endeavour has been to place each of these manifestations of our musical culture in a historical perspective. Towards this end, I have sought constantly to isolate the elements of unity from those of diversity, and elements of continuity from those of change, and to proffer plausible hypotheses for the relationship between them.

Evidently, I have not been very successful in this regard. Hardliners of different schools of thought have accused me of being excessively lenient on diversity. The "Young Turks" of the music world have labelled me a rabid reactionary, while conservatives have charged me with a liberalism verging on permissiveness. These criticisms suggest either that a descriptive-analytical perspective is not particularly palatable to connoisseurs of Hindustani music, or that I have not been objective enough. The first implication, if true, I can only lament. But, the latter implication, even if only remotely valid, I must address forthrighly.

I neither command, nor claim, sufficient scholarship to establish the legitimacy or inevitability of every tendency I have observed. When a phenomenon is observed without being explained in terms of its causation, there is a likelihood of a judgemental suggestion creeping into its recording. Such possibilities arise from the musical values I have acquired in my formative years. These values are represented by the music of a few twentieth century giants — Ustad Vilayat Khan and Ustad Ali Akbar Khan amongst instrumentalists, Kesarbai Kerkar and Ustad Ameer Khan amongst *khayāl* vocalists, and Ustad Nasir Aminuddin and Nasir Moinuddin Dagar amongst *dhrupad* vocalists. I study their recordings for the sound principles of music-making they represent, but not without my critical faculties on full alert.

I am obliged to accept that, collectively, these mid-twentieth century principles might function as a yardstick against which I judge all music. I see no reason to be apologetic about the identities of the musicians whom I regard as models. Whether this automatically establishes me as a reactionary, I do not know. But, I trust this disclosure will at least protect me against the charge of weak discernment and poor taste.

The Writer's Role

More fundamentally, however, I distrust the proposition that a yardstick of musicianship militates against a writer's role in the cultural process. A writer is, after all, nothing but a connoisseur who has decided to share his understanding with other connoisseurs. And, as such, he is a part of the watchdog mechanism, which keeps art faithful to its elevating ideals. My task, as a writer, is to help connoisseurs interpret their musical experience. Such an interpretation is inconceivable without a benchmark of quality musicianship and artistic endeavour. And, the benchmark will inevitably be one as understood by my generation of music lovers. However, I am obliged, by the ethics of my profession, to be conscious of my biases, to prevent them from intruding surreptitiously upon my observations, to respect alternative benchmarks as equally legitimate, and to recognize that no yardstick is perennially relevant. In fact, it is a part of my duty to make my readers aware of alternative benchmarks, and changing yardsticks. If I have succeeded in doing this, I will be read. If I have failed, my work deserves to gather dust on the shelves of the bookstores.

Another criticism levelled against my writings is the preponderance of commercial reasoning in the interpretation of some trends evident in the music world. I have even been charged with desecrating Hindustani music by treating audiences as consumers, recording companies and impresarios as intermediaries, and musicians as service providers in the leisure industry. My critics on this count do not challenge either my reasoning or my conclusions. Their reaction almost accuses me of having exposed some conspiracy of theirs — a conspiracy of silence on the subject.

Their discomfiture is, I suspect, rooted in collective guilt. They seem angry with me for having proven, often tellingly, the extent to which money has come to drive classical music. They are aware that societies do have a choice in the extent to which they surrender any activity to the operation of market forces. Civilized societies have found ways of insulating activities related to the life of the spirit — the soul, if you like — from the operation of market forces, and protecting them against a drift towards populism and degeneration. Most civilized societies have given such protection to religion, and many have also granted it to their performing arts traditions. As enlightened members of the community, my critics feel guilty about having neglected what they know to be their responsibility towards Hindustani music. My failure, if any, is that of having touched a raw nerve, and having evoked anger, rather than action.

This brings me to the next criticism I have encountered. I have frequently been accused of adopting a provocative, and even strident, stance in my writings in the periodicals media. My critics feel that this might deny my arguments a fair chance of being evaluated on their merits. Their observation is valid, while the consequences, if as predicted, would be unfortunate.

Towards Connoisseur Activism

The provocative titles and lead-ins to my essays are, in most cases, honest to the original provocation that suggested a topic to me, and triggered off a chain of ideas which demanded verbalization with a sense of urgency. Sharing such provocations with readers is a journalistic device appropriate to the periodicals media. It is useful for flagging the target audience, drawing the reader into the writing, focusing his attention on the subject of the text, and making the writer's position on it clear at the outset. The device is particularly suitable for a magazine like *Sruti*, whose readership is oriented predominantly towards Carnatic music. When I write for a clearly journalistic medium, I am guided by my perception of the role of the connoisseur in the cultural environment, and my desire to persuade, and even exhort, him into performing that role effectively.

Until well into the twentieth century, Hindustani music was a chamber-music art, hosted by the aristocracy, with access limited to connoisseurs, and only by invitation. Audiences were small, but their depth and width of knowledge was sufficient for the fate of musicians to depend on their approval. They performed a quality control function efficiently enough to give us the era now described as the Golden Age of Hindustani music.

In the post-Independence era, technological, political, and economic changes enlarged the size of audiences, and dramatically altered the relationship between them and the musicians. The cognoscenti amongst audiences were steadily outnumbered by the *innocenti*. The connoisseur now constitutes a hopeless minority, unable to hold the musician accountable for the quality of the artistic endeavour. He is frustrated and, understandably, angry. He is angry not only with the fact of being marginalized, but also with anyone who cares to remind him of this fact. His anger arises from a sense of helplessness, which leads to a paralysis.

Consider this piece of information provided a few years ago by the Director General of All India Radio at a closed-door meeting with the Music Forum in Bombay. When the AIR discontinued the nightly broadcast of classical music on the FM channels because it was generating no advertizing revenue, the national broadcaster received one solitary letter of protest. On reasonable reckoning, these FM broadcasts would have had at least 100,000 regular listeners in a population of about 30 million affected by the decision! Whether a 100,000 protest letters would have averted this event, is a debatable point. But, the ridiculous minuteness of the protest is indicative of the paralysis that has seized the connoisseurs of Hindustani music. And, it is this that I hope to address through the provocative stance I have adopted in my writings.

By virtue of his knowledge and involvement, the connoisseur will always remain one of the pillars of Hindustani music. Having been outnumbered as a member of the audience, he can no longer perform his quality control function effortlessly by just being a listener. His responsibility as a watchdog has now grown several fold, and his task has become more difficult. If he wishes to prevent the dawn of a Stone Age in Hindustani music, he needs to make his voice heard above the din that supports the opiates of the masses.

There could yet be hope for the connoisseur's cause, and I therefore offer no apology for attempting to jolt his conscience into activism. I may not have yet achieved the perfect balance between persuasion and provocation required for this purpose. However, at this stage of life, I cannot possibly harbour delusions of being able to change the course of cultural history.

Clarity of Purpose

What drives me is the search for a better understanding of the Hindustani music tradition — ascending the ladder of connoisseurship. Professionally, I have drifted into sharing this enterprise with others. However, reaching out beyond my professional orbit is incidental to my objectives. I explain things as I understand them, but I admit I understand them a lot better when I share what I think I understand. I will continue to enlarge my own sphere of understanding; but I will wish to share my knowledge only as long as I have readers who find my efforts rewarding.

My professional work revolves around assignments from IAM, a recording company that services a global market and is inspired and given a direction by Hindustani music enthusiasts whom I have befriended through the IAM connection, primarily products of western cultures. This orbit defines my priorities for study and writing, and could easily bias my writings for periodicals and books towards a "Western" way of understanding music.

The risk of distorted priorities seems negligible because those whom I address are guiding my attention towards the more uniquely Indian aspects of our musical tradition. And, I find that their priorities seem to be entirely consistent with my own. The risk of a bias towards a "Western" way of interpreting music — whatever that might imply — probably exists. How great this risk is, I cannot tell. But, it would have been much greater if I had been conversant with Western classical music. Since this is not so, my writing works much harder at translating Indian ideas into concepts that are intelligible to alien audiences.

This effort, as it turns out, has received an encouraging response also from Indian audiences, who have encountered some of the contents of the present book either in *Sruti*, or in other media or *fora*. This would suggest that Indian connoisseurs who read English are not very different from alien enthusiasts who read English. And, if there is any damage being done to the distinctive "Indianness" of musicological ideas, it is the English language that is doing it, and not the ethnicity of the audiences I address — either explicitly or otherwise.

This hypothesis gave me the confidence to place this book in your hands, without any need to alert you in advance about its greater value either to alien or Indian audiences. This also gives me the confidence to continue writing in English as long my readers feel I am making sense. But, some day, I would like to be able to write on music in Hindi, too, even if only to capture some of the cultural meaning which probably escapes me when I write in English.

INTRODUCTION

The Indian classical music tradition, and writings on it, can be traced back to the pre-Christian era. Since then, the melodic structures, the presentation formats and the instruments, have evolved in fits and starts, and available documentation leaves us with only a patchy picture of their evolutionary path. The systematic organization of knowledge of the various facets of the Hindustani tradition gained momentum towards the end of the nineteenth century. Significantly, that period also witnessed a great flowering of the performing tradition, often described as the Golden Age of Hindustani music. Today, at the dawn of the third millennium, the tradition is experiencing yet another efflorescence — though of an entirely different kind — and is accompanied, once again, by literary activity aimed at interpreting its content and significance.

Deepak Raja's volume — Hindustani Music: A Tradition in Transition — is a welcome overview of the post-Independaence trends in Hindustani music. It provides a panoramic, rather than encyclopaedic, appraisal of important developments in Hindustani music, and confronts us with the problems that Indian classical music faces today. At the same time, Raja has a very definite point-of-view and argues it passionately. The consistency of his viewpoint may, at times, seem questionable. He acknowledges this in his Prologue by disclosing that conservatives as well as liberals have, on different occasions, had reason to criticize his writings.

The book also has very definite structural underpinnings. It is linear, in that he begins with a series of chapters providing a contemporary overview of Hindustani music and moves towards dealing with more and more specific aspects of the presentation of the music, ending with chapters on the genres of vocal music and on instruments used in presentation. It is circular in that it begins with an assessment of the effects of populism and globalism on Indian classical music and ends with acceptance of possibly the most "populist" of instruments, one introduced very recently to Indian music from outside India, the Hawaiian slide guitar.

Raja sets out the underlying approach of his argument in the very first chapter of the book. Indian classical music has suffered from a "major discontinuity" imposed upon it, as an unintended consequence, by Indian Independence. The sudden end to the royal/feudal patronage of great musicians terminated the era of music as an economically secure and hereditary profession. The depth of musicianship previously cultivated by musicians gave way to competent artistry, even as musicians became somewhat of a commodity controlled by "market forces." The concurrent evolution of a mass market involved a concomitant dumbing down of the audience. This has left the connoisseur — amongst whom Raja counts himself — and connoisseur-quality music in a state of decline and disadvantage.

Raja, as noted, is a passionate connoisseur. He accepts the obvious fact that the continuation of the circumstances that enabled the music he cherishes is an unrealistic expectation. Great musicians and music validate themselves only in, and through the environment and means that produce them. How to achieve a return to a high standard of musicianship and artistry in a world driven by commercial considerations is the author's main concern. Although, as he acknowledges, "art-music" comprises only 2 per cent of the commercial recordings market, he sees no reason why contemporary music has necessarily to be qualitatively inferior to pre-Independence music.

The first section of Raja's book deals with the identification of the problems and their causes, which the author finds to be at the root of the dilution and mediocrity that now confront Indian classical music. The first chapter outlines the overall problem — times have changed. The traditional patronage model, which produced the greatest musicians and music, is no longer viable. Social and economic forces have caused the acceptance of a new paradigm — the mass marketplace as the arbiter of taste. Indian classical music, which thrived in the narrow upscale patronage market of music-knowledgeable *rājās* and *zamīndārs*, is now in the position of being controlled by the need to earn a living in the musically unsophisticated mass market — concerts, recordings, and teaching.

On the other hand, Indian classical music and musicians are thriving. Over the past 50 years, there has been a veritable explosion of concerts, recording companies and students. The market for Indian classical music is now larger, and no longer only Indian, but worldwide. And, there has even been minimal corporate support (e.g., the ITC-sponsored Sangeet Research Academy), and government support (e.g., Madhya Pradesh-sponsored Dhrupad Kendra). The problem, Raja finds, is the quality of the music being produced.

Raja notes, "In the totality of the scenario, the bottom-line is positive for all participants, except the *rasika* (the connoisseur)." And he lays part of the problem squarely at the door of *rasika*s themselves, whose value system he explicitly questions: they are unwilling to pay for what they want. While noting that a *rasika* will hand over Rs. 2000 to his children for a ticket to an American pop icon's concert, he will grudgingly pay only Rs. 200 for a ticket to a concert by a "superstar" Indian classical musician. On the other hand, he finds that, adjusted for inflation, at the top end, contemporary classical musicians are paid two hundred per cent to five hundred per cent more per concert than were their counterparts in the 1940s. Raja explains: "Because he is in a hopeless minority, it suits everyone to ignore him (the *rasika*) and reach out to audiences at a lower level of discernment." How much money and how many connoisseurs are needed to effect a change? There are no easy answers.

The author has considered the roles of two major emerging players in the classical music market: the government and the corporations. And, while holding out hope for help from these two sources, he, more or less, dismisses both possibilities, as, realistically, the business model for corporations and the patronage model for government are both based on principles of quantitative rather than qualitative results.

Raja then considers the musicians' point of view towards achievement in the music world and the value of producing connoisseur-quality music. The author is sympathetic with the problems of today's musicians in carving out a career. But, he is critical of the fact that many fledgling musicians promote their stature by giving themselves honorifics such as *paṇḍit* or *ustād*, whose merits audiences are not qualified to judge. Having done so, they perform to the level of their audiences' understanding, often the only level they know. Evidently, this phenomenon increases the risks of music as a profession, and provides little motivation for artists to maintain or achieve connoisseur-level abilities. The author believes that artists can, themselves, correct the ensuing inequity in the rewards system.

He acknowledges the extinction of the old model in which an artist had limited options — either to be a *paṇḍit* or an *ustād* who found royal patronage, "or a nobody with his next meal being uncertain." He advocates a new price-value relationship model, which allows a collective of musicians, rather than the audiences, to validate a musician's status. The author suggests the formation of a musician's guild that could act as a body to protect each member of the profession: an aspect of which would be a grading system for musicians, that also links fees to accomplishment levels. At the same time, he acknowledges that the profession lacks either the enthusiasm or the leadership for such a movement.

In a significant chapter dealing with the place and value of archival recordings, in raising both audience and musician standards by providing easy access to music from the past, the author also analyses the phenomena of acoustic and aesthetic obsolescence in music, and the value of digital restoration technologies. The author sees great advantage to young musicians in that "the archival movement partially corrects a significant discontinuity . . . the growing shortage of competent teachers . . . ." On the other hand, he infers, interestingly, that commercial availability of archival recordings might have a significant impact on the sales of recordings by contemporary musicians. The essay ends by acknowledging that the overall benefit of archival recordings are subject to the commercial considerations of the recording companies, which might release these recordings: "If faster or sharply focused results are desired, the music community will have to take the initiative in converting the rewards of technology into a trigger for a veritable renaissance."

Continuing the exploration of continuity and change, the book addresses the rapid loss in the last half of the twentieth century of the individuality and variety that characterized the pre-Independence and pre-technological Indian musical world. *Gharānā* uniqueness, an individuality of presentation style, was previously a musician's "wealth." Unrestricted access to this wealth, and its dilution by various socio-economic changes has fostered a homogenization of styles. The author admits to the paradox here: that the greatest vocalists of the twentieth century broke through *gharānā* barriers, and many musicians considered authentic *gharānā* stylists had actually received training from multiple *guru*s representing a multiplicity of *gharānā*s. The *gharānā*s, so it would seem, took care of continuity along with diversity, while everything else took care of itself. Excellence was not either directly or necessarily dependent on the restrictive facet of the *gharānā* system. The author concludes that we are moving towards a new model or models of "the balance between continuity and change and, between homogeneity and diversity, (which) will be decided by how audiences want art-music to relate to the world around them, and to their inner worlds."

The book has an important section dealing with specific avenues of Indian classical music presentation and understanding. The structural aspect of modern Hindustani music receives astute consideration in a chapter that deals with the logic of progression. Music, like any other language, needs commonly agreed upon structure to be understood. The contemporary trend towards shortening or truncating some aspects of structure and progression and entirely doing away with others, leads towards a situation of enjoying music — or listening to music — on the basis of vague familiarity with a phrase or theme. Without specific structural and progression formats, which are also meant to open up expansive creative possibilities, exactly the opposite will happen and is happening — performances are shorter, the content less complex, enriching, and rewarding.

With specific reference to instrumental music, the author explores the shortcomings of the trend towards widening individual instrumental idioms by borrowing from others in search of novelty, which sadly tends to result in a dilution, if not denial, of the idiom. He appears to accept the traditional notion of hierarchy in the musical arts, which accords the highest status to the vocal expression. This yardstick also determines his notion of hierarchy within the instrumental segment. By his argument, instrumental music validates itself either by getting closer to the experience of vocal music, or by exploiting the distinctive features of the instruments. After providing examples of stylistic innovations he approves of — by his yardstick — and those he questions, the author argues that as a tendency, drifting towards an "inferior" idiom in search of novelty risks creating *apaṅga* (crippled) music. His answer is not to lose sight of *aucitya*, which he defines as "a sense of propriety, of balance and moderation." His is a cry of anguish as he acknowledges that: ". . . Hindustani instrumentalists, including some of the most successful ones, might be answerable for the results of their innovative zeal."

In his chapters on *jugalbandī* and *tihāī*, the author has his say on the contemporary tendencies on the part of both musicians and promoters towards excitement, newness, and entertainment as substitutes for music of substance, and the problems of the enthusiastic public embrace of these cheap shots at art and artistry. In recent years, *jugalbandī*, far from being at its best — the intermingling and meshing of two distinct musical personalities in a way that made the sum greater than its parts — has become a promotional tool hyped as ground-breaking, innovative, refreshingly different, experimental and, rarely, if ever, rising to the level of musical promise that promoters imply or suggest as possible.

The *tihāī*, once a spontaneous, subtle, and highly improvized structural tactic, used by vocalists and instrumentalists alike as an occasional means of achieving contrast and surprise, has come to be a replacement for improvization, as a crowd-pleasing means of conveying rhythmic excitement and titillation, easily grasped by and appealing to today's unsophisticated audiences.

Part III of the book is, literally and figuratively, the heart of this book. In this section, the author presents and analyses in depth the basics upon which the melodic framework of Indian classical music is structured in theory and in performance: what a *rāga* is, what its characteristics are, what makes it identifiable and intelligible, what differentiates one *rāga* from another, the centrality of the emotional expression to the *rāga*'s aural experience. The author considers the basic components, which identify and distinguish one *rāga* from another, and how these components are used creatively to innovate compound *rāga*s that mesh in a manner that creates a distinctive new entity/*rāga*.

The association of each north Indian *rāga* with a time of day and/or season of the year is a conjunction that is unique. The author acknowledges the traditional basis and longevity of this convention and its overall value in that it further informs or refines or defines the emotional content of each *rāga*. However, he plainly confronts the fact that the entire context of performing and delivering music to audiences has changed. Today, it is entirely possible that to many listeners, *rāga*s may seem associated with other times or seasons than those with which they were originally connected, or have no specific time or seasonal association at all.

The chapter entitled "The Experience of Melody" provides a compact, although panoramic, overview of how past vocal genres, and then various instruments and their genres have defined an approach to melody that has, in Raja's estimation, become progressively more fragmented and atomized. Raja starts with the relationship between "literature, melody and aesthetics" that was integral to the vocal *dhrupad* genre as expressed in the writings of Tansen, the legendary musician at the court of Akbar in the late sixteenth century. The author then takes us through the introduction of the *khayāl* genre, its structural links with the *dhrupad* genre, and the ensuing partial liberation of melody from poetry, through the progressive fragmentation of melody by mid-twentieth century sitārists and sarodists, to the ultimate "atomization" of melody in the music played on the *santūra*.

In the penultimate section, the author provides brief histories of the development of the *dhrupad, khayāl, ṭhumarī,* and *ṭappā* genres and outlines the formal structures and vocal techniques of each genre, as we experience them today. In the course of each essay, the author is careful to include and credit the contributions and innovations of those artists primarily responsible for bringing each genre to the contemporary fulfilment of its purpose.

In the last section, the author reviews the historical usage, and physical development and construction of most of the major musical instruments in current use, except the *bāṅsurī* and the percussion instruments, and the development of the individual genres of expression unique to, and uniquely suited to, each instrument. The section also analyses the efforts to adapt the various genres and formats of vocal music to each instrument as was best suited to their abilities for expression.

Raja's book ends with a chapter on the Indian classical slide guitar. This brings him full-circle back to his initial discourse on populism and globalism, their influence and value, as he muses on the future of the Indian classical guitar: ". . . its future could well be shaped as much by the global music market as by the Indian mainstream."

June 1, 2004 **Lyle Wachovsky**

PART I

Culture, Technology and Economics

1.1

POPULISM AND RIVAL FORCES

Populism has been the most widely noticed tendency in post-Independence Hindustani music. While it has, without doubt, shaped the music-scape in the latter half of the twentieth century, it has also acquired rivals. And, it is these rivals, which are driving Hindustani music into the twenty-first century. Populism, by its very nature, is easily understood. The operation of its rivals is, however, relatively opaque. It is therefore necessary to examine populism, along with its rivals, so that we may acquire a clearer picture of the direction that Hindustani music is taking.

Independence imposed a major discontinuity on Hindustani music. The disappearance of feudal patronage exposed it to market forces, and converted something that provided a secure way of life for the truly great, into a high-risk self-employed profession for all.

As a result, classical music suffered a depletion of talent, along with a decay in the process of grooming the subsequent generations into the art. The great music disappeared along with the giants of the early twentieth century. As a legacy, what most of them left behind was not much more than the bonsai of a banyan tree — very few competent disciples, and commercial recordings, mostly of three-minute duration.

Technological advances soon enabled the creation of a mass-market for art music. By this time, however, there were neither enough musicians with strong moorings in the tradition, nor audiences with a well-defined yardstick for judging what was being dished out to them.

These forces gave rise to strong populist tendencies in Hindustani music. These tendencies have, in turn, triggered off a conservationist reaction, which insists on the sanctity of the dividing line between art and entertainment. In the fortification of this barrier, the conservationists have found an ally amongst Hindustani music enthusiasts and scholars in the US and Western Europe.

Hindustani music is now set on a path of irreversible globalization, and has raised fears of its "de-culturation." The Indian aesthete must now come to terms with this new reality.

The Emergence of a Market

By the mid-1970s, most of the towering musicians of the twentieth century had departed. Musicians with inadequate grooming in the music of the great *gharānā*s invaded the stage. From then on, musicians have been marketing their respective brands of music in a competitive, multi-media environment. The financial rewards of a career in music experienced a significant boost when, in the mid-1960s and 1970s, Europe and the US opened up in response to pioneering efforts by some of India's greatest musicians.

The post-Independence Hindustani musician now addresses an international market of considerable size and diversity. Today's market for classical music consists of 80 per cent "innocenti," and only 20 per cent cognoscenti. The rewards of addressing only the cognoscenti are now beyond the reach of most musicians, while the risk of ignoring the innocenti has become unaffordable. Hindustani music now finds it profitable to address the lowest common denominator by keeping itself accessible, intellectually undemanding, and familiar. This reality defines contemporary classical music more comprehensively than most professional musicians will care to admit.

Dimensions of Populism

For the uninitiated, instrumental music is easier to handle than vocal music because audiences are not required to come to terms with the quality of the voice delivering it, or to grapple with the poetic element. In the 1960s and 1970s, the formidable musicianship of Ustad Bismillah Khan, Pt. Pannalal Ghosh, Ustad Vilayat Khan, Pt. Ravi Shankar and Ustad Ali Akbar Khan overtook the giants amongst their vocalist contemporaries in terms of popularity. In the 1980s and 1990s, Pt. Shivkumar Sharma, Pt. Hari Prasad Chaurasia, Pt. Brijbhushan Kabra and Ustad Zakir Hussain consolidated this trend. This is reflected in the growing disparity between the concert fees of the leading vocalists and instrumentalists of comparable stature.

The decline of vocal music threatens not only vocal music, but all of classical music. This has to be so because vocal music is the principal originator of all musical ideas, and also its most authentic exponent. When the originator and the most authentic exponent ceases to attract the best talent, the art-form risks losing its ability for self-generating growth.

Partly because of the ascendancy of instrumental music over vocal music, classical music is also undergoing a melodic simplification. This trend also permits wider reach to a more diverse and less discerning audience profile. Fewer and fewer *rāgas* are now heard — from all musicians collectively, and even from each musician individually. Even in the presentation of common or popular *rāgas*, there is a tendency to simplify, compress or truncate the form of the traditional, and often complex, compositions. The principles of systematic and comprehensive *rāga* exposition have also been thrown to the winds.

The same shrinkage of variety and richness is discernible in the choice of *tālas*. *Ekatāla* and *tīnatāla* now dominate vocal music. The *baḍā* [slow tempo] *khayālas* in *jhūmarā, tilvāḍā, rūpaka* and *jhaptāla* are threatened by extinction. In instrumental music, the variety may be a little richer. However, there too, *dhamāra, cautāla,* and *ekatāla* have virtually disappeared from the concert platform. The enigmatic *ādā cautāla* is now a rarity in instrumental as well as vocal renditions.

The galloping populism of classical music is evident also in the changing role of the percussion accompanist. He is no longer in a supportive role to the process of music making. Under the guise of securing full-fledged participation in the process, he expects the freedom to intrude upon it to justify his presence. It is in the nature of rhythm to titillate and benumb the mind. Rhythm binds; melody liberates. Musicologist Dr. Ashok Ranāde has often argued that if this were not true, why would martial and disco music be heavy on rhythm and flimsy on melodic and poetic content?

It would be difficult for anyone to argue that the new celebrity status for *tabalā* players is based on a superior public understanding of the intricacies of the *tabalā* idiom. If this were so, it would have shaped a substantial market for *tabalā* solos. In fact, just the reverse is true. In the 1940s and 1950s *tabalā* exponents like Ustad Ahmedjan Thirakwa and Ustad Ameer Hussain Khan could make a living primarily as soloists and teachers. Such careers are virtually inconceivable today. With no demand for the comprehensive art of the percussionist, it could perish at the altar of audience titillation.

Musicians and their percussionists are finding it profitable to engage in a musical strip tease, unashamedly orgasmic in its aesthetic intent. Instrumentalists — more than vocalists —

are now exploiting the undiscerning majority of audiences by selling Rolls Royce bodies, fitted with Volkswagen engines. Music fit for the discos now seeks the respectability of the classical platform, and gets it.

Rāga presentations now habitually accelerate to a tempo at which neither the melodic contours of the *rāga,* nor the accentual structure of the *tāla,* can retain their respective distinctive characters. Crossing the limits of a culturally defined musicality now merits handsome rewards in terms of thunderous applause and concert engagements.

The Hindustani music scene is hurtling towards the familiar, the predictable, and the titillating. The content of music is fast falling prey to the machinations of expression. A great deal of classical music now challenges the dividing line between art and entertainment.

The Conservationist Reaction

Like all socio-cultural trends, these trends too have triggered off their own corrective mechanism. The tussle between populism and conservationism has commenced.

The populists argue that cultural change is an inevitable response to changing audience profiles and aesthetic values. It is, therefore, futile to question its validity. In the present context, conservationism has to be distinguished from conservatism. Conservationism does not resist change *per se* and is not, therefore, reactionary in its inclinations. The conservationists contend that all change is answerable to a yardstick of "propriety;" and the test of propriety neither begins, nor ends, with public acceptability. The notion of propriety, according to them, is founded on a society's concern for orderly and evolutionary change. It assumes a discernible link of continuity between the past, the present, and the future. They see their task as one of restoring the quality control mechanism which has been greatly corroded in recent years, of giving the performing art the benefit of the scholarship that led to the twentieth-century renaissance in Hindustani music, and of protecting the tradition against the consequences of discontinuity.

Attempts at re-injecting continuity into the cultural process have to contend with the absence of the early twentieth-century giants groomed under conditions, which are now, in retrospect, regarded as ideal. The near-impossibility of reviving the traditional systems of hereditary musicianship and highly personalized tutelage is also a *fait accompli*. Despite these limitations, the Sangeet Research Academy [SRA] in Kolkata has proven the possibility of creating an environment conducive to the perpetuation of the distinctive stylistic traditions even in an environment unfriendly to the forces of continuity. Another significant experiment was launched in the early 1980s, when the Government of Madhya Pradesh sponsored the Dhrupad Kendra at Bhopal to revive the medieval genre threatened with extinction. This institution has by now produced quality musicianship in significant numbers, and helped *dhrupad* to return to the mainstream concert platform.

There are, indeed, divergent opinions about the SRA and the Dhrupad Kendra as models for building institutions for replacing the traditional pedagogical model. However, the success of these institutions — whatever the magnitude — has stimulated discussion amongst musicians, musicologists, and scholars on the whole issue. This is a significant development in the field of art-music.

Another important phenomenon is the receding famine of concert-length recordings of the great masters. The restoration of old, poor-quality recordings has now become feasible and economical. Priceless old music is now hitting the market on a significant scale. Its popularity is encouraging recording companies to pursue this segment more avidly.

Individual as well as institutional archivists, who have hitherto been possessive and secretive about their collections, now realize that their treasures will have no aesthetic or commercial value as soon as the present 50-plus generation of listeners departs. They have very little time in which to get any kind of price for their labours of preservation. This realization is persuading them to surrender their gems to the recording companies for commercialization. These archives can serve as a substitute, however limited, for quality training, which has all but disappeared. More significantly, contemporary music can now be held answerable to a demanding yardstick of musicianship, which refuses to go away.

Archives, as restorers of continuity, have often been pooh-poohed on the pretext that there is no such thing as timeless music; and therefore, it is impossible to respond meaningfully to music, especially art-music, from a substantial distance in time. This argument, however, underestimates the highly creative and complex process by which the enquiring musical mind absorbs and utilizes old ideas to generate new ones.

The education of audiences is gaining momentum. In this endeavour, cultural organizations are increasingly holding public seminars, lecture demonstrations, music appreciation courses, and workshops at different levels of sophistication. These are attracting a progressively larger number of participants.

The conservationist movement is now showing signs of becoming galvanized. This phenomenon is best reflected in the activities of The Music Forum, an informal body representing all the significant segments of the classical music community in the major cities. The movement was launched in Mumbai at the initiative of the scholar-musician, Arvind

Parikh, and Shanta Gokhale, the Arts Editor of *Times of India*, with the objective of creating a healthier climate for the evolution of classical music in the city. The Music Forum movement has now spread to Kolkata, Chennai, and Delhi, and could, one day, become a formidable voice of sanity in the classical music world.

Despite isolated success stories, the magnitude of this endeavour may not be able to keep pace with the growth of the audience population and the dilution of audience discernment. The sheer magnitude of the task is sufficient to condemn it to failure.

The Unlikely Ally

The conservationists at home have, in recent years, forged an interesting alliance with Hindustani music enthusiasts in the US and Europe. The Western markets for Indian classical music might still be numerically small. But, it has a considerable presence of serious scholars within it, and even the less initiated members approach Hindustani music with respect for the seriousness of its music making process. This sensibility is able to express itself — to some extent — in their preferences because the size of the populace involved in Hindustani music is not large enough to trigger off the dynamics of a market. If there is no "market," there is no incentive for the product to pander to the lowest common denominator. In such an environment, art has a better chance of remaining true to its ideals.

In this context, the Indian Music & The West Seminar held in Mumbai in 1996 was a very significant event. Over 30 Western scholars and musicians presented papers and performances. The understanding and respect they exhibited for the essentials of Hindustani music could have embarrassed many an Indian musician and scholar.

The superiority of Western scholarship surprises nobody. The real surprise is the credible challenge posed to Indian musicians by Western performers. Several foreign performers of Hindustani music are steadily becoming household names amongst Indian connoisseurs, especially the Swiss *sarodist* Ken Zuckerman, the American flutist Steve Gorn, and the Italian *dhrupad* vocalist Amelia Cuni.

The track record of the international recording companies in producing Hindustani music is even better. The Rotterdam Conservatory of Music researched an authoritative contemporary anthology of *rāga*s, and Nimbus, a British label, published it. Navras Records, the leader in the Hindustani recordings market, is a British company, though owned by Non-Resident Indians. India Archive Music Ltd. and Raga Records Inc. [both in New York], Chhanda Dhara of Stuttgart [Germany], and Makar Records [France] have emerged as serious specialist producers of Hindustani music. Some of these companies have virtually no distribution in the Indian market. Despite the small size of the market they service — U.S., and Western Europe — their standards, across the board, can make Indian record-ing companies blush in embarrassment.

However, these are developments at the most serious end of the Indophile movement in the US and Europe. Qualitatively, what the Western "market" for Hindustani music contributes by its seriousness is largely set-off by the undeveloped state of discernment amongst audiences, and the isolation of the music from cultural meaning. It is, no doubt, significant that the commitment of some developed countries to a serious multi-culturalism should provide a strong impetus to the sustenance and growth of Hindustani music. John Naisbitt's "Global Paradox" is with us already. But, it is not clear whether this represents utopia.

India, an uncompetitive exporter of most tangible products, now takes pride in the successful and profitable globalization of its classical music. This pride is tinged with the anxiety about the paradox inherent in the situation. Hindustani music, as we understand it, is unlikely to survive without ceasing to belong exclusively to the people of Hindustan. It has become dependent on the West for economic sustenance, discerning audiences and scholarly inputs.

A significant manifestation of this phenomenon is the number of brilliant young musicians who have become so busy and successful in USA and Europe, that they have neither the time, nor the economic necessity to cultivate Indian audiences for their art. Isolated from an active engagement with the cultural meaning of their music, many of them are evolving a musical idiom that recalls the signs outside many establishments during the colonial era — "For whites only: Indians and dogs not allowed."

Under these circumstances, the anxiety about the "deculturation" of Hindustani music would be natural and, many believe, legitimate. But, if this process is irreversible, it really does not matter whether these concerns are legitimate or not. How, then, must the Indian aesthete come to terms with this reality?

Responsible musicologists often cite the example of Western classical music, which is tending to stagnate and become excessively intellectual because it has remained insular and parochial. Against this backdrop, they see the globalization of Hindustani music as a sign of its vitality, and a guarantee of its survival. This view appears to have the support of history. Hindustani music survived the second millennium because it adapted itself to the tastes of its new patrons from the Middle East, by assimilating Perso-Arabic influences.

It is inevitable that economics will drive the content and form of Hindustani music, as of every other aspect of society's artistic expression. Economically, Hindustani music is now being driven by populism at home, and elitism abroad. In both these tendencies, the performing arena allows the music to evolve free from accountability to the Indian connoisseur, who constitutes the principal element of the quality control mechanism in Hindustani music. Compared to the financial muscle of the audiences that sustain Hindustani music, the salutary presence of the conservationist forces at home will remain too miniscule, feeble and disorganized to influence Hindustani music in a substantive manner.

Of the two diversionary forces, globalism is perhaps the more insidious because it wields greater financial clout and is also pregnant with a "de-culturation" of Hindustani music. The impending divorce of music from cultural meaning, and the burgeoning presence of alien musical ideas in Hindustani music are almost a foregone conclusion. If this is the case, the Indian aesthete should derive some satisfaction from the fact that, in India as well as the Western markets, there exists a serious conservationist force, however small, to set-off alarm signals, however inaudible, when warranted.

An enlightened view of the scenario should certainly lament that the great *gharānā*s of Hindustani music have now merged into the "cocktail *gharānā*." But, this view should also permit pride in the emergence of a "Rotterdam *gharānā*," and a "San Rafael-Seniya *gharānā*," whose commitment to excellence might revitalize Hindustani music, even if it does so in ways we cannot foresee, and in ways some may not readily approve.

1.2

IF PEANUTS IS WHAT YOU PAY

DISCERNING listeners of Hindustani classical music, the *rasikas*, are an unhappy lot. They find that music no longer matches up to their standards of excellence, and that they have been reduced to a minority unable to hold music providers accountable for the quality of music in circulation.

The *rasika*'s reduction to a minority has been caused by a steady decline in the price of music to the consumer, and the resulting explosion in the size of the market. Explosive numerical growth has been accompanied, predictably, by a dilution in the discernment levels of audiences. The result of this process is a brand of music that fails to qualify as sound classical music, as understood by discerning audiences.

The process of "commoditization" of high art is not unique to India. Post-war developments in the technologies of storage and distribution have made it a global phenomenon. In the West, classical music was insulated from the forces of market-driven populism by great institutions with substantial government and corporate funding. But, a substantial contribution towards the sustenance of high art was also made by the willingness of audiences to pay exorbitant rates for a face-to-face encounter with classical music.

In India, neither government support nor corporate patronage have had any significant conservationist impact.

The onus of preserving thoroughbred music has therefore been substantially on the *rasika*. Not realizing this, he became an unwitting accomplice in the process that has driven quality music out of circulation, perhaps forever.

The Changing Context

For today's *rasika*s, the benchmark is the music that was performed between 1940 and 1950, the tail-end of the period often described as the Golden Age of Hindustani music.

In that era, the concert platform was the primary interface between musicians and audiences. The penetration of radio was below 10 per cent of urban households, while the gramophone record had perhaps not reached more than 5 per cent of them.

Other than the patron-employers of the musicians, it was the aristocracy in the major cities, which typically hosted concerts. Audiences attended free, and by invitation. The size of the audience rarely exceeded 350/400. This could be partly because amplification acoustics were scarce, and partly because selectivity based on aesthetic cultivation was an integral part of the musical culture of the era.

If this describes the "Golden Age" of Hindustani music, we would also need to accept that it offered ideal conditions for the creation of music we consider great. The music world has changed substantially since then.

With the fading away of aristocratic patronage, audiences have started paying for attendance. But, the concert platform has itself ceased to be the primary interface between musicians and their audiences. This shift has been caused by the explosive growth of the electronic media — first the radio and, later, pre-recorded music, especially after the advent of the audio cassette. If we consider the totality of these trends in terms of cost of music to consumers, we find that they are getting their music cheaper by the year.

The Economics

Let us first look at the cost of concert admissions. According to my information, the system of audiences contributing, in an organized manner, began in the early 1950s, when concerts moved out of private gatherings into large auditoria and open-air *paṇḍālas*. The highest level of concert-admission was around Rs. 100 per seat in 1961, Rs. 150 in 1971, Rs. 200 in 1981, Rs. 250 in 1991, and has settled down at Rs. 500 at the end of the last century.

If we apply an inflation-adjustment factor to these figures, we find that a front-row seat of Rs. 100 in 1961 is worth Rs. 2100 in current Rupees. Against this, we are today paying only Rs. 500 for front-row seats. If we plot a long-term trend-line on inflation-adjusted data, we conclude that the real cost of concert-admissions has been falling by 40/50 per cent every ten years.

Although the average durations of concerts have also been shrinking, they have certainly not shrunk at the rate of 40/50 per cent every ten years. To this extent, it can be proved that even the cost-per-hour of concert music has been falling significantly.

Now consider recorded music. Here, of course, the cost per unit of time has to be applied to fully understand the economics.

The 78-RPM record, with 7 minutes of music, cost Rs. 3.5 in 1958, or Rs. 0.5 per minute. The inflation-adjusted price of that record today would be Rs. 12.62 per minute.

Then came the long-playing record with 44 minutes of music at a price of Rs. 22 in 1963-64. The inflation-adjusted price of the LP today would be Rs. 9.96 per minute.

This was followed by the audio-cassette with 60 minutes of music at Rs. 20 around 1968-69. The inflation-adjusted price of that music works out to Rs. 4.12.

Then consider the present scenario of CDs with 74 minutes of music at an average of Rs. 295, and a considerable volume of quality classical music available on CDs for as little as Rs. 90. This brings the price of the contemporary CD to Rs. 1.20 per minute of music at the lower end, and Rs. 4.92 at the average.

Thus, from the 78 RPM record, which sold music at the present-day equivalent of Rs. 12.62 per minute in 1958, the cost of music on a CD has come down to Rs. 4.92 per minute in the year 2000-01 at the average, and as low as Rs. 1.20 per minute at the lower end.

What about musicians' fees? If the consumer is paying less and less for his music, is this hurting the musicians? This does not appear to be the case. According to reliable reports, in 1945, Ustad Faiyyaz Khan, and Kesarbai Kerkar, the highest paid musicians of that era, were paid Rs. 750/Rs. 1000 for a concert. Adjusted for inflation, this works out to about Rs. 85,000/110,000 at current prices [*circa* 2000-01].

These figures are shocking considering that — according to industry figures — the highest paid vocalist today is paid 250 per cent to 300 per cent of this amount, and the highest-paid instrumentalists receive as much as 500 per cent of this amount. While this data only establishes a comparison at the top end of the scale, it is indicative of the overall rise in remunerations of musicians, disproportionate to the basic level of inflation.

How reliable are the numbers? I have reconstructed the price history of concert admissions and prices of recorded music from my own memory, and the memories of senior observers of the music scene. For inflation adjustment, I have used the time-series data of the Wholesale Price Index, as published by the Reserve Bank of India. Neither of these is a perfect solution to understanding the trends in the economics of the music market. However, a similar reconstruction of history by any other raconteur, submitted to an alternative inflationary adjustment, is not likely to lead to very different conclusions. The orders of magnitude could, of course, be less dramatic.

The consumer pays less and less, while the musician gets more and more. How do the sums add up? Who makes the arithmetic work?

The sums add up because of the role of the two dominant intermediaries in the music market: the recording companies, and concert sponsors. They are both playing a progressively larger financial role in the music market — without having either the need or the desire to promote quality music.

Consider the recording companies first. Their expertise lies in making a profit on volumes. Their strategies are guided by the logic of the popular music market, which is essentially price-sensitive. They have allowed the same logic to work in the classical music segment because they have found it profitable. It is understandable that they should have no provocation to adopt a different strategy for this small market — reportedly less than 2.0 per cent of the total recordings market.

By treating the two segments similarly in their marketing strategy, they have encouraged the quantitative expansion of the classical music market. But, in so doing, they also diluted the discernment profile of listeners accessing the music, and thereby, the quality of music that would be delivered through the pre-recorded media.

Now, consider the concert sponsorship situation. Sponsorship is increasingly being offered by corporate entities for the promotion of corporate and brand personalities. To a smaller extent, this function is also being performed by government organizations towards cultural or tourist promotion. The rewards sought by a corporate or government sponsor are unrelated to the quality of music that is delivered. Their motivations would logically tilt more strongly towards quantitative reach, than the qualitative criterion.

None of the major participants in the market has had any reason to consider the qualitative dimension of the cultural process. While the classical music market is not defined by economic status, it can be argued that music is more likely to attract truly dedicated and discerning audiences when it demands an economic sacrifice, than when it is subsidized. As a corollary, when audiences pay a fair price for their music, they do not need to surrender the right to select the music to an unworthy intermediary.

The Bottom-line

In the totality of this scenario, the bottom-line is positive for all participants, except the *rasika*. Because he is in a hopeless minority, it suits everyone to ignore him and reach out to audiences at a lower level of discernment.

While the tyranny of technology and economics tends to be irresistible, the community of *rasika*s cannot consider itself blameless. It had the opportunity of creating a market segment that demands quality music and is willing to pay for it. This community of *rasika*s happily gave its kids Rs. 2000 to attend a Michael Jackson concert, but felt no pangs of guilt while paying only Rs. 200 to hear Ustad Vilayat Khan. It also loved the idea of paying less and less for concert-length recordings of Pt. Bhimsen Joshi, along with the convenience of listening to them in the comfort of home. In the process, it surrendered the right to choose the music to unworthy intermediaries.

And, now that the consequences are upon them, they are complaining. Audiences get the music they deserve; but they also get the music they pay for. To quote Peter Drucker, amongst the wisest men of our times, "If peanuts is what you pay, monkeys is what you get."

1.3

GOVERNMENT, BUSINESS AND CLASSICAL MUSIC

FOR several decades now, the State and the corporate sector in India have tried to convince us that they have efficiently taken over the patronage of Hindustani classical music from the aristocracy of the pre-Independence era. Unfortunately, such a development is neither a fact nor a foreseeable possibility.

The reasons for this are complex and fundamental. Modern governments and businesses are both managed through a bureaucratic decision-making process, which is, in its very nature, inconsistent with the demands of the patronage function. This reality operates even more mercilessly against the classical arts because their audiences constitute a microscopic minority of the population. The rewards of competent patronage of classical music, therefore, cannot enhance the legitimacy of the repositories of power and money.

If Indian society has substantial funds to divert towards the promotion of classical music, as it evidently has, it will have to find more intelligent and less destructive means of channellizing them than it has so far done.

The Traditional Patronage Model

To appreciate the issues, it is useful to identify the salient features of the traditional model of aristocratic patronage, against which we might evaluate the credentials of modern institutions.

[a] *Patron profile*: The traditional patron was a highly cultivated and discerning listener of classical music. In many cases, he was a trained, and even accomplished, musician. He was the sole and unquestioned decision maker with respect to the disbursement of his largesse — whether to musicians or to other beneficiaries.

[b] *The patronage relationship*: The relationship between the patron and the patronized musician was a personal one, in addition to being based on a discerning admiration of the maestro's music. In many cases, the patron was a formally accepted disciple of the maestro. The economics of the relationship were designed to free the maestro from all anxieties related to the comfortable maintenance of his personal establishment, which included family and disciples.

This guarantee was implicitly available not only to individual musicians during their lifetimes, but also to their descendants, as long as they lived up even reasonably well to the promise of heredity. Since such support was available to several musicians in the same court, it resulted in a spirit of healthy competition and sharing of musical ideas between musicians from different stylistic backgrounds. In addition, the patron granted "court musicians" the freedom to perform outside the patronage orbit and to get remunerated for it.

[c] *Motivations of the patron*: The patron was motivated by two desires. By way of personal satisfaction, the patron sought the unrestricted access to the music of the

maestro, perhaps including training from him. By way of public satisfaction, he sought the prestige and prominence within a community of connoisseurs through the vicarious ownership of the maestro's art-asset.

Benefactor Qualifications

With the backdrop of this patronage model, it is possible to assess how, if at all, the modern democratic State or business enterprises might qualify as a replacement for the traditional patron, whose support shaped the "Golden Age of Hindustani music."

Let us first consider the ***benefactor/patron profile***.

The State and business are both handicapped in the performance of the patronage function by the fact that they are not individuals but impersonal entities, operating under conditions of multiple-participant decision-making. While individuals can be highly cultivated and discerning listeners or students of classical music, organizations cannot. Even a hypothetical organization consisting only of connoisseurs would not nullify this argument because all modern organizations are, in their nature, bureaucratic.

A bureaucracy is, by definition, an organization wherein decision-making is distributed, impersonal, and result-neutral in terms of the identities of the beneficiaries. In such organizations, no individual can have unfettered authority over the commitment of resources. The multiple decision-maker process cannot function with a unified yardstick of discernment. As a result, the modern organization — whether the State or a business house — cannot either be an efficient judge of artistic merit, or commit corporate resources as wholeheartedly as the patronage function demands.

Let us now consider the ***benevolence/patronage relationship***.

Neither the State, nor business houses, can possibly establish any personal relationship with musicians. This is so mainly because personal relationships can only be established between individuals. But, this is also because the basis for the establishment of this specific relationship is a high level of discernment in music, accompanied by a passionate admiration for an individual maestro's art. Such a basis is inconceivable in the context of an impersonal institutional entity such as the State or a business house.

The institutional or corporate benefactor of classical music also fails to fulfil the economic criteria of the traditional patronage model. He may be lavish in his support of specific public appearances of leading musicians; but he does not guarantee to the beneficiary a life-long maintenance of his personal establishment at a decent level of comfort. As musicologist Ashok Ranade has argued [Proceedings of the Seminar on Content and Expression, Sangeet Research Academy, Mumbai, 8-9 December, 2000], the sponsorship of events is not to be confused with patronage. Concert sponsorship is contractual and event-specific, while patronage is unconditional and permanent. Event sponsorship is a business deal, while patronage is a passionate commitment. The absence of passion in decision-making is essential to the character and success of the State and business organizations. This very feature makes them incapable of matching up to the traditional patronage model.

And, finally, the ***patron's/benefactor's motives***. Neither the State nor business organizations can seek any personal satisfaction for benefaction because they are impersonal entities. Their motivations have, therefore, to be understood purely and solely in terms of public satisfaction. On this dimension as well, the two institutional types have similar perspectives.

The arithmetic of public opinion prevents governments, especially in a democratic society, from adopting a stance that genuinely addresses the needs and concerns of aesthetes who are, by definition, a small minority. The best they can do in this regard is to pay lip service to such concerns, while allowing the opinion of the masses to dominate its substantive actions.

Even in the process of acknowledging "conservationist" concerns, democratic governments are forced to justify the commitment of resources on quantitative rather than qualitative considerations. A music-festival, which costs government Rs. 5,00,000 in sponsorship, is more successful if it draws a crowd of 5000 ignoramuses than another, which cost the same amount, but attracts only 500 cognoscenti. In order to achieve numerical targets, State sponsorship is obliged to support music that caters to the lowest common denominator in public taste.

The perspective of business houses is not much different. Every business house — including its product — is a "brand" which seeks a premium position in the public mind. The objective of achieving such a position is to enable an easier commercial exploitation of the "market" so accessed. The sponsorship of a cultural event is, in effect, an exercise in "co-branding" in which a premium is created for corporate brand by associating it with a "cultural brand."

If the "cultural brand" has an appeal limited only to the cognoscenti, the co-branding exercise achieves only sub-optimal results. An encashable co-branding exercise is obviously one that maximizes its quantitative reach, independently of qualitative considerations of aesthetic cultivation. Here again, the lowest common denominator in musical values is the more obvious path to success than music to satisfy the cognoscenti.

In essence, the modern democratic State, as well as the corporate benefactor of classical music, has a lot to gain by "buying" the image of high culture, but a lot to lose by making a substantive commitment to it. If their motivations are at variance with those of the traditional patronage model, the results of their benevolence cannot possibly be compatible.

Reconfiguring Benefaction

The traditional patronage model has faded into history, and is impossible to reconfigure. In its present-day *avatāra*, benevolence acts without the discernment of the traditional patron. But, being genetically handicapped in the area of discernment, it is obliged to legitimize itself by promoting the notion that the interests of classical music are best served by "popularizing" it. Nothing more self-defeating is conceivable. An art form meant for audiences of high aesthetic cultivation cannot possibly be served by driving it towards populism.

If the experience of the West in handling such issues is any indication, our unseemly benefaction scenario is probably just one stage in the maturation of the cultural process. The West has successfully created great, autonomous institutions like conservatories, opera houses, and philharmonic orchestras which function as centres of discernment and channellize the benevolence of the State and corporate benefactors towards a close approximation to the traditional patronage model. Although these institutions were spawned in the feudal era, they have made a successful transition into becoming vehicles for modern society's commitment to cultural values.

Such developments have, by and large, escaped India. The only significant attempt to address the substantive issues under present-day conditions is the Sangeet Research Academy sponsored by ITC Ltd. In a different sort of way, the Dhrupad Kendra in Bhopal, established by the Government of Madhya Pradesh, is also a significant experiment. The success of these experiments, whatever the scale, has certainly sparked off serious discussion about the ideal institutional framework for the preservation and promotion of classical music. The debate has highlighted the need for a constructive alliance between the repositories of money and power on the one hand and forces of discernment on the other.

There are several hurdles to the proliferation of such alliances.

From the point of view of the State and corporate benefactors, classical music is only one amongst several competing demands on the treasury, all of which are more popular, and in the short run more rewarding. In addition, these institutions feel no need to question their belief that they are, in fact, making a positive contribution to classical music. It is therefore necessary for the community of musicologists, professional musicians, and the specialist media to pressurize the contemporary Indian benefactor into maturing at a faster rate.

How does one educate, coax, cajole, pressurize, chastize and seduce a benefactor, all at the same time, without risking his disinterest, displeasure and even alienation? This is a task demanding rare diplomatic skill; and the music community has to find leaders who possess it.

1.4

PAṆḌITS AND USTĀDS APLENTY!

WHAT does it take to become a *paṇḍit* or an *ustād* of Hindustani classical music today? Some audacity and a visiting card with an honorific prefix! A large number of aspiring musicians in India labour under this illusion and achieve only laughable results. In reality, the plight of such musicians, as well as their audiences, deserves sympathy. A lot of it is good talent, having no way of claiming musicianship above the ordinary, except through an absurdity. And, here are audiences, looking for good musicianship, not necessarily of super-star quality, and having no way of finding it except by risking disenchantment.

All this boils down to one simple conclusion. The collective mentality of the classical music community, in this respect, is still a prisoner of a bygone era. It has not understood that we no longer live in a world where a musician was either an *ustād* or *paṇḍit* enjoying the security of royal patronage, or was a nobody with his next meal being uncertain.

To use an automobile industry metaphor, today's music market has a place for Mopeds, Fiats, and Hondas, as well as Rolls Royces. It is also a market that allows Mopeds to grow into Rolls Royces. What the market needs is a structuring of the different segments — providing the means by which each level of excellence can be brought in contact with its prospects to conduct a transaction satisfactory to both.

Classical music is now a profession. Every profession has a market, which consists of intermediaries and consumers. The profession relates itself to its market through a graded system of value and price. The more realistic this system of grading, the more efficient the functioning of the market.

All India Radio attempts to administer precisely such a graded system of price-value relationships. The AIR system might have become a formidable force in the classical music market had AIR not decided to engineer its own irrelevance by diluting standards and insulating itself from the world outside. Today, it is possible to shape a successful career in classical music without having qualified as an AIR artist. The concert and recording markets are the bread-and-butter markets for the musician. And, it is in these markets that the forces of demand and supply require skilful management.

Today's musician is marketing a service to a complex market. The intermediaries in the market include concert and festival organizers, corporate sponsors, and the recording companies. The customers are music lovers who access the musician's art through the intermediaries. As in any other market for services, the supplier [musician] is always vulnerable to exploitation by the intermediaries. The only way to avoid exploitation is for the profession to organize itself for credibility amongst consumers.

The value of a grading system is obvious. It becomes an indication of the value that the members of the profession deliver, and justifies the prices they command in the market. From the point of view of intermediaries and customers, this becomes an indication of the value they are buying and, of how much it should cost.

From the point of view of musicians, the advantages are even greater. Once they have achieved a grade that relates to a certain market value, and the credible authority of a profession backs them, they can avoid having to negotiate rates for every engagement, and concentrate instead on cultivating their art. A graded system also becomes a ladder, ascending which becomes a worthwhile motivator towards greater effort.

As an indirect pay-off, such a system will replace the informal and inefficient quality control mechanism in today's Hindustani classical music with a formal and more efficient one. Such a formalized system of accountability for standards of musicianship must necessarily elevate standards across the board. This is the only way for musicians, as members of a self-employed profession, to protect their interests while seeking higher standards of excellence. It also happens to be the most efficient way of protecting the interests of consumers. This convergence of interests is logical because nothing promotes the interests of a profession as efficiently as protecting the interests of its clientele.

The financial clout of an organized profession can also be formidable. The collective bargaining power of a musicians' guild with respect to financial services such as loans, insurance, and medical risk cover, can be powerful incentives for concerted action. Considering the profession-related, and other benefits, many musicians will agree that musicians need to organize themselves.

Many might hope that a government body will take the initiative. If the functioning of the government's cultural institutions is any indication, this thought deserves to be dismissed summarily. Ultimately, musicians will realize that the only people competent to set up and administer such a system are professional musicians themselves. They will also realize that the unity of the entire profession backing each graded member offers the best security for the interests of all musicians.

To the extent that government support, or blessings, might be desirable, an organized community of musicians will obtain it far more easily and effectively than an unorganized one.

Consider, for instance, the legislation that gave statutory recognition to the profession of Auditors or Company Secretaries. Both these professions organized themselves into strong bodies before they were chartered by an Act of Parliament.

In the field of Hindustani music, it may seem as if nobody knows where to start. The task is, indeed, daunting. Establishing and administering such a system will require a professionally manned organization for which the members will have to pay in relation to their respective stakes in the profession. In effect, the stars and super stars will be subsidizing and supporting the rank and file of the profession, as happens in all organized professions. Every difficulty and complexity of the endeavour justifies itself by the rewards.

Today, individualistic sports like tennis, golf and even chess are lucrative professions precisely because the professionals organized themselves, and took charge of their own grading, and the sharing of spoils. These professions did not get organized after the big money came to them. The big money came after, and because, they got organized and hired the finest managerial talent to attract the money.

If musicians do not organize themselves into a guild, they will remain vulnerable to exploitation by intermediaries. If musicians shy away from defining the yardsticks of musicianship, some modern-day Aurangzeb sitting in *sacivālaya* or unqualified journalist or TV chat-show host, will start defining them. Media-savvy and well-connected musicians of questionable accomplishment will continue to promote themselves as *paṇḍits* and *ustāds* and invite ridicule towards the entire profession.

An organized profession with graded membership will, no doubt, make many musicians uncomfortable. Many will insist that in art, there cannot be any objective yardstick of accomplishment. Many will seek shelter under the argument that an organization means politics, a much-maligned and misunderstood reality. The truth, of course, is that an unorganized profession is more unfair to its members than an organized profession. The very purpose of organizing the profession is to eliminate the rewards, which the unworthy are reaping from the disorganized state of the profession.

It is fair to ask why the necessity of organized professionalism has not witnessed any concrete action. The main reason for this lapse might be that many of our senior musicians, whose mind-set still dominates the music world, grew up in the era of feudal and aristocratic patronage. A booming mass market, along with the growing power of intermediaries, are unfathomable realities for them. If they are comfortable, they see their success as a triumph of their art. If they are uncomfortable, they blame it on the failure of personal relationships — the anonymous enemy called "politics."

They are attuned to seeing their peers within the profession as rivals. It is not easy for them to start seeing their peers as potential allies, aligned in a commonality of commercial interests. To them, the notion of an audience as a market, and a concert host or sponsor as an intermediary, is alien, and perhaps even revolting.

Although our pre-Independence stalwarts and post-Independence super stars may not see the advantages of a guild organization in obvious terms, they in fact, have the most to gain. Once the floor-level of remuneration to guild members has been stabilized at a respectable level, the rewards of the seniors and the stars will accrue in higher multiples.

The stalwarts and super stars ought to encourage the post-Independence generation of promising musicians to set the ball rolling in this direction. For a variety of reasons, the young ones are more likely to provide the leadership for such a movement. The youngsters seek success in a cruel world, and are better equipped to comprehend its complexities. They understand and deploy both competition and cooperation as parts of a career strategy. When these developments will crystallize, nobody can predict. But, thanks to the alarm signals set-off by an audacious few, it could happen faster than most people imagine.

1.5

ARCHIVAL MUSIC AND THE CULTURAL PROCESS

OVER the last decade, Indian recording companies have made large investments in the acoustic re-engineering and marketing of archival Hindustani music. The activity in this market is accelerating. It is important, at this stage, to understand the cultural implications of the additional lease of life granted to archival music by the technology of acoustic restoration, and the large-scale commercialization of archival music.

Vintage music has long been available to serious seekers who could worm their way into the charmed circle of collectors and archivists. What makes this access a significant cultural phenomenon now is the commercial scale on which it has become feasible, and the acoustic quality of the product that can be delivered to the market — both results of technological advances in sound processing and storage media technologies.

I am treating 1975 as an approximate and notional bridge between archival music and the contemporary musician. This is justified by several considerations, the most important being the passing away, in 1974, of the vocalist Ameer Khan, who has emerged as the single most formidable force in the archival music market. This was also the time when two trailblazing vocalists, Pt. Kumar Gandharva, and Smt. Kishori Amonkar, spearheaded what the learned musicologist, Vamanrao Deshpande describes as the Romantic Movement in Hindustani music.

Around the same time, the first generation of post-Independence musicians emerged on the professional scene. As a watershed in the cultural life of the country, Independence is important because it is only at that point and after that the electronic media enabled, and encouraged, musicians to cultivate audiences as a replacement for the patronage-based relationship typical of the pre-Independence era. This transition was fundamental enough to alter the musician-audience relationship and the music that was on offer to audiences.

With this perspective, I refer to music recorded before 1975 as "archival music," and musicians emerging on the professional circuit after 1975 as "contemporary musicians."

Obsolescence in Recorded Music

Music, once recorded, is susceptible to two types of obsolescence with the passage of time — acoustic obsolescence, and aesthetic obsolescence.

By acoustic obsolescence, we mean the fact that every recording incorporates acoustic values as captured and reproduced by the audio technologies available at the time. These values are, presumably, acceptable to audiences of that time. But, with new developments in recording and reproduction technology, these values become progressively unacceptable to audiences accustomed to the acoustic output of later technologies. With the passage of time, therefore, the decline in the perceived quality of older recorded music can reach a stage, which denies it an audience.

By aesthetic obsolescence, we mean the fact that every piece of music represents musical values prevalent at the time when the music was recorded. The music of each era addresses audiences of that era; therefore, the aesthetic values inherent in it can be assumed to be most acceptable when the music was recorded. With aesthetic values in music responding to socio-cultural changes over time, all recorded music will inevitably drift towards unacceptability.

These two notions of obsolescence are, of course, connected. Acoustic obsolescence progressively depletes the size of audiences willing to expose themselves to a piece of recorded music. Aesthetic obsolescence progressively depletes the size of audiences able to relate to the aesthetic values incorporated in a piece of recorded music. There is a numerical relationship between the willing and the able. If we enlarge the number of people who are willing to hear a piece of archival music, we also enlarge — even if not in the same proportion — the number of those who are able to appreciate its aesthetic values.

By utilizing restoration technologies, which enable us to delay acoustic obsolescence, we are potentially also delaying the onset of aesthetic obsolescence. We accept, of course, that the technological life of a piece of recorded music is at least theoretically unlimited, while its aesthetic life is finite. Even a total nullification of acoustic obsolescence, if such is conceivable, cannot ever wish away the reality of aesthetic obsolescence.

The Archival Music Market

Archival restoration and commercialization activity today covers all segments of the art-music legacy since commercial recordings came to India in 1902. 78-RPM recordings, EP recordings, LP recordings, and pre-1975 audio-cassette productions are being re-marketed on a significant scale after being acoustically upgraded/restored. As an aesthetic force, however, the most significant segment of this activity is the commercialization of concert recordings from the pre-1975 period. By virtue of being concert-length, and by virtue of having been recorded during a face-to-face interaction with an audience, these recordings come closest to the "real thing," and therefore have the potential to exercise an aesthetic influence over contemporary tastes and musicianship which neither shorter, nor studio-made, recordings can exercise.

Art-music reportedly constitutes less than 2 per cent of the total recorded music market in the country. It is too small a segment to deserve a differentiated marketing strategy. Therefore art-music is marketed through the same volume-driven strategy as popular music. Given this reality, the large investments in the revival of vintage music would be justified only if it had begun to start selling in much larger numbers than has done for many years hitherto.

This conclusion suggests a structural change in the generational composition of the music market. This suggestion is supported by the observation that the music industry is now investing even more feverishly in the revival of vintage popular music than it is investing in vintage art-music. Obviously, music lovers above the age of 45 today, who were below 20 in 1975, have now become a large, fast-growing, and profitable market.

Life expectancies of the Indian population are growing and re-defining the market for cultural products, along with other markets. According to one estimate, the 45+ population is projected to become about 24 per cent of the population by the year 2025. If we focus these estimates more sharply towards the urban middle class, which has better access to healthcare, the 45+ age group could be heading for becoming one-third of the Indian population by 2025. This estimate can be sharpened further, even if only on a speculative basis, to support the hypothesis that as much as half of the classical music market could soon be above 45.

In any event, the 45+ age group is the natural hard core of the market for art-music for two reasons. The meditative-contemplative character of Hindustani art-music will tend to appeal primarily to audiences who have outgrown the need for frivolous music. In addition, it takes several years, indeed decades, of exposure to develop a level of comfort with Hindustani art-music. These facts automatically define the generational profile of the art-music segment as predominantly middle-aged and above.

The recent emergence of a youth market might have marginally corroded this dominance. But, the youth segment is unlikely to outnumber the "grey" segment in the near future. The importance of the "grey" market is enhanced further by its superior knowledge and discernment, which enables it to influence the preferences of the younger generations of audiences. This market would justify a product range that enables its members to grow old with the music with which they grew up. In both segments — classical and film/popular — the recording industry could be encashing the same nostalgia of the middle-aged for their youth, and the accompanying sclerosis of aesthetic values.

Generations as "Markets"

A musician does not consciously address any particular generation of audiences. However, by virtue of belonging to his/her generation, he/she represents its aesthetic values along with the values inherited as a part of the artistic tradition. The process by which these values interact to acquire a significant constituency for an individual musician's art is mysterious and variable. However, it can be argued that the constituency of every musician — no matter how popular — will be limited to a certain generational profile. At every stage in his/her performing career, a musician will inevitably fail to address, and will thereby forfeit access to, a substantial part of the art-music audience, which is either too young, or too old.

This proposition is a little easier to enunciate from the point of view of audiences. It can be observed that, in Hindustani music, audiences relate most intimately to the music that dominated their music-scape between the time they were about twenty, up to the time when they are about fifty. They remain loyal till the end to aesthetic values of music absorbed during these three decades of their lives, and find it difficult to relate to music that represents earlier or later aesthetic values.

This could be the defining paradigm of the current phenomenon. Because people are now living longer, a large volume of archival music, with a substantial residue of aesthetic life, is seeking to encash its commercial potential by enhancing its acoustic acceptability to match, or at least approximate, contemporary standards.

While this might define the commercial aspect of the present phenomenon, the issue of generations as markets, and the finite aesthetic life of music, is far less cut-and-dried than I might have appeared to suggest. In the case of music, perhaps more than other artistic expressions, artistic values are not disseminated entirely, or even largely, through direct voluntary exposure. Secondary and involuntary exposures, and even referrals and prestige suggestions, play a significant role in enhancing receptivity and creating preferences.

The osmotic potential of obsolescent aesthetic values is aided by the foundation of continuity in Hindustani music. This foundation consists of the *rāga* and *tāla* systems, and the accompanying architecture [*rāga*-presentation protocol], all of which ensure that, within limits, any recording of Hindustani music, from any era, has a decent chance of evoking willingness to exposure amongst contemporary audiences, provided its acoustic standards are acceptable. The archival music phenomenon could, therefore, be more significant than merely a technological answer to the commercial opportunity in servicing the "nostalgia" market.

Continuity and Change

Having been triggered off by demography, and made viable by technology, the archival phenomenon now participates actively in the complex interplay between continuity and change in three important ways. Firstly, it is providing competition to the recordings of the post-Independence generation of musicians. Secondly, it is reviving, in a demonstrable way, a yardstick of musicianship, which would have departed with the creators of this music, were it not for the possibility first of recording, and later, of restoration and commercial scale marketing. And, finally, it is providing valuable study material for future generations of musicians, scholars and researchers. We may now look at each of these individually.

The Challenge from the Graveyards

Pre-recorded music has taken over, from the concert platform, the primary function of delivering art-music to its audiences. On approximate reckoning, an average listener of art-music spends at least 10 times as many hours a year listening to music recordings as he spends in concert halls. According to music industry reports, recording fees now function increasingly as a lump sum multiple of an artist's rating in terms of concert fees, rather than a sales-based royalty. It would therefore appear that in geometric proportion to their market rating, contemporary musicians depend substantially on recording fees for their livelihood.

If this is true, the contemporary musician must increasingly reckon with competition from archival music on the shelves of the music stores. The challenge is more severe because recording companies have tended to sell contemporary music and archival music at the same price, and often even at lower prices. In addition to such commercial disadvantages, the contemporary musician is denied the "nostalgia premium" of the "grey" [45-plus] market, and its influence over the purchasing decisions of the younger generations of audiences. While it is possible that the flood of re-engineered archival music is expanding the art-music market as a whole, it is almost certain that it is also eating into the sales potential for the music of contemporary musicians.

The dead are, indeed, leaving less breathing space for the living. With a shrinking market share of the recordings market for contemporary music, the big contemporary names will inevitably consolidate their hold over the market, restrict the growth of the most promising second-liners, and impede the entry of fresh talent. Even if this pressure does not convert itself into a depletion of revenues in the short run, it will do so in the medium term. This is inevitable because, fundamentally, the contemporary musician is competing for the discretionary time of the music lover, and not merely for his purchasing power. Art-music is not Muzak. It is a "leisure consumption" product, and requires undivided attention — it cannot be listened to as "background music." For any given customer, the discretionary time available for art-music will always be finite. To this extent, any *a priori* preference for archival music will deny an opportunity of exposure to contemporary music. Because of this, even if the strugglers amongst contemporary musicians manage to sell more copies of recordings, this does not guarantee them proportionate exposure to further their careers.

Market access for struggling contemporary talent is being restricted not only by deceased musicians, but also by the recordings of the ageing stalwarts of contemporary music made during their peak performing years. The releases of such recordings have now emerged as valuable "retirement plans" and "pension schemes" for the ageing stalwarts of contemporary music.

The disadvantage to contemporary talent may also be aggravated by the fact that today's environment permits the exceptionally talented to access the recording and concert markets very early in life, even before their music has matured fully. In the pre-recorded market, therefore, their hesitant individuality has to struggle for acceptance in comparison with the authoritative solidity of archival music, recorded mostly during the peak performing years of the old masters.

This prognosis for emerging talent is justified by the burgeoning importance of pre-recorded music to the art-music business in its totality. To today's musician, the commercial recording is his/her advertisement, his/her "sample pack," as well as the product itself. It has now replaced the radio as the basic launch vehicle for art-musicians, and also functions as the primary builder of a national and even international presence. Without such a presence, a musician cannot develop the concert market; and without a significant presence in the concert market, he/she cannot either develop or sustain the interest of the commercial recording market, which is his/her primary source of income.

Without the spiralling effect of this interactive relationship between the concert market and the pre-recorded music market, struggling talent is tempted to gatecrash somehow, even anyhow, into the concert market, and entice the recording companies through an established concert-market presence. Such gatecrashing has to be engineered through the mass media — the undiscerning media, such as the lay press and television. This route to success requires musicians to exploit those facets of their personalities that are unrelated to their competence as art-musicians, and to invest a major part of their energy into "marketing" themselves as "brands," leaving less and less energy for their growth as musicians.

Admittedly, the relationship of the living with the living is a tough barrier for the dead to penetrate. Contemporary music therefore, can never be completely swamped by archival music. The dead cannot compete with the living for a presence on the concert platform and in the lay media. Nor can the dead reshape their music for superior acceptability with present-day audiences. But, the dead can now put the living under pressure by claiming a substantial and growing share of the purchasing power and time resources of the audience. From this perspective, archival music is now restructuring the market largely, though not solely, along generational lines. In the short run, it is putting contemporary music under economic pressure. In the long run, however, it will inevitably affect the yardstick by which audiences distinguish between good and bad music.

The Yardstick of Musicianship

Hindustani music is an improvization-dominant art form. The role of the pre-composed element has been shrinking steadily for over two centuries now, with its current durational share being as low as 10-15 per cent in the totality of a rendition. This, too, is only a notional ratio because the relationship of the pre-composed element to the improvized element is unique to each rendition. A piece of Hindustani music, as rendered, is therefore is a totally unique event, impossible to recreate, most of all by the musician himself. If it is true that the validity of any art is entirely contextual, it is true of Hindustani art-music more than any other major art-music tradition.

The continuity-and-change model of Hindustani music is inherent in its continuation as an aural tradition. The tradition has never either intended, nor attempted, to preserve even an approximate record of performed music either for replication or as a pedagogical device. And, the utility of whatever documentation was done could never go beyond an aid to memory. The aesthetic and musical values of this tradition were always intended to be transmitted from one generation to another only through what a musician performed, and what he taught during his lifetime. Having passed them on, the individual musician disappeared from the scene, allowing the interaction between future generations of musicians and audiences to shape their own musical relationship.

This model of continuity and change, "appropriate" for an individualistic and improvization-dominant art form has now been "distorted" by technology. Aesthetic values of a bygone era are now acquiring a relevance unsupported by the contemporary socio-cultural environment. That era cannot be considered either superior, or inferior, to contemporary conditions in terms of any objective yardstick. It was simply different, and cannot be recreated. But the parameters of musicianship which it enabled have now been given an additional, and if you like, "unnatural," lease of life — first by recording technology itself, and then by the technology of acoustic re-engineering of archival recordings. Consciously or otherwise, contemporary audiences could now begin to hold contemporary musicians accountable to these parameters of musicianship that are holdovers from a previous era.

The "yardstick" notion has two dimensions. Firstly, it refers to the phenomenon of something acquiring *a priori* value merely by virtue of having once been lost. It is not subjected to critical evaluation before it is accorded a premium. It is considered valuable merely because it cannot be revived or replicated, and is beyond reach. Secondly, we are dealing with the unstated assumption that everything in this world is drifting away from being "as it was intended to be," and the farther back you go into the past, the closer you are to "things as they were intended to be." By implication, therefore, whatever is closer historically to the "original" is assumed to be closer to the ideal.

With a substantial co-existence of archival music along with contemporary music on the shelves of the music stores and in our homes, this generalized "nostalgia premium" acquires a power beyond the validation of personal experience. This extra-experiential racial nostalgia operates through the agency of the 45+ age group of audiences, who wield great influence over the tastes of the younger listeners, and validate musical values that go much farther back into history.

As an operative reality in the cultural process, this premium to antiquity, divorced from the socio-cultural context of music, has been made possible by the acoustic acceptability of vintage music to contemporary audiences. As a result of this intervention of technology, the contemporary listener is willing to give vintage music an equal chance of shaping the values that enable the mind to distinguish good music from bad. Consequently, the balance between the forces of continuity and the forces of change is being tilted in favour of the former.

The "Virtual Guru"

Perhaps the most significant facet of the phenomenon under review is the emergence of archival music as study material for aspiring musicians. In this role, archival music is filling — even if only partially — the large vacuum in the availability of competent *gurus*.

It is obvious that recorded music cannot function as a total substitute for a competent *guru*. It can only provide a stylistically coherent model of performed music. It cannot inculcate, in the student, either the ideation process or the principles of music-making which make that music possible. Under ideal conditions, therefore, archival music should be a supplementary source of guidance, complementing the efforts of a real-life *guru*.

The optimal use of archival music as study material might require a quality of personalized guidance even rarer than a traditional *guru*. Such a revolution in the process of grooming Hindustani musicians is inconceivable for quite some time to come. Therefore, archival music will influence the music of future generations driven largely by the individual predilections of aspirants. This scenario might appear pregnant with highly unmusical consequences. However, the results may not be uniformly unseemly.

The most obvious results of such a situation could be the mushrooming of Xeroxes, and even laughable caricatures, of the great musicians of the past. Such tendencies are already visible with respect to the influence of some of the modern masters, who are no more. This is not too frightful a prospect.

The *guru-śiṣya paramparā* in Hindustani music was not very different from a reliance on pre-recorded music in its explicit intent. In that system of aesthetic indoctrination, a substantial amount of teaching and learning energy was invested in shaping the *śiṣya* as a decent Xerox of a *guru*. Mercifully, the endeavour failed in most cases because of three human imperfections: imperfect perception, imperfect retention, and imperfect reproduction. Because of these imperfections, the traditional system became an effective instrument of continuity within change. Because of the possibility of repetitive exposure, a pre-recorded archive removes some of these imperfections, and enhances the risk of producing Xeroxes and even caricatures.

With a much larger volume of each departed musician's archive being commercially available, there is bound to emerge a breed of musicians which can adopt, from archival music, the principles of music making, and evolve an expression without the need to ape the archival cliché. Even if this prospect did not exist, this risk need not bother us because the Hindustani tradition has always refused to grant any credibility to Xeroxes. Moreover, for every hundred Xeroxes, the tradition would still be capable of producing one brilliant original.

The other obvious consequence of the emerging scenario is the possibility of aspirants indiscriminately absorbing a multiplicity of stylistic influences from archival sources. This has the potential for shaping music that is no more than an incoherent patchwork of clichés, lacking in substance. But, since we cannot wish away the onslaught of technology, we might look at the more acceptable possibilities arising from it. History will bear witness that the Hindustani tradition has consistently produced great originals who could integrate diverse influences into an aesthetically coherent whole. Indeed, the greatest names in pre-Independence music were, almost without exception, disciples of multiple stylistic lineages.

The intervention of technology in effect enables the Hindustani tradition to resume the transmission of aesthetic values and the skills of musicianship, disrupted for over two generations because of a growing shortage of competent *gurus*. Even if the conditions for the exploitation of archival material as a pedagogical device are not ideal, its availability on a commercial scale constitutes a definite empowerment of every aspiring musician.

Optimism about the intelligent, rather than mindless, utilization of the archival resource is justified by the emerging profile of musicians. Increasingly, professional musicians belong to highly educated families, and have acquired significant academic credentials, though not necessarily in music. They have the intellect, and the keenness, to establish an interactive relationship with scholarship in the field of music, and to acquaint themselves with its output. Such a profile greatly reduces the risk of absurd results.

The Big Picture

Essentially, the archival revival movement corrects a significant discontinuity imposed on the Hindustani music tradition by the growing shortage of competent teachers in the post-Independence period. In the cultural process, the forces of continuity have now been strengthened through an infusion of a powerful source of traditional aesthetic values. As recording companies encash the commercial opportunities opened up by the demographic patterns of the market, Hindustani music could now be revitalized by the restoration of the continuity, which was lost during the second half of the twentieth century. Contemporary musicians may now find it possible, and even necessary, to forge a stronger link between the music of the present and the music of the past. Such a link may become a prerequisite to establishing their credibility amongst the influentials of the music market. The forward march of romanticism and post-modernist tendencies could now be arrested, at least for the moment. These pressures are primarily the creations of the technologies of acoustic restoration of archival recordings, and the feasibility of their low-cost commercialization and distribution on a national scale.

This phenomenon also has larger implications for the contemporary music-scape, which the contemporary musician should welcome, rather than fear. The present music scene reveals three categories of impoverishment in comparison with the pre-Independence era. The variety of genres represented by quality musicianship has shrunk drastically. The pre-modern *dhrupad* and the semi-classical *ṭhumarī*, for instance, stand considerably depleted. Within each genre, there is a diminution in the variety of *gharānā*s represented by quality musicianship. And, across genres and *gharānā*s, the total number of *rāga*s and *bandiśa*s being performed on the concert platform, or available on pre-recorded media, is dwindling.

All these losses may be partially recovered by the return of vintage music to the shelves of the music stores.

A serious musician, at any level of accomplishment, remains forever a student of music. He seeks and values a "reference library" that aids the ideational process, and enables him to enrich the musical product that he delivers. To this extent, the accelerated commercialization of archival music can be expected to enrich the totality of the environment for Hindustani music through its influence on listeners as well as contemporary musicians.

What we are witnessing today is a market-driven phenomenon. The logic of the recording companies will necessarily be different from that of those who are concerned about the preservation and revival of the artistic tradition. The music community can, therefore, expect only limited and slow benefits from the initiatives of the recording companies. If faster or sharply focused results are desired, the music community will have to take the initiative in converting the rewards of technology into a trigger for a veritable renaissance.

1.6

A REQUIEM FOR THE GHARĀNĀS

OVER the last half a century, stylistic pedigree and genealogy have emerged as the least clearly understood, and the most insidiously exploited facet of our musical culture. The truth or otherwise of *gharānā* claims made by individual musicians is not the issue, because these are verifiable in every case. The issue is whether the claims carry any substance in terms of musical value, and what we may legitimately infer from *gharānā* linkages in the contemporary context.

What is a Gharānā?

The word *gharānā* is used to denote a distinctive style of rendering *rāga*-based music in the modern genres of Hindustani music. The *gharānā* system or tradition is most clearly defined in the *khayāla* genre of vocalism, and has been a formidable force in shaping Hindustani music for two centuries. The *gharānā*s had their forerunners in the four *banī*s [literally, dialects] of medieval *dhrupad* music, which ruled Hindustani art-music between the fourteenth and eighteenth centuries. But, even pre-*dhrupad* music recognized several *mata*s [literally, ideologies], acknowledging the existence of diversity.

Stylistic diversity in musical expression is virtually written into the script of Indian culture because of the large number of racial-ethnic-linguistic groups that inhabit the sub-continent. A degree of homogeneity was probably achieved during the Mogul era, when musician communities were concentrated in and around Delhi, and were supported by the patronage of the Imperial court. After the Mogul Empire disintegrated, musicians migrated to the smaller principalities under British protection in search of alternative patronage. Once art music was allowed to intermingle with the local cultures under conditions of relative isolation, the essential diversity of Indian culture re-surfaced effort-lessly and got crystallized in the form of *gharānā*s.

Considering the powerful forces working in favour of diversity, it is truly remarkable that the essential core of Hindustani music has remained uniform throughout non-peninsular India, and stable for centuries, with diversity manifested largely in the manner of rendition. The melodic and rhythmic content of Hindustani music originates in the *rāga*s and *tāla*s of the system, which are common to all *banī*s of *dhrupad* and the *gharānā*s of post-*dhrupad* genres. The architecture of *rāga*-presentation is determined by the genre that is performed. It is only in the manner and mode of rendition that the tradition exhibits considerable diversity. This diversity needed names for identification. The word *gharānā* emerged as the most appropriate for this purpose.

The word *gharānā* is derived from *ghara* [house/home, from the Sanskrit noun: *gṛha*]. In Hindi and Urdu, *gharānā* is a collective noun denoting those who live under the same roof; therefore, a family, a lineage, a clan. The first significance of the term is thus derived from heredity, or ties of kinship.

The names of *gharānā*s are most commonly the names of places, such as Agra, Rampur, Gwalior, Jaipur, Atrauli, Kirana, Indore, etc. The second significance of the term, therefore, derives from the place of origin. Because the nomenclature implies the existence of distinguishing features, it recognizes that the distinctiveness of each *gharānā* is attributable, in considerable measure, to its place of origin.

Gharānās named after their places of origin almost always have the names of one, sometimes two, towering personalities treated either as their founders, or landmark personalities. The Kirana *gharānā* of the *khayāla* is, for instance, associated with the name of Abdul Kareem Khan, considered the fountainhead of the distinctive style. Likewise, the Jaipur-Atrauli *gharānā* of *khayāla* reveres Alladiya Khan as its founder, and the Etawah *gharānā* of the *sitāra* and *surabahāra* treats Imdad Khan as its landmark personage.

Thus, we have three different, historical factors, converging to define a *gharānā* as a stylistic distinctiveness or an ideology of music making, exhibiting signs of continuity over several generations. In plain language, once upon a time, there was a great musician, whose music was different from those who lived in other villages or cities. He groomed his sons as musicians and they sang a lot like him; and their music was also different from the music of those who lived in other places, and in the same respect as their father's was. And, this went on for several generations, as long as conditions were favourable.

Favourable Conditions

This caveat is important — "as long as conditions were favourable." Conditions do change, and often change radically enough to nullify the cultural meaning we attach to certain historical facts. This is why we need to examine the conditions that favoured the perpetuation of certain well-defined styles in the rendition of Hindustani music.

The scrutiny must relate to the basic notions defining *gharānās*. It is easy to appreciate the appearance of a great musician whose style influenced many other musicians of his own generation as well as the next. But, beyond this, the phenomenon requires some exploration. Why did the sons and nephews of musicians need, or want, to become musicians? And, why did the style of a musician from Gwalior, and his sons and nephews, need to be, or end up becoming, distinctly different from that of their corresponding generations from Agra or Jaipur?

Hereditary musicianship was a creation of genetic, familial, as well as economic factors. Genetic factors were conducive to the transmission of the musical sensibility, subject to the naturally determined pattern of probabilities. The risks associated with this mode of transmission were systematically reduced by a preference for marital alliances between the progeny of professional musicians. The concern for this risk was so great, especially amongst Muslims, that the community of professional musicians even permitted marriage between first cousins. The notion of the art as an asset, and the desire to keep it "in the family" encouraged in-breeding.

The children of musicians thus grew up in an environment dominated by the practice of music. Familial factors ensured that a great deal of learning of music took place involuntarily. The voluntary aspect of hereditary musicianship responded to the attractions of feudal patronage. The employment of *nawābs*, *mahārājas*, and *zamīndārs* under British protection, promised lifelong economic security, and constituted the most attractive market for musicians. Patrons were few and the supply of talent was unlimited, resulting in an intensely competitive situation for musicians.

The greatest amongst musicians were, of course, wooed by the most powerful amongst princes; but the rest struggled for survival. The "market" for art music was too small to support its pursuance as an independent self-employed profession. Under these conditions, it was natural that patronage be regarded as an "asset" to be protected and, if possible, bequeathed to direct descendants. The incentive for doing so arose from the lack of widespread access to formal education, and the predominantly feudal-agrarian economy, which severely limited career options.

For musicians enjoying feudal patronage, the chances of bequeathing the patronage asset were perceived to be the greatest if they could turn their children into their own musical clones. The patron's heir, also chosen by heredity, and aesthetically nurtured on the senior musician's art, would — in all likelihood — also accept the heir to the musician's stylistic legacy. This likelihood made it attractive for the sons of musicians to be inducted early into the ownership of the art-asset and put through a rigorous process of aesthetic indoctrination. This process struck deep roots in the musical culture because the "market" — feudal patrons — rewarded its products. It often became a matter of "national" pride. A king could legitimately boast of his army, his elephants, his jewels, his palaces and even his *gharānā* of music.

Even without its cloning intentions, hereditary musicianship would have qualified as an eminently suitable vehicle for the Hindustani tradition, which requires the musician to perform the simultaneous roles of composer and performer. The demands of this duality have grown exponentially over the second millennium, as the role of the pre-composed element has shrunk, and that of the improvised elements has grown. As a corollary, the notion of a *rāga* has risen to progressively higher levels of abstraction. The combination of these tendencies has left the art with no effective mode of transmission other than the aural. Involuntary familial exposure to the art during the most formative years, accompanied or followed by a voluntary submission to the rigors of grooming, was therefore uniquely promising as a pedagogical culture.

Predictably, heredity could not retain exclusive control over the music world for long. Despite the painstaking "genetic engineering" practised by professional musicians — and perhaps also because of it — heredity turned out to be an unreliable guarantee of musicianship potential. In all probability, patronage also became progressively disenchanted with heredity, and more categorically committed to musicianship. Therefore, with the exhortation of patrons, and often under their orders, musicians began to groom promising talent beyond the orbit of kinship. But, since the nature of the art demanded intensive and involuntary exposure, and the "market" demanded stylistic continuity, the mentor-pupil relationship cast itself into the parent-child model of cohabitation, and total subordination verging on servility.

Although stylistic cloning was the explicit intent of this art transmission system, it could not possibly have been its result. In addition to the "generation gap," such as might have existed, three imperfections inherent to aural transmission took care of the element of change — imperfect perception, imperfect retention, and imperfect reproduction. Therefore, by and large, the system did not produce clones; but it did produce musicians who explicitly attempted continuity, while inevitably representing change. Depending on the quality of talent each *gharānā* produced, the strong bias towards continuity resulted in the progressive refinement and enrichment of the salient features of its style, in addition to giving the music a greater degree of aesthetic coherence. These processes yielded a variety of musical styles defined by a genealogy of tutelage, only partially coinciding with heredity.

Such an outcome was possible because, by and large, each lineage pursued its special interests relatively insulated from other lineages. Partial protection against dilution and disorientation came from the self-righteous and dogmatic attitudes that were cultivated during the period of grooming. These fortifications worked because of the appalling backwardness of the country in terms of transport and communications. Even early twentieth century accounts of great musicians report that they took leave of their princely employers to go on concert tours, that could last several months, and even a couple of years.

The Golden Age of Hindustani Music

The *gharānā*s thus came to be distinctive stylistic lineages of post-*dhrupad* art music, shaped by feudal patronage, heredity, a rigorous pedagogical environment relying substantially on aesthetic indoctrination, and a backward economy starved of education, career options, transport and communications. The result they delivered was a variety of distinct musical styles within the same genre of music, with each style possessing an aesthetic coherence arising from a set of fundamentally held and assiduously cultivated musical values. The distinctive features of the *gharānā*s have been the subject of considerable scholarly attention.

V.H. Deshpande [1987 2nd edn.] offers a conceptual framework for the aesthetic classification of the *gharānā*s of *khayāla* music. He classifies *gharānā* styles on a continuum defined by rhythmic orientation and melodic orientation as the two polarities. Amongst the *gharānā*s considered by him, he places the Agra at the rhythmic orientation polarity, and Kirana at the melodic orientation polarity. At the exact mid-point of the continuum, he places Alladiya [Jaipur-Atrauli] as a complex fusion, and Gwalior as a simple fusion of the two orientations. Patiala is placed towards the melodic orientation pole, but considerably short of Kirana. The Indore/ Bhindi Bazar *gharānā* of Ameer Khan, falls between Patiala and Kirana, close to the melodic orientation pole.

This blossoming of the *khayāla* genre in various hues and fragrances, represented by towering musicianship in all the *gharānā*s, made it possible for the century preceding India's Independence [1947], to be described as the "Golden Age of Hindustani music." However, the *gharānā* system had exposed its limitations even before Independence.

Chinks in the Armor

Deshpande [1987] points out, with stunning validity, that the greatest vocalists of the Golden Age had been, almost without exception, disciples of multiple *gharānā*s. Evidently, the *gharānā* system was incapable of supporting the flowering of true genius, and forced it to seek a diversity of exposure in search of its own voice. This phenomenon suggested that stylistic loyalty to a single *gharānā* was no guarantee of quality musicianship and could, indeed, be an inhibitor of exceptional potential in so highly individualistic an art as Hindustani music.

Chinks in the *gharānā* armor expanded into gaping holes from the dawn of the twentieth century, when the print and electronic media weakened the hold of the personalized *guru-śiṣya* relationship over the art-transmission process.

In the first quarter of the century, V.N. Bhatkhande published his near-encyclopaedic re-interpretation and documentation of the Hindustani music tradition. From a pedagogical perspective, the most important aspects of his work were the development of an eminently usable notation system, the documentation of *rāga* grammar, and the publication of a large repertoire of *bandiśa*s with notations. His contemporary, Vishnu Digambar Paluskar also published highly reliable documentation of *rāga* grammar and *bandiśa*s. Paluskar, however, made a more immediate impact on the accessibility of musical knowledge and performing skills by setting up Gandharva Mahavidyalaya, India's first music university. In its early years, this university trained a virtual army of musical missionaries to run music schools all over the country.

Collectively, Bhatkhande and Paluskar provided a large part of the knowledge-base and the institutional framework to create an alternative pedagogical environment. They partially liberated the art transmission process from the one-to-one, personalized, *guru-śiṣya* relationship. But, even within the one-to-one relationship, they freed it partially from aural transmission. Their work enabled ample and unselective access to musical knowledge, made it less dependent on aural transmission, took some of the tyranny out of the teacher-taught relationship, and thus weakened the forces, which created the "cloning effect" characteristic of the *gharānā* phenomenon.

The momentum of homogenizing forces in the musical culture was greatly enhanced by the appearance of the radio and the gramophone record in the early years of the twentieth century. The electronic media ended the isolation of the different *gharānā*s from each other by making the music of every musician accessible to every other musician and aspirant to musicianship. These media also enlarged the market for art music. By the time the cost-effective audio-cassette made its appearance with concert-length recordings in the 1960s, pre-recorded music was emerging as a "virtual *guru*." Hereafter, technology and commerce worked in tandem to demolish traditional barriers to the acquisition of musical knowledge and skills, talent's entry into musicianship, and to the public's access to music.

However, even before this development, Independence and the launch of a parliamentary democracy had demolished the bulwark of the *gharānā* system — the feudal aristocracy. The demise of the feudal aristocracy was far more significant than is commonly recognized. In addition to the dispossession of a patron class, this transition took away an important quality control mechanism operating in Hindustani music. In the feudal era, only the finest musicians secured sinecures of patronage. And, once they were appointed in the service of a court, they became models of musicianship for the laity, with the most promising talent within their territories gravitating to them for grooming. This process of automatic matching of talent to opportunity took a beating when the princely states were abolished.

Democratic India forced musicians to migrate from the smaller towns to the big cities. Economic development started offering musicians' children alternative career options. Heredity, already abandoned as the exclusive entry criterion, gave way to a talent-based selection system for grooming. But, the anonymity of urban life could not guarantee the automatic gravitation of the most promising talent towards the greatest musicianship. Even when such relationships did get forged, the stresses of managing self-employment left the greatest musicians depleted of energy and time for teaching. With the best of intentions, the rigorous institution of personalized tutoring, that had sustained the *gharānā* system in the feudal context, could not be supported in the urban context.

These factors, coupled with easier access to music through the electronic media, corroded the two most important features of the *gharānā* system — stylistic distinctiveness of the different *gharānā*s, and the aesthetic coherence in the music of each musician nurtured by a *gharānā*. These trends obliged Prof. Bonnie Wade [1984] to observe that the epitaph for the *gharānā* system was about to be written, if it had not been written already. This observation was valid not only for *khayāla* vocalism, for which it was intended, but also for the lineages of instrumental music, which have exhibited a comparatively lower level of stylistic diversity.

The Gharānā "Brands" Today

In the contemporary context, then, what does it mean, when a musician claims your attention as a stylistic descendant of Miyā Tānsen, or as the twentieth generation in an unbroken lineage of musicians?

First, what it does mean. It means that the musician has not drifted into music purely because of heredity, or by the absence of alternative careers, but chosen music as a voluntary pursuit. It also means that he has submitted himself to apprenticeship under an "authorized" teacher of a particular *gharānā*, and has been formally accepted into it. It implies that he accepts his accountability for adherence to the stylistic features for which his lineage is known.

Now, let us consider what his claim does not necessarily mean. It does not mean that his tutelage with his *guru* has been sufficiently long and intensive for him to internalize the aesthetic coherence and stylistic distinctiveness for which the lineage is respected. And, it can certainly not mean that his music is substantially free from all stylistic influences other than seniors of his own lineage.

A majority of musicians born in free India will be embarrassed into silence by this interpretation of their *gharānā* claims. Amongst the leading *khayāla* vocalists of the younger generation, there is, admittedly, still a reasonable presence of *gharānā* linkages. In most cases, however, either the tutelage links are tenuous, or the lineages themselves are stylistically blurred, or the music flouts the hallmarks of the professed *gharānā*. These facts do not detract from their outstanding musicianship on dimensions of aesthetic coherence or stylistic distinctiveness. But they do demonstrate the marginalization of the *gharānā* as a determinant of style.

From the trends we observe, we are obliged to infer that, increasingly, the lineage of a musician can only be as relevant as that of a lawyer or a medical specialist, whom we, in India, trust in relation to his heredity, education, and apprenticeship. What do we need to know before we permit any of them to prove their worth to us? Whose son is he? What is his education? Whose student/apprentice is/was he? Did his father/mentor have a track record of producing illustrious protégés? What is/was his father's/mentor's specialization? And, what is his specialization?

Even if all these questions are answered satisfactorily for a musician, they do not, and cannot, establish a musician's talent, competence and integrity, any more than that of a lawyer or a surgeon. These, we can assess only by the manner in which they conduct themselves, and the competence with which they relate to our needs. This is, no doubt, bad news for music lovers who are looking for easy short-cuts to assessing musicianship, and imagined *gharānā* affiliations to be the key to it. Their only consolation is that misjudging musicianship is far less hazardous than misjudging the competence of a medical or a legal consultant.

Beyond two generations of probable relevance, *gharānā*s are now little more than misleading history for audiences, and an academic indulgence for critics. This truth calls for neither lament, nor rejoicing. Hindustani music is built on the foundations of continuity within change. This reality will remain operative as long as Hindustani music remains an improvization-dominant tradition, impossible to transmit without a substantial dependence on the aural experience. The same is true of stylistic diversity. It existed before the *gharānā*s emerged, and will remain as long as India remains a multi-racial, multi-ethnic, multi-linguistic sub-continent.

With the fading away of the *gharānā*s, one model of continuity and diversity is being driven into history by political, social and economic changes. An alternative model, or perhaps a multiplicity of models is replacing the *gharānā* model, even if the emerging configuration of forces cannot yet be conceptualized. In the future, as in the past, the balance between continuity and change, and between homogeneity and diversity, will be decided by how audiences want art-music to relate to the world around them, and to their inner worlds.

PART II

Form, Idiom and Format

2.1

ARCHITECTURE IN MODERN HINDUSTANI MUSIC*

IN Hindustani music, architecture would refer to the structural aspect of a performance that enables it to consummate its function — communicating the emotional content of a *rāga*, utilizing its melodic personality as the trigger for the emotional experience. Architectural values in classical music are more durable, and less culture-specific, than extra-architectural values because they are based on insights into the nature of the creative and auto-suggestive processes of the musician as well as the cognitive-responsive processes of audiences.

By the middle of the twentieth century, the vocal as well as instrumental manifestations of Hindustani music had cast themselves into a mature and sophisticated architectural model, which acknowledged its *dhrupad* legacy while also carving out a post-*dhrupad* evolutionary path. This model inspired the golden age of vocal music in the first half of the twentieth century, and instrumental music in the latter.

In the last few decades of the twentieth century, however, the music being rendered by a majority of the post-Independence generation of musicians has begun to suggest a

---

* [Reproduced with the consent of Sangeet Natak Akademi, New Delhi, from *Sangeet Natak*, Vol. XXXVI, Number 1, 2001.]

considerable weakening of the structural model hitherto established. It appears almost as if "creator and spectator are locked in a conspiracy against history, geography, and specificity, which may be considered liberating or destructive . . . but which is entirely without precedent in the history of the arts" [Kenneth McLeish, 1993].

Theoretically, it can be argued that all art, and therefore all change in artistic expression, is automatically legitimate because it is a "natural" response to the socio-economic environment. In the same vein, it can also be argued, as long as it has an audience, contemporary artistic expression can be assumed, *a priori*, to have remained culturally relevant. Such assumptions may not, however, be entirely valid when the magnitude of discontinuities is abnormal enough to threaten the fundamental aspects of an artistic tradition. At such times, it could become important to acknowledge the breakdown of the mechanism that sustains the relationship between the arts and cultural meaning, and to aid its restoration.

An important part of this mechanism is a constant dialogue between the parallel traditions of scholarship and performance. In the interest of such a dialogue, it may be helpful to take another look at the modern architectural model of Hindustani music performance.

The Architectural Metaphor

Le Curbusier [Towards a new architecture] describes a building as a machine to live in; nothing more, nothing less. To him, the plan, i.e., the functional organization of spaces, is everything; any element that does not derive inevitably from the plan is either sculpture or ornamentation, and therefore redundant to the essence of architecture. Drawing loosely on this conceptual framework, any artefact can be seen as having an architectural component, a sculptural component, and an ornamentational component. Here, architecture would refer to the manner in which the creation *functions*; the sculptural aspect would refer to the way it *looks*; and the ornamentational to the way it *pleases*.

In relation to music in general, one might say that all music has elements of architecture, sculpture and ornamentation, though their relative weightage would vary from one piece of music to another. The metaphor can provide a useful framework for understanding Hindustani music too. For instance, at a macro level, genres of Hindustani music can be classified as being architecture-dominant [*dhrupad*], sculpture-dominant [*khayāla*] or ornamentation-dominant [*ṭhumarī*]. Then again, within the same genre, the musical temperaments of individual musicians can be described as architecture-oriented [Kesarbai Kerkar or Ameer Khan], sculpture-oriented [Omkarnath Thakur or Roshanara Begum], or ornamentation-oriented [Bade Ghulam Ali Khan].

By extending this analogy to the micro level, individual *rāga*-renditions can be broken down into architectural, sculptural and ornamentation facets. For the purpose of this discussion, we shall isolate the architectural, or structure-functional, aspect of *rāga*-rendition from its stylistic aspects.

Function and Structure

What is the "function" of a Hindustani music rendition? Its function is a comprehensive exploration of the chosen *rāga*. In this context, comprehensiveness encompasses the melodic as well as emotional character of the *rāga* rendered.

The melodic and emotional facets of a *rāga*'s personality are not distinct from each other, but intimately linked. The melodic facet of each *rāga*'s personality is pregnant with a well-defined emotional charge that does not require either a name or conscious awareness. To the Indian mind, this proposition is valid *a priori*. From this arises the proposition that the architecture of a rendition enables the effective exposition of the melodic facet of a *rāga*'s personality and thereby maximizes the probability of releasing the emotional charge inherent in it.

The primacy of architecture — rather than sculpture or ornamentation — as the repository of durable values has almost intuitive appeal because the functionality of any structure is based on principles that are either universal or reasonably stable in their validity. For instance, a residence in which the main entrance is through a bathroom or a kitchen, or a home with three bedrooms and twenty bath-rooms, would be a piece of bewildering architecture in any era. Then again, in a society that respects privacy, a home with one bedroom leading into another, which leads into yet another, would be considered dysfunctional.

This analogy is valid with respect to classical music. But, there is a small difference. In Hindustani music, though not necessarily in architecture, the bewildering is automatically dysfunctional because the central vision of the creator needs to be intelligible before the creation can function as an object of aesthetic appreciation, or evoke an emotional response. Architecture in Hindustani music, then, refers to the manner in which a musician selects its elements or movements, and organizes them for exploration of the chosen *rāga* — explicitly for intelligibility, and implicitly for eliciting the desired emotional response.

In the post-*dhrupad* era, Hindustani music has acquired an overall linearity of progression, encompassing subordinate cyclicities within it. It is through this overall linearity that Hindustani music seeks to make itself comprehensible.

The Linearity of Progression

The primary linearity drives the music simultaneously through the following progressions, and arranges the different movements, sequentially, in progressive sequence:

(a) from the melodically simple to the melodically complex

(b) from lower levels of *svara*-density towards higher levels of *svara*-density

(c) from the rhythmically simple towards the rhythmically complex

(d) from lower beat-densities [tempi] towards higher beat-densities

(e) from the relatively unstructured towards the more structured

Anyone trained formally in the psychology or education will recognize these principles as being fundamental to learning, comprehension, and retention. As a demonstration of this principle in Hindustani music, consider the formal structure of *khayāla* presentation, consisting of a *baḍā khayāla* and a *choṭā khayāla*.

The *baḍā khayāla* commences with the *bandiśa* and the *ālāpa*, which is very low in melodic density [*svara*s intoned per minute], is rendered at a very slow tempo [usually below 30 beats per minute-bpm], and is rhythmically unstructured. The next stage of development could be a *bola-bāṇṭa*, rendered at a slightly stepped-up tempo [perhaps up to 40 bpm]; the melody is slightly more complex, denser in terms of *svara*s intoned per minute, and corresponds better to the beats of the rhythmic cycle. The third stage of the development could be *tāna*s, which are even higher in melodic density and melodic complexity, are sung at a tempo stepped up even further, and involve melody corresponding more systematically to the beats of the rhythmic cycle. This linear progression of melodic and rhythmic density and complexity is elevated to a still higher level in the *choṭā khayāla*, which may commence at 160 bpm, and accelerate to 240 bpm before it closes.

The overall linearity of progression is important because it is consistent with the way the human mind works. If its unidirectional flow is not maintained, the comprehension of the music ceases to be effortless. To the extent that the listener is required, intermittently, to focus his cerebral faculties to comprehend the music, he becomes less responsive to its emotional charge.

This unidirectional flow is equally important for the musician himself because, in an improvization-dominant art form, the musician is also his own audience. He is absorbing the music sequentially even as it is being created, and responding cumulatively to it much the same way as the audience is. The deliberateness of the structurally meticulous approach is, therefore, essential to the autosuggestive process by which the musician "works himself" into the realm of the *rāga*'s emotionality. A disciplined adherence to the linearity cannot, of course, guarantee either the musician's transportation into a different realm, or that of his audience; but it certainly maximizes the probability of such an event.

In the *baḍā khayāla*, for instance, once the rendition has progressed to the *tāna* stage, the musician cannot retrogress into *bola-bāṇṭa*, or alternate between *bola-bāṇṭa* and *tāna*s, except for an occasional breather, or to create an element of surprise. If he does so, he is not only disturbing the process of comprehension by the audience, but also upsetting the process by which he leads himself into the emotional content of the *rāga*'s personality from its melodic facet.

Such a musician is in poor control over his own cerebral, aesthetic, and emotional processes, and cannot therefore exercise any significant control over his music. This is why the connoisseur of music is unwilling, or perhaps unable, to distinguish between a musician who is steadfast in his adherence to the principle of linear progression and one whose music touches the heart.

The Cyclicity of Melodic Exploration

While the linearity of the structure addresses itself to the universal psychology of human comprehension, the cyclicity protocol governs the more culture-specific and *rāga*-specific aesthetic values. As a culture-specific feature, it confirms the cyclical notion of time common to all ancient civilizations [*Time: Rhythm & Response*, Marie-Louise von Franz, 1978]. As a *rāga*-specific requirement, it ensures that the melodic personality of the *rāga* is fully explored, and the probability of eliciting the target emotional response is maximized.

Cutting across the central strand of linear progression, or superimposed upon it, *rāga*-presentation involves two cyclicities — the cyclicity of melodic exploration within each movement, and that of the rhythmic cycle, wherever operative. From the architectural angle, the model for melodic exploration is more significant because it is relevant for the classical genres of Hindustani music, irrespective of the existence or absence of central linearity.

At least since Miyā Tānsen [*Sangeet Chintamani*: KCD Brihaspati, 1989], Hindustani music has had a four-stage melodic development protocol. Tānsen recommended a *pada* [from Sanskrit *padya*, or poetry] of four stanzas. There would be no sanctity to the number four unless the stanzas were intended also to be composed differently, with each having a specific melodic-aesthetic function. Collectively, just as the poetic verses in a *pada* are intended as a complete expression of an emotional statement, the four parts of the melody are intended as an aesthetically satisfying exposition of the *rāga*. Significantly enough, Tānsen also prescribed that the *rasa* of the poetry and that of the *rāga* should be in perfect consonance.

Therefore, we have four melodic movements, with their distinctive melodic patterns: *sthāyī, antarā, sañcārī, ābhoga*.

(a) *Sthāyī*: Melodically, this is understood as covering the lower half of the melodic canvas: from the lower octave up to the mid-point of the middle octave. By convention, the melodic development commences at base — *sa*, descends to the bottom of the lower octave, and then ascends upwards towards base — *sa* and beyond.

(b) *Antarā*: Melodically, this is interpreted as covering the upper half of the melodic canvas: between the mid-point of the middle octave and the outer limit of the higher octave. Here, the higher octave *sa* receives special emphasis as a climactic point of ascent from the mid-octave region.

(c) *Sañcārī*: *Sañcāra* in Sanskrit means disseminating, or dispersing over distances. The term negates the idea of both, the ascending progression characteristic of the *sthāyī-antarā* and the winding-up notion in the fourth part, the *ābhoga*. *Sañcārī* is necessarily a free flowing movement covering the entire melodic canvas, usually at a slightly accelerated pace.

(d) *Ābhoga*: The word means satiation and completion. The connotation here is of winding up, wrapping up, and rolling up the canvas opened up systematically by the *sthāyī* and *antarā*, and then painted in detail by the *sañcārī*. Here, there is disagreement over the proper melodic structure, but none about what the word means or the melodic intent.

There do exist some differences of opinion over the melodic form and sequencing of the *sañcārī* and *ābhoga*. These differences are insignificant in the face of the fact that contemporary musicians have all but dropped these concepts of melodic exposition from their treatment of a *rāga*. On a close scrutiny of *bandiśa*-renditions in contemporary instrumental music, it is evident that, increasingly, the *antarā* too is falling into disuse. It is conceivable that, in the near future, even the *sthāyī* will be truncated, and all that will remain of the *bandiśa* is the *mukhaḍā* [the opening phrase of the *sthāyī*].

Music is a language. The rules of grammar, whether in a spoken language or in music, have the purpose of aiding communication without requiring great learning either on the part of the sender or the receiver of the communication. If the emotional statement inherent in every *rāga* is to be understood, the aid of grammar is required. The current grammar of each *rāga* prescribes rules to ensure that even an undistinguished musician can do a fair job of communicating its emotional content. The four-stage melodic development can be seen, therefore, as a similar risk-control device because it can also ensure that every *rāga*, no matter what its character, has an equal and adequate chance of being successfully rendered.

Particularly important in this respect is the directional and regional character of *rāgas* [*aṅga-prādhānya* and *diśā-prādhānya*]. Some *rāgas* are *āroha-pradhāna*, while others are *avaroha-pradhāna*. Then some *rāgas* are *pūrvāṅga-pradhāna*, while others are *madhyāṅga-pradhāna* or *uttarāṅga-pradhāna*. These facets of a *rāga*'s personality risk being underemphasized if a musician sacrifices the *sañcārī* and *ābhoga* movements, which are spared from mandatory ascending-descending protocol. A recognizable melodic outline of a *rāga* can, of course, be presented without the *sañcārī* and *ābhoga*; and this is indeed being done most of the time in contemporary Hindustani music. The abbreviated form, however, cannot qualify as a *rāga*-exposition because a *rāga* is more than a melodic entity.

A *rāga* is an aid to the contemplation of a particular facet of the human mind, and carries within itself the "racial memory" of experiencing certain emotions. Our *rāga*s are archetypal entities, pregnant with not only deep cultural meaning, but also have a universal component of meaning. Thus, every *rāga* is an isolation of one aspect of man's mind for elaborate exploration. If this were not so, a *rāga* would be no different from a song — incapable of contemplation.

The Econometric Model

It is possible to visualize the superimposition of cyclical melodic expositions onto the central linearity of progression using the classic time-series graph in econometrics. As its central tendency, there is a secular trend-line of progressive enhancement of melodic density and complexity. Cutting across this trend-line are cyclical melodic expositions of each movement, which would also provide for random distortions of the cycles [see Graph 1].

In the "Hindu" notion of time, linearity is only a myopic

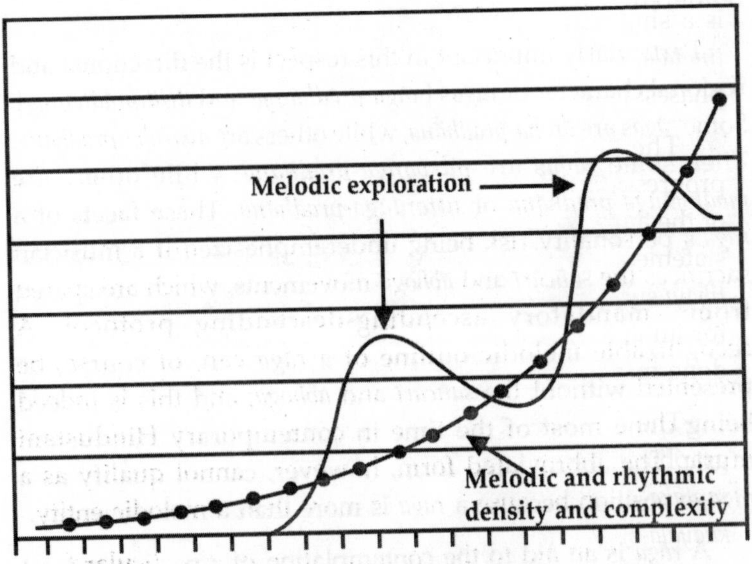

Graph 1 : Performance Duration

view of the essential cyclicity of time. As a model of time, this graph, with a dominant linear tendency, and subordinate cyclical tendencies, suggests a "non-Hindu" socio-cultural foundation. This suggestion has historical validation because modern Hindustani music is a fusion of "Hindu" musical ideas with Perso-Arabic [Islamic] influences. In this respect, it represents a departure from the architecture of the medieval *dhrupad* genre, which was closer to the Hindu roots of our musical tradition, and which isolated the dominant cyclicity of the *pada*-rendition from the predominant linearity of the preceding *ālāpa*. The econometric model is especially interesting because it finds an oblique echo in the cultural process.

A Case Study

In June 1991, Ustad Vilayat Khan recorded his creation, *rāga Sanjh Saravali*, for India Archive Music Ltd., New York [IAM CD 1040]. For its architecture, this recording will qualify amongst the classics of recorded Hindustani music. The music is a single-piece *vilaṁbit* [*baḍā*] *khayāla*-style presentation in *tīnatāla*, lasting seventy-four minutes. The rendition is in three phases: [a] *ālāpa*, [b] *laya-banta*, and [c] *tāna*s.

The recording was analysed manually for melodic progression and the progress of the tempo. For the purpose of the analysis, the performance was divided into 119 musical statements, separated from each other either by a *mukhaḍā*, a *tihāyī* substituting for a *mukhaḍā*, *antarā*, or a *tihāyī* substituting for an *antarā*. The notation of every melodic statement was done manually.

The melodic span of each musical statement was plotted graphically with a scaling of tonal frequencies to the *mandra-saptaka sa* = 1. The melodic plot of the entire 74-minute *baḍā khayāla*-style presentation is shown in Graph 2. Graph 3 plots the tempo of the performance, measured from the beats of the *tabalā* accompaniment throughout the performance, using a stopwatch.

In Graph 2, it is observed that Ustad Vilayat Khan takes the *ālāpa* through his elaborate version of *sthāyī, antarā, sañcārī* and *ābhoga*. He then re-establishes the *bandiśa* with a *laya-banta*

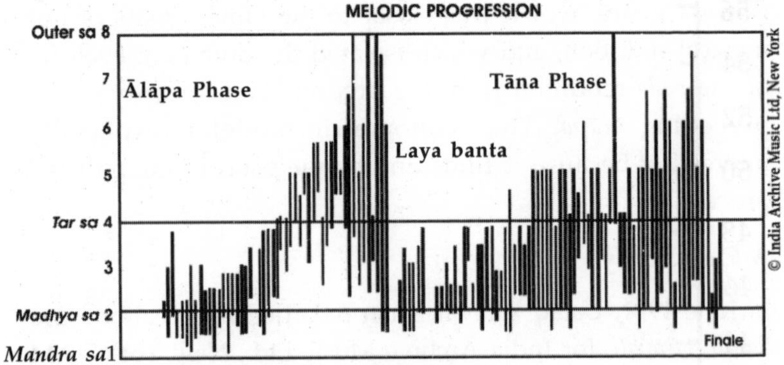

Graph 2

movement, and then launches the *tāna*s section. It is also worth noting that the melodic plot of the *tāna*s section is almost a mirror image of the *ālāpa* section, suggesting that the same conceptual framework of *sthāyī, antarā, sañcārī* and *ābhoga* also guides the melodic pattern of his *tāna*s. A careful listening of the recording will reveal that the progression logic is not limited only to the melodic span of the *tāna*s, but also covers the melodic density and complexity dimensions.

In Graph 3, we observe that the *ālāpa* is rendered at 36 bpm. There is a small *joḍa*-type section at 40 bpm, which steps up to 44 bpm in the *laya-banta* movement. The *tāna*s begin at 46 bpm, and step up gradually to 64 bpm, just prior to the anti-climactic finale.

This analysis establishes that the music of the living greats does follow the structural approach. On this basis, one can argue that the architecture of their presentation holds an

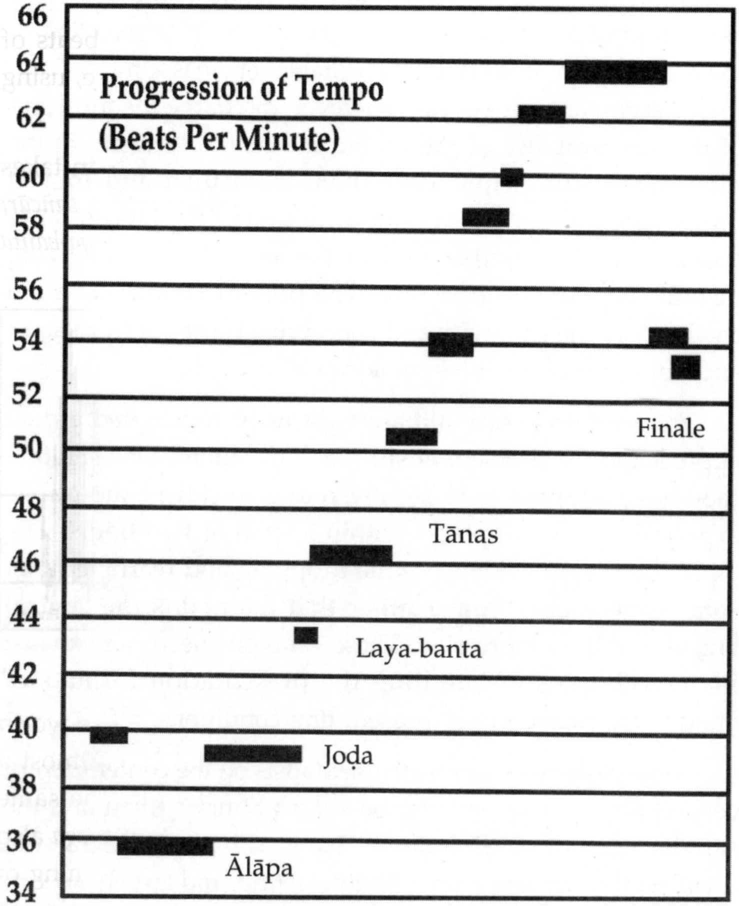

important clue to the greatness of their music. This analysis also suggests that their approach to music making is potentially decipherable, and that the econometric model presented above is a suitable representation of the architecture of modern Hindustani music.

The Duration Factor

In defence of the short-cuts and disorder in vogue on the contemporary concert platform, it has been argued that concert durations no longer permit a leisurely and comprehensive exposition of a *rāga*. Under such conditions, a telescoping of the presentation protocol is unavoidable. There is some validity to this argument. It does not, however, discharge the musician of the responsibility of preserving the central linearity of the movements and sequencing them in distinct and logical progression. It also does not absolve him of the obligation to build the cyclicities that lead to the aesthetically satisfying melodic exploration of a *rāga*. The present conditions are a challenge to the creativity and conceptual clarity of musicians, and not a license for musical jaywalking.

The modern greats still amongst us have adopted a dual approach to the problem of shrinking durations. One solution they have adopted is to simply refuse to satisfy the public expectation of three pieces within a span of two hours. The other solution in evidence is the dropping and rearranging of some movements in a manner that maintains the central linearity of the progression. These solutions need not exhaust the possibilities of handling the presentation formats of Hindustani music under present-day conditions.

Some of the younger instrumentalists on the contemporary concert platform — notably the sitārist Shujaat Khan and the sarodist Tejendra Majumdar — have addressed these issues intelligently, and come up with interesting, and largely acceptable, solutions. This leaves other young musicians no credible excuses for structural waywardness.

The Argument

It cannot be anyone's argument that great musicians inexorably submit every rendition of every *rāga* to the cyclical discipline of melodic exploration and the linear sequencing of individual movements. If this were so, their music would be boring beyond description. The contention is that, like a great architect, the great musician never loses sight of the functionality of his artefact, and is a disciplined presenter of his art. He selects his elements in consonance with his central vision, arranges or sequences them meticulously for effortless comprehension, and allows the melodic treatment of every movement to release its emotional charge.

At the highest level of musicianship, the soundness of architecture is therefore a fundamental differentiator between durable and ephemeral music. Interestingly, however, the same quality can also serve as a discriminator between music and merely pleasant sounds at the lowest level of musicianship.

The issue of structure is worth reiterating at this stage in the history of Hindustani music because the current attack on structured music is an attack on the *rāga*. Without the systematic and elaborate exploration of *rāga*s by exceptional musicians, the Indian musical mind would have been unable to develop and sustain the *rāga* as an archetypal entity, and an inexhaustible reservoir of creative energy. The archetypal stature of the *rāga* cannot survive without the deliberateness and elaborateness of its expositional protocol. Structural wantonness in the presentation of Hindustani music will cause a *rāga*-presentation to degenerate either into a random juxtaposition of familiar phrases, or into an exercise in tonal kaleidoscopy.

Contemporary crusaders for innovation might be permitted to liberate their music from architecture as well as the archetypal *rāga*; but only after they have come up with an acceptable and intelligible alternative within the Hindustani tradition. Until then, their music will have to acknowledge that a concern for structure has neither exposed any internal contradictions, nor militated against change, nor proven the uselessness of form in Hindustani music.

2.2

INSTRUMENTAL IDIOMS AṄGA OR APAṄGA?

AN important facet of post-Independence Hindustani music has been the eclipse of vocal music by instrumental music in terms of popularity. The boom in instrumental music has brought to the forefront many instruments, which were, until recently, not accepted on the mainstream concert platform. On the other hand, traditional instruments too have attempted, with varying degrees of success, to develop new musical languages and idioms in order to cater to a new generation of audiences.

The flute and *sāraṅgī* are now following the *sitāra aṅga* [glimpse/facet/idiom]. The *santūra* is playing a combination of *sitāra* and *tabalā* idioms. The *sitāra* is moving towards the *gāyakī aṅga* [vocalism]. Instrumental music is in a state of flux, and demands an assessment of its endeavours and the resultant tendencies.

These trends are neither new nor, in themselves, disturbing. Originally, Indian art music regarded instruments capable only of accompaniment to vocal music. It pays to recall that even the venerable *rudra vīṇā*, the grandmother of several Indian instruments, was once considered a *śuṣka vādya* and forbidden for solo performance. Since instrumental music developed as a significant solo art form, musical ideas and practices have been freely exchanged between vocal and instrumental music, and even between the different instruments. The cause for anxiety lies in the experimental frenzy evident in recent years, which will impoverish, rather than enrich, instrumental music.

Instrumentalists are increasingly willing to deny the ergonomic and acoustic character inherent to their respective instruments. The result is a growing variety of instruments, and a shrinking variety of idioms; a growing range of sounds accompanied by a shrinking diversity of content.

When musicians deviate radically from the native or natural idioms of their instruments, they can easily create music which is at war with itself. This appears to be happening on a considerable scale now, and audiences are expected to hail such stylistic and idiomatic innovations as new *aṅgas*, even when their aesthetic value qualifies them as *apaṅga* [crippled]. In such a confused environment, the music community needs to develop a well-considered perspective on the issues.

Source Material of the Hindustani Tradition

The source material of contemporary Hindustani music is traceable to three principal music-making models in art-music:

The gāyakī [vocal] model: This model is based on melodic continuity, and the dominance of the melodic element over the rhythmic element.

The rudra vīṇā/taṅtakāra model: In this model, plucking of the strings serves as the mode of sound activation. The act of plucking creates an element of melodic discontinuity as well as rhythm. Though within limits, the *taṅtakāra* model offers a large range of stylistic and idiomatic options in terms of the balance between the melodic and rhythmic elements.

The pakhāwaja/tāla-vādya model: In this model, sound activation occurs via the striking of the surface of the instrument, and is intended to create rhythmic patterns. The melodic content of its music, if any, is incidental and limited.

The three main models, therefore, are: the music of melodic continuity, the music of melodic discontinuity, and the music of rhythm. Until recently, the wind and bow instruments did not have either a significant solo presence or stature in art-music. Hence, they cannot be said to have an independent music-making model that has evolved as a tradition.

A fourth, and hybrid, model developed as a combination of the second and third models. This model arose from the music of the *saroda*'s ancestor, the *rabāba*. The *rabāba* is a plucked instrument, but has a resonator covered with animal skin, which gives it an acoustic facet akin to a *tāla-vādya*. The Kabuli *rabāba* came to India with *paṭhāna* soldiers, who played martial tunes on it. These features encouraged a percussive-melodic model of music making in which the rhythmic element dominates the melodic element.

Adoption and Adaptation

As instrumental music developed into a solo art form, the various modern instruments adopted the three basic models. Adoption was accompanied by adaptation, and further development designed to exploit their distinctive acoustic character. Through the first half of the twentieth century, wind and bow instruments followed the vocal model because the music of melodic continuity was their obvious territory.

The *sitāra* adopted and adapted the *rudra vīṇā*/*taṅtakāra* model because this is where it logically belonged. The present-day sophistication of *sitāra* music owes a great deal to the mature *rudra vīṇā* legacy.

In the early stages of its hundred-year history, the *saroda* developed its idiom as a refined version of the *rabāba*. In the next phase, it took two different directions. Ustad Alauddin Khan steered it towards the *rudra vīṇā* model, while Amjad Ali Khan's father, Ustad Hafiz Ali Khan and Mohammad Ameer Khan [the *guru* of Pt. Radhika Mohan Maitra], reinforced and refined the percussive bias of its *rabāba* legacy. By its very nature, the *saroda* could not do away with the *taṅtakāra* idiom altogether. But, under the influence of Ustad Ali Akbar Khan, it drifted away from the percussive-melodic model. Soon thereafter, the *santūra* took over the percussive-melodic model, and emerged as a significant instrument on the art-music scene.

The *tabalā* has, from the very beginning, been a protégé of the *pakhāwaja*; hence its language has evolved as logically from its predecessor's as the *sitāra*'s has from the *rudra vīṇā*.

Until the 1970s, this pattern of appropriate and logical evolution of musical languages prevailed amongst modern instruments. Thereafter began the movement that poses issues of *aucitya*, and of the distinction between *aṅga* and *apaṅga*.

Deviations and Innovations

The most controversial trends are apparent in the music of the wind and the bow instruments, which have moved sharply towards the *taṅtakāra* model. By virtue of their design and sound-activation technology, however, the wind and bow instruments are suited for the music of melodic continuity and the subordination of the rhythmic element to the melodic element. Wind instruments were designed as an acoustic enhancement of the human breath; and bow instruments were designed explicitly as the closest possible mechanical approximation to the musical capabilities of the human voice.

In the Indian tradition, the vocal musical expression has the highest ranking. There are good reasons for this. On purely technical considerations, no instrument can match the acoustic and melodic potential of the human voice. As a vehicle for musical ideas, too, the vocal expression ranks supreme as a unified and unfettered expression of the body, the mind, and the soul, being activated by *prāṇa*, the human breath or the life force. This also makes it the most potent device for spiritual pursuits, thus emphasizing the meditative-contemplative foundations of our art-music tradition. Hence, vocal music is regarded as the originator of all melodic ideas, and also their most authentic exponent. Against this yardstick, every other musical expression is considered a compromise.

Playing *sitāra* music on the flute or *sāraṅgī* is an issue in *aucitya* because the instruments were not designed for it. The transgression is more significant because they have deserted a superior model in favour of music belonging to an inferior category of instruments. The much-touted *taṅtakāra aṅga* on the flute or *sāraṅgī* is, by this yardstick, an *apaṅga*.

Against this backdrop, what can we say of the *gāyakī aṅga* [vocalized idiom] on the *sitāra* popularized by Ustad Vilayat Khan? Melodic discontinuity is inherent in the *sitāra*'s design. A rhythmic element is built into its character by the required frequency of sound priming. By extracting longer acoustic sustain from the instrument, and reducing the frequency of fretwork and strokes, the *gāyakī aṅga* sitārist executes melodic expressions strongly suggestive of singing. This is accompanied by a variety of other devices to magnify the illusion of a vocal performance.

Against the human voice as the yardstick, the *sitāra* is an inferior vehicle for the musical idea. In the *gāyakī aṅga*, the musician enables the instrument to transcend its limitations, and to simulate the aural experience of a superior musical expression. This innovation adds something to the acoustic and musical potential of the *sitāra*.

The *gāyakī aṅga* on the *sitāra* deals in the aesthetics of illusion — illusion of a superior experience — whose purpose is to evoke a sense of marvel. As a response, marvel is distinct from laughter, which is the aim of mimicry and caricature.

Ustad Bismillah Khan has often given us glimpses of the *taṅtakāra aṅga* on the *śehnāyī* with plectrum stroke effects like *dir-dir-da*, and *da-dir-dir-dir*. His is not an idiomatic shift into an inferior melodic experience. He merely offers fleeting illusions evoking a sense of marvel; but they never become a caricature of the *sitāra* or *saroda*, eliciting laughter. Bismillah Khan is never guilty of *aucitya-bhaṅga*.

The aesthetic of illusion does not raise issues of *aucitya* because, in this case, the protagonist does not deny his own identity.

Aucitya in Innovation

Contemporary music offers outstanding examples of *aucitya* as a perfect congruence between the ergonomic-acoustic character of the instrument and its idiom. The most outstanding examples are the *saroda* idiom of Ustad Ali Akbar Khan and the *santūra* idiom of Pt. Shivkumar Sharma. Both play percussive-melodic instruments, and have developed idioms that make brilliant use of melodic discontinuity as a musical element.

Towards the end of the last century, the *saroda* started its journey as an extension of the *rabāba*. In the 1930s, the legendary "Baba" Alauddin Khan, and his brother, Ayet Ali Khan, re-engineered the instrument into a sophisticated and versatile acoustic machine. Baba also introduced elements of *rudra vīṇā* music into the language of the *saroda*. But, the development of an idiom that truly exploited the instrument's unique character had to wait until Ali Akbar Khan.

Khansaheb Ali Akbar retained the inevitable moorings of

saroda music in the *taṅtakāra* idiom, but revolutionized everything else. The Ustad's contribution to the evolution of the distinctive *saroda* idiom is encyclopaedic. But, one feature stands out. It is the dramatic use of geometric and kaleidoscopic tonal patterns, exploiting the semi-polychord facet of the *saroda*.

This feature not only enhances the melodic language of the plucked-lute family of instruments, but also exploits the multiple timbres available on the different strings. This development is uniquely appropriate to the *saroda*, and merits documentation as a classic example of *aucitya*. Ali Akbar Khan gave the *saroda* a language distinctive enough to place it beyond the magnetic fields of the vocal expression as well as other instruments.

In the same mould is the *santūra* idiom of Pt. Shivkumar Sharma. The *santūra* had a Persian idiom, an Afghan/Kashmiri idiom, but no idiom in Hindustani art music. Shivkumarji saw in this staccato, percussive-melodic, polychord the potential for a scintillating musical language, with an emphasis on geometric and kaleidoscopic tonal patterns and an accentuated rhythmicality.

Pt. Shivkumar Sharma follows the *sitāra/taṅtakāra* protocol for *rāga* presentation. But, the content of his music is a *tabalā* connoisseur's delight. While the average listener is enraptured by the acoustic charm of his *santūra*, cultivated listeners gape in awe at his melodic-rhythmic interpretation of the *tabalā* idiom — *peśakāras*, *quaidās*, *bandiśas* and *cakradāras*. Like Ustad Ali Akbar Khan, Pt. Shivkumar Sharma is the originator of an idiom uniquely suited to his instrument.

Some kind of perspective emerges from this discussion. The more recent percussive-melodic instruments, like the *saroda* and the *santūra*, have freed themselves substantially from the shadow of the mature traditional models, and developed their own musical languages. What the *saroda* and the *santūra* are doing today is an affirmation of their acoustic character.

The *sitāra* continues to build on the foundations provided by the *rudra vīṇā* idiom. It is attempting to enhance its acoustic capabilities, along with the shaping of a more sophisticated idiom. The *tabalā*, likewise, continues to build upon its *pakhāwaja* legacy.

Amongst the major instruments of contemporary music, it is the wind and bow instruments, which seem to be groping for an evolutionary direction. The best they have come up with, so far, is a denial of their ergonomic-acoustic character, a stifling of their melodic potential, and an abandonment of the vocal ideal to which they traditionally belong.

Fortunately, the wind and bow categories can boast of one splendid exception. Consider how seamlessly Dr. N. Rajam has integrated ideas from the *taṅtakāra* idiom into the traditional vocalism of the violin. Her *drut bandiśa*s end with a *jhālā*. But it is a *jhālā* for the violin, and not a sitārist's *jhālā*. It is a *jhālā* in concept but not in technique. It conjures an aural experience of a *jhālā*; but, unlike the *sitāra jhālā*, it does not involve 480 wrist-movements per minute.

Dr. Rajam's music demonstrates the possibility of enhancing the idiomatic richness of the music of wind and bow instruments without raising issues of *aucitya*. Her music, and that of Ustad Ali Akbar Khan and Pt. Shivkumar Sharma, have also established the viability of an instrumental idiom liberated from an *a priori* ideal in vocalism. But, as these precedents suggest, a worthwhile direction can emerge only from a discovery and exploitation of the distinctive character of each instrument.

The argument here is that, as a tendency, drifting towards an "inferior" idiom in search of novelty risks creating *apaṅga* music. An original solution to this problem must certainly be feasible. But, until it emerges, it might be in the interests of *aucitya* that the wind and bow instruments stay with their traditional, and logical, home in the vocal model.

Aucitya — The Idea

As an aesthetic yardstick, *aucitya* is, admittedly, a dynamic concept. What was *anucita* a hundred years ago has probably become *ucita* today; and what we might consider *anucita* today, could well be accepted as *ucita* a few decades from now. Our notion of *aucitya* must, therefore, allow for change. While accepting this caveat, we need to understand *aucitya* as an idea, which is much bigger, and far more fundamental, than our immediate concerns.

The *aucitya* yardstick is not satisfied by acceptability to the public. *Aucitya* is a sense of propriety, of balance and moderation. It demands a clear perception of a unique identity and destiny. It assumes a sense of history and attributes sanctity to the strand of continuity between the past, the present and the future. It implies a faith in the value of evolutionary rather than revolutionary transformations, and a sense of responsibility towards orderly change.

Aucitya is not the voice of status-quoism as much as it is of sanity. In its widest sense, *aucitya* is the yardstick by which oriental societies judge the conduct of their leaders in all fields of human endeavour, including the cultural. It is in this sense that many Hindustani instrumentalists, including some of the most successful ones, might be answerable for the results of their innovative zeal.

2.3

THE JUGALABAṄDĪ RACKET

NOT a season passes, nowadays, without the announcement of a "first time ever" *jugalabandī* concert between one big-name musician and another. Most of these turn out also to be the "last time ever" events involving the pair. The conclusion is obvious: Audiences are seduced by the promise, and cheated by the product. This does not appear to discourage either big-name musicians or their concert organizers. They seem surprisingly eager to risk their credibility repeatedly for the rewards of a one-night stand. For the organizers of such events, as well as audiences lured by them, a little background could be useful.

A duet, as a presentation format, is fundamentally inconsistent with the meditative-contemplative character of Hindustani music. Being a predominantly improvized form, it can assume only one musician. Any accompaniment, whether drone, melodic or rhythmic, must function under his/her control.

In contrast, Carnatic music can support the duet format on a larger scale, allow a larger orchestra, and also permit a freer interaction amongst the members of the ensemble. The difference arises from the role of the pre-composed element in the music. In contemporary Hindustani music, the pre-composed element has only a marginal role. Because of this, a soloist with a skeletal ensemble is the norm; a pair of collaborating performers is a rarity; and a successful and durable duo is a phenomenon.

Despite the hurdles, a number of extraordinary duet performers have, in recent years, trained our ears to the duet as an engaging presentation format. A quick survey reveals some patterns. A more authoritative and comprehensive survey is undoubtedly possible, but considering the burden of evidence, it is unlikely that it would reveal radically different patterns.

Jugalabandī Patterns

In all, sixteen significant partnerships, representing different degrees of acknowledged success, are considered. The sample is based on the significance and stature of the musicians involved. The list has some overlaps, with musicians like Ustad Ali Akbar Khan and Ustad Vilayat Khan having partnered several instrumentalists over the years.

The sixteen partnerships fall into four categories:

[a] Traditional vocal, i.e., *dhrupad* and *khayāla*;

[b] Traditional instrumental, combining instruments of the same basic organological classification [*sitāra / saroda* and *sitāra / surabahāra*];

[c] Modern instrumental, combining organologically dissimilar instruments [e.g., *sitāra / śehnayī* or *santūra /* flute];

[d] Experimental, which fall in none of the above categories and are still at an experimental stage of evolution.

The largest, the most successful, and the most durable category is the traditional vocal, with six duos. Without exception, these pairs are brothers not far removed from each other in age, and trained simultaneously by the same *guru*, in most cases their father.

The traditional instrumental category reports four winning partnerships. They have ties of shared tutelage, but not necessarily of kinship. In this category, one exception is significant — the brief but memorable collaboration of Ustad Vilayat Khan and Ustad Ali Akbar Khan in the 1950s.

The modern instrumental category has three partnerships. Amongst these, Bismillah Khan/Vilayat Khan and Shivkumar Sharma/Hariprasad Chaurasia have been sensational successes, while the Bismillah-VG Jog team did not get far. None of these pairs shares a bond of common *guru*s or even *gharānā* affiliations.

The fourth category, with four experimental partnerships, is a mixed bag. This could be a gross understatement of the numbers in this category. And, any number will become obsolete before any listing of this category is published. This category includes duets of the flautist, Hariprasad Chaurasia with Hindustani as well as Carnatic vocalists, and Dr. Balamuralikrishna's Carnatic/Hindustani dialogues. Their success and durability are still a question mark.

The Burden of Evidence

On historical evidence, the success rates of duet pairs can be attributed predominantly to the acoustic compatibility of the music of the duo, and also to stylistic affinity acquired from a common *guru*. Ties of kinship between them could be a conducive, though not critical, success factor. However, if the team-mates are individually of the highest calibre, and admire each other, acoustic compatibility becomes a non-issue, as does kinship or shared tutelage.

The majority of non-starters amongst duet concepts belong to the "experimental" category. On the other hand, the traditional vocal and the traditional instrumental categories continue to produce winning duos in every generation.

The modern instrumental category can perhaps withstand some experimentation because, provided other ingredients of success are in place, the chances of success are reasonable.

Significantly, in many cases, studio recordings of instrumental duets have been more consequential than live concerts. This is understandable. Once the essential ingredients of a satisfactory aural experience are in place, a successful duet is a product of a partial surrender of individual freedom, careful planning, and intuitive anticipation. The studio context is more conducive to such a process than a live concert. Considering the growing sophistication of audio engineering, the studio recording could become an even more powerful vehicle for duet-music in the future, and perhaps even redefine the ingredients of a successful duet product.

Consider this "duet" concept. There exists, in the archives of a recording company, an unpublished duet of Ustad Vilayat Khan on the *sitāra* with himself on the *surabahāra*. He first recorded the *sitāra* track, put on the headphones, and recorded the parallel *surabahāra* track. This could be an indication of duet products of the future. Similar "duets" of other leading instrumentalists are now conceivable.

Though the aesthetic acceptability of such electronically engineered duets remains untested in the market, their potential for acoustic compatibility and "teamwork" cannot be matched by the finest duet recorded in real-time. However, audio engineering alone does not appear to provide a surefire route to success considering that even impressively coordinated and "processed" duet recordings by second-level musicians have failed. This suggests that, in a duet, Indian audiences are not content merely with a pleasant sound and the absence of confusion: they want to feel the simultaneous and distinctive presence of two great musicians for the cost of one concert in terms of time and money invested.

These factors make duet concerts a demanding proposition in Hindustani music, with only maestros having a decent chance of success. This also makes duet concerts prohibitively expensive and financially risky. Both musicians charge their full fees, sometimes insist on two percussionists, and could even demand a premium for playing a duet. No wonder, then, that the duets format invites so much experimentation, and the experimental events are backed by so much media hype.

Experimentation and Propriety

In itself, experimentation can hardly be questioned — all artistic endeavour thrives on it. Questions of propriety, however, arise when experimentation ignores the fundamental character of the art form and the motives for pursuing it are apparently more commercial than artistic.

This conservative line of argument can be challenged on the grounds that it considers the durability of a duet concept or partnership the essential validation of its value and success. It might also be contended that dynamic audience profiles and changing audience tastes demand continuous experimentation, unfettered by pre-conceived, and probably invalid, notions about what is "proper," and what is not.

We do, however, need to interpret the evidence of the marketplace. The experimental *jugalabandī* product appears to fail consistently in delivering what it promises. Time and again, it fails to generate a repeat purchase demand on a credible scale. One may therefore ask whether the "experimental" product fulfils a genuine cultural need. If the marketeer is neither fulfilling a genuine consumer need, nor produces evidence of repeat purchase demand, he probably has no business to be in the business.

The market, which has seemingly encouraged the *jugalabandī* racket, is itself giving discouraging signals. Audiences are now disenchanted with the untested duet product and are becoming highly selective about concert attendance. As the competition intensifies between the concert platform and pre-recorded music for a share of the music lover's discretionary time, the experimental *jugalabandī* concert must inevitably lose out even faster to the superiority of concert alternatives, and to pre-recorded *jugalabandīs*. The writing is on the wall for the new breed of *jugalabandī* impresarios who believe that a sucker is born everyday.

2.4

TIHĀYĪS . . . AND THE RAPE OF MELODY

In recent years, the melodic *tihāyī*, a triplet melodic device, has emerged as a significant musical expression, especially in instrumental music. As a melodic expression of rhythmic intent, it belongs to the same category as puns in literature. The pun is a form of humour, and has its own aesthetics. Increasingly, however, the melodic *tihāyī* is either being used excessively, clumsily and mechanically, or is being deployed as a piece of titillation and entertainment.

Fortunately, the aesthetic deployment of the melodic *tihāyī* is still alive in circulation to enable us to document its musical meaning and distinguish between different levels of musicianship.

A melodic *tihāyī* takes shape when a melodic statement is rendered thrice in a row in such a manner as to convert the resulting pattern into a rhythmic statement. The melodic *tihāyī* was probably inspired by the rhythmic *tihāyī* form in percussion. Percussion itself is believed, by some, to have developed the *tihāyī* in response to the needs of accompaniment to *Kathaka* dance.

An expanded form of the *tihāyī* is the *cakradāra*, which consists of melodic statements in multiples of three, with two or more *tihāyī*s dovetailed into each other. There are several dovetailing patterns in vogue, the most common being the same *tihāyī*, rendered thrice.

Interestingly, some orthodox *gharānā*s of music frown upon the *tihāyī* and *cakradāra* as melodic expressions. One of the objections is that the *tihāyī* form belongs to the territory of dance, an "inferior" art form. Others regard it as a childish display of arithmetical prowess, which, in their opinion, represents a mediocre level of musicianship. Though some of these reservations ring true even in the context of present-day instrumental music, we need to acknowledge that these are prejudices carried over from an era dominated by vocal music, especially the poetry-dominated vocal music of the *dhrupad* era. Where the poetic form is held sacred, one can plausibly regard the rhythmic use of melody as an intrusion upon the aesthetics of melody as well as poetry. This might, incidentally, explain why the melodic *tihāyī* does not feature significantly in Carnatic music, which is dominated by pre-composed *kṛti*s.

In contemporary Hindustani music, the modern *khayāla* genre does not accord the same sanctity to the communication of literary meaning as the mediaeval *dhrupad* did, and Carnatic music still does. Moreover, the *sitāra, santūra,* and the *saroda* dominate the contemporary Hindustani environment. These instruments have a built-in rhythmic element in their music because of the need for plucking or striking of the strings for sound activation. The melodic *tihāyī* is predominantly and legitimately their territory. The dominance of these instruments of percussive-melodic tendency is now a reality. We must, therefore, accept the triplet melodic-rhythmic form as an integral part of contemporary music, and appreciate its use as a musical device.

The Logic of Tihāyīs

In all ancient civilizations, great sanctity is attached to the number "Three." Hindu mythology treats the number as representing *trimūrti*, the holy trinity of Brahmā, Viṣṇu and Maheśa, respectively the Creator, Preserver, and the Destroyer of the Universe. Likewise, the Judaic-Christian tradition pays its obeisance to the Father, Son, and the Holy Ghost. But, for listeners of Hindustani music, it is unnecessary to get so esoteric about the *tihāyī*.

According to musicologist Ashok Ranade [via a private interview with the author], the number of times a melodic line is repeated in a *tihāyī* has a very specific significance. There is an aesthetic relevance to three, which cannot be replaced by two, or four, or eight or ten. The appeal of the *tihāyī* [triplet] lies in its ability to create and release aesthetic tension within a short span of time, and thereby function as an interesting punctuation.

The first time any melodic statement is rendered, it merges with the melodic landscape. On the first repetition [second iteration], it evokes bewilderment. On the second repetition [third iteration], however, it reveals its intent by fulfilling its rhythmic function, and thus releases the aesthetic tension. From this logic, one can appreciate that if a *tihāyī* culminates with any number of iterations, other than three, it performs no aesthetic function at all.

The melodic *tihāyī* probably originated as a convenience. As Hindustani music emerged from its pre-composed origins to evolve as an improvization dominant art form, such a device became necessary. Musicians often found themselves completing a round of improvizations a few beats before they could rejoin the pre-composed *bandiśa*. In their search for an appropriate melodic device for filling this gap, they drew upon the resources of the percussion idiom. Over time, this joinery device acquired a sophistication of its own. And, along with sophistication came an attention-enhancing character appropriate for its place in the logic of *rāga* presentation.

The propriety of its attention-enhancing character arises from its placement at the transition from one kind of progression/logic to another. The *tihāyī* is used when the music is making a transition from the linear or unfettered logic of the improvizations to the cyclical framework of the *bandiśa*.

Placement, Function, and Aesthetics

As a piece of joinery, the *tihāyī* is encountered in two placements: one, as a replacement for the *mukhaḍā,* and the other, as a replacement for the *āmada*. The *mukhaḍā* is the opening phrase of the *bandiśa* which culminates at the *sama*. The *āmada* is the phrase which precedes the *mukhaḍā*.

The *mukhaḍā tihāyī* can start from any beat of the rhythmic cycle but must, by definition, end on the *sama*. In its melodic structure, it will usually — though not always — end on the *svara* on which the *sama* of the composition's pre-composed *mukhaḍā* falls. Only by fulfilling these requirements can it logically be followed by the pre-composed follow-through of the *mukhaḍā* of the *bandiśa*. *Cakradāra*s are most frequently used in the same manner as *mukhaḍā tihāyī*s, although their use in *āmada* placement is not ruled out.

The *āmada tihāyī* can, likewise, start on any beat of the cycle, but must, by definition, end on the beat before the commencement of the *mukhaḍā*, and generally on a *svara*, from where a smooth transition to the pre-composed *mukhaḍā* of the composition is possible.

There also exists a third *tihāyī* placement, the *baḍhata tihāyī* [the progressive *tihāyī*], mainly found embedded in *behlava* improvizations in instrumental music. Rhythmically, this *tihāyī* is structured like a *mukhaḍā tihāyī,* but does not link the improvizations to the composition. Instead, it is followed by further improvizations. Thus, the function of the *baḍhata tihāyī* is merely to link a free-flowing improvization with the rhythmic cycle, and not with the melodic-rhythmic frame of the composition. This *tihāyī* is generally used when the musician takes up a prolonged improvization, covering several rounds of the rhythmic cycle. Appropriately for its role and placement, the *baḍhata tihāyī* is generally short, and melodically and rhythmically un-dramatic.

The placement of a *tihāyī* determines its melodic-rhythmic structure, and its intrusiveness. Obviously, the *mukhaḍā tihāyī*, which replaces the single most important melodic phrase of the composition, and arrives at the *sama*, tends to be the most intrusive. By the same logic, the *āmada tihāyī* is less intrusive than the *mukhaḍā tihāyī*, and the *baḍhata tihāyī* is the least intrusive.

The *tihāyī* appears to have no fixed rules for structuring. Several *gharānā*s have an inventory of pre-composed rhythmic *tihāyī* patterns, which they adapt melodically to different *rāga*s and mathematically to different *tāla*s. The pre-composed *tihāyī*, however, can fail to make the desired impact if handled only mathematically, without due consideration to the overall tenor of the presentation, and the melodic-rhythmic structure of the improvizations into which they are dovetailed.

The Aesthetic and the Grotesque

In the music of the great masters, we see the *tihāyī* in its intended form — as a masterpiece of spontaneous melodic-rhythmic improvization. In recent times, the most brilliant use of the *tihāyī* is attributed to Ustad Ali Akbar Khan and Ustad Vilayat Khan. Elderly connoisseurs go into raptures recalling the *tihāyī*s they have heard from these luminaries in the 1960s and early 1970s, their peak performing years.

Every one of their *tihāyī*s was unique and spontaneous. Very often, even the most astute audiences failed to notice the appearance of *tihāyī*s in their performances until the triplet formations were well into the third iteration — it was almost as if their *tihāyīs* took shape in their minds unbeknownst even to themselves. Their culmination seemed as much of a surprise and a delight to the *ustāds* themselves as it was to the audiences. So intuitive, and formidable, was the command they displayed over melody and rhythm that, they could pick up any phrase from any *rāga* on any beat of the rhythmic cycle, and construct from it a *tihāyī* or *cakradāra* of unfailing rhythmic accuracy.

Recently, the present author had occasion to review a recording by a young sitārist which had a 14 minute presentation of a slow-tempo *bandiśa* with 18 *tihāyīs*, one every 45 seconds. The *tihāyīs* had replaced the improvizations as the content of the music. Arithmetic had replaced music. And, such instances abound. Today, one sees a real danger that the appropriate and elegant use of the melodic *tihāyī* or *cakradāra* will depart from Hindustani music along with some of our living legends. This is a disturbing prospect.

It is fair to ask why we should concern ourselves so much with the *tihāyī* form, which constitutes such a small part of a *rāga* presentation. Such a query will amount to asking why careful attention should be paid to the joinery in a piece of furniture. And, the answer is obvious. Functionally, it is the joinery that holds the piece together, and makes it stable. Aesthetically, if so designed and crafted, the joinery can also make it more beautiful.

Your carpenter will tell you that, in a piece of furniture, the joinery should ideally be invisible. An avant-garde designer might convert the joinery into a major design feature. But, neither your friendly neighbourhood carpenter, nor the award-winning designer, will allow the joinery to replace the substance of the artefact, or become dysfunctional.

The grotesque has a place in art. But, when art becomes grotesque, it gets derailed from its elevating ideals.

PART III

The World of Rāgas

3.1

THE RĀGA-NESS OF RĀGAS

EVEN a casual listener of Hindustani music is aware that the word *rāga* is used to describe the melodic facet of a piece of music. He also knows that a *rāga* is not a pre-composed melody. The same *rāga*, performed by different musicians, or by the same musician on different occasions, can sound entirely different while yet retaining a strong basis in familiarity. He also knows that there are hundreds, perhaps thousands, of *rāga*s in circulation, and that experienced listeners can distinguish one *rāga* from others. From this, most listeners can infer that a *rāga* is, broadly, a melodic structure, tight enough to remain distinct and identifiable, and yet loose enough to form the basis for considerable individual freedom.

This inference is not wrong. But, it jumps the first step in understanding the notion of a *rāga* — the word *rāga* itself. The word *rāga* does not have a musical or melodic meaning at all; it has only an emotional meaning. In Sanskrit, and in most Sanskrit-based Indian languages, the word *rāga* is normally encountered as a suffix: *anu-rāga* = attraction/affinity or *vai-rāgya* = indifference/apathy/detachment. The meaning of the suffix becomes clearer by tracing the root of the noun *rāga* to the verb *rañjana*, to colour, or to tinge. When we colour, or tinge, something, we contribute to it a subjective element, which warrants a subjective response. In behaviourist terminology, therefore, the notion of the *rāga* deals with the totality of the communication process — generation of "stimulus" as well as the elicitation of "response." The word has come to describe a melodic structure, the stimulus, because the music world has accepted a correspondence between the stimulus and the response, and feels comfortable in using the word *rāga* to describe the former.

This leads to the proposition that the *rāga*, as commonly understood, is a melodic representation of an emotional statement and a vehicle for its communication. But, since music is capable of communicating a whole range of human emotions, we must reckon with a qualitative aspect of the emotional response that each melodic structure is associated with. The notion of a *rāga* is, therefore, inseparably linked with the concept of *rasa*, crudely translated as "the essence." The Indian aesthetic tradition bases its understanding of this aspect on the eight-way *rasa* classification of Bharata in the treatise on the performing arts [*Nāṭyaśāstra*, 200 BC]. Different *rāga*s are associated with different categories of emotional states based on the accumulated experience of Indian society. These associations have yet to be either validated or rejected — even in a culture-specific context — by the application of modern psychometric tools.

The *rasa* issue is a little more complex than it appears at first. Each *rāga* is pregnant with more than one *rasa*; one of them is dominant, while others are subordinate to it. Another perspective on the same issue is that a *rāga* expresses different *rasa*s at different tempi, different levels of melodic density, and in the different regions of the melodic canvas. To this extent, a musician has a choice in terms of which of the *rasa*s should dominate his presentation, and he exercises this choice by the manner in which he presents the *rāga*.

Even if you regard them as fanciful or arbitrary, these psycho-acoustic associations remain the basis on which the

Hindustani musician undertakes his music making endeavours. He assumes the *rasa*s of the *rāga* to be inherent or implicit in the melodic structure, determines — either consciously or otherwise — which of them should dominate his rendition, designs every facet of the presentation accordingly, and "works himself" into the appropriate emotional state by auto-suggestion. The auto-suggestive process is aided by a host of related associations that *rāga*s have come to acquire in the Hindustani tradition. These include mythological, historical, and environmental [time of the day, seasons, etc.] associations, which enable a *rāga* to be visualized, personified, and occasionally, even deified as an object of contemplation. To this extent, the *rāga-rasa* relationship is germane to our understanding of the notion of a *rāga*.

This leads to the proposition that a *rāga* is the melodic stimulus, believed to have a high probability of inducing a well-defined emotional state in the performer and eliciting a similar emotional state amongst his audiences. And, it is, of course, a melodic structure, tight enough to remain distinct and identifiable, and yet loose enough to form the basis for considerable individual freedom. But, why does Indian tradition require *rāga*s, when the art music traditions of other mature civilizations have produced great music even without such a device?

The only answer to this question is cultural. The notion of a *rāga* exemplifies the oriental concern for evolutionary, rather than revolutionary, change. It reflects the special genius of Indian society for balancing continuity with change, conformity with individuality, and discipline with creativity. When manifested in a specific artistic expression, such as a music performance, this genius ensures that the aesthetic experience enjoys the benefits of familiarity along with novelty for all times to come. But, accepting that the cultural process is an open-ended historical process with no pre-determined destination, the tradition accepts that, in time, everything changes. Each generation of musicians and audiences is free to choose the parameters of continuity/discipline/conformity/familiarity, and impose on them their own parameters of change/creativity/individuality/novelty. *Rāga*s have thus evolved as ever-growing and ever-changing repositories of aesthetically coherent melodic ideas. Since the advent of recording technology, *rāga*s have become even richer as sources of melodic ideas, without losing their propensity for reflecting changing aesthetic values.

*Rāga*s can, and do, change over even relatively short periods of time. For instance, only 200 years ago, the scale that we recognize as Kāfī today, was called Bhairavī. When, and how, the old Bhairavī dropped its *śuddha re* and *dh* in favour of the *komala svara*s, to acquire an entirely different melodic personality, is a subject for conjecture. And, Bhairavī's transformation, as everyone knows, continues unabated even in our times. The Bhairavī-Kāfī transition is rather drastic compared to that of many other *rāga*s, which have changed substantially, but not so radically.

This brings us to the proposition that, for every generation of musicians and audiences, each *rāga* is defined by a set of features, which constitute its current "grammar" — features that make the *rāga* identifiable, and distinct from other *rāga*s. Considering that Hindustani music grants the musician the simultaneous roles of performer and composer, and every performer cannot be a great composer, the grammar of the *rāga* protects the performance against aesthetic incoherence, while also shielding audiences against possible bewilderment. These rules of grammar have assumed greater importance as Hindustani music has moved towards presentation formats providing progressively greater improvizational freedom to the performing musician.

The present writer's understanding of these rules draws on three sources — authoritative modern and contemporary texts, the *guru*s who have taught him music, and his own analysis of over a hundred *rāga*s recorded by over 50 prominent musicians. For explaining *rāga* grammar, the present writer has found it efficient to segment the rules into two categories — melodic grammar and aesthetic grammar. By melodic grammar is meant the selection, sequencing, and relative importance of *svara*s in a *rāga*, while aesthetic grammar refers to aspects of shaping a distinctive aural and emotional experience in performance. Aesthetic grammar is prescriptive more than mandatory.

Admittedly, this distinction is unacceptable to the conceptual framework of linguistics because, if anything is called grammar, it can only be mandatory, and anything that is discretionary does not qualify as grammar. In the conceptual framework of musicology, too, the distinction is probably debatable because both facets of *rāga* grammar have aesthetic implications, and classifying only one of them as "aesthetic" is indefensible.

However, for those who are not performing Hindustani musicians, the distinction appears to aid comprehension for two reasons. Firstly, a *rāga* can remain identifiable and distinct even by adherence only to the melodic grammar, while ignoring its aesthetic grammar. Secondly, aesthetic grammar is more susceptible to different levels of adherence, and different interpretations, by different members of the same generation of musicians, and is more likely to change over a period of time than melodic grammar. Aesthetic grammar may therefore be considered a facet of usage — a means of sharpening or fine-tuning the aesthetic intent of melodic grammar — and thus fall on the borderline between grammar and literature.

The Melodic Grammar of Rāgas

Melodic grammar begins with the permissible *svaras* of a *rāga*. The vast majority of *rāgas* utilize a minimum of five *svaras*. The few *rāgas*, which use four *svaras*, are performed only rarely — obviously due to their limited melodic potential. On this basis, *rāgas* are classified into *catusvara* [quadratonic], *auḍava* [pentatonic], *ṣaḍava* [hexatonic] and *sampūrṇa* [heptatonic]. *Rāgas* which use a different number of *svaras* in the ascent and the descent are described by a dual description such as *auḍava-sampūrṇa* or a *ṣaḍava-sampūrṇa*.

In this classification, Indian theory does not habitually double-count the *komala* and *tīvra śrutis* of the same *svara* when both are used. For communicating this feature to readers cultivated in the Western traditions, the present writer has found it useful to use terms like "hyper-hexatonic" or "hyper-heptatonic" for such *rāgas*.

Although the *svaras* permitted in a *rāga* constitute the basis of its melodic grammar, and are therefore mandatory, they are subject to an occasional influence of aesthetic grammar. This dimension arises from the practice, in some *rāgas*, of non-standard intonation, deploying pitches [relative to the fundamental/scale-base] other than the standard pitches for the *svaras* as defined in Hindustani music. Many of these prescriptions are based on sound principles of acoustic correspondence between *svaras* even if musicians advocating the practice cannot always articulate them. But, some of them might well be purely aesthetic. In *rāga* Purīya, for instance, some *gharānās* prescribe the intonation of *komala re* in the microtonal region below the standard frequency of *komala re*. In a similar deviation, the *komala ni* of *rāga* Aḍānā is prescribed at a pitch between the standard *komala* and *śuddha ni* frequencies.

Such instances abound in Hindustani music. Non-standard intonation of *svaras*, though not usually rendered in Hindustani notation, is not a figment of imagination. It is a very explicit part of the grammar of some *rāgas*. It is documented in several texts on *rāga*-grammar, and perpetuated by the personalized system of aesthetic indoctrination prevalent in Hindustani music. Its advocates also practice it with explicit intent. However, it is unclear whether this feature of *rāga*-ness, prescribed selectively, should be classified as melodic grammar, which is mandatory, or aesthetic grammar, which is prescriptive. Only a substantial survey of performances of relevant *rāgas*, using contemporary pitch measurement equipment, can resolve this issue.

The second dimension of melodic grammar of a *rāga* is its scale, consisting of the *āroha* [ascent] and the *avaroha* [descent]. Although a simple sequential listing of the permissible *svaras* in ascending and descending order is often encountered, it is misleading because it fails to account for the sequence in which the *rāga* permits their deployment. On these grounds, there exists a strong and valid opposition to the very notion of a simple *āroha-avaroha* as being representative of a *rāga*'s melodic personality. This objection is particularly potent because the same scale can deliver a multiplicity of *rāgas*, as in the case of Mārwā, Purīyā and Sohinī. It seems legitimate, therefore, to accept a *rāga*'s *calana* [skeletal phraseology] as a superior alternative.

The *calana* is a set of phrases, generally arranged in ascending and descending formation. Most *rāgas* can be adequately represented by a *calana* of eight or fewer phrases. This device is indeed superior to the simple, sequential, scale because it provides the essential building blocks of the melody. It always includes the *pakaḍa* [signature/catch phrase], which identifies the *rāga* beyond reasonable doubt. Collectively, the *calana* phrases represent the identifiable and distinctive melodic personality of the *rāga*. They achieve this status by also incorporating several elements fundamental to defining the *rāga*'s melodic grammar.

The first such element is the sequence in which the permissible *svara*s can be used for phrasing. The phrasing structure also reflects the permissible *alpatva/bahutva* [abbreviated/elongated intonation] of the *svara*s within a phrase and also the manner of their treatment or intonation. The second important element is the identification of the *nyāsa svara*s of the *rāga* — *svara*s permitted for use as terminal or resting points in the phrasing. The *nyāsa svara*s are often critical to the differentiation between *rāga*s using an identical set of *svara*s. The distinctive aural experience of Mārwā, for instance, is considered safe with only two permissible resting/terminal points: *dh* and *ṛe*. Any other terminal point in phrasing can cast an unintended shadow of either Purīyā or Sohinī on the *rāga*.

Two of the *nyāsa svara*s — the most frequently used, and the second most frequently used — are the *vādi* [primary dominant] and the *saṁvādi* [secondary dominant] *svara*s of the *rāga* respectively. The *vādi* and the *saṁvādi* are generally located in different halves of the scale. The *vādi-saṁvādi* notions, memorized unquestioningly by students of music theory, are often a musicologist's nightmare. Far too often for comfort, the present writer has found even Bhatkhande, the father of modern *rāga* grammar, circumspect and tentative about the identity of the *vādi-saṁvādi svara*s of *rāga*s. In addition, authorities often differ on this subject. In many cases, authorities have identified *nyāsa svara*s, but shied away from naming either the *vādi* or *saṁvādi svara*s, sometimes both.

Approaching this problem from an empirical and analytical perspective is not always more helpful. The present author's attempt at verifying the melodic personality of the popular and seemingly non-controversial *rāga*, Ahīra Bhairava, was an eye-opener. He surveyed eight recordings of the *rāga* by the biggest names in contemporary Hindustani music. He found that only four of the eight maestros treated *ma*, the documented *vādi svara* of the *rāga*, as even a *nyāsa svara*. Of these, only two made a special effort to give it the status even of a probable *vādi*. Only one musician had squarely, and explicitly, treated *ma* as the *vādi* of the *rāga*.

This need not mean that the texts are wrong or confused. Nor need it imply that leading musicians perform the *rāga* incorrectly. It could merely suggest that the dialogue between theory and practice required of a vibrant art music tradition has ceased to function, and that the *vādi-saṁvādi* notions now require fresh thinking, probably along with several other notions of *rāga* grammar. If the *vādi-saṁvādi* are indeterminate for some *rāga*s, it might be necessary to accept this reality. If this is found to occur on a large scale, we might even shift this facet of *rāga*-ness out of mandatory/melodic grammar, treating it as a facet of prescriptive/aesthetic grammar. The intuitive and conceptual appeal of the *vādi-saṁvādi* notions is, however, so strong, that music theory will probably persist with their mandatory status, and performance will continue to handle music as it has always done.

Most modern authorities on *rāga*s have documented the above aspects of *rāga* grammar. Selectively, rather than systematically, some texts have ventured beyond them into what the present writer has described as the "aesthetic grammar."

The Aesthetic Grammar of Rāgas

The aesthetic grammar of a *rāga* is related partially to its melodic grammar, and partially to the *rasa* associated with the *rāga*. This is why the present writer has described it as lying on the borderline between grammar and literature.

The basic concept in aesthetic grammar is the location of the *rāga*'s centre of gravity or its epicentre. This is normally defined as a tetrachord [a set of four *svaras*], which ought to dominate the aural experience of the *rāga*. Unlike Western music, which defines only two tetrachords, with the scale split into equal and mutually exclusive halves, the Hindustani system defines the *rāga*'s centre of gravity assuming three overlapping tetrachords — the *pūrvāṅga* [lower tetrachord: *sā-re-gā-mā*], the *madhyāṅga* [middle tetrachord: *gā-mā-pā-dh*], and the *uttarāṅga* [upper tetrachord: *pā-dh-nī-sā*].

The region defining a *rāga*'s centre of gravity is clearly related to the *vādi svara* of the *rāga*, logically and usually the most frequent terminal point for the phrasing. It is important to define such an epicentre as a region, in addition to its focal point [*vādi*], in order to avert the risk of its dilution by a disproportionate amount of improvizational energy being invested outside this region. If, for instance, a musician tarries substantially in the lower tetrachord in Sohinī, he exposes the *rāga* to a risk of confusion with Mārwā or Purīyā. This risk remains significant even if his phraseology adheres strictly to Sohinī because, as acoustic experiences, these *rāga*s are anchored in different regions of the melodic canvas.

Even for *rāga*s, which do not have so fragile a *rāga*-ness, the systematic development of a melodic centre of gravity is important. Mārwā, for instance, is performed equally effectively with its centre of gravity in the *uttarāṅga* of the lower octave, and the *uttarāṅga* of the middle octave. But, a choice needs to be made. Likewise, Kedāra is equally emotive with its epicentre in the *madhyāṅga* and the *uttarāṅga*. But, again, a choice is necessary to make. Making the choice is important because it often distinguishes a piece of effectively rendered music from merely competent music. It is interesting to observe how, on a bad day, unfocused or indecisive handling of a *rāga*'s melodic centre of gravity has marred the performances of even the greatest musicians.

A broader version of the epicentre/centre of gravity notion is the notional scale-base. Fundamentally, all *rāga*s make melodic sense only in relation to the scale-base at the *madhya saptak sa* and a scale of *sa* to *sa*. Yet, some *rāga*s are most effectively rendered assuming a different scale base. The scale-base of Ghārā, for instance, is explicitly defined as the lower-octave *pa*. Mārwā, Purīyā, and Sohinī are also good, though less dramatic, examples. The contemporary Mārwā is most effectively performed assuming the scale-base at the lower-octave *dh* [Scale: *dh* to *dh*]. It is differentiated from Purīya with the scale base at the lower-octave *nī* [Scale: *nī* to *nī*], and Sohinī with its scale base at the middle-octave *gā* [Scale: *gā* to *gā*].

In this context, the present writer recalls a remarkable recording of Sohinī by Pt. Shivkumar Sharma. Throughout the performance, he totally avoids melodic execution in the region below the middle-octave *gā*, using the scale-base at *sā* merely to provide the scalar reference point for the *rāga* to make melodic sense. This is, of course, a rare instance of fastidiously sound music. But, it demonstrates the logic of a notional scale-base as an important operating principle for the aesthetic integrity of some *rāga*s.

Related to these prescriptions are biases in favour of specified melodic directions. Certain *rāga*s are described as *āroha-pradhāna* [ascent-dominated] while others are described as *avaroha-pradhāna* [descent-dominated]. Learned texts frequently refer to the relationship between the melodic centre of gravity of a *rāga* and its directional bias. Bhatkhande, for instance, virtually equates *rāga*s with their epicentre in the *uttarāṅga* with those that are descent-dominant. Contemporary practice does not support so sweeping a generalization. But, there is ample justification for regarding the directional dominance of melodic movements as an independent, and additional, discriminator between *rāga*s.

The operation of this discriminator can be seen clearly, once again, in the treatment of Mārwā, Purīyā and Sohinī by great musicians. Mārwā renditions tend to be dominated by descending phrases; Purīya phrasing tends to be almost equally split between ascending and descending phrases, while Sohinī renditions tend to be dominated by ascending phrases. This prescription is neither far-fetched, nor imaginary. The present writer has verified its validity through a phrase-by-phrase notation of these three *rāga*s, recorded in succession by Ustad Vilayat Khan on a CD due for publication by India Archive Music, New York. On this recording, the maestro has demonstrated, in quantifiable terms, the creation of the desired directional biases by the use of ascents structured as strings of descending phrases, and descents structured as strings of ascending phrases.

This consecutive rendition of Mārwā, Purīyā, and Sohinī by Ustad Vilayat Khan is significant also for its demonstration of the other two aspects of aesthetic grammar discussed here. A melodic plot of the renditions of the three *rāga*s also demonstrates the use of different notional scale-bases, and different melodic centres of gravity/epicentres as differentiators between *rāga*s using the same set of permissible *svara*s. The Vilayat Khan rendering suggests that the deployment of these devices is probabilistic in nature. No *rāga* presentation can entirely forego any region of the melodic canvas, or entirely ignore the universal scale-base at *sa*, or entirely neglect ascending or descending melodic phrasing. But, the great musician, because of the clarity of his musical vision, engineers an unequivocal aural image of the *rāga* in the listener's mind through a multi-dimensional reinforcement of the melodic idea which best expresses the emotional statement he wishes to make.

This brings us back to where we started — that a *rāga* is a melodic representation of an emotional statement, and a melodic vehicle for its communication. An understanding of its *rāga*-ness helps the musician to create a stimulus, which has a high probability of attaining a well-defined emotional state for himself, and of inducing a similar emotional state amongst his audiences. Truly great music, like great literature, tends to transcend grammar, often liberating it from itself. When this happens, grammar gets re-written. But, for the less epochal moments in music, the grammar — as understood in each era — remains the stepping-stone to literature.

3.2

RĀGA CHEMISTRY AND BEYOND

CLASSICAL music audiences often encounter *rāga*s in a deliberately modified, rather than pure, form. The transformations are created by systematically pushing the melodic features of familiar *rāga*s beyond their recognizable boundaries. When confronted with the unfamiliarity of these aural images, the listener seeks clues to their musical intent in their nomenclature. The names rarely help because no naming conventions exist. And those that exist are vague, because the various categories of transformation have not been codified.

Some would frown upon a classification-codification approach to understanding *rāga* transformations on the grounds that it militates against the creative process. On the other hand, the need for audiences to understand and classify the departures from the familiar cannot be wished away. If they are likely to drift towards some metaphoric understanding anyway, they might welcome some help.

In the present writer's efforts at deciphering the melodic intent and content of *rāga* transformations, he has found the rudiments of chemistry useful. The chemical metaphor is not out of place because, while transgressing its recognizable boundaries, a *rāga* is exposed to an interaction with the entire universe of *rāga*s, each with its own melodic identity. A "chemical" reaction takes place between the base *rāga* and the *rāga*-universe, and the base *rāga* is transformed. The resultant melodic entity retains some "native" features of the base *rāga*, while acquiring features "alien" to it. The new melodic entity lends itself to categorization in the language of chemistry on the basis of how the "native" and the "alien" are reflected in the resultant melodic entity.

Rāga transformations appear, broadly, comparable to three types of derivative chemical entities — allotropes, compounds, and emulsions. This list is limited by the totality of the present writer's exposure to music, and by his ignorance of chemistry. As a useful starting point for an analyst of greater competence, let us consider the chemical metaphor through contemporary examples.

The Allotrope

In the mid-1980s, Ustad Vilayat Khan recorded a *rāga* called Vilayat Khani Kānadā for HMV in India. In the early 1990s, he rechristened it Enayet Khani Kānadā as a tribute to his father, the legendary Ustad Enayet Khan, and recorded it for India Archive Music, New York. Both recordings, considered independently and together, constitute the basis of this description.

This *rāga* is a melodically enhanced version of Darbārī Kānadā. It uses the *śuddha gā* and *nī svaras*, in addition to the *komala gā* and *nī svara*s "native" to Darbārī Kānadā. The phraseology of the *rāga* is identical to that of Darbārī Kānadā. Darbārī phrases using the "native" *ga/ni svara*s alternate with the same phrases using the "alien" *śuddha svara*s.

As a result of the *śuddha ga* usage in the lower tetrachord, the *rāga* is exposed to a similarity with Mālguñjī. Likewise, in the upper tetrachord, the *śuddha nī* usage can suggest Candrakauṅs. But, the *ustād* navigates these regions so skilfully that there is no chance of the resulting melodic entity conveying a suggestion of either Guñjī-Kānadā [Mālguñjī+Darbārī Kānadā] or of Candramukhī Kānadā [Candrakauns+Darbārī Kānadā].

The dominant melodic idea or aural image of the *rāga* remains anchored firmly in Darbārī Kānadā. In its totality, Vilayat Khani Kānadā/Enayet Khani Kānadā is an individualistic, special, or idiosyncratic version of Darbārī Kānadā; nothing more, nothing less. The closest approximation to this configuration in chemistry is that of an allotrope.

Allotropes are different physical forms of the same element. Coal and diamond are both, for instance, allotropes of Carbon. They differ in the way the atoms bond with each other and arrange themselves. In addition to differential physical characteristics, allotropes are also supposed to exhibit different chemical properties. This would be true of Darbārī Kānadā and Enayet Khani Kānadā. In isolated passages, Enayet Khani Kānadā, does throw seductive glances at Guñjī-Kānadā and/or Candramukhī Kānadā. With a slight shift in handling, Enayet Khani Kānadā could easily become a compound of two or three *rāga*s. Vilayat Khan, however, does not allow this to happen.

Before we consider melodic compounds, let us consider the contemporary Bhairavī, whose melodically enhanced form has driven the original [early twentieth century] form, called *śuddha* Bhairavī, out of circulation.

Is the modern Bhairavī an allotrope of the *śuddha* Bhairavī? This question probably points towards to the evolutionary path of the *rāga*. In the early twentieth century, when *śuddha* Bhairavī of *komala re-gā-dh-nī svara*s accepted the *śuddha re* and *dh svaras* as a melodic enhancement, the modern Bhairavī with a minimum of nine *svara*s would have been considered an allotrope of *śuddha* Bhairavī. Today, with Bhairavī permitting the use of all twelve *svara*s, and the *śuddha* Bhairavī almost out of circulation, we do not need to think of the two *rāga*s as allotropes, even though such a description would be conceptually valid. In less than a century, Bhairavī has enlarged is *svara*-material by five *svara*s, and we still call it Bhairavī.

A similar path can plausibly be traced by Darbārī Kānadā, if the Vilayat Khani/Enayet Khani Kānadā transformation strikes deep roots in the musical soil, and displaces today's Darbārī Kānadā. We cannot predict whether this will happen, nor can we be sure that it will not. If it happens, the surviving melodic entity might still be called by the same old name — Darbārī Kānadā — even though it will not be Darbārī Kānadā as we know it today.

The point to note here is that the evolution of a *rāga* may start with the emergence of an allotrope, with the allotrope ultimately driving the original out of circulation, but retaining the name of the original. To the extent that grammarians document *rāga*s periodically, the evolutionary path may be traceable. But, in the absence of an effective dialog between scholarship and musicianship, nomenclatures of melodic entities will remain at the mercy of musicians responding to the need of audiences for a basis in familiarity.

The Compound

A compound *rāga* comes into being when two *rāga*s are fused together in such a manner as to retain both their melodic personalities in the compound so created. In the compound *rāga*, there is no distinction between "native" and "alien" melodic features. Both are explicitly present, though their relative presence in the aural experience may vary from musician to musician, and even from concert to concert for the same musician.

Some musicians and scholars have argued that the purpose of compound *rāga*s is to obliterate the individual identities of the component *rāgas* by merging them into a novel resultant entity. However, this view is not supported either by the practice of compound *rāgas*, or by the conventions pertaining to the fusion of *rāgas* for the purpose of creating compounds.

A compound is a substance formed from two or more elements chemically united in fixed proportions. In Hindustani music, the compounds, answering to this definition, are used for fusing two *rāgas*, and are the most commonly encountered *rāga* transformations.

In theory, the fusion is done by one of the two classical methods. The directional fusion results from the ascent of one *rāga* being fused with the descent of the second *rāga*. The scalar fusion deploys one *rāga* in the lower tetrachord and the other *rāga* in the upper tetrachord. Theoretically, thus, the "fixed proportions" requirement of the molecular structure in a compound is met.

Amongst the popular compounds, the Kānadā group *rāgas*, other than Darbārī Kānadā [the primary Kānadā], generally correspond to the directionally fused category. Kāfī Kānadā, for instance, is a fusion of the Kāfī ascent with the Darbārī descent [*nī-pā-gā-mā-re-sā*]. Likewise, Candramukhī Kānadā is generally a fusion of Candrakauns ascent with the Darbārī descent.

The compounds fused at the scalar midpoint belong mainly to the Bahāra and Malhāra group. This is because Bahāra and Malhāra are both ascent-oriented and upper tetrachord dominant *rāgas*. They are highly eligible for fusion with *rāgas* whose melodic soul resides in the lower tetrachord, or are descent oriented. Bāgeśvarī-Bahāra, Bhairava-Bahāra and Deśa-Malhāra are examples of this category.

The existence of fusing conventions should not convey the impression that compound *rāgas*, like the *rāgas* in their pure form, have a clearly defined grammar. Firstly, any two compatible *rāga*s can be fused either directionally or at the mid-point of the scale, thus resulting in at least two feasible variants of the same compound. Secondly, considering that a compound *rāga* is the product of the creative urge to enlarge the melodic potential of one of the two component *rāga*s, musicians differ substantially from each other in the manner in which they treat the fusion.

The conventions pertaining to fusion have other limitations, too. A formalistic approach to the fusion would be hopelessly inadequate for fusing two *rāga*s, like Aḍānā and Bahāra [in the compound *rāga*, Aḍānā-Bahāra], both of which have ascending phrases that constitute their respective signatures, and also have their melodic soul residing in the upper tetrachord. A strict directional fusion of the two would be insufficient for solving the aesthetic problem. The total solution, in such cases, has to allow both the *rāga*s to express their melodic signatures, even though this implies a substantial duplication of *rāga* identities in the upper tetrachord and in ascending motion.

In the real world, therefore, while the classical conventions for the formation of *rāga* compounds serve as important guidelines, the music, as performed, might often treat the phrases of the component *rāga*s as the building blocks of the fusion rather than conform to classical conventions. This brings us to the third type of *rāga* transformation, the emulsion, which explicitly configures phrases rather than scalar regions or directional motions.

The Emulsion

In chemistry, an emulsion is a fine dispersion of minute droplets of one liquid in another in which it is not soluble or miscible. The droplets are so small that they remain suspended indefinitely in the suspension medium, unaffected by gravity. If, however, the force of gravity is greatly increased in a high-speed centrifuge, the suspension can be broken down into its components.

In a *rāga* transformation of the emulsion type, the phrase, rather than the scalar canvas, determines the fusion of component *rāga*s. Typically, the melody is constructed fusing the distinctive phrases of the component *rāga*s as its building blocks. Because of this, the emulsion is clearly, and explicitly, decipherable as a tapestry of phraseologies borrowed from the component *rāga*s.

In rendition, the *rāga* emulsion is the most difficult form of transformation because of the constant *rāga* switching it demands. Because of this, it has emerged as a forte of the Jaipur-Atrauli *gharānā*. Vocalists trained in this *gharānā* perform all *rāga* combinations in the emulsion format, almost totally shunning the compound form. This special penchant for the difficult and the challenging has made musicians from this *gharānā* the foremost exponents of combinations of three or more *rāga*s, for which the emulsion form is ideal, and unavoidable.

Amongst the most memorable achievements in this category, as performed by Jaipur-Atrauli singers, are Kesarbai Kerkar's renditions of Sampūrṇa Mālkauṅs, a blend of Mālkauṅs, Bāgeśvarī and Kāfī, and of Khat, claimed to be a blend of six different *rāga*s, of which the predominant are Deśī, Jaunpurī and Suha Kānadā. Concert recordings of Kesarbai Kerkar's renditions of these *rāga*s have been in grey market circulation for several years now.

The Jaipur-Atrauli practice of adhering exclusively to the emulsion approach suggests that the conceptual framework of chemistry holds the clue to the various options for the tonal and melodic enhancement of the mature *rāga*s.

Chemistry Defines Options

To demonstrate this point, let us consider the ramifications of *sampūrṇa* [heptatonic] Mālkauṅs as a *rāga* enhancement concept.

Mālkauṅs is a pentatonic [*auḍava*] *rāga*, omitting *re* [2nd] and *pā* [5th] *svaras*. When its transformation is intended to be a "*Sampūrṇa* [Heptatonic] Mālkauṅs," it must, by definition, be enhanced to include the two missing *svaras*, *re* and *pā*. This enhancement can be effected by any of the three transformations listed here.

An allotrope of Mālkauṅs, which includes the use of *re* and *pa*, has been performed by several vocalists and instrumentalists. Their interpretations differ greatly from each other. But the treatment, in all cases, ensures that the resultant melody remains rooted in the Mālkauṅs character, and avoids the risk of even momentary confusion with other mature *rāgas*.

If a musician wishes to present a heptatonic [*sampūrṇa*] version of Mālkauṅs as a compound, he can perform Kaunsi-Kānadā, which is most commonly a blend of Mālkauṅs with Darbārī Kānadā. Kaunsi-Kānadā is a *sampūrṇa* [heptatonic] Mālkauṅs because it uses *re* and *pa* in addition to the Mālkauṅs *svara* material; but it also a compound because it fuses Mālkauṅs and Darbārī Kānadā. In Kaunsi-Kānadā, the two *rāgas* are more commonly fused directionally, in the form of a Mālkauṅs ascent and a Darbārī Kānadā descent. Theoretically, however, Mālkauṅs in the lower tetrachord and Darbārī Kānadā in the upper tetrachord, or the other way round, are feasible alternatives.

And, finally, we have Kesarbai's version of *sampūrṇa* [heptatonic] Mālkauṅs which is an emulsion of Mālkauṅs, Bāgeśvarī and Kāfī, constructed with alternating and interlocking phrases from all the three *rāgas*.

The Rāga-Mālikā

In recent years, the subtlety and complexity of the *rāga* enhancement idiom has often been confused with the popular *rāga-mālikā* [literally, a link-chain of *rāga*s] form of presentation. This confusion requires to be cleared. In the *rāga-mālikā* form, a series of *rāga*s is presented, in sequence, without a break. The common practice is for the musician to commence with one *rāga*, and to take a detour into a series of different *rāga*s before returning to the original *rāga* before closing the rendition.

In this format, there is no attempt to forge a new melodic entity. There are no conventions for linking the *rāga*s. The transition from one *rāga* to another can be made at any point, almost at will. The only link, a tenuous one at that, is forged by using one *svara*, or a phrase, which is important to both the sequentially linked *rāga*s. The critical feature of this form, therefore, is not the comprehensive skill and aesthetics of *rāga* chemistry, but the momentary delight of a near-imperceptible transition from one *rāga* to another.

In an interview with a leading American producer of Hindustani music in 1991, Ustad Vilayat Khan claimed that the origins of this form could be traced to a practice prevalent in the royal courts of early twentieth century. It was common, in that era, for princes to invite musicians from other courts for a few weeks at a time to perform at their courts. During these visits, visiting musicians performed at the host court over several evenings in a row.

During such visits, the visiting musician occasionally performed one *rāga* for an entire evening, drifted into a second *rāga* before ending the concert, and picked up where he had left off on the next evening. The same procedure was evidently repeated every evening until the last evening of his performing visit. On the final day, the musician would drift back, imperceptibly again, into the *rāga* with which he commenced his guest-appearance at the court.

Though further details about the traditional techniques of *rāga-mālikā* presentation are not available, it would appear that it emerged as an attention-holding device for a concert that was intended to stretch over several evenings. By drifting into a second *rāga* before ending an evening's rendition, the musician probably wanted to ensure a return of the same audience to hear him the next evening.

On the modern concert platform, this elaborate procedure has been abbreviated to suit its compulsions, which generally permit only two hours even to the most distinguished musicians. In the contemporary context, therefore, the *rāga-mālikā* is no more than a convenient format for presenting glimpses of several *rāga*s within a single presentation merely because there is insufficient time for a relaxed and comprehensive display of musicianship.

The contemporary *rāga-mālikā* is, therefore, a mechanical device not to be confused with the products of *rāga* chemistry. Even if the name suggests something more ambitious, it is merely a link-chain of *rāga* fragments.

Beyond Chemistry

While chemistry is a useful aid to the understanding of *rāga* enhancement practices, they are a part of a creative process aimed at shaping a novel aesthetic experience. It is worthwhile, therefore, to consider the cultural and aesthetic issues that lie beyond chemistry. Why is it that, despite the literally thousands of mature *rāga*s in existence, musicians appear to be attracted towards *rāga* enhancement devices? The question probably has two answers — one aesthetic, and the other practical.

The aesthetic answer lies in the individuality of the aesthetic product the musician creates with *rāga* enhancement devices. Conventions for this process do exist, but what is delivered in a transformed *rāga* presentation is an individualistic creation. To the musician's mind, the rendition of such a creation may not seem like an alternative to a *rāga* rendered within its recognizable melodic boundaries. It is simply his creative choice and individual statement, requiring no validation beyond the musical sense it makes to his audiences.

The practical answer probably lies in the fact that the range of *rāga*s in circulation at any given time is limited. Every generation of audiences, and indeed of musicians too, is familiar with only a limited number of *rāga*s. In the first quarter of the twentieth century, V.N. Bhatkhande presented compositions of one hundred and eighty-one *rāga*s, of which he described only forty-five as being *prasiddha*. The remaining were classified as *aprasiddha*. A contemporary enumeration of popular *rāga*s may be even smaller than that of Bhatkhande's. Because of this phenomenon, a musician is naturally more confident of sharing a novel aesthetic experience through an unfamiliar juxtaposition of familiar aural images than he would be with a rare *rāga*. By the same logic, *rāga* chemistry would probably be far too demanding for contemporary audiences. This may be why *rāga* allotropes, compounds and emulsions are tending to get eclipsed by the *rāga-mālikā*, a mechanistic pretender which can provide only flashes of surprise, without the sustained aesthetic delight characteristic of true *rāga* chemistry.

Under conditions of diluted musicianship and audience profiles, it is tempting to suspect that the practical has overshadowed the aesthetic consideration. As a cultural phenomenon, then, the progressive shrinkage of the familiar, along with the growing popularity of populist formats like the *rāga-mālikā*, could be depleting the vastness and richness of the living *rāga* tradition.

Rāga Chemistry and You

What can the chemistry of *rāga* enhancement mean, personally, for you? This depends on the kind of listener you are. The connoisseur needs to comprehend music at the cerebral level and also respond at the emotional level. For such a listener, an understanding of the inner workings of the music might be a precondition to its enjoyment. On the other hand, a listener who is untrained in *rāga* grammar, but is merely sensitive, can enjoy the novelty of the aural experience independently of its chemical analysis.

To a musically sensitive mind, the enjoyment of music arises from its aesthetic coherence. This is precisely what a *rāga* enshrines. A *rāga* is a well-defined musical idea, whose aesthetic coherence has been matured by the accumulated talent and compositional imagination of several generations of musicians. In our musical tradition, which requires every musician to be a performer as well as composer, the *rāga* functions as a "quality control" device for the compositional facet of the artistic endeavour.

When a musician decides to transgress the framework of a mature *rāga*, or to blend two or more *rāga*s to create a novel melodic entity, he is setting aside — though only partially — the compositional contribution of his ancestors, and enlarging his own role as a composer. In such a situation, it does not matter what name he gives the novel melodic entity, or whether the new entity is an allotrope, a compound, or an emulsion. The music has to be accepted on its own terms, with aesthetic coherence and emotional appeal as the only criteria for judgement.

3.3

RĀGAS: RIGHT AND WRONG

SENIOR musicians are often found criticizing other musicians for incorrect renderings of *rāga*s. Likewise, critics and scholars frequently pull up musicians for performing a *rāga* improperly. Even the discerning listener is often bewildered by the crossfire. Every objection to a particular treatment of a *rāga* cannot be valid; nor can every objection be invalid. Some efforts at developing a rational viewpoint on the subject of *rāga* authenticity are, therefore, in order.

As a backdrop to this issue, we must appreciate the socio-economic context in which music practice evolved up to the nineteenth century. The major seats of musicianship were the courts of the feudal aristocracy, which patronized great musicians. These principalities were isolated from each other by primitive modes of transportation, and communication. This was an era without radio, without telephony, and without mass-distributed pre-recorded music. Very few musicians knew precisely what their neighbours, just a couple of hundred miles away, were singing.

Considering these features of the nineteenth-century environment, it is the similarities in the treatment of *rāga*s between different *gharānā*s and musicians that are more surprising than the dissimilarities between them. Although all *gharānā*s sang music derived from the same musical tradition, most musicians of that era had imbibed it through personalized, oral transmission. The documentation of the tradition was not accessible to a majority of these musicians, partly because much of it was in an archaic language, and partly because scholarship was scarce amongst professional musicians.

The vast area of similarity in the presentation of music was evidently based on the very strong framework that Hindustani music inherited in the twentieth century. This framework probably belonged to *dhrupad*, or its predecessors, with their strong bias in favour of the pre-composed element. The differences probably began to surface as the post-*dhrupad* genres eclipsed the pre-composed element and expanded the role of improvization.

The whole issue of grammar and/or "right" or "wrong" interpretations of *rāga*s gathered momentum in the late nineteenth/early twentieth century when scholars started documenting the consensus between major musicians on the melodic features of the *rāga*s they heard. Bhatkhande provided, for the first time in recent history, the conceptual-analytical framework for defining the essentials of *rāga*-ness. This was a priceless contribution, because any art form ensures orderly evolution for itself only by interacting with a parallel body of scholarship.

A rational viewpoint on *rāga* authenticity must, therefore, balance the demands of Hindustani classical music as a performing tradition with the demands of theoretical soundness. Such a perspective becomes easier to develop once we recognize the categories of issues that arise in the debate on *rāga* authenticity.

Nomenclature

Vocalists of the Jaipur-Atrauli *gharānā* sing a *rāga* called Khambāvatī, which is identical to Rāgeśrī as understood in all other *gharānās*, and is also at variance with the grammar of Khambāvatī as documented by early twentieth-century authorities. Does this make the Khambāvatī of the Jaipur-Atrauli musicians "wrong"?

If the commonly understood Rāgeśrī and the recognizable or documented Khambāvatī were very similar *rāgas*, it would imply that the Jaipur-Atrauli musicians do not recognize the subtle distinction between the two *rāgas*. Since this happens not to be the case, a sane view would be to judge the Jaipur-Atrauli Khambāvatī on the yardstick of the commonly understood Rāgeśrī, and allow the *gharānā*'s musicians, if they so wish, to call it Khambāvatī. After all, you cannot lynch a musician for giving a different name to a well established and coherently rendered melodic entity!

Consider another similar, though not identical, example. The Candrakauṅs sung by Agra *gharānā* vocalists is very different from the *rāga* that is understood as Candrakauṅs by other *gharānās*, and audiences in general. It is, in fact, a *rāga* unique to this *gharānā*, and performed only by its musicians. Does the Agra *gharānā*'s Candrakauṅs become "wrong" merely because audiences, in general, do not associate it with their notion of Candrakauṅs?

The sane view here is to judge the *rāga* by the basic yardsticks of *rāga*-ness. Firstly, is it distinctive enough from other *rāgas* to warrant independent status as a *rāga*? Secondly, is it an aesthetically coherent and pleasing melodic entity? If the *rāga* passes these two tests, it should be evaluated by the yardstick of its own grammar, rather than by the grammar of Candrakauṅs as sung by other *gharānās*.

Rare Rāgas and their Compounds

Śuddha Chāyā is the dominant component in the popular compound *rāga*, Chāyānat. Likewise, Bhīm is the dominant component of the compound *rāga*, Bhīmpalāsi. Similarly, *rāga*

Alhaiyā is a component of the popular *rāga*, Alhaiyā Bilāwal. Śuddha Chāyā, Bhīm and Alhaiyā, and other similar *rāga*s, are performed only rarely in their pure form because they are almost indistinguishable from their more popular compounds.

The problem does not end here. In some *gharānā*s, many compositions in these *rāga*s are performed in both forms, the pure form and the compound form. Moreover, some compositions in the compound form can be easily mistaken for the pure form, and vice versa. As a result, one may find that Bhīm, or Alhaiyā, or Śuddha Chāyā performed by one musician may sound quite different from the same *rāga*s performed by another musician. Alternatively, you could find two different names describing two pieces of music, which you find indistinguishable in terms of their *rāga*-ness!

In such cases, what is the rational view to adopt? This problem really has no solution. The only sensible stance is to ask the musician how his interpretation of what he has performed differs from its pure or compound twin, and accept the explanation as valid if his rendition is consistent with the melodic definition.

Creative License

There exists a concert recording of Bihāg by Pt. Omkarnath Thākur, in which he has used phrases like *gā-re-sā* and *gā-re-nī*, treating *re* as a full-bodied *svara*, rather than the subliminal accidental considered proper in the *rāga*. There also exists an unpublished recording of Bhīmpalāsi by Ustad Ameer Khan, in which his ascent into the *uttarāṅga* follows the Gawoti pattern rather than the distinctive Bhīmpalāsi pattern. Are we to conclude from these recordings that these luminaries were not adept at these *rāga*s?

In such cases, the most reasonable response is to recall the tens of times these greats rendered these *rāga*s in perfect consonance with their grammar as commonly accepted. In a specific context, great musicians have a variety of "reasons" for deviating from the familiar, and they are not accountable to us for their exercise of creative license. If, however, a particular creative license becomes a habit with a musician, it may, or may not, raise fundamental theoretical issues.

Take the instance of Omkarnathji's treatment of the *re svara* in Bihāg. Let us suppose he habitually treated the *svara* in this idiosyncratic manner. What would be a reasonable view on this?

The yardstick, in this context should be two-fold: Does the resultant melodic entity remain well within the recognizable boundaries of the *rāga*? Does the resultant melodic entity steer clear of the risk of confusion with another established *rāga*? As long as these two conditions are met, the apparent transgression should be acceptable either as a creative license, or an individualistic interpretation adding to the richness of the *rāga*.

It is the acceptance of such passable transgressions by audiences and the community of musicians that contributes to the evolution of *rāga*s.

Rāga Evolution

*Rāga*s do change and evolve. And, some of this evolution takes place because great musicians leave a stamp of their own personalities on the *rāga*s they perform. The *rāga* Mārwā, for instance, was performed largely as an *āroha-pradhāna rāga* with its centre of melodic gravity in the *uttarāṅga* until its rendering by Ustad Ameer Khan on a long-playing record. Since then, Mārwā has acquired a strong *pūrvāṅga-pradhāna* melodic identity.

On the melodic features of this *rāga*, Ustad Ameer Khan would appear to be at variance with early twentieth century scholars like Bhatkhande. Can we, by this yardstick, pronounce Ustad Ameer Khan as being in error?

A more significant case of *rāga* evolution is *rāga* Lalit, which, according to Bhatkhande, utilizes the *śuddha dh svara*. This will come as a surprise to most contemporary listeners because Lalit no longer uses *śuddha dh*. In fact, a lot of contemporary musicians consider the use of the *śuddha dh* in Lalit as the signature for Ādī Basant/Śūddha Basant, in addition to other aspects of *rāga* grammar.

Consider also Kesarbai Kerkar's two available recordings of Tilak Kamod. In one of them, she has performed the early twentieth century form of the *rāga* which deploys the *śuddha* as well as *komala ni svaras*, while in the second, she performs the new form, with only *śuddha nī*. Those, who have not been exposed to the old form, will conclude that Kesarbai did not know the distinction between Tilak Kamod and Deśa. Audiences are not expected to be familiar with the evolutionary paths of all *rāgas* over a century or more. But, such instances should alert us to the risks of rushing into judgements with respect to *rāga* authenticity.

Another facet of *rāga* evolution is the tendency amongst musicians to simplify the rendition of *rāgas* by introducing phrases which current grammar does not permit, but are contextually not inconsistent with the *rāga*'s melodic personality.

Consider, for instance, the *uttarāṅga* ascent of Kedāra. The theoretical position approves of *mā^-pa-sa'*. Over the years, musicians have varied this ascent to include *mā^-pā-dh-nī-sā* as well as *mā^-pā-nī-sā*. Taken in isolation, these phrases can be mistaken for phrases of other *rāgas*. However, in the context of a Kedāra rendition, with appropriate phrases preceding or succeeding them, they do not create any dissonance amongst listeners.

The rational view is to accept that *rāgas* are not static melodic entities. Their strength lies precisely in their ability to evolve in response to the creative visions of maestros, and the acceptance of it by changing audience tastes. Theory will, as always, be a couple of steps behind practice. In a performing tradition, theory can document practice, but it cannot expect to dictate it.

Grammatical Propriety

Some *gharānās* permit the use of phrases such as *re-pā-gā* and *pā-sā-dh*, in Darabārī. Although this usage is increasingly rare, the users of these phrases would include musicians who are otherwise considered theoretically sound.

Several objections have been raised against such usage. *Re-pā-gā* provides a strong suggestion of Malhāra, while *pā-sā-dh* belongs to Asāvari. Because the two phrases are perfectly congruent in first-fourth correspondence, it is also argued that they compete with Darabārī's own congruent set of distinctive phrases: *gā-mā-re* and *dh-nī-pā*, with oscillated treatment of *gā* and *dh*.

Here, the yardstick of distinctiveness comes into sharp focus. These two phrases provide strong suggestions of other, mature *rāgas*. In addition to this, they conflict with a similar, though distinctive pattern fundamental to the melodic character of Darabārī. The resultant melodic entity therefore appears to breach the recognizable boundaries of Darabārī as presently understood.

Let us consider another, though less dramatic, instance of probable impropriety in a seemingly non-controversial *rāga* like Yaman. In recent years, many musicians, including the most respected, have considered it permissible to use *re* as a *nyāsa svara*, the terminal point of a phrase, in this *rāga*. This has been questioned on the grounds that, *re* being adjacent to *gā*, such usage dilutes the dominance of the *vādi*, the pivotal *svara* of the *rāga*.

This argument has instant theoretical appeal because the idea of *rāga*-ness cannot be reduced to a mere scale, and every permitted *svara* cannot qualify as a *nyāsa svara*. On closer scrutiny, however, the objection might appear draconian. The treatment of *re* as a melodic focus, as commonly practised, neither suggests another mature *rāga*, nor pushes the melodic entity beyond the recognizable boundaries of Yaman. It can therefore be considered a facet of the *rāga*'s evolution through the enlargement of its melodic potential. Whether this usage actually dilutes the prominence of the *vādi svara* may depend a lot more on specific treatment of melody by a musician than on the theoretical position on propriety.

The Bottom-Line

Where does this discussion leave us? It must leave us with a great deal of caution, and even diffidence, about sitting in judgement over *rāga* authenticity. But, it does identify a handful of issues, which frequently place a question mark over a musician's interpretation of a *rāga*. The question to consider, then, is: Who applies the yardstick; and, with what motivation?

What novices perform is of no consequence to anyone; and undiscerning listeners do not have the knowledge to apply any yardstick to what they hear. The *rāga* authenticity issue is, therefore, between the greatest musicians of each generation, and the corresponding generation of cognoscenti. The cognoscenti use the weapon of *rāga* grammar to enforce upon their aural experience a comfortable degree of familiarity. The great musician, on the other hand, is under no obligation to dish out repackaged doses of the familiar and is driven by the urge to liberate literature from grammar.

If we accept that today's grammar is derived from yesterday's literature, and today's literature will rewrite grammar for tomorrow, the two parties to this issue must always be in a state of debate. The debate, in fact, represents the dialectic that guides our musical tradition along its evolutionary path.

Considering the significance of this process, responsible participants in it need to raise the level of debate above the nuts and bolts of a *rāga*'s familiar melodic identity. They must come to grips with the fundamentals of *rāga*-ness, while accepting that a *rāga* does not exist in isolation, but takes shape in performance, and its boundaries are redrawn by every rendition.

At the fruitful level of debate, the crucial issues are: Is the melodic identity — no matter by what name called — sufficiently distinctive? Does it steer sufficiently clear of the risk of confusion with other well established melodic entities? Is it consistent in its painting of the melodic canvas? Is it aesthetically coherent? Does it make a discernible emotional statement? Once we raise the debate to such issues, words like "right" and "wrong" will either acquire their appropriate meaning, or become irrelevant.

3.4

KEDĀRA AT SUNRISE?

KEDĀRA AT sunrise is an outrageous idea for a majority of Indian connoisseurs. But, the time may have come for them to reconsider the time-theory of *rāga*s, and get prepared for Hindustani music to loosen its strictures on account of time-related prescriptions for the performance of *rāga*s.

In Hindustani music, every *rāga* is prescribed for performance during a specific three-hour time-slot of the twenty-four hour daily cycle. Musicologists have, for long, challenged the validity of the convention, as well as the assumptions underlying the adherence to it. They are now joined by a substantial segment of music lovers, who ask why the timings of concerts — generally between sunset and midnight — should limit the variety of *rāga*s they hear on the concert platform.

It is interesting that Carnatic music, a product of the same tradition as Hindustani music, follows no such prescription. Even in the age-old tradition of *Havelī Sangīta*, the *dhrupad* of the Vaiṣṇava temples, compositions in Mālkauṅs — regarded as a late evening *rāga* — are sung routinely during the *śrīṅgāra darśana*, around ten in the morning. Consider also the fact that, inside a modern auditorium, environmental conditions are identical at any time of the day and throughout the year. Also note, that there is no way of controlling the time of the day or night, or part of the year, during which audiences will listen to pre-recorded music, which is now the primary vehicle for the delivery of music. Therefore, a debate over the validity of the conventions is legitimate.

Despite the unresolved issues surrounding the time theory, significant Hindustani musicians have not, so far, deviated blatantly from its prescriptions on Indian soil. With more and more of their earnings coming from foreign as well as uninitiated Indian audiences, their deviations could begin soon. We have, therefore, to prepare ourselves for resolving the imminent conflicts between our rationality and conventional notions of artistic propriety.

Tradition represents the accumulated experience of a society, even if its logic is opaque to us. Over a period, practice can deviate imperceptibly from the logic, and the deviations somehow get accepted. In its totality, our response to music is, therefore, a complex combination of culturally conditioned, and universal aesthetic values and tendencies.

We can neither accept traditional notions merely because they represent the accumulated wisdom of society, nor reject them merely because their logic is not transparent to us. With this perspective, we need to consider the time theory of *rāga*s, and how it can fit into our understanding of music.

The fundamental concept in Indian aesthetics is *rasa*. *Rasa* refers to the specific state of mind that any artistic endeavour elicits, communicates, or reflects. Every *rāga* — loose and coherent at the same time — is a tool by which the musician maximizes the possibility of eliciting the target emotional response from his audiences.

On what basis has tradition assumed a correspondence between a *rāga* and its *rasa*? This assumption is validated by experience and general acceptance. The experience also leads tradition to believe that each pattern of melodic stimuli has the highest probability of eliciting the target emotional response during certain hours of the day/night or during certain seasons of the year. Thus has evolved a performing tradition, which assumes, broadly, a three-way correspondence between melodic patterns [*rāga*s], emotional states [*rasa*s] and environmental and climatic variables.

Many non-musical factors do, of course, influence our receptivity and response to a musical presentation. But, a musician can only control musical variables; and this is what the performing tradition helps him to do. In doing so, the tradition attempts to harmonize musical variables with environmental variables, based on its understanding of the relationship between the two. At the root of these prescriptions is the oriental notion that man is most at peace with himself when he is at peace with nature. Arbitrary and even fanciful as these prescriptions may appear, they relate music to a reality whose relevance the latest researches in physiology are beginning to vindicate.

The proposition is that our bodily and emotional states respond constantly to changes in the quality of sunlight, and climatic factors such as humidity and temperature. If this proposition is acceptable, it is logical that there should be specific environmental conditions most conducive to each category of emotional experience. Our performing tradition has attempted to stabilize its understanding of these probabilities with the benefit of centuries of trial and error.

This configuration of ideas came closer to "scientific" respectability when Prof. V.N. Bhatkhande [2nd edn., 1970, pp. 21-23] observed a relationship between *rāga* forms and their time-specific prescriptions. Since then, other scholars and musicians have identified additional patterns,which provide some support for the time-theory of *rāga*s as an evolved parameter in the classification matrix.

The Theory

The Hindustani performing tradition divides the day into eight equal parts of three hours each. The musical clock is standardized with the notional interval between sunrise and sunset being assumed to be 12 hours, or consisting of four 3-hour parts. Each *rāga* is assigned its most appropriate part of the day [after sunrise] or night [after sunset] for performance. Some *rāga*s are prescribed for performance in the twilight zone — around sunrise or sunset. And, there are some *rāga*s, though very few, which are permitted for performance at any time of the day or night.

Even for *rāga*s associated with seasons of the year, the time of the day is considered a binding prescription. The seasonal prescription dominates the selection. But, the time of the performance is not allowed to contravene the time-based principles of classification.

For instance, Bahāra, the *rāga* of spring, and Malhāra, the *rāga* of the rainy season, both use the *komala svara*s of *gā* and *nī*. Therefore, unless they are performed as compounds of morning *rāga*s, they are performed after sunset, though only during the appropriate season. These seasonal *rāga*s, and their compounds, can be performed along with non-seasonal *rāga*s of the appropriate time-segment.

The tonal commonalties between *rāga*s prescribed for different times, and the pattern of transitions, reflect the movement of the sun along its geocentric path. Although a *rāga* is defined by a large number of rules designed for aesthetic coherence, the time theory is discussed primarily with respect to the basic aspect of *rāga* grammar — its *svara* material. As a basic classification based on *svara* material, *rāga*s are divided into three categories:

1. *Rāgas that use the flat svaras of re and dh* [*2nd and 6th*]

These *rāgas* are prescribed for performance either around sunrise or around sunset. The suppressed/debilitated microtones of the *re* and *dh* are suggestive of the semi-awake condition, and are believed to have an aesthetic affinity with the quality of light in the twilight zones. Some senior vocalists also report that, during these periods, the throat muscles tend to become loose, and the accurate rendition of *śuddha re* and *dh svaras* becomes difficult. There could, therefore, also be a physiological basis for this pattern.

The twilight periods — sunrise and sunset — have a very deep cultural meaning. For instance, *rāgas* of the twilight zone are also called *rāgas* of the *godhūli belā* [*go* = cows + *dhūli* = dust + *belā* = time]. This is the time when the cows raise a lot of dust on the village roads either on their way out to the grazing pastures at sunrise, or on their way home at sunset.

To the Indian mind, this is an emotionally charged description. The cow plays a pivotal role in India's primarily agrarian economy, and is held sacred. The sanctity of the cow, and of all the activities associated with dairying as an occupation in the rural context, has been reinforced in mythology by the depiction of Lord Kṛṣṇa as Gopāla [the Divine Cowherd].

There also exists a tradition, in many parts of the country, of lighting a lamp before the earthen water-pot in the household around sunset, as a mark of welcome and respect for the spirits of the ancestors, which are believed to visit the family home to quench their thirst. Sunrise and sunset are also times when the typical Hindu family congregates around the altar to offer its prayers.

As a combination of economic forces, ancestor worship sentiments, and religious sentiments, and of course, as a natural response to the quality of light, the Hindu mind has given this group of *rāgas* a strong bias in favour of the devotional fervour. In the Hindu mind, sunrise and sunset are appropriate times for acknowledging the glory of God.

Of the three major classifications, the Time-*rāga-rasa* equation appears to hold most consistently for the Group 1 *rāgas*.

2. *Rāgas that use the śuddha* [*natural*] *svaras of re and dh* [*2nd and 6th*]

These *rāga*s are prescribed for performance after the first group, that is, between 7 and 10 a.m. and between 7 and 10 p.m. This prescription sees the stepping up of the *re* and *dh* *svara*s from *komala* [flat] to *śuddha* [natural] as symbolizing the completion of the night-to-day or day-to-night transition that commences in the twilight. There could well be a physiological basis for this, too.

3. *Rāgas that use the flat svaras of gā and nī* [3rd and 7th]

These *rāga*s are prescribed for the remaining parts of the day/ night: 10 a.m. to sunset and 10. p.m. to sunrise.

In addition to these three indicators of the time dimension in the performing tradition, the use of the *mā* [4th] plays an important role. This, however, is a weaker and less consistent pattern than the first three.

The Indian scale works a notion of seven *svara*s. The 4th [in a frequency ratio of 1 : 1.33 to the scale-base] is therefore, notionally, the mid-point of the Indian scale, with three *svara*s below it, and three above. The solfa symbol *mā* is itself an abbreviation for *madhyama*, which means mid-point.

It has been observed that, largely, *rāga*s performed during the day [sunrise to sunset] use the *śuddha mā svara*, either solely or as the dominant of the two *mā svara*s when both are used. As the sun approaches dusk, the *tīvra mā* appears on the scene, and even dominates the melody until late into the night.

It is important to note that these are not rigid rules. They cannot be so, simply because the primary classification of *rāgas* is based on *rasa*, and not on *svara* material. And, the Indian aesthetic sensibility is far too mature to assume a mechanistic correspondence between *svara*-material and the emotional content of all its melodic potentialities.

Even the *rasa* classification of *rāgas* is merely indicative because the *rasa* of a *rāga* can be as much a matter of interpretation as of the intrinsic psycho-acoustic propensity of the *svara* material. Different musicians, of comparable stature can, and do, interpret the same *rāga* in obviously different *rasas*.

The Time Theory is, then, an effort by musicologists to identify the patterns of commonality between *rāgas* prescribed by tradition for performance during different parts of the day. They are pointers to the possibility that certain *svaras*, or combinations of *svaras*, might have a higher probability of communicating certain emotions appropriate to certain times of the day/night than others.

A Rational Perspective

The theory, as understood so far, falls short of being a comprehensive and fully organized system of relationships. Some psychometric experiments have been conducted to verify the association of melodic patterns with time-slots in the audience mind. The results are, so far, only tentative in their affirmation.

Quite irrespective of what any kind of scientific enquiry says about these psycho-acoustic notions, it will not change the way different categories of audiences feel music. It might, therefore, be necessary for the "believers" to accept that, maybe, the Time theory works for them because they have Indian bodies, and Indian minds, of a particular generation, responding under the sunlight quality and climatic conditions characteristic of the Indian subcontinent.

The generational issue might be more important than is easily appreciated. Generations brought up on pre-recorded music, and in acoustically and environmentally engineered auditoria, may be relatively insensitive to compliance with the time theory, and consequently unsympathetic to it.

Climatic conditions, too, cannot be an insignificant factor. If the Hindustani and Carnatic traditions are derived from a common source, the time theory was probably common to them until their bifurcation. Why did the Carnatic tradition abandon the theory, while the Hindustani tradition retained it? It can be hypothesized that, by virtue of being closer to the equator, the southern states experience a far lower level of variation in climatic conditions within the day and between the different seasons than the northern, non-peninsular, states do. This could be the reason why the *rāga* Hiṇḍolam/Mālkauṅs does not suggest, to Carnatic audiences, as radical a contrast with the *rāga* Bhairavī/Hanumatoḍī in aesthetic value and emotional content, as it does to Hindustani audiences.

Once we appreciate this logic, it can be extended farther. A Sunrise Sonata composed in Kedāra by a Swedish composer need not raise eyebrows even with cultivated Hindustani audiences, because a Swede's relationship with sunlight is radically different from ours.

As Hindustani music addresses an increasingly diverse global audience, the musician becomes progressively incapable of controlling the time and environmental conditions attendant to the performance. Thus, as the context of the musical experience undergoes a fundamental transformation in terms of audience profiles and the environmental conditions, conservative connoisseurs may have to ease their strictures further. Why should it be wrong for an Indian to perform Kedāra at the Bhairava hour, but okay for a Swede to do so?

Those who cannot make this attitudinal transition could soon find themselves in an indignant minority, unable to come to terms with the programming strategies that guide music performance on the contemporary platform. The emerging reality will not show any deference to whether their conservatism is subjective or objective; rational or irrational. It will confront them with a simple choice between the dissonance of concert-attendance and the comfort of "proper" enjoyment of music through pre-recorded media at home.

3.5

THE EXPERIENCE OF MELODY: FROM DHRŪPAD TO SANTŪRA

WHETHER we hear Mālkauṅs in a *dhrupad* recital, or in a *khayāla* performance, or on the flute, *sitāra, saroda,* or *santūra,* we relate easily to the *rāga* in each of these modes of presentation. This is more remarkable than it seems at first sight. Each of these is a different genre with its distinctive architecture, treatment of melody and way of relating the melody to the non-melodic facets of music. Collectively, these genres add to the overall richness of the melodic experience of Hindustani music. And, as alternatives available to our generation of listeners, they oblige us to acknowledge the robustness of our *rāga*s, which sustain their *rāga*-ness across several categories of melodic experience.

But, there is yet another way of looking at this diversity. It evolved sequentially, and not simultaneously, and represents an identifiable tendency over the centuries. Considering the phenomenon in a historical perspective, we can observe some patterns in the changing music-scape. These patterns suggest a progressive fragmentation of the melodic experience, and a growing emphasis on non-melodic facets of music. This trend has implications for the direction the experience of melody can take in the future.

Such a linear-historical perspective can be aided by recognizing the significant stages in the evolution of the melodic experience in Hindustani music. The first is, obviously, the era dominated by *dhrupad* as a vocal art form — up to the early nineteenth century. The *khayāla* as the dominant interface between musicians and their audiences defines the second stage — mid-nineteenth to mid-twentieth centuries. The third stage is defined by the emergence of the fretted lute, the *sitāra*, as the major force in Hindustani music — late nineteenth century onwards. The fourth stage is characterized by the influence of the semi-polychord, the *saroda* — starting from the 1950s. And, the most recent stage was heralded in the mid-1970s, with the ancient bamboo flute making a radical departure from its traditional idiom, and the meteoric rise of the *santūra*, a polychord.

Melody in Dhrupad

Miyā Tānsen, the landmark figure in Hindustani music [sixteenth century], prescribed four criteria for an acceptable *dhrupad* composition. A *pada*, according to him [a] should have four rhyming stanzas of verse, [b] should have been composed by a learned *guru*, [c] can represent any of the *rasa*s and [d] the emotional content of the poetic element should be consistent with that of the *rāga* in which the *pada* is composed [Brihaspati K.C.D., *Sangeet Chintamani*, Sangeet Karyalaya, Hathras, 1st edn. 1989].

In this prescription, we have a multi-dimensional concept of a *rāga*. It starts with the *rasa*, which is explicit in literature. It then ensures that the *rasa* of the poetry determines the candidate *rāga*s in which it can be composed. It thus links the explicit *rasa* of the poetic element with the *rasa* assumed to be associated with the melodic personality of the *rāga*. It then goes on to define the number of stanzas of poetry — and hence melodic lines — that are necessary for the *rasa* implicit in the *rāga* to completely express itself. And, finally, it ties all these facets together by prescribing that only a musician with a respectable command over poetry, melody, and aesthetics should be considered eligible for the role of a composer.

This firm three-way relationship between literature, melody, and aesthetics, which obviously assumed vocal music as the primary manifestation of *rāga*-based art-music, left nothing to chance. The composition was made a total vehicle for the communication of the emotional content of the *rāga*, implicitly as well as explicitly. The faithful conversion of the composer's musical vision into performance was ensured by the evolution of *dhrupad* as a genre with a strong pre-composed tendency, with stringent control over the improvizational freedom conceded to the performer. [Ashok Ranade "Perspectives on Dhrupad," *Journal of the Indian Musicological Society*, 1999, ed. Deepak Raja and Suvarnalata Rao]

By making the composer the controller of literature, melody and aesthetics, and by virtually subordinating the performer's role to that of the composer, *dhrupad* made poetry and melody the joint repositories of *rāga*-ness. But, if both have to work together, and only together, poetry becomes the driver of melody because it conveys explicit meaning, and permits melody to acquire its phonetic and syntactical structure and meaning — semantic as well as musical — only by association with itself.

This feature is reflected in the notion of *rāga-svarūpa* [the *rāga* form], zealously espoused by *dhrupad* vocalists, as the repository of *rāga*-ness, as distinct from such notions in the other genres. Although a precise definition of this notion is not available, it appears to consider a melodic line, rather than a melodic phrase, as the basic building block of melody. A melodic line consists of a string of contiguous phrases, in adjacent regions of the melodic canvas. Such continuity in the sequencing of phrases was necessary for preserving the integrity of the poetic form in rendition, the communication of its literary meaning, and completeness of the intended musical communication. This approach can be described as the "narrative path" to shaping the melodic experience.

Melody in Khayāla

Compared to *dhrupad*, which is a poetry-dominant genre, the *khayāla*, its one-time rival and ultimate successor, is a melody-dominant genre. The *khayāla* form partially liberated melody from poetry through several of its features. It truncated the role of poetry in terms of verbiage as well as importance. The *khayāla* genre also introduced the use of vowels [*ākāra*], *saragama* [solfa symbols] and meaningless consonants [*tarānā*] as alternative articulations available to the vocalist, and granted much greater improvizational freedom to the performer. In addition, it introduced *tāna*s, or high-density melodic runs, which almost entirely liberated melody from poetry, moving music towards a higher degree of abstraction.

Having freed melody partially from the grip of poetry and explicit meaning, the *khayāla* form could develop the notion of *calana*, or skeletal phraseology, as the repository of *rāga*-ness. The *calana* of a *rāga* is a set of melodic phrases permitted in a *rāga*, which collectively establish its distinctiveness. But, since the *khayāla* form did not entirely dispense with poetry, each melodic phrase still had to correspond to a poetic word, which was mostly either tri-syllabic, or was bi-syllabic with a monosyllabic preposition attached to it. A melodic phrase, as represented in the *calana*, thus came to be understood as a tonal contour with a minimum of three points corresponding to a minimum of two intervallic transitions.

With relative freedom from poetry, the *khayāla* form was able to explore sequencing options for melodic phrases, which were fragments of what *dhrupad* implies in the notion of *rāga*-

svarūpa. This freedom led to two new approaches to shaping the melodic experience — the symmetric and the geometric. In the symmetric sequencing of phrases, the phrases have similar melodic contours, but the three points defined by them do not need to seek an identical tonal geometry. The symmetric sequencing can be similar to *alaṅkāra*s [practice exercises] such as *re-mā-gā/gā-pā-mā/mā-dha-pa/pā-ni-dha*. In the geometric sequencing, however, the sequencing explicitly seeks congruence in terms of frequency ratios of the *svara*s utilized in the sequential phrases. Example: *sā-ni-re-sā-ni-sā/pā-mā/dha-pā-mā-pā/sā-'ni/re-sā-'ni-sā*.

The *khayāla* form did not explicitly abandon the "narrative approach" to the sequencing of phrases. But, by permitting the *rāga*-ness to express itself through smaller units through the notion of *calana*, it opened the door for the first significant fragmentation of the melodic experience. For conceptual clarity, the *calana* might be described as the "Phraseological approach" to melody.

Melody on the Sitāra

The emergence of the *sitāra* as a major solo instrument heralded two directions in the evolution of Hindustani music. Firstly, melody itself had to compete with other musical elements — rhythmicality and texture. Rhythmicality was inherent in the fact that the *sitāra*'s technology of sound activation demanded a certain minimum frequency of strokes, and the *cikarī* [set of drone strings tuned to the upper tonic] needed to be used as an intermittent filler of silences. Both these were perceptible and potentially rhythmic interruptions of melody. Texture emerged as a significant feature of the aural experience partially because of the *cikarī* and partially because, although the *sitāra* is a monochord [entire melody executed on one string], the non-melodic strings, other than the *cikarī*, are also involuntarily activated. Over a period, rhythmicality and texture were both raised to a level of high art by the two contemporary giants, Ustad Vilayat Khan and Pt. Ravi Shankar. Secondly, melody itself, freed entirely from poetry, could now seek newer expressions.

In seeking these directions, Pt. Ravi Shankar and Ustad Vilayat Khan explored different paths. Starting from the mid-1960s, Ravi Shankar began a limited use of harmony, executing melody simultaneously on two strings to deliver chords. Vilayat Khan, on the other hand, commenced explorations in stroke-craft for the manipulation of timbre. In order to heighten the acoustic impact of these explorations, the *ustād* explored *svara* combinations in isolation and in pairs, sequenced occasionally in geometric relationship, but often in random juxtaposition.

These patterns deviated from the *khayāla*-based notion of melodic contours as defined by a melodic phrase of three points and two intervallic transitions. Being almost staccato, they neither had a clearly defined melodic contour, nor represented a distinct intervallic transition. Since they were not even phrases, they couldn't form a string that might be construed as narrative. For the same reason, they could also not be classified as either geometric or symmetric. The only appropriate description for them is "kaleidoscopic."

Thus, with Vilayat Khan on the *sitāra*, we arrive at a stage of evolution, which permits melody to ignore the notion of phrasing, and adds "kaleidoscopic" *svara* juxtaposition, to the existing notions of narrative, and phraseological melody to the shaping of the musical experience. Vilayat Khan's explorations in kaleidoscopy imply that the melodic phrase has ceased to be the sole repository of *rāga*-ness. It permits *rāga*-ness to be defined merely by the permissible *svara*s, not necessarily in a prescribed sequence, but conforming to some astutely conceived principles that keep the melodic experience within the recognizable boundaries of a *rāga*.

However, what Vilayat Khan introduced to the *sitāra* in the late 1970s and the 1980s was already in an advanced stage of development since the 1960s, on an instrument better equipped for the purpose — the *saroda* in the hands of Ustad Ali Akbar Khan.

Melody on the Saroda

Unlike the *sitāra*, which is a long-necked monochord, the *saroda* is a short-necked semi-polychord. None of the strings of the *saroda* gives it a large enough canvas to cover two octaves. The instrument habitually executes the melody over three strings, often four. Because of the metallurgical features and tension levels of the different melodic strings, the *saroda* delivers different timbres in different regions of the melodic canvas covering two or three octaves.

The *saroda* was re-engineered into a sophisticated acoustic machine in the 1930s by Ustad Allauddin Khan and his brother, Ustad Ayet Ali Khan. Khansaheb Ali Akbar was the first musician to fully exploit the different timbres available to a sarodist. And, because timbres could be best be isolated by making the melody discontinuous, the *ustād* developed a kaleidoscopic approach to shaping the melodic experience.

But the *ustād*'s music, as also that of other sarodists, introduced another vital change into the music-scape. The sarod was derived from the Kābulī *rabāba*, an instrument on which *paṭhāna* soldiers played martial tunes. The percussive punch of the strokes was an integral part of the *rabāba* idiom because of its leather-cladding over the stomach cavity which receives the impact of the plectrum.

Khansaheb Ali Akbar loosened the grip of the percussive punch over *saroda* music, and drove the instrument sharply towards melody. But, because of its construction, the *saroda* retained its bias towards the percussive element. The *ustād*'s unmatched mastery over rhythm created the combination of multiple timbre exploitation, a heightened rhythmicality and kaleidoscopic *svara* patterns which has now become the distinctive language of the *saroda*. This combination was the ideal setting for the emergence of the *santūra*.

Melody on the Flute

The flute is a breath-activated instrument. Being such, melodic continuity is its natural idiom. Appropriately, the music of Pt. Pannalal Ghosh [1911-60] remained anchored in the vocalized *khayāla*-inspired idiom, though a drift towards the *sitāra*/*saroda* idiom was evident in his *bandiśa*s. These tendencies culminated, starting from the mid-1970s, in the music of Pt. Hariprasad Chaurasia. Chaurasia followed the melodic discontinuities characteristic of the *sitāra*, and *saroda* idioms. This includes a substantial reliance on staccato intonation and symmetric, geometric, and kaleidoscopic melodic strategies.

Melody on the Santūra

The *santūra* is a polychord, on which each string-set delivers only one *svara*, and melody has to be executed by a series of mallet strokes, each on a separate string-set. The rhythmicality of the music is inseparable from its melodic execution. Being a staccato instrument, it can deliver only an approximation of a continuous melodic expression characteristic of Hindustani music. Because of its mechanical uniqueness, the kaleidoscopic *svara* pattern is the natural habitat of the *santūra*. Melodic discontinuity is as effortless a feature of the instrument as is its rhythmicality. Thus, the *santūra* is the rightful heir to the percussive-melodic idiom, which was once the preserve of the *rabāba*-inspired *saroda*.

But, the *santūra* has some other features, which permit it to explore a musical territory beyond the capabilities of the *saroda*. Melody is understood as a sequential delivery of *svara*s, but the polychord *santūra* can deliver different *svaras* even simultaneously. By virtue of being hammer-driven, and having a small physical frame about the size of an adult musician's forearm, the *santūra* permits the two hammers to execute harmony [simultaneous execution of acoustically related *svaras*] and polyphony [the simultaneous execution of different melodies].

The *sitāra* and the *saroda* had already introduced an involuntary rhythmicality into the experience of melody, and permitted isolated *svaras* in kaleidoscopic juxtaposition to become carriers of *rāga*-ness. In both these directions, the *santūra* surpassed them by subordinating melody to rhythmicality, and by atomizing the melodic experience. With the *santūra*, *rāga*-ness could be totally atomized, and pushed into a territory beyond melody, and into a region so far alien to Hindustani music.

What the Trends Imply

In historical perspective, we trace the origins of our story to the narrative approach of the melodic experience in *dhrupad*, with *rāga-svarūpa* or complete melodic lines functioning as the repositories of *rāga*-ness, jointly with the poetic element. This feature gets diluted with the emergence of *calana*, or melodic phrasing, as the repository of *rāga*-ness in the *khayāla* form, and the entry of the symmetric and geometric approaches to their sequencing.

Then comes the era of the plucked lutes — *sitāra* and *saroda* — which brought in rhythmicality, texture, and even a limited use of harmony. But, more significantly, it saw the beginning of the melodic phrase of well-defined melodic contour being splintered, and its fragments being arranged even randomly into kaleidoscopic patterns. In the current phase, this fragmentation was neither arrested nor reversed by the flute, which chose to adopt the melodic approaches of the *sitāra* and the *saroda*, rather than stay with the vocalized *khayāla*-based idiom. It gained further momentum with the entry of the *santūra* which atomizes the melodic experience, permitting the *rāga* to be treated as a mere scale, with other facets of *rāga* grammar slipping into relative irrelevance.

Collectively, these different levels of melodic experience through which Hindustani music expresses *rāga*-ness, imply an enrichment of the musical experience. But, in historical perspective, they suggest melody getting progressively fragmented, and competing increasingly with non-melodic facets of the musical experience. The atomisation of melody, and the imposition on it of a need to compete with non-melodic [non-sequential] *svara* configurations are both alien to Hindustani music, and are redefining its character.

This line of thought might seem alarmist considering that each of these levels of melodic experience is related to different genres of vocal music or instruments of different ergonomic-acoustic capabilities. These levels need not, therefore, necessarily reflect the drift of all of Hindustani music in the direction suggested by these trends. If this were plausible, it would be a consolation. However, this is not how the cultural process works.

In art, whatever the tradition permits, it tends to encourage. It is the possible that defines the direction rather than the acceptable. The acceptability follows the possible once it is a *fait accompli*.

The *khayāla*, for instance, has the narrative path of *dhrupad* available to it; but its distinctiveness is best expressed in the symmetric and geometric sequencing of phrases, and hence this is the direction *khayāla* has tended to take. The *saroda* has the narrative, the symmetric, and the geometric melodic strategies available to it; but it tends to drift towards a marked use of the kaleidoscopic to emphasize its individuality.

Likewise, the *santūra* has the narrative, the symmetric, the geometric, and the kaleidoscopic melodic paths available to it; but its inclination appears to be towards the atomization of melody and the search for extra-melodic pathways to musical ideation and expression. These observations demonstrate the tendency of each genre of vocal music to define itself by its distinctive features, and the tendency of every instrument to define its idiom as a genre, which reflects its own distinctive features.

The Concept of a Genre

What, after all, is a genre? With respect to literature, the notion of a genre

> emphasizes the ways in which certain patterns, themes, structures, and styles may be identified, despite the differences in storyline or plot. In this way, we can understand genre as a kind of scaffolding, which "contains" and shapes individual variations. The key elements of a genre text, therefore, are repetition, recognition, and familiarity. Given these factors, the part played by the audience or reader in recognizing and responding generically identifiable texts is seen as crucial.
>
> — Casey, Bernadette, in Kenneth McLeish, 1993.

Broadly, this description is also useful for art-music.

A genre evolves around the repetitive occurrence of certain patterns, themes, structures, and styles, leading to recognition and familiarity amongst audiences. Considered from this perspective, it can be argued that although the *rudra vīṇā* plays *dhrupad*, it does so only with respect to the architecture of the music. Only superficially, for instance, can we describe the *jhālā* of the *rudra vīṇā* as corresponding to the *drut ālāpa* of the vocal *dhrupad* form. In every respect, other than the architectural, music of the *rudra vīṇā* constitutes an independent genre because, without exploiting its distinctive ergonomic and acoustic features, it would not justify itself as a solo instrument. The same can be said of the wind and bow instruments, which ostensibly present music in the *khayāla* genre.

This argument is equally valid for the *sitāra, saroda* and *santūra* idioms. Only superficially do they perform the same genre: Each of them conforms to the same *rāga*-presentation protocol [architecture], derived from the shared essential discontinuity inherent in their sound activation technology. However, they differ in their approach to sculpture and ornamentation and, indeed, in the unique aural experiences they conjure with the different movements they have devised for the expression of their distinctiveness. Without doing so, they would not validate their presence on the concert platform. Thus, *sitāra* music, *saroda* music, and *santūra* music are all distinct genres of Hindustani music, the term being considered in its strictest theoretical meaning. And, to the extent that these genres exploit the distinctive characters of the instruments, their relative presence on the concert platform, and in the pre-recorded media, shapes the music-scape of the era.

The Concept of a Music-Scape

Just as cities have landscapes shared by different genres of architecture in a certain proportion, and this landscape changes over time, societies have a dynamic music-scape, representing a mix of different genres of music. In the mid-1950s, for instance, the art-music segment of the north Indian music-scape was dominated by *khayāla* vocalism, while *dhrupad* was almost fading into history, and *sitāra* and *saroda* music were beginning their ascent. In the 1960s and 1970s, the music-scape came to be dominated by *sitāra* and *saroda* music. In the 1980s, *khayāla* almost took a backseat, with the emergence of Hawaiian guitar, the *santūra* and the flute substantially enlarging the share of instrumental music in the musical culture. In the 1990s and thereafter, *dhrupad* showed some signs of revival, the *khayāla, sitāra* and *saroda* did not considerably enlarge their shares of society's musical mind, while the flute and the *santūra* evidently stole a march over other instruments in terms of visibility on the musical horizon.

When any genre moves towards becoming the dominant genre on the music-scape of an era, two things can be said about it. Firstly, that it is a better reflection of the aesthetic values of contemporary audiences than genres with a lower, or a shrinking, share of mind. Secondly, that its dominance will influence the aesthetic values of audiences as well as of the other genres which appear to be losing share-of-mind to it. The distinctive tendencies of the emerging dominant genre will, under such conditions, tend to gather momentum amongst the minor and receding genres, thus reshaping the entire music-scape in consonance with the predominant aesthetic values of the ascendant genre.

The distinctive characteristics of the *santūra*, the most meteoric ascendant on the musical horizon, revolve around the splintering of the *rāga* form, a heightened rhythmicality, and exploration of supra-melodic region of musical experience rather than a melody-dominant experience characteristic of Hindustani music so far. These characteristics are now guiding the evolution of *santūra* music as a genre. Their exploitation appears entirely compatible with the bewildering fragmentation of the human experience in all facets of human life. Alvin Toffler describes this situation as "Future Shock," heralding an era, which Peter Drucker calls "The Age of Discontinuity." It is the era that gave respectability to post-modernism, and imparted near-cult status to literary figures like Jacques Derrida and film-makers like Jean Luc Goddard.

The wider dispersion of these aesthetic values is also evident. Now that the *saroda* and the *santūra* have made the kaleidoscopic *svara* pattern acceptable in Hindustani music, even the music of melodic continuity — *khayāla*, flute and *sāraṅgī* — has started aping it. The *joḍa* played on the *sitāra* by some *sitārists* of the younger generation already shows the marked influence of the *santūra* genre.

On the *santūra* itself, the experimental zeal of the younger musicians is now producing a musical experience that is almost literally breathtaking. Now that Pt. Shivkumar Sharma has introduced the judicious exploration of harmony and polyphony, the second successful generation of *santūra* players, like Tarun Bhattacharya, appear to have developed an obsession for all the musical possibilities of an atomised tonal canvas.

The *santūra* is not the villain of the piece. It merely represents a historical and socio-cultural direction. Contemporary tendencies in *santūra* music reflect a progressive crystallization of this inevitability, because a distinct move in this direction is apparent in the other genres, too. The entire music-scape is reshaping itself, altering our society's experience of melody, and the very notion of *rāga*-ness.

A *rāga* is predominantly a melodic entity. Its aesthetic value, or *rasa*, does depend partially on its tonal geometry. But, the *rāga* itself is much more complex than tonal geometry. The defining characteristic of a *rāga* is *rasa*; and *rasa* requires a categorical, sequential, relationship to be established between the *svaras* deployed. Thus, it would seem that the farther we go from the purely sequential arrangement of *svaras*, the farther we are drifting from the *rāga* as a vehicle of emotional meaning.

With this prospect staring us in the face, we need to raise basic questions about Hindustani music. In the emerging music-scape, what melodic expression, or expressions, can be considered the repository[ies] of *rāga*-ness? What principles of *rāga* grammar can be applied to ascertain the quality of the emerging melodic experience? And, what happens to the *rāga-rasa* relationship once music crosses the boundaries of melody into something else? Or are we on the threshold of an era in Hindustani music devoid of *rāgas*, as we understand them?

Alarm and Reassurance

After this line of thought was originally published under the present author's by-line in *Śruti*, learned friends called to express disagreement with it. The burden of their criticism was that the argument was unduly alarmist. They based this view on two premises.

The first was that the argument credits the *santūra* with far greater significance on the music-scape than it either has, or can possibly have. They acknowledge Shivkumar Sharma as a towering musician; but they see the *santūra* as a footnote in the history of Hindustani music, rather than a significant long-term presence.

The second was that cultural phenomena have a cyclical, rather than linear, trajectory. When the trend towards the fragmentation of the melodic experience crosses the limits of a culturally defined musicality, audiences will once again want its "wholeness" and, indeed, a wholesomeness, restored to it.

Both these objections are pregnant with wisdom, and welcome for their reassuring implications. The author would rather be proved alarmist than see his critics being proven myopic or complacent.

PART IV

The Major Genres

4.1

AN INTRODUCTION TO DHRUPAD

THE term *dhrupad* [*dhruva* = immutable/fixed + *pada* = Hymn/verse] refers to a genre of *rāga*-based music which dominated Hindustani music between the fifteenth and the eighteenth centuries. Its distinguishing features are [a] a deliberate, unhurried style of presentation involving graceful, rounded — rather than angular — melodic contours, [b] an austere, rather than ornate, approach to melodic phrasing and *rāga* elaboration, [c] the sanctity attached to the literary component and the melodic structure of the verses, and [d] a highly structured method of melodic development, tending towards a pre-composed art form. Because of the poetic bias of the genre, the conceptual aspect of *dhrupad* music has its moorings in vocal music. However, instrumental music, mainly the *rudra vīṇā* [popularly known as the *bīna*, a fretted stick-zither], dance, and even theatrical performances, have also been associated with the *dhrupad* tradition.

Contemporary authorities consider *dhrupad* the successor of the *prabandha gāna* genre [eleventh century AD]. *Prabandha gāna* [*prabandha* = organization/structure, *gāna* = song/singing]

Note: Adapted from sleeve-notes for recordings written by the author for India Archive Music Ltd., New York, and a paper titled *Dhrupad: An Introduction*, published by the author in the *Journal of the Indian Musicological Society*, Issue of 1999.

enjoyed great popularity between the eleventh and thirteenth centuries. From the fourteenth century onwards, *dhrupad* replaced *prabandha gāna*, reaching peak status and popularity between the fifteenth and eighteenth centuries. *Dhrupad* is, therefore, described as a medieval genre.

Raja Man Singh Tomar [ascended 1483] of Gwalior, who patronized excellence in the performing art as well as scholarship, is considered a landmark figure in *dhrupad* history. Gwalior and the neighbouring principality of Rewa, which the legendary Miyā Tānsen [1491-1583] once served, were the original centres of *dhrupad* music. The Golden Age of *dhrupad* commenced when Emperor Akbar [Reign: 1542-1605], invited Tānsen to the Imperial Court. Later, Vr̥ndāvan and Mathurā established their own *dhrupad* schools. In the south, the patronage of Sultan Ibrahim Adil Shah II, a contemporary of Emperor Akbar, made Bijapur a major centre of the *dhrupad* genre. At its zenith, *dhrupad* held sway over the whole of non-peninsular India.

According to Parjnananda, while *dhrupad* was still at its peak, Perso-Arabic religious music was influencing some lesser-known streams of *prabandha gāna*, to shape the modern, *khayāla* genre. Thakur Jayadev Singh, another distinguished scholar, traces the origins of the *khayāla* to the *rūpakālapti* genre, known to have been in practice from the eighth/ninth centuries. In knowledgeable contemporary circles, it is widely believed that the *khayāla* emerged as a fusion between *dhrupad* itself and *qawwālī*/Kaul music, a devotional genre associated with Islamic Sufi sects. Quite irrespective of which of these theories is accepted, there is little doubt that *dhrupad* and *khayāla* have been contem-poraries and rivals for a substantial part of *dhrupad*'s dominance over Hindustani music.

Dhrupad was debilitated by the decline of its strongest patron, the Mogul Empire, in the early nineteenth century. At that stage, leading musicians — so far concentrated in Delhi and its neighbourhood — began migrating to smaller principalities in search of alternative patronage. This process created new centres of *dhrupad* music, mainly in the fertile Indo-Gangetic plains of eastern India, but also exposed *dhrupad* to a diverse musical environment. In their new environments, many lineages of *dhrupad* musicians diverted their energies to the *khayāla* genre, and virtually spearheaded its ascendancy over the receding *dhrupad* genre.

In the early years after Independence, the *dhrupad* genre was frequently described as "a museum piece." This description was probably more appropriate to the art of the *rudra vīṇā* [*bīna*], than to the vocal art. The vocal art still boasted of a reasonable presence on the concert platform along with quality musicianship. Even amongst *khayāla* singers, *dhrupad* had remained relevant as an essential part of training — the repository of the sciences of breath control and intonation.

The *dhrupad* revival, such as is evident, was fuelled primarily by the following the genre acquired in Europe and other Western societies. It began when the Indologist, Alain Daneilou, and the UNESCO, introduced the pre-eminent *dhrupad* vocalists, Nasir Aminuddin and Nasir Moinuddin Dagar, to Europe. The success of this effort made *dhrupad* a unique phenomenon in art music — losing ground in its home and acquiring an enthusiastic following amongst alien audiences.

The West's recent enthusiasm for *dhrupad* was repeating *dhrupad*'s history of 500 years ago, when its adoption by another foreign race, the Moguls from Central Asia, gave it a long lease of life in the face of a challenge from the rival *khayāla* genre. Although the two contexts are not strictly comparable, this recurrence could suggest features that give *dhrupad* a greater universality of appeal than its rivals and successors.

In the 1970's and 1980's, as the Indian currency depreciated speedily against the major international currencies, *dhrupad*'s growing international constituency stimulated a great deal of activity in India. An important part of the action was a substantial inflow of fresh talent, especially into the vocal art, which was the more vibrant of the two streams of *dhrupad*. By the end of the twentieth century, the art of the *bīna* had become a "museum piece," while the vocal art of *dhrupad* could boast of a small group of credible musicians at home, who were dependent largely on the Western market for their livelihood.

An Aesthetic Perspective

Dhrupad, the performing art, evidently developed from the migration of an older tradition of devotional songs performed in the *Vaiṣṇava* temples to the secular environment presided over by the feudal aristocracy in medieval north India. [Thielemann, Selina, *Journal of the Indian Musicological Society*, 1999, ed. Deepak Raja & Suvarnalata Rao] Because of this background, it retained its bias in favour of the poetic form. The *dhrupad* genre is therefore anchored to the melodic-poetic axis, in contrast to the *khayāla* genre, which revolves around the melodic-rhythmic axis giving the literary component only a subordinate role.

The poetic bias also explains the tendency of *dhrupad* towards being a pre-composed genre of music. This tendency is significantly manifested in its principles of melodic organization and the correspondence between the melodic structure and the poetic form. For melodic organization, the *dhrupad* tradition prescribes a four-stage development. In contemporary terminology, they are called [a] *sthāyī*, [b] *antarā*, [c] *sañcārī* and [d] *ābhoga*. Although compositional formats vary, each step is conceived with a well defined aesthetic function. The *sthāyī* and the *antarā* unfold the melodic canvas in progressive sequence from the lower octave to the upper, while the *sañcārī* summarizes the *rāga*'s melodic profile, and the *ābhoga* "winds up" the *rāga* exposition, folding back the melodic canvas. Although this protocol pertained initially to the composition of the melodic-rhythmic shell of the poetic form, it has been accepted as a general principle, valid also for the elaborate *ālāpa* that precedes the presentation of the composition in contemporary *dhrupad*. This protocol continues to be treated with great respect in the post-*dhrupad* genres, and is conspicuous in the performances of the greatest musicians of our times.

Corresponding to this principle of melodic development, Miyā Tānsen laid down that a *pada* should have four rhyming stanzas, The majority opinion amongst fifteenth and sixteenth century scholars favoured a three-stanza *pada*. In more recent times, the *pada*, as performed, has shrunk to just two stanzas — the *sthāyī*, and the *antarā*. The literary component of the *pada*s has been predominantly in praise of Hindu Gods and Goddesses. Many *pada*s were written on musicological themes. As *dhrupad* became a resident of the princely Courts, *pada*s also came to be composed in praise of emperors and princes.

In recent times, several lineages of *dhrupad* practitioners have veered away from the melody-poetry axis towards the melody-rhythm axis, forsaking the primacy of the literary element. But, the derailment was probably less widespread than was made out to be. For, the *dhrupad* mainstream did, indeed, incorporate different sub-streams called *banī*s [lit. languages/dialects] with their respective stylistic biases.

Stylistic Diversity

Raja Man Singh Tomar's treatise [*Māna-Kūtūhala*] mentions the four *banī*s. In his time, these classifications were based on the language/dialect in which the *pada* was written: "Gaurhar" from Gwalior, "Dagar" from the Dangar region near Delhi, "Khandar" from the Khandar region, and "Nauhar" from the dialect spoken by the Nauhar community. In later years, the four *banīs* came to signify stylistic distinctions.

Dhrupad musicians of the Gauhar Banī concentrate their musical energies on the *śānta rasa* [the tranquil emotional state]. Dagar Banī emphasizes the *mādhurya* [tenderness] and *karuṇā* [pathos] *rasas*. The Khandhar Banī expresses the *vīra rasa* [the sentiment of valour]. And, finally, Nauhar Banī specializes in the music of *adbhut rasa* [the sentiment of surprise/marvel]. Up to the time of Tānsen [sixteenth century], practitioners of each of the *banīs* chose *rāgas* and poetry in accordance with their emotional/stylistic biases. In later years, however, this integrity of approach lapsed, and musicians began to adopt multiple *banīs* in their musical demonstrations.

In terms of musical expressions, a differentiation between the *banī*'s is indicated from an observation by Ustad Vilayat Hussain Khan, the scholarly vocalist of the Agra *gharānā*. According to him, the Khandhar is replete with heavy *gamakas* [a magnified *vibrato*]; Nauhar combines *gamakas* with brisk passages; Dagar presents its music with aplomb; Gauhar, patronized by Miyā Tānsen, is devoid of *gamakas*, and moves primarily with graceful *Mīṇḍa* [smooth intervallic transitions using grace notes].

The different Banīs of *dhrupad* ceased to retain their formal identities in the sixteenth century after the death of Miyā Tānsen, and merged into the new Seniya *gharānā*, with Tānsen himself as the titular fountainhead. This was merely a "political" alignment, and even Tānsen's immediate descendants could not entirely ignore the stylistic variety they had inherited. The lineage of his son, Bilas Khan specialized in the Gauhar *banī*, and partially patronized Dagar *banī*. The lineage of his son-in-law, Misri Singh [Naubat Khan] were specialists of the Khandhar and Dagar *banīs*.

Although contemporary *dhrupad* musicians profess allegiance to *banīs* through their stylistic lineages, the stylistic distinctions between them are, by and large, no longer discernible. This could be because, due to the shrinkage in the number of *dhrupad* practitioners over the last century, aspirants to the art have had to draw on a multiplicity of sources for their musical ideas and melodic technique, including the modern *khayāla* idiom. As a result, the only viable classification in contemporary *dhrupad* vocalism is between aggressive styles revolving around the poetic-rhythmic axis, and relatively softer styles anchored to the poetic-melodic axis.

Gharānās of Dhrupad

The diversity of approach and style in *dhrupad* is now represented by five major *gharānās* practising the genre. [Selina Thielemann, "Classical *dhrupada*: the principal *gharānās*," *Journal of the Indian Musicological Society*, 1999, ed. Deepak Raja & Suvarnalata Rao]

[a] ***The Dagar gharānā***: This is the oldest *gharānā* of classical *dhrupad*, having been founded by Nayak Haridas Dagar in the sixteenth century. Its descendants converted to Islam during the eighteenth century. In recent times, its most eminent representatives have been vocalists, Nasir Moinuddin Dagar [1919-66] and Nasir Aminuddin Dagar [1923-2002] and the *bīna* maestro, Zia Mohiuddin Dagar [1929-90].

[b] ***The Darbhanga gharānā***: This *gharānā* was founded in the eighteenth century by two brothers, Radha-Kr̥ṣṇa and Karttaram, whose descendents have carried the "Mallik" surname. In the post-Independence era, the most distinguished musicians of this lineage have been Ramchatur Mallik [1906-90] and Vidur Mallik [1936-2002].

[c] ***The Bettiah gharānā***: Though founded in the seventeenth century, this *gharānā* flourished during the nineteenth century, and wielded tremendous influence over *dhrupad* in the entire eastern region. Musicians of Bettiah are believed to have taught the founders of the once influential Bishnupur *gharānā* in Bengal. Bettiah is represented, on the contemporary concert platform, by Indrakishore Mishra [born 1957].

[d] ***The Talwandi gharānā***: This *gharānā* originated in north-west India, now in Pakistan, and is currently based in Lahore. Although its music is entirely based on *dhrupad*, it has "Islamized" its poetic content. Very little is known about its contemporary musicianship.

[e] ***The Mathura gharānā***: This is the oldest *gharānā* of Havelī Sangīta, the *dhrupad* tradition of the Vaiṣṇavite temples. Though its members have stepped out of the ecclesiastical environment for a nominal presence on the concert platform, their art has not made a complete transition to the elaborate format of contemporary *dhrupad*.

It may be noted that only three of these *gharānā*s — Dagar, Darbhanga, and Bettiah — have a significant presence on the contemporary concert platform.

Melodic Expressions in Dhrupad

The *ālāpa* in the *dhrupad* genre, considered the soul of the genre, has often been described as a "journey into pure sound." This is a poetic description of the genre's substantial reliance on the individual *svara*, rather than a phrase, as the basic building block of melody. The *dhrupad ālāpa* displays a preference for single intervallic transitions, and relationships between two *svara*s. Individual transitions may, however, touch several tonal and micro-tonal bases on their path. In contrast, post-*dhrupad* genres favour greater melodic agility, and rely more on phrasing involving two or more intervallic transitions, and relationships between three or more *svaras* at a time. In its vocal manifestation, this philosophy of the *dhrupad ālāpa* converts the yogic practice of *prāṇāyāma* [breath control/ mastery over the life force] into a science of intonation. As an approach to musical expression, the practice of this science is associated with each intonation being backed by the controlled power of exhalation, resulting in a sense of introspection, serenity and repose.

The inventory of expressions in *dhrupad* manifest this technique of breath control along with the resultant melodic continuity, and the austerity of expression consistent with a meditative art form. *Dhrupad* thus rules out the more agile and ornate melodic expressions typical of the vocal genres that succeeded it. An important manifestation of this distinction is its elephantine gait. The pedagogy of *dhrupad* contains a large inventory of melodic expressions. However, four basic techniques may be mentioned here.

For convenience of comprehension, these expressions may be classified into: [a] melodic continuity, and [b] melodic discontinuity. The melodic continuity expressions consist of the *mīṇḍa*, *sūta*, and *gamaka*, while the discontinuous expression is limited primarily to the *khaṭakā*.

The *mīṇḍa* is a continuous intervallic transition from one *svara* to another. Its melodic contour can be concave or convex; but never angular. This is the primary melodic expression in *dhrupad*, and emphasizes the near-absence of disjunct or staccato expressions. Generally, the word *mīṇḍa* is used for a short-to-medium span intervallic transition.

The broad-span continuous intervallic transition, generally devoid of obvious concavity or convexity, and corresponding to a complete exhalation, is called a *sūta*. The *sūta* may be unidirectional or bi-directional within the same exhalation. The *sūta* generally traverses tonal distances more briskly than a *mīṇḍa* does. This vocal expression is believed to have been borrowed from the *ghasīta* [literally, dragging] technique of the *bīna,* which is executed with a glide of the fingers across the fretboard under a single stroke of the plectrum. The aural experience of the *sūta/ghasīta* is that of a *svara* being dragged from tonal point to another point at a considerable distance.

The *gamaka* creates a pulsating or quivering effect — a magnified *vibrato* — by repeatedly attacking a *svara* from a lower *svara*. The melodic contour of a *gamaka* is concave. The *gamaka* is generally used for distances of up to two, and occasionally three *svara*s. The *gamaka* is ideally suited for medium-to-high density melodic execution. In high-density execution, it approaches staccato intonation.

Perceptible melodic discontinuity in *dhrupad* is handled primarily with the *khaṭakā* [lit. jerky motion] expression. It is deployed for short-span intervallic transitions, most commonly in descending melodic motion. A *khaṭakā* represents a sudden, jerky drop of intonation from one *svara*, to a lower *svara*, with a momentary break in exhalation.

The Tālas of Dhrupad

In response to a query, Selina Thielemann, the eminent *dhrupad* scholar, wrote [e-mail of October 18, 2002]:

> *Dhrupad* compositions are set basically to six *tāla*s: *Cautāla* [12 beats], *Dhamāra* [14 beats], *Rūpaka* [7 beats], *Tīvra* [7 beats], *Jhapatāla* [10 beats], and *Sulatāla* [10 beats]. Ustad Fahimuddin Dagar would accept these as the only six *tāla*s employed in *dhrupad*. Compositions in *Matta tāla* [18 beats] are of recent origin. I only know of a few such compositions composed by the Gundecha Brothers. This is the information for classical *dhrupad*.

> However, devotional *dhrupad* [*dhrupad* performed in the temples of the Vaiṣṇava sects] is performed strictly in *Cautāla.*

Despite the variety of *tāla*s reported by Ms. Thielemann, contemporary *dhrupad* restricts itself almost entirely to *cautāla, dhamāra*, and *sulatāla*.

Rāga Presentation Structure

In the *dhrupad* genre, the established model for *rāga* presentation prescribes two phases. Phase I is solo, and without percussion accompaniment. Phase II is performed to accompaniment by the *pakhāwaja*, the double-conical barrel drum. The solo Phase I has three stages of development:

[a] ***The vilaṁbita [slow tempo] ālāpa***: This is a free-flowing, anarhythmic exposition of the *rāga*'s melodic personality, structured in consonance with well-established rules of melodic progression. Its character in vocal and *bīna* renditions is identical, except that the vocal rendition uses meaningless consonants such as *tā, nā, rī* as articulation. The *vilaṁbita ālāpa* has two movements — the *sthāyī*, rendered in the lower half of the melodic canvas, and the *antarā*, rendered in the upper half. The *sthāyī* begins with improvizations around the tonic accompanied by a few phrases identifying the *rāga* beyond reasonable doubt. It then descends into the lower octave, thereafter ascending step-by-step up to the mid-octave region. The *antarā* begins in the mid-octave region, ascends into the higher octave with a restful pause *en route* at the upper *sā* [tonic], and descends finally to the tonic. In rare cases, a musician may decide to append a *sañcārī* and/ or *ābhoga* movement to the *vilaṁbita ālāpa* as a "winding up" movement, deploying broad-span melodic

phrasing, bypassing the discipline of step-by-step melodic progression typical of the *sthāyī* and the *antarā*.

The melodic progression in the *dhrupad ālāpa* often appears less methodical than that of the modern *khayāla* genre. This is because it habitually progresses in broader melodic spans. This feature arises from the notion of the *rāga*'s melodic personality in *dhrupad*, shaped by the melodic lines of the *pada*s the musician has learnt, which in turn are shaped by the poetic lines of the verse. This feature of *dhrupad* relates to the "narrative" experience of melody in *dhrupad*, contrasted with the "symmetric" and "geometric" experience enabled by the shorter-span phrasing and progression typical of the *khayāla* genre, [Refer: *The Experience of Melody — From dhrupad to Santoor*, Chapter 3.5]

[b] ***The madhya laya* [*medium tempo*] *ālāpa***: With this stage in the *ālāpa*, a pulsation enters the melody. This corresponds to the nomenclature and melodic-rhythmic character of *joḍa* on the *bīna*. In the vocal manifestation, the *madhya laya ālāpa* utilizes meaningless consonants such *nom, tom, ta, nā, rī*, etc., to heighten the rhythmicality of the aural experience, and to mimic the regular frequency of strokes on the *bīna*, its traditional accompaniment. For this reason, this stage onwards, the unaccompanied solo rendition is often described as the *nom tom ālāpa*. This *nom tom* phonetic is a remnant of what was once a rhythmic chanting of the name of Lord Viṣṇu — *oṁ hari ananta nārāyaṇa*. The distortion probably took place either due to the aversion of Moslem musicians to chanting the name of Hindu gods, or purely because of phonetic convenience in rendition. The *madhya laya ālāpa*/*joḍa* is structured

to a simple pulse at the rate of one to two beats per second, and typically uses broader-span phrasing strategies than the *vilaṁbita ālāpa*. The *madhya laya ālāpa* also generally conforms to the principles of melodic progression in two movements — the *sthāyī* and the *antarā*. The valedictory *sañcārī/ābhoga* movements are rare in the *madhya laya ālāpa*, though an approximation to them may be found in the third phase, the *druta ālāpa*.

[c] ***The druta [fast tempo] ālāpa***: This corresponds to the nomenclature and melodic-rhythmic structure of the *jhālā* on the *bīna*. The vocal rendition of the *druta ālāpa* retains the use of meaningless consonants for convenience of high-density melodic-rhythmic articulation. The *druta ālāpa* is performed at a stepped-up tempo relative to the *madhya laya ālāpa* — at a pulsation rate of four beats per second or higher. In the vocal rendition, this requires the articulation to shift from a two-beat pulse to four-beat and eight-beat patterning of the meaningless consonants. The *druta ālāpa* also conforms to melodic patterning on the basis of *sthāyī* and *antarā* movements, but tends to deploy broader spans of phrasing than the earlier two movements of the *ālāpa*. In rare cases, it may be stepped up a notch to form a fourth tier of the unaccompanied solo presentation. The fourth tier, when present, approximates the free-flowing *tāna*s of the post-*dhrupad* genres.

In mid-twentieth century recordings, and in contemporary *dhrupad* concerts, the *druta ālāpa* is occasionally found to have been rendered to *pakhāwaja* accompaniment, with distinctly titillating results. This practice would appear to militate against the austerity of the genre, and could represent an attempt by recent and contemporary musicians to revive audience interest in a dying art form.

A durational analysis of *dhrupad* performances [Selina Thielemann, *The Darbhanga Tradition*, 1st edn. 1997, Indica Books, Varanasi] establishes the three/four-tiered *ālāpa* as consuming over 60 per cent of the duration of a *rāga* presentation. Presentations in *dhamāra* and the minor rhythmic cycles may, however, frequently devote a lower share of duration to the *ālāpa*.

The *ālāpa* is followed by a Phase II, consisting of a pre-composed *pada*, along with improvizations thereon. The *pada* may be set to any of *tāla*s accepted in the *dhrupad* tradition. The percussion-accompanied Phase II has two stages of development:

[a] ***Complete rendition of the pada, in both its parts*** — The *sthāyī* and the *antarā*, and *sañcārī-ābhoga*, if present. In case of *pada*s in *dhamāra* and the minor *tāla*s, contemporary practice permits some improvisatory movements to be inserted between the *sthāyī* and the *antarā*.

[b] ***Improvisatory movements***: In *pada* rendition, orthodox *dhrupad* permits only such forms of melodic improvization, as would protect the integrity of the poetic element.

> Improvizations in *dhrupad* consist of a sequence of rhythmic variations [*layakaaree*] within the metric cycle based on either the division of beats [*laya-bāṇṭa*] or divisions of the words [*bola-bāṇṭa*] . . . the use of solfa syllables or embellishments on the vowel "aa," as characteristic of the *Khayāla*, are prohibited. *Layakaarees* in slow tempo consist of stretched notes; the syllables are extended to note values longer than or equal to

> those of the basic composition. In medium tempo, the syllables are grouped into two or three per beat, and the *layakaarees* are sung [at] approximately double the speed of the composition, suggesting a speed approximately four times faster than the composition. Some singers may further speed up, to the eighth degree, in which case the comprehensibility of the syllables may be disturbed. . . . In some *dhrupad* traditions, it is common practice to repeat the basic composition at various levels of speed ranging from double speed to the sixth or eighth degree but never slower than the composition itself.
>
> — Thielemann, 1997, *ibid.*

Variants on the Rāga Presentation Structure

For vocal music, as well as the *bīna*, the above model for *rāga* presentation is generally followed for the first/main *rāga* in a concert, which will have a *pada* set to *cautāla* of 12 beats. With this as the basic format, several variants have been common in recent/contemporary *dhrupad* practice. The choice of the format depends greatly on the time available for the performance, and the inclination of the performer [Thielemann, 1997, *ibid.*]

[a] Three-tier *ālāpa*, followed by a *pada* in *cautāla* — the primary *dhrupad* format.

[b] Three-tier *ālāpa*, followed by a *pada* in *cautāla*, and then by a *dhamāra* composition in the same *rāga*.

[c] Three-tier, or even single-tier *ālāpa*, followed by a *dhamāra* composition.

[d] Three-tier or single-tier *ālāpa*, followed by a *dhamāra* composition and a *sulatāla* composition.

[e] A three-tier *ālāpa*, followed by a *cautāla* composition, and a *sulatāla* composition.

The Ensemble for Dhrupad Performance

In vocal as well as *bīna* presentations, the ensemble for contemporary *dhrupad* performance is austere. It consists of a pair of *tānapūrā* for drones, and *pakhāwaja* as percussion accompaniment. *Bīna* accompaniment for vocal performances, once the norm, is now rare. Up to the middle of the twentieth century, *dhrupad* vocalists, like contemporary *khayāla* singers, occasionally performed with a *sāraṅgī* as melodic accompaniment. However, with the growing shortage of *sāraṅgī* players, especially those trained in *dhrupad*, this practice has fallen into disuse.

A special note has to be taken of the role of *pakhāwaja* accompaniment in a *dhrupad* recital, which varies considerably from the role of the *tabalā* in post-*dhrupad* music. While, the basic composition is being performed, the *pakhāwaja* behaves very much like *tabalā* accompaniment for *khayāla*, providing the metric structure [*ṭhekā*] of the *tāla*. But, once the *pada* rendition is over, and the improvizations begin, each of them takes off on his independent improvisatory trip, often competing with the other in the invention of increasingly complex rhythmic variations.

This feature of *dhrupad*, coupled with the excessive rhythmic bias in the improvisatory movements of *pada* rendition, obliged late nineteenth/early twentieth century musicologists like V.N. Bhatkhande and D.L. Roy [Ranade, *JIMS*, 1999] to compare *pada* rendition to a wrestling bout between the musician and his percussionist. They pronounced it an unpleasant aural experience that could only doom the genre to an untimely demise. It is now believed that *dhrupad* succumbed to this obsession in an attempt to resist the challenge posed by the *khayāla* genre. Although some contemporary *dhrupad* musicians have tried to resist a drift in this direction, they do not seem to be unanimous about this being a problem waiting to be solved.

A Structural Analysis

This structure of a *dhrupad* performance can be interpreted in two different ways:

Firstly, the *dhrupad* format represents a sequential separation of the strictly melodic from the poetic-rhythmic. The *ālāpa* is pure melody. It has *laya* [pulsation] but no *tāla* [cyclical rhythmicality]. The *pada*, on the other hand, is dominated by poetry. The manipulation of the melodic and the rhythmic elements, beyond the confines of the basic frame of the composition, is severely restricted. In comparison, the *khayāla* requires the simultaneous manipulation of the melodic, the rhythmic, and the poetic elements right from the beginning.

Secondly, the *dhrupad* format represents a sequential separation of the linear progression of music from the cyclical flows. The progression of the *ālāpa*, from the lower octave to the higher, from a subtle *laya* to the explicit, and from a slow tempo towards the higher, is a predominantly linear structure. The *sañcārī* and *ābhoga* sections of the *ālāpa*, as originally conceived, had an element of cyclicity. However, with these two movements having fallen into disuse, the *dhrupad ālāpa* has become a linear melodic entity. While the *ālāpa* is linear, *pada* rendition is cyclical in its structure. The poetic-melodic-rhythmic shell of the presentation is cyclical. Improvizations, whether melodic or rhythmic, remain within a restricted periphery of the melodic-rhythmic-poetic frame of the composition, and are therefore largely cyclical.

In *dhrupad*, therefore, the *ālāpa* moves in a well-defined direction, while the *pada* goes nowhere. *Khayāla*, in comparison, plunges simultaneously into the linear and cyclical flows of the musical idea. It progresses simultaneously on the melodic and the rhythmic dimensions in terms of density and complexity. The *khayāla* is therefore continuously going somewhere. *Khayāla* progresses towards a destination that appears to justify the musical endeavour more categorically than *dhrupad*.

The notion of "going nowhere," or "going somewhere," and the implications of this notion for the build-up and release of anticipatory tension, defines an important structural divide between the medieval *dhrupad* and the modern *khayāla* forms.

The Nature of Appeal

Dhrupad is frequently considered more "intellectual," while the *khayāla* is considered more "emotional" in its appeal. This view needs to be reconsidered.

A significant justification for *dhrūpad's* "intellectual" label might rest on the richness and sanctity of its poetic element, relative to the *khayāla*. Most scholars are agreed that the richness of *dhrupad*'s literary content is now history, and its significance too has shrunk substantially over the centuries.

The *dhrupad* genre has been described as *svarāśrita* and *padāśrita*. By this description, its soul lies in its melodic and poetic elements, and the relationship between the two. Since a *rāga* is a melodic vehicle for an emotional statement, and the poetic element of the *pada* imparts explicit meaning to the emotional communication of the melody — refer to Tānsen's tenets enumerated above — the elicitation of an emotional response would appear to be the predominant aesthetic intention of *dhrupad* as a genre.

Another way of looking at this issue is the level of freedom *dhrupad* allows the musician in the different departments of musicianship. The constraints on improvizational freedom — melodic, rhythmic or poetic — are so great that the only real freedom musicians enjoy is in the soul-power and the emotional intensity with which they imbue their music. Whatever a genre permits, it encourages. By shutting the doors to freedom in most departments, *dhrupad* focuses the musical energies upon the most fundamental dimension of musicality: helping the aesthetic impact of *svara*-delivery to transcend its known psycho-acoustic parameters.

The aesthetic ideal of *dhrupad* would appear to be the experience of the *svara* as *svara* [*sva*=the self + *ra* = illumination]. For achieving this result, medieval musicological texts have defined ideal *svara*-delivery as a product of two qualities: *anūraṇana* and *dīpti*. Neither of these terms is satisfactorily translated. Their intent is, however, to relate voice production and *svara*-delivery to the auto-suggestive and personality-transforming potential of the act of music making. This deduction again appears to support an "emotional" label for *dhrūpad* more than an "intellectual" one.

As a genre, *dhrūpad* invests an extraordinary proportion of musical energy into the acoustic and aesthetic cultivation of voice production and *svara*-delivery. Consequently, the individual *svara* becomes as basic a unit of the musical expression as the phrase that it constructs.

The phrase, as a unit of music, has an element of design in it, which defines the relationship of the expression to a *rāga*. Pattern recognition is largely a cerebral process. When, as in *dhrupad*, the individual *svara* receives focused attention, it enables its aesthetic enjoyment, independently of the phrase and the *rāga*. A *svara* in isolation, by virtue of its momentary, and even illusory, isolation from the phraseological context, is a more probable stimulus for an emotional response than an intellectual one.

The comparison with *khayāla* points towards another aesthetic dimension of *dhrupad*. *Khayāla* requires the simultaneous manipulation of the melodic with the poetic and the rhythmic, and of the linear with the cyclical. A genre requiring the simultaneous manipulation of two or more variables is intellectually more absorbing and demanding than a genre that isolates them for sequential handling. By this logic, again, the structure of the *khayāla* can be considered more "intellectual" than that of *dhrupad*.

Considering the totality of these factors, a contemporary view would justify an "emotional" label for the *dhrupad* genre, and an "intellectual" label for *khayāla*. The caveat to any such labelling temptation is, of course, that it identifies biases and tendencies without necessarily providing the basis for a mutually exclusive classification.

Dhrupad Today

The epilogue to a global survey of *dhrupad* [*Journal of the Indian Musicological Society*, Annual Issue of 1999, ed. Deepak Raja and Suvarnalata Rao], assessed *dhrupad* with the following observations:

> The decline of *dhrupad*, and its surrender to the *khayāla* wave, is a socio-cultural phenomenon, reflecting changing audience profiles, and aesthetic values. *Dhrupad* probably declined in popularity because of its resistance to change, restrictions on individual creativity, and its failure to accommodate changing audience tastes. Comprehensive *rāga* presentation in Hindustani music needed to do somthing to avert extinction. It did so by loosening the rigid *dhrupad* format, and found a ready solution in the already mature rival, the *khayāla* form.
>
> Some *dhrupad gharānās*, however, resisted the *khayāla* wave, and persisted with the *dhrupad* format. Their tenacity was rewarded with the opening up of the European market for Hindustani music in the 1960s, and subsequent revivalist attempts at home. Thanks to these efforts, young vocalists with respectable performing standards have partially restored

the genre to the mainstream concert platform. These musicians are attempting to impart to *dhrupad* a greater acceptability amongst contemporary audiences. In creating an audience for their music, their focus seems to include Indian audiences nurtured in the Carnatic tradition, and receptive audiences in Europe and the US.

Their efforts appear to be winning back mature Hindustani audiences who had either rejected *dhrupad* as an unpleasant experience or who had not heard quality *dhrupad* for a long time. For the newer audiences, especially the younger and uninitiated audiences, *dhrupad* is a novel experience, but more accessible than *khayāla*. In south India, *dhrupad* claims acceptance because of two factors: a general opening up of the Carnatic-oriented market to Hindustani music, and the similarity of the *dhrupad* format to the *rāgama-thānama-pallavī* format in Carnatic music.

In the domestic music market, with an ample availability of other genres of classical and semi-classical music, audience preferences or loyalties are not shaped by the genre as much as by individual musicianship. In Europe and the US, on the other hand, there appears to be a genre-based following for *dhrupad*. Driven by economics, *dhrupad* is now evolving primarily within an orbit defined by Indian musicians, and trans-culturally receptive Western audiences, enthusiasts, musicians, and scholars. Today, European and American audiences and students largely sustain the livelihood of Indian *dhrupad* performers. *Dhrupad* is moving towards becoming a European and American genre of Indian origin, performed largely by Indians, but increasingly also by Western musicians. The larger implications of this reality have yet to be ascertained.

This configuration of tendencies is unique in the history of Hindustani music. Never before has a genre been pronounced dead in India, experienced so shaky a revival with hard-core home audiences, and become popular enough with alien audiences to become so totally dependent on them. This makes *dhrupad* one of the enigmas of cultural anthropology.

4.2

AN INTRODUCTION TO KHAYĀLA

The *khayāla* is the dominant genre of mainstream vocal music today, and has been so for over two centuries. Because of the primacy of vocal music in the Hindustani tradition, it has also had a considerable influence on the evolution of instrumental music. The word *khayāla* is of Perso-Arabic origin, and has been variously translated as idea, imagination, subjectivity, individuality, and impression. All these connotations are consistent with the character of the genre. Bhatkhande suggests that the term may have originally denoted licentiousness. [*Bhatkhande Sangeet Shastra*, vol. I, 5th edn., 1981] This suggestion has some merit considering the vast creative freedom accorded to the musician by the *khayāla*, compared to the highly disciplined formalism of its medieval predecessor, *dhrupad/dhamāra*.

> Among all Hindustani vocal genres, the *khayāla* provides its performers the greatest opportunity and challenge to display the depth and breadth of musical knowledge and skills. Its essence lies in the manner in which artists take the characteristics that distinguish *khayāla* as a genre, make those choices that lie within their group traditions, summon their own creative

Note: Adapted from a backgrounder for incorporation in commentaries on *khayāla* music produced by India Archive Music Ltd., New York.

> individuality, and create a unique *khayāla* at each performance. [Bonnie C. Wade, 1st edn., 1984]

The *khayāla* genre is distinguished from other major genres of Hindustani vocal music — *dhrupad* and *ṭhumarī* — by a linear [progressive] intensification of melodic and rhythmic densities and complexities, and a cyclical treatment of melodic and rhythmic elements within the central linearity of rendition.

The Plastic Arts Metaphor Applied to Khayāla Music

Every artefact can be seen to have an architectural element, a sculptural element, and an ornamentational element. The architectural element relates to the structural and functional relationship between the parts. The sculptural element deals with the contours it defines from a reasonable distance. The ornamentational element concerns itself with features that endear the artefact to the viewer from close quarters. Architecture deals with the manner in which an artefact *functions,* sculpture, with the way it *looks*, and ornamentation, with the way it *pleases*.

In general, one might say that all music has elements of architecture, sculpture and ornamentation, with their relative weight varying between the different genres, and even between the different styles/*gharānā*s within the same genre. Using this framework for understanding the principal genres in Hindustani music, *dhrupad* can be described as architecture-dominant; *khayāla* can be described as sculpture-dominant; and *ṭhumarī* can be described as ornamentation-dominant. [Refer chapter 2.1]

Interestingly, however, what differentiates the *khayāla* genre from *dhrupad* and *ṭhumarī* most conclusively is its architecture. The architecture of *khayāla* vocalism is characterized by an end-to-end linearity, shaped by a progressive intensification of tonal and beat densities and complexities in its rendition. It is probably this unidirectional flow of musical energies that enables the artistic effort to focus itself sharply on the melodic effort, and thus to define *khayāla* as a sculpture-dominant genre.

This linearity of architecture distinguishes *khayāla* from both *dhrupad* and *ṭhumarī*. But, the difference between sculpture and ornamentation being one only of perspective, the sculpture-dominant character of *khayāla* still needed protection from a drift towards the ornamentation characteristic of the *ṭhumarī* genre. It is by this logic of differentiation between the genres that *khayāla* evolved as a genre unidirectional in its architecture, elaborate in its approach to sculpture, and judicious in its deployment of ornamentation.

History and Evolution

The legendary thirteenth-century poet-musician Amir Khusro is popularly credited with the invention of the *khayāla* form. This belief is conceptually fallacious because no individual can be credited with the creation of a genre. This attribution of even an initiating role to Amir Khusro is contentious. The architecture and stylistics of the *khayāla* form apparently pre-date Khusro by several centuries. Thakur Jaydev Singh traces the *khayāla* form to the *rūpakālāpati* form within the *sādhāranī śailī* of vocal music in practice in the eighth/ninth centuries. He credits Amir Khusro, however, with giving it a Perso-Arabic name, introducing it to the patronage of Muslim rulers, and encouraging its practice amongst singers of *qawwālī*, a form of Sūfī religious music. [*Nibandha Sangeet*, ed. L.N. Garg, 2nd edn., 1989]

The *khayāla* represents a fusion of older Indian musical traditions with Perso-Arabic influences starting from the twelfth/thirteenth centuries. The genre acquired some stature under the patronage of the Sharqui *sultāns* of Jaunpur [fifteenth century], and attained maturity and sophistication under the patronage of Emperor Mohammad Shah of Delhi [eighteenth century]. Since then, the *khayāla* has eclipsed the medieval *dhrupad/dhamāra* genre, and replaced it as the predominant genre of mainstream vocal music.

Sultan Hussain Sharqui [reign: 1458-99] of Jaunpur encouraged the evolution of a *kalāvantī khayāla* based on musical forms prevalent in his region as distinct from the *khayāla* inspired by the *qawwālī* encouraged by Amir Khusro [1253-1325]. The immortal composer Niamat Khan "Sadarang" in the employ of Emperor Muhammad Shah, reportedly composed *khayālas* as a challenge to the supremacy of *dhrupad/dhamāra*, by recasting poetic and melodic material drawn from the medieval genre.

The medieval *dhrupad/dhamāra*, which dominated the mainstream between the thirteenth and the eighteenth centuries, and the modern *khayāla* genre, which overtook it in later years, have thus been contemporary rivals for almost the entire period of *dhrupad/dhamāra* dominance. Ashok Ranade, the eminent musicologist, has argued that, neither of the two can be described as having been derived from the other, though both would have influenced each other to some degree. *Dhrupad/dhamāra* evolved as a highly formal and disciplined art form with a tendency towards being a predominantly pre-composed genre of music. In a parallel development, the *khayāla* evolved as a predominantly improvized form, and a vehicle for individual creativity. [*Journal of the Indian Musicological Society*, 1999]

The Gharānās of Khayāla Music

The century preceding India's Independence, which witnessed the flowering of the *khayāla* genre in various hues and fragrances, is often described as the Golden Age of Hindustani music [V.H. Deshpande, *Indian Musical Traditions*, 2nd edn., 1987]. Its foundations were laid in the sunset years of the

Mogul Empire [mid-eighteenth century], when a vast resource of musicianship emigrated from Delhi and its environs towards smaller principalities in search of patronage. Several of these feudal principalities, protected by India's new British rulers, became patrons to lineages of musicians [*gharānā*s], which cultivated distinctive musical styles within the broad framework of the *khayāla* genre.

For a variety of reasons, *gharānā*s of *khayāla* music have come to acquire their names either from the principalities where they were cultivated, or from the name of a towering vocalist, who is recognized as the founder of the distinctive style of *khayāla* music.

Vamanrao Deshpande recognizes six distinct *gharānā*s as stylistic lineages: Agra, Gwalior, Jaipur-Atrauli, Patiala, Indore, and Kirana. [V.H. Deshpande, *ibid.*]. Prof. Bonnie Wade recognizes six significant *gharānā*s of *khayāla* music. They are Gwalior, Agra, Sahaswan/Rampur, Alladiya Khan [also known as Jaipur-Atrauli], Kirana, and Patiala. She considers the Indore/Bhindi Bazar *gharānā* too close to Kirana to qualify as an independent *gharānā*. She, however, acknowledges its principal exponent, Ustad Ameer Khan, as being amongst the towering individuals whose music she does not identify with any of the major *gharānā*s. [Bonnie C. Wade, 1984]

Deshpande [*ibid.*] cautions enlightened opinion against glorifying the *gharānā* system and placing an undue premium on stylistic conformity amongst its followers. He reminds us that the greatest vocalists in recent memory, almost without exception, acquired their art from more than one *gharānā* or *guru*, and openly credited their accomplishments to the multiplicity of influences.

Deshpande [*ibid.*] offers a conceptual framework for the aesthetic classification of the *gharānā*s of *khayāla* music. He classifies *gharānā* styles on a continuum defined by rhythmic orientation and melodic orientation as the two polarities. Amongst the *gharānā*s considered by him, he places Agra at the rhythmic orientation polarity, and Kirana at the melodic orientation polarity. Placing them at the exact mid-point of the continuum, he regards Alladiya [Jaipur-Atrauli] as a complex fusion, and Gwalior as a simple fusion of the two orientations. Patiala is placed towards the melodic orientation pole, but considerably short of Kirana. The Indore/Bhindi Bazar *gharānā* of Ameer Khan falls between Patiala and Kirana, close to the melodic orientation pole.

With specific reference to the two polarities, Agra at the rhythm oriented end, and Kirana at the melody oriented end, Deshpande [*ibid.*] observes that rhythm is the principle of motion, while melody is the principle of repose. The bias towards the rhythm end indicates animation, playfulness, and dynamism, while a bias towards the melody end is soothing, tranquillizing, and even depressing.

Prof. Wade [*ibid.* 1984] adopts a more elaborate framework for comparing *gharānā* stylistics. The dimensions she lists are

[a] Voice–vocal technique, voice quality, range, ornamentation

[b] Preferences with respect to *rāga*s

[c] Preferences with respect to *tāla*s

[d] Preferences with respect to compositions

[e] Preferences with respect to performance tempo, and its acceleration

[f] Balance between rhythmic and melodic elements

[g] Structure of slow-tempo *khayāla* presentation

[h] Preferences with respect to improvisatory movements and types of articulation

[i] strategies with respect to slow-tempo and medium/fast tempo *khayāla* presentations.

Although these dimensions have been proposed as a differentiator between the musical styles of the different *gharānās*, they are equally applicable as a framework for analysing *khayāla* music at an individual level.

The Ensemble for Khayāla Performance

The minimum ensemble for a *khayāla* performance consists of a drone [*tānapūrā*] and a percussion accompaniment [*tabalā*]. A majority of concert performers today use two *tānapūrās*, along with a melodic accompaniment provided either by a *sāraṅgī* or a *harmonium* player. In addition to this standard ensemble, some vocalists accompany themselves on a *svaramaṇḍala*, a harp belonging to the box-polychord family. Ustad Bade Ghulam Ali Khan was the first significant vocalist to use the *svaramaṇḍala*. Several eminent vocalists, notably, Smt. Kishori Amonkar and Pt. Jasraj, have followed his example.

The *tānapūrā*, *svaramaṇḍala*, and the melodic accompaniment — *sāraṅgī* or *harmonium* — perform a very significant and complex role in *khayāla* music. Their role relates as much to aiding the music making processes of the vocalist, as to enriching the totality of the musical experience for audiences.

The Format of Khayāla Presentation

The *khayāla* genre subsumes three categories of compositional format: the slow-tempo *baḍā khayāla* [major *khayāla*] and the medium-to-fast tempo *choṭā khayāla* [minor *khayāla*], both based on a piece of poetry, and *tarānā*, a medium-to-fast tempo compositional form structured around meaningless sound syllables borrowed mainly from the stroke patterns of the plucked instruments [e.g., *da, ra, dir*] and beat patterns of percussion [e.g., *dha, tirkit, dhin*].

The *khayāla* genre permits the musician considerable freedom in structuring his presentation. Different *gharānās*, and even individual musicians, have their own predilections in terms of the presentation format. Contemporary *khayāla* presentation does, however, tend to follow one of the two principal presentation formats:

The most common format in *khayāla* presentation is a *baḍā khayāla* in *ekatāla* [12 beats], or *jhūmarā* [14 beats] or *tilwāḍā* [16 beats] or *tīnatāla* [16 beats] followed by a *choṭā khayāla* in *tīnatāla* [16 beats] or *ekatāla* [12 beats]. In such a presentation, the rendition almost always begins with either an *auchara,* a brief free-flowing introduction of the *rāga*'s melodic personality, or merely a *rāga-vākya,* a couple of phrases seeking to achieve no more than identification of the *rāga*. An *auchara-baḍā khayāla-choṭā khayāla* presentation can last 35-45 minutes. In rare cases, the vocalist might add a third composition, a *tarānā* in the same *rāga*. This extension could consume an additional ten to fifteen minutes, bringing the total duration to about an hour.

In a less common format, deployed mainly by Agra and Gwalior vocalists, the slow-tempo *baḍā khayāla* is omitted. In its place, the vocalist presents an elaborate, three/four tiered, *dhrupad*-style *ālāpa* without percussion accompaniment, followed by a *choṭā khayāla*. In such cases, the *khayāla* rendition generally begins at a medium tempo, and accelerates gradually to reach the normal, brisk, *choṭā khayāla* tempo. It is rare for such presentations to end with a *tarānā*.

An even less common format in contemporary *khayāla* presentation is a single medium-tempo composition, normally without an elaborate *ālāpa*. The composition is generally in *rūpaka tāla* [7 beats] or *jhapatāla* [10 beats], and sometimes *tīnatāla* [16 beats]. The rendition is generally maintained at the same tempo throughout, with only marginal acceleration, if at all. This format is generally avoided for the first or main *khayāla* rendition in a concert. This type of medium-tempo *khayāla* presentation rarely lasts more than 20 minutes.

Melodic Expressions in the Khayāla Genre

Melodic execution in Hindustani music, essentially, avoids abruptness in intervallic transitions. This feature has been described as "conjunct" melody, as distinct from the "disjunct" melody found in Western music. In medium and high *svara*-density expressions, as also for the expression of explicit rhythmicality, staccato expressions are, however, frequently encountered.

The theory of music performance describes at least ten forms of melodic execution/intervallic transitions [*Sangeet Kaladhar*, Dahyalal Shivram, 2nd edn., 1938]. Other texts have larger inventories. The definitions from the texts are imprecise, and vary from text to text. The categories of melodic contours encountered in contemporary *khayāla* rendition would, however, outnumber all inventories considered together.

The principle categories of intervallic transition/phrasing/melodic expressions are:

[1] ***Mīṇḍa***: The *Mīṇḍa* is the basic form of intervallic transition in *khayāla* music. It involves a melodically continuous dragging of one *svara* to another, touching all the microtones along the path without allowing any of them to be perceived as having been explicitly intoned.

[2] ***Kaṇ***: The words means "fraction." When an intervallic transition between *svara*s involves a fractional use of the first *svara*, it is called a *kaṇ*. A generous use of the *kaṇ* is considered more proper in the semi-classical *ṭhumarī* renditions than in *khayāla*.

[3] ***Murkī***: Like the *kaṇ*, the *murkī*, too, is used more generously in the *ṭhumarī* genre. The *murkī* involves

the execution of a phrase normally using at least three *svaras* in brisk, wrap-around, jerky expression, as in *pā-mā^-dhā-pā*. The *khayāla* generally deploys single-loop *murkīs*. Multiple-loop *murkīs* are used in the *ṭhumarī* genre.

[4] ***Gīṭakīrī***: The brisk and explicit intonation of three or more adjacent *svaras*, whether in ascent or descent, without a jerk or wrap-around melodic motion, is called a *gīṭakīrī*.

[5] ***Khaṭakā***: The word means "a jerk." This melodic expression is generally used for a transition between *svaras* at least two/three *svaras* apart, and in descending transition. The expression drops from the higher *svara* to the lower *svara*, with a jerk. This is specially useful in *rāgas* such as Gaud Sarang [Descent: *sā'-pā-mā-gā/re-gā-re-mā-gā-pā-re-sā*. The *sā-pā* and *pā-re* transitions in Gaud Sarang require the *khaṭakā* expression almost as mandatory for *rāga* identification.

[6]. ***Gamaka***: The *gamaka* expression arises from a repetition of the same *svara* at a medium-to-high *svara*-density. Taking the support of the lower *svara* without its explicit intonation, the musician repeatedly hammers the target *svara* to create the *gamaka* expression.

[7]. ***Jamajama***: This expression also uses two adjacent *svaras* with one being emphasized by repetition, and differs from the *gamaka* in that the *jamajama* explicitly intones both the adjacent *svaras*, as in *gā-mā-mā/gā-mā-mā/gā-pā-pā/mā-pā-pā*.

These categories of melodic expression define the sculptural and ornamentational facets of a vocal recital. *Gharānās*, and individual musicians, differ in their preferences in this regard. These preferences, collectively, constitute a major part of the "stylistics" of *khayāla* music.

The Poetic Element in Khayāla Vocalism

The role of the poetic element in *khayāla* has been a subject of some bewilderment as well as debate. The song texts of *khayāla bandiśa*s are primarily in Braj *bhāṣā,* a dialect of Hindi spoken in and around Mathura. *Khayāla*s are, however, sung by musicians and heard by audiences from all parts of the country, most of whom do not understand the literal meaning of the poetry. Despite this, *khayāla*s lyrics in other languages have not been as popular, and Braj *bhāṣā* verses have not been translated into either mainstream or regional languages. Moreover, a large number of vocalists, including the greatest, have been casual about the articulation of the poetic element, treating it almost on par with the meaningless consonants of a *tarānā*. And, yet, there is no general revolt in the music world against the apparent assault on the integrity of the *bandiśa,* or on the listener's rights. These facts do not reflect a blind adherence to tradition as much as they acknowledge the role of the poetic element in *khayāla* vocalism.

Deshpande [*ibid.,* 1987] has argued, persuasively, that the art of singing could achieve its highest level of perfection in *khayāla* because, in this genre, the poetic element surrendered its literary function to its musical function. This musical function has several dimensions. The phonetic and syntactical structure of the poetry imparts concrete form to the *bandiśa,* independently of its semantic significance. It enhances the musical value of the *bandiśa* by adding a psycho-phonetic dimension to the psychoacoustics of the melodic-rhythmic shell. The semantic significance of the poetry activates the auto-suggestive process of the musician, helping the music to explore the emotional content of the *rāga.*

Deshpande's argument is supported by the fact that the twentieth century has witnessed equally great *khayāla* music from vocalists who treated *khayāla* verses rather casually, and those who systematically exploited its semantic significance.

Khayāla gives the individual musician the choice. No wonder *khayāla* lyrics are written by musicians rather than poets, and rarely command respect as poetry.

Articulation in Khayāla Music

The *khayāla* genre deploys three categories of articulation:

[a] ***Bola***: The poetic form, representing a vast range of themes, which holds together the melodic and rhythmic elements in the composition [*bandiśa / cīẓa*].

[b] ***Saragama***: The use of solfa symbols as textural consonants in the improvisatory movements.

[c] ***Ākāra***: The vowel *ā*, used in the improvisatory movements.

The *tarānā* does not use the poetic form in the main body of the *bandiśa/cīẓa*. However, there exists a tradition of inserting Persian and Urdu *rubāīs* [verses] into the *tarānā* as a relief from the otherwise meaningless consonants constituting the phonetic element of the form. In the improvisatory movements, the *tarānā* form is permitted the use of *saragamas* as well as *ākāra*.

These three forms of articulation have collective, as well as individual, roles in the rendition of *khayāla* compositions. At the purely phonetic level, they provide the musician with three distinct textural devices. The poetic form is a balanced and unpredictable mix of vowel and consonant articulations, generally with a bias towards the softer consonants. The *saragama* device uses only consonants, and the range is limited to seven. The *ākāra* has only one vowel, though individual styles can occasionally vary the articulation slightly. Collectively, the three devices contribute to the textural richness of the phonetic component of *khayāla* music.

The three forms of articulation also represent three different levels of abstraction in terms of meaning. The poetic form represents explicit meaning, which interacts, potentially, with the melodic element of the phrasing in the expression of its emotional content. The *saragama* represents musical meaning, by virtue of direct correspondence between the intonation and the articulation. The *ākāra*, being a vowel phonetic, is totally abstract, with the meaning being provided only by the melodic contours of the intonation.

The deployment of the three forms of articulation is guided by aesthetic considerations, and by the stylistic predilections of individual *gharānā*s and vocalists. The poetic form is, for instance, used predominantly in slow and medium *svara* density movements. This is because high-density melodic expressions can jeopardize the integrity of the poetic form and the intelligibility of explicit meaning.

The *saragama* is used predominantly in medium density movements. In such movements, it provides a textural option for the poetic form, and greater freedom for melodic-rhythmic improvization than the poetic form will permit. It tends not to be used in very high-density melodic movements because consonants militate against high-frequency articulation, in addition to being less pleasing than vowels.

The *ākāra* articulation is the most versatile, but is also the most demanding in terms of lung-power, and is therefore used selectively. Being a vowel form, it is most useful in movements where the melody is not required to express an explicit rhythmicality. Such movements are the low *svara*-density *ālāpa*, which is free from explicit rhythmicality, and the high-density *tāna*s where the rhythmicality is built into the fixed ratio between the *svara*-density of the melody and the tempo [beat-density] of the rhythmic cycle at the particular stage of rendition.

The Structure of Compositions

Baḍā and *choṭā khayāla* compositions, and also *tarānā* compositions, have two stanzas, represented by two melodic sections: the *sthāyī*, and the *antarā*. The *sthāyī* is, as a rule, centred in the lower half of the melodic canvas, except when the melodic centre of gravity of the *rāga* falls in the *uttarāṅga*. The *antarā* is identifiable by a deliberate ascent to the upper tonic, with its follow-through centred in the upper half of the melodic canvas. The *antarā*, however, ends with a descent to base-*sā*. The two parts together represent a comprehensive map of the *rāga*'s melodic personality. The *sthāyī* also functions as the nucleus of the *khayāla* presentation — the basic theme or refrain to which the rendition returns, repeatedly, after each round of improv-izations.

Khayāla Presentation Protocol

The *baḍā khayāla* rendition begins with the presentation of the *sthāyī* and *antarā* of the *bandiśa*, and is followed by improvisatory movements, woven around the *sthāyī*. It is not uncommon, however, for the *antarā* to be introduced after the first improvisatory movement.

The *baḍā khayāla* uses three improvisatory movements, each distinct in the melodic-rhythmic structure. The sequencing of these movements is in consonance with the convention of progressive enhancement of melodic and rhythmic density and complexity. In recent times, it has become customary to match this progression, at each transition, with a perceptible stepping-up of the basic tempo of the *tāla* performed by the percussionist.

[a] ***Ālāpa***: The *ālāpa* is a free-flowing, rhythmically unstructured improvization of low melodic density, in which the melodic lines attempt no correspondence with the beats of the *tāla*. The *ālāpa* acknowledges the rhythmic cycle only at the end of each round of

improvizations, when it has to rejoin the *sthāyī*. For the purposes of articulation, an *ālāpa* can either use the poetic element of the song [*bola-ālāpa*], or the abstract *ākāra* [the vowel form *Ā*], or a combination of the two. In rare cases, solfa symbols [*saragama*] are also found in the *ālāpa*.

[b] ***Bola-laya* [*articulation in correspondence with rhythm*]**: The *bola-laya* movement is also referred to as *bola-bāṇṭa* [emphasis shifts on the poetic element]. *Bola-laya/bola-bāṇṭa* is a pulse-driven movement of medium melodic density, which introduces a moderate degree of correspondence, and even playful interaction, between the articulation, the melodic contours, and the beats of the rhythmic cycle. For articulation, a vocalist can use either the poetic form, or *saragama* [solfa symbols], or a combination of the two. Only in rare cases is the *ākāra* articulation encountered in the *bola-laya* movement.

[c] ***Tānas***: *Tāna*s are highly structured melodic runs of medium-to-wide melodic span, and high *svara*-density. They achieve a strong correspondence between their melodic contours and beats of the rhythmic cycle, and can exhibit a lively interaction with them. The melodic structure of *tāna*s is derived from a typology that has matured over centuries of evolution. For articulation of *tāna*s, a vocalist can use either the poetic element of the *bandiśa*, *saragama* [solfa symbols], or *ākāra*, or a combination of the three.

For those familiar with the medieval *dhrupad* genre, it is easy to see that the improvisatory movements of the *baḍā khayāla* correspond to the *vilaṁbita*, *mahālaya*, and *druta ālāpa* of a *dhrupad* presentation. Structurally, though not historically, the *baḍā khayāla* inserts the *ālāpa* of a *dhrupad* rendition into the rendition of the pre-composed *bandiśa* as a chain of improvisatory movements. With this structural departure from the *dhrupad* format, the *baḍā khayāla* permits the simultaneous manipulation of the melodic and rhythmic elements, and creates a presentation format with an end-to-end linearity of melodic-rhythmic progression. This structural alignment is accompanied by a substantial enlargement of freedom in the choice of textural, sculptural as well as ornamentational devices to establish the *khayāla* as a distinctive genre of vocal music.

The *bandiśa ṭhumarī*, a lively vocal form, originally evolved as an accompaniment to footwork-dominant sub-forms of *kathaka* dance, inspires the second *bandiśa*, the *choṭā khayāla*. The *bandiśa ṭhumarī* is characterized by a one-to-one correspondence between the poetic, the melodic, and the rhythmic elements. This makes the form ideal for rendition in the faster tempi.

A *choṭā khayāla* presentation begins with the rendition of the *sthāyī* and the *antarā* and is followed by the improvisatory movements. Here again, it is common for the *antarā* to be introduced after a few rounds of improvization rather than immediately after the *sthāyī*. In rare cases, one may encounter elements of *ālāpa* and *bola-laya* in the *choṭā khayāla* too. However, in consonance with the tempo and the aural flavour of the *choṭā khayāla*, the improvizations are dominated by *tāna*s, generally rendered at a *svara* density at least twice the beat-density of the rhythmic cycle. In the *tāna*s, the vocalist has the same choice of articulation as in the *baḍā khayāla*. *Tarānā* renditions follow the same format as the *choṭā khayāla*, except that the absence of poetry, and the availability of meaningless consonants for articulation might encourage a greater display of rhythmic dexterity and virtuosity.

The Typology of Tānas

The melodic patterns in *tāna*s are constructed from five basic patterns. [i] *Baḍhata* [ii] *Laḍīguṭhāva* [iii] *Sapāṭa* [iv] *Chūta* [v] *Hopping Tānas*.

Baḍhata* [*progressive*] *Tānas: There are two concepts of *baḍhata* or progression in *tāna* construction. The first is to construct them in progressively ascending melodic waves, each wave ascending further upwards than the previous one. The first wave ascends from a certain base, mostly base *sā*, ascends upwards up to a point, returns to base, ascends again, this time a little farther, returns again to base, and so on. The second approach to *baḍhata tāna*s is patterned as a series of short *tāna*s woven around one melodic focus after another in ascending order, without returning to base *sā* after each ascent, but instead reverting to the *sthāyī*. The phraseology of *baḍhata tāna*s can either be flat-out or zigzag. Their identifying feature is the progressive unfurling of the melodic canvas. *Baḍhata tāna*s are, by their nature, appropriate for the ascent.

Laḍīguthāva* [*chain-knitting*] *Tānas: *Laḍīguthāva* is a special category of *baḍhata tāna* in which the melodic development moves progressively upwards, but continuously without returning to a base, using a very complex web of inter-locked patterns woven around each *svara* along the path. Their identifying feature is the complexity of the melodic web in progressive ascending or descending motion. *Laḍīguthāva* is perhaps the most demanding *tāna* pattern because of short spans of improvizations and their seamless knitting into an ascending chain. This requires a total mastery over the melodic features of the *rāga*.

Sapāṭa* [*flat-out*] *Tānas: *Sapāṭa tāna*s ascend or descend in a cascading motion, with straight-forward runs on the *rāga* scale without any twists and turns, with a single intonation supporting the execution of every *svara* on the intended melodic path. They have the desired impact when their melodic span covers at least one full octave. *Sapāṭa*s are rendered in ascending as well as descending movements.

Chūta* [*leaping*] *Tānas: *Chūta tāna*s are constructed by establishing a geometric [generally first-fifth or first-fourth] tonal relationship between phrases of short melodic spans, delivered in different regions of the melodic canvas. Their structure appears to leap from *svara* to distant *svara* in the process of generating waves of corresponding phrases. The *chūta* pattern can be descending or ascending; but a set of *chūta-tāna* waves will generally be rounded off by a descending *sapāṭa*.

***Hopping Tāna*s**: These *tāna*s, generally found in ascending formation, hop across alternate *svara*s, often repetitively. For example, *sā-gā-sā-gā, re-mā-re-mā, gā-pā-gā-pā, mā-dhā-mā-dhā,* Depending on the grammar of the *rāga*, these *tāna*s may skip more than one *svara* in each hop. For obvious reasons, they are sometimes referred to as two-by-two *tāna*s. The hopping/ two-by-two *tāna* is also inspired by one of the *alaṅkāra*s. It acquired the status of a *tāna* variety primarily as a speciality of the Jaipur-Atrauli *gharānā* vocalists, particularly, Kesarbai Kerkar.

Amongst other *tāna* structures, a significant, but simplistic in construction, is the *alaṅkāra tāna*. *Alaṅkāra*s [lit: ornamentation] are a large group of practice exercises of varying complexity given to students with the dual purpose of training them in the precise delivery of *svara*s irrespective of the order in which they are arranged, and preparing them for the techniques of improvisation fundamental to Hindustani music. *Alaṅkāra tāna*s are recognizable by their symmetric progression such as: *sā-re-gā-gā, re-gā-mā-mā, gā-mā-pā-pā, mā-pā-dhā-dhā.*

The Aesthetics of Tānas

In the architecture of the *khayāla* genre, the *tāna*s represent a culmination of melodic density and complexity. The advanced level of melodic density automatically makes the *tāna*s a display of virtuosity, and in the advanced level of complexity, the musician has the opportunity of demonstrating his virtuosity, imagination, as well as aesthetic sensibility. But, the issue of aesthetics in *tāna*s is much larger than complexity.

At every level, melodic density has a different psycho-acoustic implication. Pt. Omkarnath Thakur [1897-1967], for instance, refused to sing *tāna*s in Nīlāmbarī, because they would militate against the *rasa* of the *rāga*. Swimming against the tide of generalized expectations of *khayāla* presentation protocol, he established Nīlāmbarī as one of his most memorable and popular *rāga*s.

The character of the *rāga* is also an issue in the selection of *tāna* patterns. The melodic personality of every *rāga*, and also its emotional charge, are residents of its *calana*. The *calana* of each *rāga* limits the musician's options in terms of patterning strategies for *tāna*s. *Rāga*s with a zigzag *calana* cannot, for instance, support the *alaṅkāra* or *sapāṭa tāna* patterns. Such *rāga*s could, on the other hand, be ideally suited for the hopping or *laḍīguthāva* pattern.

Another major issue of aesthetics in *tāna*s is the level of melodic density [intonations per second]. Above a certain level of *svara*-density, some *tāna* patterns will tend towards an unmusical aural experience. And, there is a threshold of *svara* density beyond which all *tāna* patterns will sound unmusical. The frontiers of musicality are, of course, fluid. But, they demand respect from each generation of musicians.

The issue of aesthetics in *tāna*s stands at the borderline between art and entertainment. If taken seriously by musicians, it can often restrain the demonstration of virtuosity. The greatest of musicians have been guilty of opting for virtuosity at the cost of aesthetics, and the most highly cultivated amongst connoisseurs have been guilty of forgiving them.

Trends in Khayāla Vocalism

The *khayāla* genre has been defined by its "formal aloofness." However, the history of the genre in the twentieth century is replete with vocalists — all of formidable stature — who have deviated either from its formalism or its aloofness, or both. Of the two deviationist tendencies, the revolt against aloofness shows a greater resemblance to a movement. Deshpande [*ibid.*] describes it as a romanticist movement, comparable to a similar movement in Western classical music. The movement argues in favour of explicit emotional stimuli in art music, in addition to the architectural and sculptural variables of the aural experience. The phenomenon is particularly relevant to *khayāla* vocalism because of the freedom it gives the musician, and the premium it accords to his role as a composer over that of a performer.

Stylistically, the recent history of the *khayāla* can be viewed in three phases. The first phase covers the pre-Independence era, dominated by Ustad Faiyyaz Khan. The second phase covers the quarter of a century thereafter, with several giants straddling the *khayāla* platform, approximately ending with the demise of Ustad Ameer Khan in 1974. The third phase begins with the trailblazing emergence of Pt. Kumar Gandharva and Smt. Kishori Amonkar.

At the dawn of the last century, Ustad Abdul Kareem Khan [1872-1937] had already paved the way for a combination of classicism with romanticism. In the next generation, Ustad Faiyyaz Khan [1886-1950] took the process farther, though with an entirely different style. On a partial review of his radio broadcasts, it appears that he adopted a mildly informal approach to *khayāla* architecture, in addition to introducing elements, which were explicitly solicitous of an emotional response. Expressions typical of the *ṭappā* genre, derived from the songs of camel drivers in north-west India, entered *khayāla* music for the first time in Faiyyaz Khan's renditions. On the evidence of 78-RPM records, the same appears to be broadly true of Pt. Ramkrishna Vaze [1871-1945] Pt. Omkarnath Thakur [1897-1967], partially their contemporary, was a fastidious formalist, but a die-hard romanticist.

In the second phase, Pt. D.V. Paluskar, [1921-55], Kesarbai Kerkar [1890-1977], and Ustad Ameer Khan [1912-74] were exemplary models of formalism as well as aloofness. This phase witnessed a solitary deviant, Ustad Bade Ghulam Ali Khan [1903-68]. He was, broadly, in the Faiyyaz Khan mould, with an informal approach to architecture, and an inclination towards seductive ornamentation, and emotionally potent musical communication.

Amongst significant vocalists of the third phase, Pt. Bhimsen Joshi [born 1922] stands alone as the bulwark of the *khayāla*'s formalism and aloofness. In this phase, Pt. Kumar Gandharva [1925-92] rebelled against both, aloofness as well as formalism. His junior by a few years, Smt. Kishori Amonkar [born: 1931] has remained steadfast in her respect for *khayāla* architecture, while rebelling against its aloofness. Their approximate contemporary, Pt. Jasraj started as a follower of the fastidious classicist, Ustad Ameer Khan, but has drifted steadily away from the formalism as well as aloofness of *khayāla* vocalism.

The significant aspect of romanticism in the third phase was the consolidation of the infusion of melodic expressions characteristic of the semi-classical, folk, regional, and popular genres of music into *khayāla* vocalism. As a result, *khayāla* was faced with a blurring of the stylistic divide between genres of vocal music.

In all probability, these tendencies had their socio-cultural logic. By this time, several leading performers of the semi-classical and romantic *ṭhumarī* and allied genres —

Siddheshwari Devi, Rasoolan Bai, Begum Akhtar, Bade Ghulam Ali Khan, Barkat Ali Khan — had departed from the scene, leaving the genres starved of quality musicianship. Simultaneously, *khayāla* singers with *ṭhumarī* training had also faded away. Emotionally satisfying genres were beginning to disappear from the art-music platform. Around the same time, Jagjit Singh, an outstanding singer of the *ghazal*, a poetry-dominated genre, was enhancing its melodic content to corner a part of this vacant space. The *khayāla*, at that stage, attempted to fill the vacuum with a dual strategy — allowing *khayāla* itself to drift towards a more explicit and ornate emotionalism, and adopting the highly stylised *bhajana* as a tail-piece replacement for the *ṭhumarī*. Little wonder, then, that by the dawn of the twenty-first century, the *ṭhumarī* is all but extinct, and the distinctiveness of the *khayāla* is sustained almost entirely by its architecture.

The resilience of *khayāla* architecture cannot be taken for granted considering that it has been breached by some of the most formidable vocalists of the twentieth century. For the moment, the opinion-makers of the art-music world are committed to its structuralism. However, a more permissive music establishment is likely to emerge soon out of the cultural discontinuities imposed by Independence. As a result, a more complete expression of post-modern tendencies can now be considered imminent in *khayāla* music.

4.3

AN INTRODUCTION TO ṬHUMARĪ

THE *ṭhumarī* is a modern genre of semi-classical music, which originated as an accompaniment to the *kathaka* genre of north Indian dance, and evolved later as an independent art form. Its name is traced to *ṭhumakā* in Hindi and its dialects, an onomatopoeic expression representing the sound of the graceful steps of a dancer with ankle bells.

The genre subsumes two sub-genres — a brisk and lively form called the *bandiśa ṭhumarī* and a leisurely, sentimental form called *bola-banāo ṭhumarī*. The latter is allied closely to *dādarā, caitī, kajrī* and other semi-classical forms, which are highly stylized versions of the folk music of the Benares region. Though the *bola-banāo ṭhumarī* is a later development, the two sub-genres evolved probably in response also to different choreographic formats — the *bandiśa ṭhumarī*, to footwork dominant formats, and the *bola-banāo ṭhumarī*, to mime dominant formats. The *bandiśa ṭhumarī* started moving towards the mainstream in the eighteenth century, reached its zenith in mid-nineteenth-century Lucknow, and was near extinct by the early twentieth century. The *bola-banāo ṭhumarī*

Acknowledgement: This essay draws generously on the authoritative work of Prof. Peter Manuel of the City University of New York. *Ṭhumarī — in historical and stylistic perspectives*, 1st edn., 1989, Motilal Banarsidass, New Delhi. The present author also acknowledges with gratitude Prof. Manuel's consent for this reliance, and his suggestions on the coverage of the subject.

flowered in nineteenth century Benares, acquired the stature of a mainstream genre in the early twentieth century, and is now seemingly heading for extinction.

Kathaka dance as well as the *ṭhumarī*, evolved in the neighbourhood of Mathurā, the birthplace of Lord Kṛṣṇa. Thematically, both genres are immersed in the *bhakti* movement, and the amorous joys of Rādhā, a cowherd's daughter, and her divine paramour, Kṛṣṇa. Their legendary romance, defining the ambiguous zone between the accessible and the unattainable, became a metaphor for man's spiritual quest. The cultural expressions of the metaphor thus came to have a female protagonist, anguished by separation from her beloved, and yearning for union with him.

The *ṭhumarī* genre represents the refinement and stylization of folk sources from the Brij [Mathurā/Vṛndāvan] region by courtesans in response to the entertainment needs of a cultivated aristocracy. Until the end of the nineteenth century, courtesans were the predominant performers of both, the *kathaka* genre of dance, and the *ṭhumarī* genre of vocal music. To this extent, the alluring qualities of the genre also reflect the manipulative intent fundamental to the relationship between courtesans and their clients.

Along their evolutionary path, the two *ṭhumarī* sub-genres [*bandiśa ṭhumarī* and *bola-banāo ṭhumarī*] have interacted intimately with the art-music mainstream, and may be seen as informal and romanticist manifestations of the very aesthetic forces that were driving classical music into the modern period. Superficially, the *bandiśa ṭhumarī* corresponds to the *choṭā* [*druta*] *khayāla*, and the *bola-banāo ṭhumarī* to the *baḍā* [*vilaṁbita*] *khayāla*. Unlike, *khayāla*, however, the *ṭhumarī* genre is dominated by its poetic element. The *bandiśa ṭhumarī* revolves around the poetic-rhythmic axis with a subordinated role for melody, and is thus closer to the music-making philosophy of the medieval *dhrupad* genre. The *bola-banāo ṭhumarī*, on the other hand, revolves around the poetic-melodic axis, with a subordinated role for rhythm. To this extent, it is unlike *khayāla* as well as *dhrupad*.

Using the architectural metaphor, *ṭhumarī* may be classified as an ornamentation-dominant genre, differentiated from *dhrupad*, which may be considered architecture-dominant, and the *khayāla*, which qualifies as a sculpture-dominant genre.

Sources of the Ṭhumarī Tradition

As a genre performed in accompaniment to interpretative dance, the *ṭhumarī* tradition is traceable to Bharata's *Nāṭyaśāstra*, the ancient text on dramaturgy, and its description of a dance-form called *lāsya*. It was a solo female dance, accompanied by female singers and an orchestra. The dancer interprets accompanying songs describing the lover, and complaining about him. The dancer's technique was primarily *abhinaya* [mime], and portrayed *śṛṅgāra* [amorous] and *karuṇa* [pathos] *rasa*s. A similar dance and music form, called *paṇika*, appears in the ninth-century work, *Dattilam*. In eleventh-century texts, there are references to a dance of folk origin, called "Dombika," deriving its name from the Domb gypsies, who made a living as singers and dancers, and whose art was adopted by the courtesans of that era. On this evidence, scholars suggest that the *ṭhumarī*, as an artistic tradition, could be as ancient and continuous as *khayāla* and *dhrupad*.

The precursors of the *ṭhumarī* genre were associated with the pre-modern stage in the evolution of *kathaka* dance. The word *kathaka* derives from a community of professional storytellers of the same name, going back to the pre-Christian era. This community specialized in narrating stories from the Hindu myths with the help of mime and accompaniment. The *kathaka*s were Kṛṣṇa devotees, and deeply absorbed in the cult of Rādhā and Kṛṣṇa.

The folk-material for *kathaka* dance and the *ṭhumarī* came from three medieval dance-and-music traditions — *carcarī, rāsak* and *Holī. Carcarī* was an erotic dance, accompanied by music sung to songs in the present-day Kāfī scale and the *cañcara tāla*, which is, to this day, amongst the mainstays of the *ṭhumarī* genre. The *rāsaka* was an erotic fertility dance performed to the accompaniment of music in *rasa tāla*, which coincides with *kehervā*, a major *tāla* of the *bola-banāo ṭhumarī* genre. This form apparently evolved into the *rāsa-līlā* of the Kṛṣṇa cult, whose exponents shaped *kathaka* dance and *ṭhumarī* genres. *Hori* as a dance-and-song form was also called *Horī-Dīpacaṇḍī, Dīpacaṇḍī* being another name for *cañcara tāla*.

It would appear that these folk genres had considerable acceptance amongst the nobility — Hindu and Muslim — in medieval India. The patronage of genteel society induced their adoption and refinement by courtesans. In this process they absorbed the influence of the *khayāla* tradition without losing their moorings in the folk traditions.

The folk anchorages are evident in the choice of *tāla*s as well as the melodic framework within which the genre functions. Even in the deployment of *tāla*s, which are considered "classical," the *ṭhumarī* has retained an accentual pattern that is distinctively folk in its spirit. Despite the *khayāla* influence, both *ṭhumarī* forms have remained within the melodic orbit of amorphous folk-derived modal entities, which dominated its precursors. The differing melodic biases of the two sub-genres may reflect the difference between the aesthetic values of eighteenth and nineteenth-century Lucknow and nineteenth and twentieth-century Benares, the dance forms each related to, and their respective patronage profiles.

Stylistic Evolution

By the eighteenth century, the *bandiśa ṭhumarī* had achieved a mature form, was performed primarily as accompaniment to *kathaka* dance, but increasingly also as an independent genre of music. At its zenith during the reign of Wajid Ali Shah [1822-87] in Awadh, the *ṭhumarī* was a medium or fast tempo *tīnatāla* composition, but occasionally in *rūpaka* or *ekatāla*, rendered with *bola-bāṇṭa, tāna*s and *layakārī*. However, by this time, the genre was no longer rendered exclusively in the fast tempo.

Throughout the nineteenth-century, the *kathaka-ṭhumarī* form was performed primarily by courtesans. The presentation format consisted of two sub-forms. One was the sitting format in which the courtesan sat on the floor, sang a verse, and then enacted it, deploying mime and the language of the torso. Following such a presentation, she would stand up and then render a footwork oriented dance item.

The sitting format of *kathaka-ṭhumarī* rendition achieved a totality of involvement in direct interface with her audience. It also enabled exceptional vocalists, who no longer had the figure for dancing, to continue longer in the profession. The intimate context of the sitting format, conducive to the delivery of the emotional experience, could have encouraged the slowing down of the tempo of rendition, and thus paved the way for the *bola-banāo ṭhumarī*.

With growing sophistication in dance as well as *ṭhumarī*, there emerged different categories of courtesans — those who only sang and those who only danced. The role for a specialist singer opened the door for male vocalists as accompanists, and stimulated the evolution of its independent idiom.

In the early twelfth-century, the Lucknow-style *bandiśa ṭhumarī*, which already had an affinity with the *choṭā khayāla*, virtually merged with the classicist genre. Its place was taken by the slow-tempo *bola-banāo ṭhumarī*, which bore a superficial resemblance to the *baḍā khayāla*. This development took place primarily in Benares, and also partiallv in nearby Gayā. Both these cities had an ample patronage base amongst the local aristocracy. By the late nineteenth century, conditions were conducive for Benares, already an important *kathaka-ṭhumarī* centre, to spearhead the fructification of emerging tendencies.

The *bola-banāo ṭhumarī* of Benares is, in fact, performed as a part of a cluster of sub-genres derived from the folk music of the region. In its allied forms like *caitī, kajarī, fāguna,* etc., the melody is so simple and predictable that its *rāga*-ness is questionable. And yet the presentation is stylized and sophisticated enough to make even its folk origins immaterial. While the *bandiśa ṭhumarī* relied primarily on the formal *tīnatāla,* the *bola-banāo* adopted the informal and folksy *kehervā, dādarā* and *dīpacaṇḍī* as the primary *tāla*s. It dropped the rhythmic cleverness of the *bola-bāṇṭa* and the virtuosity of *tāna*s typical of *bandiśa ṭhumarī*s, and stuck to the poetry-melody axis for its delivery of musical value. For rhythmic excitement, it borrowed the *laggī* practice from folk music, which permits the percussionist to demonstrate his musicianship in brief interludes, and as the finale of a *bola-banāo ṭhumarī* rendition.

The most significant aspects of Benares *ṭhumarī*'s stylistic tendencies in the early twentieth century were the steady deceleration of the tempo of rendition, a sharper focus on the emotive and melodic treatment of the song-text to the practical exclusion of virtuoso vocalism, and a heightened emphasis on the folk melodic and rhythmic elements in the *ṭhumarī,* along with its allied sub-genres.

The period from 1920 to 1960, regarded as the Golden Age of Hindustani music, was a significant period for the *ṭhumarī* genre. The entry of the gramophone record and the radio in the early twentieth century, and the growth of the urban middle class created a larger and qualitatively different market for Hindustani music. The *ṭhumarī* came out of the courtesan districts, and entered the concert hall and people's homes. While the erotic and the aesthetic were both important to the courtesan's salons, the erotic became inappropriate in the new context, and the aesthetic gained ascendancy. The *ṭhumarī* shed its stigma as leading *khayāla* singers added it to their repertoire, and enriched it immensely.

As a result, a full concert of semi-classical music typical of the Benares tradition disappeared from the scene. With the virtual cannibalization of the *ṭhumarī* tradition by the *khayāla* platform, the specialist *ṭhumarī* singer, as a distinctive class of musicians, started becoming extinct. This represented a considerable depletion of the musical culture, considering that the great Benares courtesans could hold an audience for two hours with a feast of semi-classical music. Such a concert would begin with a 30-minute *bola-banāo ṭhumarī*, followed by a *ṭappā*, and then by a *dādarā*, a *bandiśa ṭhumarī*, a *caitī*, a *kajarī*, and end with another *bola-banāo ṭhumarī*.

Another significant consequence of the *ṭhumarī*'s migration to the concert hall was the disappearance of the sitting format of *kathaka-ṭhumarī* presentation. The format was unsustainable because a sitting performer suffers poor visibility beyond a few rows in an auditorium. This loss of intimacy and immediacy of artistic communication impoverished the choreographic as well as musical arts.

The *ṭhumarī* genre evolved almost hand-in-hand with the *khayāla* genre, to wean away audiences from the medieval *dhrupad* genre. It emerged as a significant romanticist genre, and undertook a steady deceleration in the tempo of rendition in order to become a more effective vehicle for sentimental musical ideas. Its trajectory has been synchronous with the decline of feudalism and the rise of bourgeois capitalism. In these developments, Peter Manuel sees a parallel with the socio-economic conditions that led to the rise of the romanticist movement [*Parlando Rubato*] in Western classical music. He equates *dhrupad* with the feudal values of heroism, and the *khayāla* and *ṭhumarī* as reflecting the relaxed mores of bourgeois society.

Ashok Ranade, sees the evolution of the *ṭhumarī* within the framework of a dialectic process in the musical culture. He argues that, at each milestone in its recent history, the Indian musical tradition has tended to create parallel genres, one with a formalistic tendency, and the other giving the musician a wider scope for individual creativity. According to him, *khayāla* and *ṭhumarī* were both reactions against the rigidity of the medieval *dhrupad* genre. The evolution of the *ṭhumarī* gathered momentum when the *khayāla* began to crystallize as a formalistic genre. In the most recent stage, while the *ṭhumarī* was defining unprecedented degrees of individual creative freedom, it was challenged by its own antithesis in the *ghaẓal*, a relatively *rāga*-neutral genre, but with a substantial role for the pre-composed element. [Ashok D. Ranade, "Perspectives on *dhrupad*", *Journal of the Indian Musicological Society*, Issue of 1999, ed. Deepak Raja and Suvarnalata Rao].

Landmark Personalities

Men, who have been patrons, composers, and teachers of the *ṭhumarī-kathaka* arts, ironically, dominate the roster of landmark personages. The primary reason for this is the culture of anonymity that characterizes the world of courtesans. Though many courtesans belonged to eminent lineages of artists, matrilineal pedigree did not have sufficient respectability to give them a place in history. Only with the advent of recording industry in the early twentieth century did their art achieve recognition.

The *ṭhumarī* attained its zenith in eighteenth-nineteenth-century Awadh [Lucknow]. The Lucknow tradition is traced back to one Prakashji, an exponent of the *rāsa* form, who migrated from Allahabad and secured the patronage of Nawab Asafuddaula [reign 1775-97]. Prakashji's sons, Durga Prasad and Thakur Prasad became tutors to the next Nawab, Wajid Ali Shah and ushered in the flowering of the *ṭhumarī* and *kathaka* dance as state-supported arts. Durga Prasad had two sons, Kalkaji Maharaj and Binda Din Maharaj [1836-1917]. The latter is credited with having introduced *ṭhumarī* to *kathaka* dance by composing *ṭhumarī*s specifically as support for interpretative dance, and making it the pre-eminent song form accompanying *kathaka* performance.

Wajid Ali Shah was undoubtedly a pivotal patron of the *kathaka-ṭhumarī* renaissance. Under the tutelage of Durga Prasad and Thakur Prasad, he became a formidable dancer. He trained with Sadiq Ali Khan to become a fine vocalist. He penned three volumes of song-texts for the *ṭhumarī*, *dādarā*, *khayāla* and *sadra* genres of vocal music. He scripted a Vaiṣṇavite dance drama called "*Indra Sabhā*" in Urdu, with songs in Braja *bhāṣā*. His *ṭhumarī* composition *bābul morā naihara chūṭo jāye* is amongst the immortal classics of modern music. In 1856, an entourage of 160 musicians accompanied Wajid Ali Shah to Calcutta, when British mercenaries exiled him with a privy purse worthy of his status. This exodus took the *ṭhumarī* to eastern India, and contributed greatly to its popularity.

Wajid Ali Shah's artistic passions were ably supported by Sadiq Ali Khan [1800-1910], a vocalist in his employ, descended from a lineage of *qawwālī* singers, associated with the early days of the *khayāla* genre. He devoted his energies to refining the *bandiśa ṭhumarī*. He reportedly also initiated the deceleration of the tempo, thus laying the foundations of the *bola-banāo ṭhumarī*. His genius attracted some of the most talented musicians of his era as disciples. In addition to *ṭhumarī* exponents and composers, the list includes *khayāla* singers like Inayet Hussain Khan [1849-1919] of the Sahaswan *gharānā*, Ramakrishna Vaze [1871-1945] of the Gwalior *gharānā*, and the legendary *harmonium* exponent, Bhaiyya Ganpat Rao [1852-1920].

In this flowering, a pivotal role is attributed to Bhaiyya Ganpat Rao of Gwalior. He was trained in *dhrupad*, *khayāla* and the *rudra vīṇā*, but fell in love with the newly arrived *harmonium* and the *ṭhumarī* genre. He studied the *ṭhumarī* with Sadiq Ali Khan and Khurshid Ali Khan of Lucknow. Remarkably enough, he helped shape the incipient *bola-banāo ṭhumarī* by performing it on the eminently unsuitable *harmonium*, overcoming its technical limitations. Under his influence, the *harmonium* fast replaced the traditional *sāraṅgī* as the standard melodic accompaniment for *ṭhumarī*. Under the pseudonym "Sughar Piya," he composed a large number of *ṭhumarī*s, which became immensely popular. Some of the greatest *ṭhumarī* singers of his times were his students. Amongst them were great courtesans — Gauhar Jan, Jaddanbai, Malka Jan — and male vocalists — Mauzuddin Khan [1840-1926], Mir Irshad Ali, and Babu Shyam Lal.

Though independently of Ganpat Rao, his contemporary, Jagdeep Mishra of Benares performed a similar pioneering role in the evolution of the *bola-banāo ṭhumarī*. Mishra belonged to a family of hereditary *kathaka* exponents, and is considered a co-founder of the Benares *bola-banāo* tradition.

In the Benares tradition of specialist singers, the last few greats in the twentieth century were Girijashankar Chakravarty [1878-1948] in Bengal, a disciple of Bhaiyya Ganpat Rao, and the Benares courtesans, Rasoolan Bai [died 1974], Siddheshwari Devi [1908-77], and Badi Moti Bai. While Girijashankar trained some outstanding *ṭhumarī* singers like Naina Devi [died 2002], the courtesans created an enviable niche for themselves on the concert platform.

Siddheshwari Devi was, by far, the most outstanding semi-classical vocalist of her times. She had studied *khayāla* and *ṭhumarī* with her aunt Rajeshwari Bai, Siyaji Mishra [a *sāraṅgī* player], Bade Ramdasji of Benares, Inayet Hussain Khan of Lahore, and Rajab Ali Khan of Gwalior [1875-1959]. The leisurely classicism of her *ṭhumarī* renditions brought them almost on par with the *baḍā khayāla*. In stature and popularity, Rasoolan Bai came next to Siddheshwari Devi. She had studied primarily with *khayāla* vocalists, *sāraṅgī* players and *kathaka* exponents. She was famous for her *ṭhumarī*s, *dādarā*s, and *ṭappā*s. Her melodic range and imagination were limited, but achieved tremendous depth of expression. Badi Moti Bai, was a disciple of Siyaji Mishra, Mithailal Beenkaar and Mauzuddin Khan. Her singing bespoke her solid classical training, but lacked the leisurely appeal of Siddheshwari Devi.

Another significant vocalist from the courtesan tradition of the *ṭhumarī* was Begum Akhtar [1914-74] of Faizabad. She had studied *khayāla* with Wahid Khan and Ata Khan of Kirana *gharānā*, and also from some Patiala maestros. She performed *ṭhumarī, ghazal, dādarā,* and the allied folk genres. Her *ṭhumarī*s were said to have been a combination of the Benares and Punjab styles. In contrast to the *baḍā khayāla*-like expansiveness of Siddheshwari Devi's *ṭhumarī*s, her *ṭhumarī*s were short, up to about ten minutes each. She devoted her energies primarily to the melodic development of the *ghazal*, a more poetry dominant form than the *ṭhumarī*, and enriched its melodic content enough to bring it almost on par with the *bola-banāo ṭhumarī*. She was a trendsetter in the evolution of the *ghazal* genre, which later cornered part of the aesthetic space of the *ṭhumarī*.

In the early twentieth century, the *bola-banāo ṭhumarī* entered the mainstream through the musicianship of *khayāla* singers, primarily as a tailpiece. Abdul Kareem Khan [1872-1936], the founder of the Kirana *gharānā* of the *khayāla*, spearheaded this trajectory. He virtually redefined the *ṭhumarī* by taking the erotic, and partially the folk, out of the Benares *bola-banāo ṭhumarī*, and replacing it with an intense poignancy and devotional fervor. He made the *ṭhumarī* respectable in the *khayāla* world. The second and third generations of his lineage continued the dissemination of his style of *ṭhumarī*.

In the generation after him, the Agra *gharānā* titan, Faiyyaz Khan [1886-1950] became immensely popular by adopting the erotic manner of the courtesan's salons in *bola-banāo ṭhumarī* rendition. He also revived the Lucknow style of *bandiśa ṭhumarī*, and gave it an additional lease of life by training his foster-son, Sharafat Hussain [1930-85], as a brilliant exponent of the genre. In the succeeding generation, the brothers from Patiala, Bade Ghulam Ali Khan [1903-68] and Barkat Ali Khan, revolutionized the *bola-banāo* genre with their "Punjab *aṅga*" *ṭhumarī*. Because of greater visibility, Bade Ghulam Ali was the more important of the two.

Like Abdul Kareem Khan, Bade Ghulam Ali came from a *sāraṅgī* background, and exemplified formidable musicianship. His *ṭhumarī*s were rich in ethnic flavours from his native Punjab and the neighbouring Rajasthan, Sindh, Kashmir and the North-West Frontier. He is also credited with popularizing *ṭhumarī*s in *tāla*s other than the traditional *dīpacaṇḍī* [14 beats], by adding *dādarā* [6 beats], *kehervā* [8 beats], and *mughlai* [7 beats] *tāla*s.

Other than Kirana vocalists who adopted the *bola-banāo ṭhumarī* in a big way, the other eminent *khayāla* singers who performed the *ṭhumarī* with great élan around the middle of the century were Vilayat Hussain Khan of Agra [1885-1962], Mushtaq Hussain [1878-1964] of Rampur-Sahaswan, Rehmat Khan of Gwalior [died 1922], and Kesarbai Kerkar of Jaipur-Atrauli [1892-1977]. However, none of them contributed significantly to preserving or enhancing the distinctive identity of the genre. In fact, after Bade Ghulam Ali Khan, the *ṭhumarī* renditions of *khayāla* singers were increasingly criticized for not being sentimental enough. Soon thereafter, the *khayāla* itself started drifting towards a more explicit communication of sentimental values, thus depriving the *ṭhumarī* of its *raison d'être*.

Poetry in Ṭhumarī

The role of the poetic element in *ṭhumarī* is much greater than its role in the *khayāla* genre, but considerably smaller than its role in the *ghazal* genre. The *khayāla* genre can treat the poetic element as a mere textural articulatory element, while the *ghazal* genre demands respect for the autonomous literary quality of the poetry.

Although the *ṭhumarī* revolves around the poetic-melodic axis, the poet-composers have been primarily musicians and only secondarily poets. Except in rare cases, the verse is of mediocre literary value, but an excellent vehicle for musical expression. *Bandiśa ṭhumarī*s of considerable poetic merit are attributed to Lallan Piya [died 1925] and Sanad Piya, two composers from Lucknow. Their compositions are still heard occasionally, but as *khayāla*s.

The great majority of *ṭhumarī* verse is written in Braja *bhāṣā*, the dialect of Hindī spoken in the region around Mathurā. Between the fifteenth and nineteenth centuries, this dialect was the primary literary vehicle of the Hindī-speaking region of the country. Braja *bhāṣā* was also the primary language of the medieval *bhakti* movement, which dominates the literature of the *ṭhumarī* genre. This movement was a rebellion against the stranglehold of the priestly class over the ecclesiastical affairs of the laity. It emphasized a personal God with whom a devotee could establish an emotionally intense relationship without the need for intermediaries. The movement found its most potent vehicle in the legendary romance between Rādhā and her divine paramour, Kṛṣṇa. At an abstract level, this movement came to represent man's spiritual yearnings, with

God symbolizing the active principle and therefore the male principle, and man the passive and female principle.

Early *bhakti* poetry of saints such as Sūrdās, Mīrābaī, Kabīr, Nānak, Jāyasī, and Tulsīdās [fourteenth to seventeenth centuries] had great depth and vitality. In later years [seventeenth to nineteenth centuries] the poetry gave way to artificiality and shallow sensuality. The *ṭhumarī* grew primarily out of the devotional/romantic songs of the *bhakti* cult of this latter period.

Predominantly, *ṭhumarī* poetry belongs to the *śṛṅgāra rasa* — the romantic/erotic sentiment, in the eight-way classification of *rasa* [emotional/sentimental states] in Indian aesthetics. Even within this broad theme, the emphasis is on *viraha*, the pangs of separation from the beloved, and the longing for union. The explicit focus on the man-woman relationship with a female protagonist brings *ṭhumarī* poetry under the purview of the theory of *nāyikā bheda* [Sanskrit for: classification of heroines] in Indian dramaturgy. *Nāyikā bheda* identifies eight different situations in the amorous relationship [10 according to some authorities]. These are not merely academic concepts for the thematic classification of verses, but an active part of the performing tradition. They aid contextual visualization and guide the auto-suggestive and communicative process of the performer, especially when the rendition is accompanied by an element of mime or dance.

The eight basic situational classifications [*aṣṭa-nāyikā*] are:

- *Vasakasajjā*: One dressed up for union with the beloved
- *Virahotkaṇṭhita*: One distressed by separation from the beloved
- *Svadhīnabhartṛkā*: One who dominates her lover/ holds him subservient
- *Kalahāntaritā*: One separated consequent to a quarrel

- *Khaṇḍitā*: One enraged by her lover
- *Vipralabdhā*: One deceived by her lover
- *Proṣitabhartṛkā*: One with a sojourning lover
- *Abhisārikā*: One on her way to a rendezvous with her lover

Texts belonging to the above classifications have been identified in major anthologies of *ṭhumarī* verse. Of the last two categories, instances are rare:

- *Pravatsyātpatikā*: One distressed by news of her lover's departure
- *Āgatapatikā*: One returning joyfully from her lover's abode.

There are, indeed, *ṭhumarī*s that are not classifiable under any of the above situational categories. The romantic aspects get de-emphasized more frequently in *bandiśa ṭhumarī*s in order to accommodate physical imagery required to support choreographic portrayal. Legendary amongst composers of such *ṭhumarī*s was Binda Din Maharaj of Benares [died: 1917].

Rāgas in Ṭhumarī

The melodic framework of the genre derives from a group of relatively undifferentiated modal entities, almost certainly of folk origin. There is, indeed, a group of *rāga*s in Hindustani music which are typically *ṭhumarī rāgas*, although the genre does occasionally deploy a few *rāga*s found in the classical genres. The major *ṭhumarī rāga*s are: Dhāni, Tilaṅg, Śivrañjanī, Bhairavī, Khamāja, Pilū, Ghārā [including its transposed variants, Madhyamse Ghara and Pañcamse Ghara], Zillā, Kāfī, Pahārī, Mañja Khamāja, Mānd, Kauśi-Dhānī, Sindhūra, Jaṅgula and Bihārī. However, two significant *rāga*s of the *ṭhumarī* and allied semi-classical genres — Deśa and Tilaka Kāmod — are also found in the mainstream classical genres. We may add

Jhinjhotī and Bhairavī to this group, though they still remain minor in the mainstream vocal genres.

There is a substantial relationship of tonal geometry and phrasing congruence between several of these *rāga*s, especially Khamāja, Bhairavī and Kāfī, three immensely popular *rāga*s of the genre. This relationship makes it possible for a phrase from one *rāga* to be sung in the other *rāga*s, though with reference to a different scale-base. This creates a recurrence of the same melodic contours/motifs through the genre, makes the genre more accessible, and contributes to its stylistic distinctiveness.

The treatment of the melody in *ṭhumarī* renditions reflects their coherence within well-defined melodic settings many of which have fluid boundaries within their group. Despite the relative informality of grammar, the crossing of boundaries is judicious and tasteful. *Ṭhumarī* rendition is not permitted to degenerate into a *rāga-mālikā*.

Tāla in Ṭhumarī

The nineteenth century *bandiśa ṭhumarī* relied almost entirely on the formal *tīnatāla*. Some *bandiśa ṭhumarī*s were rendered in "Punjābī *tīnatāla*," a dented version with a pronounced swing to it. This version, almost certainly of folk origin, was to later play a bigger role in the *bola-banāo ṭhumarī*. The *bandiśa ṭhumarī* was a genre for the medium to fast tempo, with an explicit rhythmicality. In rendition, it also involved a lively interaction between the poetic-melodic and rhythmic elements. This equation between the different elements changed dramatically as the tempo of the *bandiśa ṭhumarī* decelerated. The *bola-banāo ṭhumarī* took over and drifted closer to folk genres, and the genre itself became a vehicle for overt sentimentalism. Rhythm was now relegated to the back seat.

Cutting through the maze of multiple nomenclatures and multiple versions, and in contemporary language, the *bola-*

banāo ṭhumarī primarily uses *cañcara* or *dīpacaṇḍī* of 14 beats in 3+4+3+4 subdivision, *kehervā* of eight beats in 4+4 subdivision, *dādarā* of six beats in 3+3 subdivision, and *tīnatāla* of 16 beats, rendered in a stylized, or probably folk, manner. This version of *tīnatāla* is, even today, known by several names — *sitārākhanī, addhā, punjābī,* and *qawwālī*. This idiom is an asymmetrical and dented interpretation of the symmetrical [4+4+4+4] subdivision of the *tāla*. The *sitārākhanī/addhā/punjābī/qawwālī,* generally played in medium tempo, interprets the 4-beat subdivision in the *tāla* as an 8-beat subdivision, and renders it with percussion strokes falling on the 1st, 4th and 7th markers of the notionally 8-beat subdivisions. Peter Manuel observes that this interpretation of the *tīnatāla* brings its rhythmic experience remarkably close to the 14-beat *dīpacaṇḍī*.

Amongst the *tāla*s used in the *ṭhumarī* genre, *dādarā* of six beats poses a special problem because this happens also to be the name of a genre of vocal music belonging to the *ṭhumarī* family.

Dādarā, The Genre

Dādarā is currently the only genre in Hindustani music, other than *dhamāra,* which bears the name of the *tāla* in which it is performed. This suggests the primacy of the rhythmic element to its character and aesthetics. Though this is helpful, it does not differentiate it clearly from the *bola-banāo ṭhumarī*. For, the *dādarā* genre itself is not performed exclusively in the *dādarā tāla,* but also in others, all of which are used in *bola-banāo ṭhumarī* — *kahervā* of eight beats, *mughlai* and *rūpaka* both of 7 beats, and a fast *cañcāra/dīpacaṇḍī* of 14 beats.

According to its enthusiasts, the *dādarā* genre does have some distinguishing features. It is performed at a faster tempo than the *bola-banāo ṭhumarī,* and has an explicit rhythmicality in rendition. Both these features are in contrast to the *bola-banāo ṭhumarī,* which is rendered at a leisurely pace and revels in the sentimentality of a subdued rhythmicality. Other clues have been suggested. But, none of them is more categorical. This situation probably leaves the *dādarā* substantially, though not entirely, at the mercy of arbitrary classification.

Ensemble for Ṭhumarī Performances

As a genre of vocal music, divorced from its function as accompaniment for *kathaka* dance, the ensemble for the *ṭhumarī* in the latter half of the twentieth century has been similar to the modern *khayāla* genre. One *tānapūrā*, but occasionally two, as the drone, accompanies the vocalist. Melodic accompaniment is provided either by a *sāraṅgī* or a harmonium player, and percussion accompaniment is the *tabalā*. A supporting vocalist has been encountered less frequently in the *ṭhumarī* than in the *khayāla*.

In the choreographic context, the orchestra is known to include a plucked instrument [*sitāra* or *saroda*], and sometimes also the bamboo flute.

Bandiśa Ṭhumarī: Structure and Rendition

The word *bandiśa*, in this context, denotes a poetic-melodic-rhythmic composition. The name *bandiśa ṭhumarī* suggests two important features — firstly, that it is a tightly composed piece of music, and secondly, that the pre-composed element dominates its rendition. As it evolved independently of the choreographic context, it acquired a substantial improvisatory component, which makes it indistinguishable from a *choṭā khayāla*. By the early twentieth century, when gramophone records arrived in India, the *bola-banāo ṭhumarī* had overshadowed the *bandiśa ṭhumarī* and had also begun to influence its performance. Even the earliest 78-RPM recordings of the genre, therefore, bear no resemblance to the original. The description here relies substantially on secondary sources.

Despite being dominated by the pre-composed element, *bandiśa ṭhumarī*s do not consistently exhibit a high level of originality in their melodic-rhythmic structure, although their poetry is generally of superior literary value than on *bola-banāo ṭhumarī*s. One famous Lucknow composer, Lallan Piya, is known to have set at least fourteen different lyrics to the same melody in *rāga* Kāfī. However, several *bandiśa ṭhumarī*s do exhibit rhythmic cleverness, a feature particularly useful in the choreographic context.

The *bandiśa ṭhumarī* is generally composed in *madhya-laya tīnatāla*. However, compositions in *rūpaka, jhapatāla* and *ekatāla* have also been in practice. The composition is generally in two parts, *sthāyī* and *antarā*. The *sthāyī*, usually of two poetic-melodic lines, is occasionally of three lines. In the shorter *tāla*s, such as *rūpaka* and *jhapatāla*, the *sthāyī* can be longer. The *antarā* is generally at least as long as the *sthāyī*, in most cases two or three poetic-melodic lines. There are also *bandiśa ṭhumarī*s with several *antarā*s, all performed to identical melodic contours.

In the austere format of rendition, the vocalist merely renders each part of the composition several times in sequence and repeatedly, without any improvizations whatsoever, but occasionally at a progressively higher tempo in each successive iteration. In such a rendition, each line may undergo some melodic variations without damaging the integrity of the poetic form, and without straying too far from the melodic contours of the pre-composed form.

In the more elaborate form, the vocalist follows up the rendition of the complete pre-composed form with melodic-rhythmic improvizations upon it in a manner that would challenge the dancer's interpretative skills. This form of *bola-bāṇṭa* or *layakārī* is almost certainly derived from the *dhrupad* genre. An enhancement over this level of improvizations is a duet between the vocalist and the percussionist [or, theoretically, the dancer too] in which the percussionist and/ or the dancer attempt to accompany, anticipate, and even outwit the rhythmic intentions of the vocalist's *bola-bāṇṭa*.

Contemporary *kathaka* maestros, like Birju Maharaj, have performed *bandiśa ṭhumarī*s using *bola-bāṇṭa* as well as *bola-banāo* improvizations. This innovation is still consistent with the text-dominant character of the *ṭhumarī*, and with its original function as accompaniment to interpretative dance.

Bola-banāo Ṭhumarī: Structure and Rendition

The name of this sub-genre suggests its basic features — that the poetic element [*bola*] is the driver of the rendition, and that the rendition concentrates on the emotive and alluring embellishment [*banāo*] of the text. For this reason, the *bola-banāo ṭhumarī* has also been called the *artha-bhāva* [*artha* = meaning + *bhāva* = emotions] *ṭhumarī*. By implication, and by contrast with the *bandiśa ṭhumarī*, the pre-composed element is de-emphasized in the *bola-banāo* sub-genre. The *bola-banāo ṭhumarī* is performed at a much slower tempo than the *bandiśa ṭhumarī*. In the choreographic context, this form was appropriate for dance formats devoid of fast or intricate footwork. By the early twentieth-century, it stabilized at a rendition tempo approximately twice the beat-density of the contemporary *baḍā khayāla*.

The *bola-banāo ṭhumarī* is not a pre-composed entity in the sense of having a stable poetic-melodic-rhythmic shell constituting the nucleus of the rendition. The song-text is stable, though the musician has the freedom to insert exclamatory expressions [e.g., *ho rāma*/O my Lord or *sāvariyā*/ beloved] during rendition, almost at will. The same song-text has been found set to different *rāga*s, and the same poetic-melodic shell has been found sung in different *tāla*s and at different tempi. Even an established poetic-melodic entity is not predictably recognizable beyond the *mukhaḍā*. The rendition of the *mukhaḍā*, generally a four-beat phrase, is syllabic, and sustains a degree of correspondence with the beats of the rhythmic cycle. Other than this, the entire rendition is a free-flowing interaction between poetic, melodic, and rhythmic elements.

The *bola-banāo* song texts are generally more compact than those of the *bandiśa ṭhumarī*. The song-text is in two parts, described as *sthāyī* and *antarā*, more by convention than melodic logic. Unlike a *bandiśa ṭhumarī* or a *khayāla* composition, the two parts of a *bola-banāo ṭhumarī* are not necessarily anchored in different regions of the melodic canvas. In a majority of the cases, the *sthāyī* and *antarā* are both located in the same region of the canvas, with one of them having a slightly broader span than the other. This feature exploits the psycho-acoustics of relative pitch for sharpening the emotional communication of the song-text. Such concentration of poetic, and acoustic energies is appropriate in a genre that is explicitly sentimental in its character.

The format of rendition in *bola-banāo ṭhumarī* follows broadly the following order. The rendition is preceded by a solo [unaccompanied by percussion] free-flowing *ālāpa* of upto two minutes outlining the melodic features of the *rāga*. Thereafter, the *sthāyī* begins with percussion accompaniment. After the *sthāyī* has been rendered a couple of times, the *bola-banāo* improvizations begin. The progress of the improvizations is systematic, though informal. They begin with the lower octave, and progress gradually upwards. When they have reached an appropriate point in the *uttarāṅga*, the *antarā* is rendered. After the *antarā*, there is a *tabalā* solo interlude, called a *laggī*, which is always in the 8-beat *kahervā* or the 16-beat *tīnatāla*, irrespective of the *tāla* in which the *ṭhumarī* is rendered. After the *laggī*, the rendition may either come to a close, or return to the *ṭhumarī* for further *bola-banāo*, and further rounds of *laggī* interludes. Generally, all *bola-banāo* renditions end with a *laggī*.

The stylistic nuances of the *bola-banāo* process owe their character to the salons of the courtesans where the art evolved. In that context, the rendition was erotic allurement with the aim of obtaining the patronage of the wealthiest, handsomest, or otherwise most desirable members of genteel society. Vocalism of such explicitly manipulative intent, when accompanied by the enticement of mime and gesture, corresponded uniquely to the "counterfeit" nature of aesthetic emotion, the artifice that is central to all art.

As described by Peter Manuel, the *bola-banāo* process uses segments of the song-text as a platform for a luxuriant and leisurely melodic ornamentation, with the purpose of making the words come to life. The *ṭhumarī* genre tends to rely heavily on the *kan*, *khaṭakā* and *murkī* type of ornamentations, including strings of *murkī*s resembling the melodic mischief of the *ṭappā*, a genre inspired by the songs of camel drivers from India's north-western regions. Another typically *ṭhumarī* style idiom is the *pukāra* [lit: a cry], which generally leaps from the mid-octave region to the upper tonic, and descends summarily to its starting point. These modes of melodic execution are so intimately associated with the *ṭhumarī* genre, that their use in the *khayāla* genre has been considered inappropriate.

Ṭhumarī in Instrumental Music

Considering the primacy of the poetic element as one of the defining features of the *ṭhumarī* genre, a *ṭhumarī* rendition on the instruments is an apparent contradiction. This is not entirely so because the *ṭhumarī* also represents a distinctive musical style. By adopting its musical elements — *rāga*s, *tāla*s, tempi of rendition, modes of melodic ornamentation, composition formats, and improvizational conventions — instrumental music has developed a "*ṭhumarī* style," which is sufficiently distinct from the *dhrupad* and *khayāla* inspired idioms in instrumental music. As a result, there has emerged a distinctive *ṭhumarī* style in instrumental music, which may possess greater vitality today than the *ṭhumarī* as a vocal genre.

The *ṭhumarī* genre has had the most profound influence on the idiom of the *sitāra* and the *saroda*, the two instruments that rose to prominence in eighteenth and nineteenth century Lucknow, the home of the *kathaka-ṭhumarī* renaissance. The *sitāra* inherited its original idiom from the *rudra vīṇā*, the primary instrument of the medieval *dhrupad* genre. However, while the *rudra vīṇā* could support only unidirectional strokes, the *sitāra* enables bi-directional strokes. In the early stages of developing its own idiom, the *sitāra* developed the slow-tempo Masit Khani composition format, named after Masit Khan, a Delhi-based sitārist. However, being ergonomically superior to the *rudra vīṇā*, the *sitāra* was in search of an agile idiom. Ghulam Raza Khan, a late eighteenth century Lucknow sitārist, developed such an idiom by a direct and immensely successful transposition of the *bandiśa ṭhumarī* composition format onto the stroke pattern of the *sitāra*.

The nascent *saroda*, an important part of the Lucknow court under Nawab Wajid Ali Shah, had already inherited a bi-directional stroke pattern from its ancestor, the *rabāba*. Thus, along with the slow tempo Masit Khani format, the *sitāra* and the *saroda* came to adopt the medium-to-fast tempo Raza Khani format as standard repertoire. Although both instruments have considerably diversified their repertoire in the twentieth century, the Masit Khani and Raza Khani formats remain, to this day, the mainstays of *sitāra* and *saroda* music.

The flowering of the *ṭhumarī* style in the music of the plucked instruments is attributed to the lineage of Ustad Sahebdad Khan, the great grandfather of the contemporary sitārist, Ustad Vilayat Khan [born 1928]. Sahebdad Khan was a *sāraṅgī* exponent and a *khayāla* singer, who commenced the family's mastery over the plucked instruments — the *sitāra* and the *surbahāra*. The earliest recordings of Raza Khani format *ṭhumarī* on the *sitāra* are those of his son, Ustad Imdad Khan [1848-1920], followed in later years by his grandson, Ustad Enayet Khan [1894-1938].

The execution of the vocal idiom on the *sitāra* reached its highest level of sophistication in the hands of Ustad Enayet Khan's son, Ustad Vilayat Khan, who has not only adopted and adapted compositions from both the *ṭhumarī* sub-genres, but also successfully captured their musical experience in entirety, across all movements. The totality of his "*ṭhumarī* experience" also gains a lot from his brilliant vocalization of *bola-banāo* along with its rendition on the *sitāra*. Ustad Vilayat Khan's *ṭhumarī*-inspired idiom has been imitated by a host of *sitāra* and *saroda* players not only of his own stylistic lineage but also of the rival lineages.

The other major instrument to be influenced by the *ṭhumarī* genre was the *sāraṅgī*, which had become the standard accompaniment to the *ṭhumarī* as well as the *khayāla* by the nineteenth century. The *sāraṅgī* player has been an important link between the worlds of *ṭhumarī* and *khayāla* which, in any event, have never been totally isolated from each other. However, economic considerations probably drove the *sāraṅgī* player much closer to the world of courtesans, and consequently towards a stylistic bias towards the *ṭhumarī*. As a result, the austere *dhrupad* genre almost ignored the *sāraṅgī*, while many a competent *sāraṅgī* player has been disqualified from accompanying even *khayāla* singers. These reservations are, however, immaterial in the context of a *sāraṅgī* solo. As a soloist, a *sāraṅgī* player can do greater justice to a *ṭhumarī* rendition than any other instrumentalist, and is acceptable if his *khayāla* renderings admit an ornate sense of melodic design resembling the *ṭhumarī*.

The *ṭhumarī* genre has also partially inspired the content and style of *śehnāyī* music, largely because of the towering influence of Ustad Bismillah Khan, who hails from Benares, the home of the *bola-banāo ṭhumarī*. Being a ceremonial instrument which addresses an involuntary audience of indeterminable profile, the *śehnāyī* came to acquire a repertoire dominated by folk and regional music. When Bismillah Khan raised the *śehnāyī* to the status of a concert instrument, he also made the *dādarā, kajarī, caitī*, and *fāguna* songs of the Benares region an integral part of *śehnāyī* repertoire. Appropriate to the concert hall, he developed an improvizational idiom inspired by the *bola-banāo* family of songs. *Śehnāyī* players all over the country adopted this style until the regional and folk music of other parts of India began to compete with Bismillah's Benares for a place in *śehnāyī* repertoire.

Like the *śehnāyī*, though to a far lesser degree, the *bāṅsurī* [the bamboo flute], has conceded a significant place to the *ṭhumarī* and other semi-classical genres in its repertoire. This pattern is attributed to the phenomenal musicianship of two maestros, Pannalal Ghosh [1911-62] and Hariprasad Chaurasia [born 1938]. Ghosh tended to perform *bola-banāo ṭhumarī*s more frequently in the traditional *dīpacaṇḍī* [*cañcara*], while Chaurasia has an affinity for *kehervā, rūpaka* and *dādarā*.

The Ṭhumarī Today

Although the *ṭhumarī* remains an integral part of *kathaka* dance, the limits of the present author's competence oblige him to restrict this contemporary appraisal to its status as an independent genre of vocal music.

At the time of this writing [July 2003], the genre can claim only two vocalists of stature — Girija Devi [born 1929] and Shobha Gurtu [1925-2004] — who are exclusively devoted to the practice of the Benares tradition of *ṭhumarī* and its allied genres, such as *dādarā, caitī, kajarī*, etc. No heirs to their mantle are yet visible on the horizon.

Amongst the leading *khayāla* exponents, the notables amongst fine performers of the *bola-banāo ṭhumarī*, are Pt. Bhimsen Joshi [born 1922] Ustad Niyaz Ahmed Khan [1928-2002], Parveen Sultana [born 1948] and Prabha Atre [born 1932]. The *bandiśa ṭhumarī*, interestingly, appears to be experiencing a minor revival. The younger male vocalists, like Rashid Khan, Ulhas Kashalkar, and Ajoy Chakravarty perform *bandiśa ṭhumarī*s with great competence, distinguishing them astutely from the *choṭā khayāla*. Female vocalists of the younger generation have virtually abandoned the *ṭhumarī* genre altogether. This is important because, on the *khayāla* platform, women now outnumber men several times over.

On probabilistic reckoning, no more than one in twenty vocal music concerts in contemporary Hindustani music ends with either a *bandiśa ṭhumarī* or a *bola-banāo ṭhumarī*. Around the middle of the twentieth century, the *ṭhumarī*'s share of the tailpiece position was at least five times greater than it is today. With the complete concert of semi-classical music revolving around the *ṭhumarī* having disappeared long ago, and its presence on the *khayāla* platform having shrunk dramatically, the *ṭhumarī* appears to be faced with extinction.

When we encounter such a situation, it is appropriate to look at the genre from two angles — as an occupant of a specific niche in the concert repertoire, and as an occupant of a well-defined aesthetic space. Both these issues are relevant to considering *ṭhumarī* in the present-day context.

Two factors have predominantly influenced the emergence of *ṭhumarī* substitutes in the tailpiece position — the de-emphasis of the romantic/erotic element in the concert hall context, and emergence of western state of Maharashtra as the home of *khayāla* vocalism. The state has a rich regional tradition of literature and music, with which classical musicians have, traditionally, maintained a strong link. Maharashtrian musicians have a relatively lower level of empathy with the language and stylistic values of the *ṭhumarī*, both of which are inseparably linked with the ethnicity of a small part of Hindī speaking India. It is therefore natural that a poetry-driven musical genre like the *ṭhumarī* would appear less attractive to Maharashtrian vocalists than viable alternatives.

Interestingly, the younger male vocalists who are reviving the *bandiśa ṭhumarī*, are all based in Kolkata, which has a long-standing relationship with the *ṭhumarī* because of Wajid Ali Shah's exile in that city a century and a half ago.

Because of Maharashtra's dominance over the *khayāla* platform, the tailpiece position has increasingly been taken up by classicist renderings of *bhajanas* [devotional songs] composed by the major poets of the *bhakti* movement, by folk devotional genres from Maharashtra such as *abhaṅgas* and *kīrtanas*, and semi-classical songs from the Marāṭhī theatre, called *nāṭya saṅgīta*. Most of these *ṭhumarī*-substitutes possess some features of either the *bola-banāo* or the *bandiśa ṭhumarīs*, and fill a part of the aesthetic space earlier occupied by the *ṭhumarī*. None of them, however, occupies the entire aesthetic space of the *ṭhumarī*. This is to be expected, because the *ṭhumarī* was a unique product of a unique environment in a bygone era, and is probably unsustainable, in its original form, in the present-day context.

However, the aesthetic space the *ṭhumarī* occupied cannot disappear with the eclipse of the genre. The space exists, but can apparently not be occupied by a single genre. The encroachment into this space began around the middle of the last century when the Benares *bola-banāo* tradition was in full bloom, and originated from the classical as well as the light music ends. Starting with Bade Ghulam Ali Khan, *khayāla* vocalism moved towards a libertarian approach to architecture, an ornate sense of sculpture and ornamentation. In a sense, he was the forerunner of the romantic brigade — Kumar Gandharva, Kishori Amonkar, and Pt. Jasraj — who rebelled against either the formalism of the *khayāla*, or its aloofness, or both, thus driving the classicist genre closer to the emotional expressiveness of the *ṭhumarī*.

The other significant encroachment of the *ṭhumarī*'s aesthetic space came from the *ghazal* end, with Begum Akhtar as its high priestess. Inspired by her music, Jagjit Singh, Mehdi Hassan, along with several others, substantially widened the scope of melodic improvisation in *ghazal* rendition and raised it to a level of sophistication comparable to a *ṭhumarī*. However, the subsequent generations of *ghazal* singers have impoverished the genre in terms of melody as well as the poetry. The implications of this vacation of the *ṭhumarī* space by the *ghazal* are too early to ascertain.

The instrumental manifestations of *ṭhumarī* aesthetics appear to be in good health. However, they cannot substantially alter our assessment of the health of a text-dominant romanticist genre. Without the benefit of a crystal ball, the *ṭhumarī* today appears as nearly extinct as *dhrupad* did half a century ago. This may precisely be the issue. As *dhrupad* itself proved, genres of music do not simply vanish. They merely go underground, transform themselves, and surface again to reclaim audiences. When conditions are favourable, the *ṭhumarī* might have a good chance of doing so.

4.4

INTRODUCTION TO THE ṬAPPĀ*

LIKE the *ṭhumarī*, the *ṭappā* is a modern semi-classical genre of folk derivation, which flowered in Lucknow and Benares. However, while the *ṭhumarī* evolved from the cultural manifestations of the *bhakti* movement around Mathurā-Vṛndāvan, the *ṭappā* owes its inspiration to the songs of camel drivers in Punjab and India's North-Western Frontiers. The acceptance of the genre in genteel society by the late seventeenth century appears to have been synchronous with that of the *ṭhumarī*. Although the genre was practised by lineages of *kathakas*, and by courtesans, it gained early acceptance amongst *dhrupad* and *khayāla* vocalists. As a result, the genre has escaped the social stigma that the *ṭhumarī* and its allied genres had to endure before semi-classical music entered the concert platform.

The pioneering role in the refinement of the folk idiom into a stylized genre is attributed to one Shorie Miya, whose signature appears at the end of many popular *ṭappā* compositions. "Shorie" was, apparently, the name of the wife of the *ṭappā* innovator, Ghulam Nabi, the son of Ghulam Rasool, an eminent *khayāla* vocalist in the employ of Nawab Asafuddaula [reign 1775-97] of Awadh [Lucknow]. Ghulam Nabi was trained in *khayāla* vocalism, but did not have a voice suitable for the genre. He apparently travelled extensively in Punjab, mastered the *ṭappā* idiom, and matured it enough to return to Lucknow, and achieve distinction at the Awadh court. The genre continued to enjoy the patronage of the Awadh rulers during the reign of the *kathaka-ṭhumarī* enthusiast, Wajid Ali Shah [1822-87].

Thereafter, it has had a trajectory similar to the *ṭhumarī*. It struck roots in Lucknow and Benares, acquired a significant following in eastern India probably through Wajid Ali's entourage in exile, and established itself as a companion to *khayāla* vocalism. In present times, though performances of the *ṭappā* are none too frequent, the genre appears to have withstood the pressures of the *khayāla*-dominated environment better than the *ṭhumarī*.

Historical Outline

This outline relies on the biographical sketches included in the epic work *Indian Music*, by Dr. Thakur Jaydev Singh [1st edn., Premlata Sharma, ed.], and a paper presented by Prof. Rohit Desai, archivist of Nadiad [Gujarat] at the Faculty of Performing Arts, Baroda University, in January 2003. The clues and links are far from categorical. However, some patterns can be discerned.

Shorie Miya [Ghulam Nabi] had four significant disciples: Prasiddhu Maharaj, Miya Gammu or Gammu Khan, Tarachand, and Mir Ali Saheb. Gammu Khan's son, Sadi Khan [Sadiq Khan?], and Babu Ramsahay [died 1850], another eminent *ṭappā* singer, taught one Prasiddhu Maharaj, a member of the *kathaka* community — unlikely to be the same Prasiddhu tutored by Shorie Miya — who together with his brother Manohar Maharaj, founded the Prasiddhu-Manohar lineage. Like several lineages of *ṭappā* singers, this lineage claimed significant musicianship in the mainstream genres of vocal music but, as an exception, also instrumental music. Prasiddhu's great-grandson, Ramkrishna Mishra taught and performed in Calcutta till 1955.

Gammu Khan's son, Sadi Khan/Sadiq Khan left Lucknow to settle in Benares, thus making the city an early partner in the evolution of the genre. His presence encouraged the leading courtesans of the era to master the art. The Prasiddhu-Manohar lineage also originated in the city, and made a significant contribution to the propagation of the *ṭappā*. Throughout the nineteenth and twentieth centuries, the courtesans of Benares remained important repositories of the *ṭappā* art. Of great importance to the surviving *ṭappā* tradition of Benares are the names of Bade Ramdasji [born 1896], a *khayāla* singer, who trained several famous twentieth-century vocalists in the *ṭappā*.

The *ṭappā* entered the Gwalior *khayāla* lineage fairly early in its history. Natthan Peer Baksh [early nineteenth century], the founder of the Gwalior lineage, apparently studied the *ṭappā* with Shakkar Khan and Makkhan Khan, two famous disciples of Shorie Miya's father, Ghulam Rasool. Natthan Peer Baksh' grandsons, Haddu Khan and Hassu Khan [died 1859], apparently adopted the *ṭappā* into the *gharānā*'s repertoire. Haddu Khan's son, Rehmat Khan [died 1922], was a formidable *ṭappā* singer. Haddu Khan's son-in-law, Inayet Hussain Khan, founder of the Sahaswan-Rampur *gharānā* of the *khayāla*, and his heirs, Mushtaq Hussain and Nissar Hussain, were also eminent *ṭappā* performers.

Hassu Khan's disciples, Devji Buwa, and Raoji Buwa perpetuated the *ṭappā* tradition in the Gwalior lineage. In the succeeding generation, Balkrishna Buwa Ichalkaranjikar brought the *ṭappā* into the *khayāla* mainstream in Maharashtra, while Narayan Buwa Phaltankar introduced the *ṭappā* style to the performance of *abhaṅga*s [Marāṭhī devotional songs]. With their contribution, the *ṭappā* genre struck deep roots in the cultural soil of Maharashtra. The Gwalior *khayāla* lineage values its *ṭappā* repertoire as a means of cultivating exceptional vocal agility. Gwalior vocalists worked closely with musicologist, V.N. Bhatkhande, to document *ṭappā* songs, thus contributing to the stature of the genre as also its survival.

Through the nineteenth century, Lucknow remained active in the *ṭappā* genre, with Nawab Hussain Khan [died early nineteenth century], and Chhajju Khan [died 1870] on record as great practitioners of the art. In the late nineteenth century, eastern India exhibited great enthusiasm for the genre, with the performing and scholarly contributions of Gopeshwar Bannerji of Vishnupur [born 1878], Raja Sourendra Mohan Tagore of Jorasanko [1840-1914], and Bholanath Bhatt of Darbhanga [1891-1971]. Gwalior also remained an important centre of the *ṭappā* well into the twentieth century, with Balasaheb Guruji [died 1919] and his disciple Nanu Bhaiyya Telang [died 1948] distinguishing themselves.

According to Prof. Rohit Desai, approximately 100 *ṭappā* recordings have been published in the twentieth century. A limited discography identifies some of the most significant *ṭappā* singers of recent times. [Desai, Rohit, and Mehta Sharadchandra: *Ṭhumarī, dādarā, horī, caitī & kajarī*, A selective discography, Indian Musicological Society, Baroda, 1990]. Though the document does not claim to be comprehensive, it gives a reasonable picture of the *ṭappā* scene. The overwhelming majority of the named *ṭappā* singers are specialist singers of the semi-classical genres: Badi Motibai, Doanni Jaan, Girija Devi, Hiradevi Mishra, Rasulan Bai, Savita Devi, Siddheshwari Devi, Vidyadhari Bai, and Shobha Gurtu. The few *khayāla* singers named in the discography are Yunus Husain Khan [Agra], Mushtaq Hussain Khan [Rampur-Sahaswan], and Sharafat Hussain Khan [Agra].

Salient Stylistic Features

The identifying feature of the *ṭappā* is a vivacious, and even mischievous, treatment of melody. The melody is not only naughty within itself, but also in relation to the beats of the rhythmic cycle, and occasionally even rhythmically clever. The bouncy ethnicity of *ṭappā* melody has often been compared to a ride on the back of a camel. This interpretation of the camel-driver's song has intuitive appeal, even if its oblique attempt at explaining the melodic features of the genre is not convincing.

The primary devices for achieving the melodic effervescence of the *ṭappā* are strings of intricate symmetric phrases creating brisk *ṭāna*-like passages, and *gītakīrī*, coupled with dramatic twists and turns, and frequent shifts in *svara*-density between melodic lines and sets of phrases. A *ṭappā* is so distinct a musical experience that it is easy to identify it with minimal familiarity, though difficult to describe. As a starting point for the entirely unfamiliar, a *ṭappā* may be described as an impish rendition of a *choṭā* [*druta*] *khayāla*, but considerably more puckish than a *bandiśa ṭhumarī*.

*Ṭappā*s are composed mainly in *ṭhumarī rāga*s, such as Bhairavī, Khamāja, Deśa, Kāfī, Jhinjhotī, Pilū, Barwā. They are generally set to 16-beat variants of the *tīnatāla*, such as *addhā*, *qawwālī* and *sitārakhanī*. A few *ṭappā*s have also been composed in *ekatāla*. In *ekatāla* as well as *tīnatāla*, *ṭappā*s are sung in medium tempo. This tempo is mandated by the need for the genre's simultaneous indulgence in melodic and melodic-rhythmic playfulness. The lyrics are mostly in Punjābī or Sindhī, the languages of the north-west, and centred around the tragic romance of Hīra and Rāñjhā, an important part of the folklore of the Punjab region. Shorie Miya, however, enlarged the thematic content of *ṭappā* lyrics, and included general romantic themes, as also philosophical themes in his *ṭappā*s. Compositions sporting the signature of "Shorie" Miya are still the most popular, though the genre has benefited from the contributions of several composers thereafter.

Because of its accent on complex melody, the *ṭappā* cannot accord any significance to its poetic element. *Ṭappā* lyrics are short — either two lines or two stanzas with two short lines each — and simple. As in *khayāla bandiśa*s, the two sections are anchored in different regions of the melodic canvas, and function as *sthāyī* and *antarā*. Many *ṭappā* songs also have a melodically distinct *mañjha* section between the *sthāyī* and the *antarā*. A *ṭappā* is generally rendered relying only on the poetic-melodic form as the basic material. *Ākāra tāna*s and *bola-bāṇṭa/layakārī* of the *khayāla* variety, occasionally also found in *bandiśa ṭhumarī*s, are not found in the *ṭappā*. Its *bola-tāna*s have no identity independent of the lyrics. They are dominated by symmetry, and eschew other melodic patterns typical of *khayāla*.

The symmetry of *ṭappā tāna*s is typically expressed in overlapping ascending or descending waves of phrases. Examples in Bhairavī: Descending: *ni-sā-re-sā-ni-dhā, dhā-ni-sā-ni-dhā-pā, pā-dhā-ni-dhā-pā-mā, mā-pā-dhā-pā-mā-gā*. Ascending: *gā-re-re-sā-re, mā-gā, gā-re-gā, pā-mā-mā-gā-mā, dhā-pā-pā-mā-pā*. This symmetrical pattern may sometimes include shifts of *svara* density. A consistent feature enhancing the knotted character of *ṭappā* passages is the looped or bi-directional phrases used to build the melody. This feature is best exploited in highly malleable *rāga*s like Bhairavī, and Kāfī, where intricate phrasing within short melodic spans can help create bewildering and even stunning effects. The demands of lithe melodic execution may explain why, only one *khayāla gharānā* has taken to the *ṭappā* in a significant way, and, other than this, the genre has been the preserve of female singers.

As a challenge to musicianship, the *ṭappā* tests the agility of the vocalization mechanism, and the fertility of the melodic imagination. Less obviously, though more meaningfully, the *ṭappā* also tests the vocalist's command over *rāga* grammar and the rhythmic element. A *ṭappā* singer is required to use the laxity of grammar in *ṭhumarī rāgas* and the melodic freedom granted by the genre to establish the character of the genre. But, this has to be achieved without letting the basic *rāga*-ness of the *rāga* recede out of focus. The demands on the rhythmic skill arise from the pattern of melodic structuring typical of the genre. Once a *tāna* pattern has been commenced, it has to be carried through at least two more symmetric iterations in different regions of the melodic canvas before the improvization can return to the pre-composed shell of the rendition. The dovetailing of intricate *tāna* clusters with the *bandiśa* requires consummate rhythmic skill.

Although the *ṭappā* apparently relied on the *bandiśa ṭhumarī* and the *choṭā khayāla* for its format, it has, in turn, influenced the *khayāla* genre by giving birth to a hybrid form, the *ṭap-khayāla*. This form is normally rendered in the "classical" *rāgas*, but has the distinct vivacity of the *ṭappā* in its treatment of melody. *Ṭap-khayālas* enjoy considerable stature because of their demanding aesthetics, and are performed in several *gharānās* of *khayāla* vocalism.

The Ṭappā Today

The presence of the *ṭappā* on the contemporary concert platform is slightly better than that of the *ṭhumarī*. While their relative relegation to the background may have some common features and causes, the *ṭappā* can be viewed individually.

The major repository of *ṭappā* musicianship was the courtesan tradition of Benares, which specialized in the semi-classical genres such as the *ṭhumarī, dādarā, caitī* and *kajarī*, along with the allied folk-based genres of the region. This tradition was a unique product of its environment and its times, and has been speeding towards extinction, taking the *ṭappā* along with it.

The other significant repository of *ṭappā* musicianship is the Gwalior *khayāla gharānā*. From the second quarter of the twentieth century — after Omkarnath Thakur — this *gharānā* was unable to produce front-ranking musicians. In an effort to re-invent itself, it drifted towards the aggressive, rhythm-oriented, vocalism of the Agra *gharānā*. One of the results of the Gwalior-Agra confluence was the gradual disappearance of the *ṭappā* from Gwalior repertoire. Traditional Gwalior vocalism is all but extinct. The *khayāla gharānā*s, which gained ascendancy in the post-Independence era — primarily Kirana and Jaipur-Atrauli — ignored the *ṭappā* in favour of either the *ṭhumarī* or *bhajana*s. Bengal, once an important *ṭappā* centre, is yet to produce front-ranking vocalists with any interest in the *ṭappā*.

On the contemporary platform, the *ṭappā* qualifies primarily as a tailpiece to a *khayāla* rendition, as an alternative to a *ṭhumarī*. The dominance of the *khayāla* platform by vocalists from Maharashtra has caused this role to be handed over to *bhajana*s and *nāṭya saṅgīta*. One of the keys to this phenomenon, though not a major key, may be that *ṭappā* lyrics are written in Punjābī or Sindhī, languages understood by even fewer people than Braja *bhāṣā*, the language of the *ṭhumarī*.

Despite its limitations, several features suggest a better chance for the *ṭappā*'s survival than that of the *ṭhumarī*. The poetic element plays a far smaller role in the aesthetics of the *ṭappā* compared to the *ṭhumarī*, or even the *khayāla*. In addition, the *ṭappā* is not sentimental in its treatment of the melody. *Ṭappā* melody relies on vocal technique and melodic imagination, and not the communication of cultural meaning through poetry. To this extent, the *ṭappā* is probably less "parochial" than the *ṭhumarī*. Because of Ṭappā's excessively ornate treatment of melody, *khayāla*, the dominant mainstream genre, cannot encroach upon the *ṭappā*'s territory as easily as it could upon the *ṭhumarī*. Nor can the poetry-dominant genres like the *ghazal* compete for its aesthetic space from the other end. The revival of the genre, therefore, depends more on the interest of musicians and the acceptance of the genre by contemporary audiences. Indicators of these factors deserve attention.

The current scene can claim the towering presence of Girija Devi [born 1929], and Shobha Gurtu [1925-2004] as specialists of the semi-classical genres who have excelled at *ṭappā* rendition. Amongst established *khayāla* vocalists, the significant *ṭappā* exponents are Laxman Krishnarao Pandit [born 1932] and Malini Rajurkar [born 1941]. This picture looks dismal. But if we look for a ray of hope, Manjiri Asnare-Kelkar [born 1971], a successful *khayāla* vocalist, is reviving a constituency for the *ṭappā*.

Her induction into the genre is interesting. Manjiri belongs to a thoroughbred Maharashtrian family, and had her initial training in the Gwalior tradition. Early in her grooming, she became a fan of Malini Rajurkar, especially of her *ṭappā* renderings. She acquired all available *ṭappā* recordings of Malini, painstaking took down notations, verified lyrics with published sources, and started performing them with great success [interview with the author on 5 May 2003]. She later became a disciple of Madhusudan Kanetkar, the Jaipur-Atrauli *gharānā* stalwart, who studied the *ṭappā* specially to be able to help her organize and polish her renditions.

These may be unorthodox conditions for the continuity of a genre, and this individual case might be no more than a straw in the wind. But, Manjiri's success with the *ṭappā* confirms several promising features of the genre. Most of all, it establishes its "non-parochial" character, the possibility of acquiring respectable proficiency without expert supervision, and the genre's continued appeal amongst audiences. These factors justify greater optimism for the *ṭappā* than for the *ṭhumarī*.

PART V

The Major Instruments

5.1

THE RUDRA VĪṆĀ*

RUDRA vīṇā [commonly called the *bīna*] is an instrument of entirely Indian origin and considerable antiquity. It is revered because of its association with Rudra [Lord Śiva], the Originator of the performing arts. According to legend Śiva created the instrument inspired by the reclining image of Pārvatī, his Divine Consort. A categorical description of Lord Śiva's craftsmanship is not available from mythological texts. Nevertheless, the instrument now called the *rudra vīṇā*, has inherited the legend, and its magical beliefs have been acceptable to several mystical cults — Hindu as well as Moslem. This feature of the *bīna* may be attributed partly to Śiva as an archetype, but largely to the *bīna*'s design and ergonomics.

The neuro-acoustics of *bīna* playing are well documented in the Indian mystical tradition. Such phenomena arise from the experience of intimate physical contact between the instrument and the musician during the act of playing. In the traditional posture, the *bīna* has a larger part of its body in contact with the musician's body than any other Indian instrument — touching the temple above the left shoulder, across the torso, and under the right armpit. And, each instrument is tailor-made to achieve a perfect fit to the musician's dimensions. As a result of this intimacy of contact, the vibrations generated in the act of playing on the *bīna* are magnified by the instrument, and transmitted back to the musician's body at critical neurological centres. The musician is thus a recipient of the physical vibrations of the *bīna*, along with its acoustic output. At its best, *bīna* music enables the musician to enter a trance-like state, which falls broadly within the category of mystical/religious experiences.

By organological classification, the *bīna* belongs to the fretted stick zither family of chordophones, fast heading for extinction on the Indian subcontinent. It is the progenitor of the idiom of the plucked lutes — fretless as well as fretted — which succeeded it as vehicles of the Indian art-music tradition. From the point of view of Indian organology, therefore, the distinction between the stick zithers and the plucked lutes is insignificant.

Organology

According to the organologist, Deva [B.C. Deva], India has a long tradition of stick zithers in art, as well as folk music. The tradition goes back to the *ghoṣaka* and the *ekatantrī vīṇā*, both single-string, single-gourd, fretless instruments documented from the fifth century AD. Like the modern *bīna*, the *ekatantrī*, first named in eleventh-century texts, was a revered instrument, being often called *bramha vīṇā* — associated with Brahmā, the Creator. The *ekatantrī* required the sound to be activated by right-hand plucking, and the melody to be executed by the left hand stopping of the string at different points along the bamboo stem with a small piece of bamboo. This instrument is considered the forerunner of contemporary fretless zithers such as the *vicitra vīṇā* [*batta bīna*] in Hindustani music, and the *goṭṭu vādyam* in Carnatic music.

The addition of frets to fretless zithers is believed to have taken place around the eleventh century AD. This development gave rise to the *kinnarī vīṇā* with multiple gourds as chamber resonators. The *kinnarī vīṇā* came in two forms — the *bṛhat* [major] *kinnarī* with three gourds, and the *laghu* [minor] *kinnarī* with two gourds. The fretted, twin-gourd, *laghu kinnarī* is now considered the direct parent of the *bīna*. Having evolved in the twelfth or thirteenth centuries, the *bīna* is a creation of the middle ages, whose art has evolved over less than a millennium.

History

The art of the *bīna* is associated with the *dhrupad* genre of art music. The *bīna* originally accompanied vocal *dhrupad* recitals. The content of their music thus came to be identical in melodic and rhythmic respects, as also in the philosophy of music making. It was common, amongst families of musicians, for the children to be groomed in the vocal as well *bīna* arts, the choice of profession being left to their individual predispositions. But the two arts also evolved their independent performing domains, which allowed both to express their respective endowments. By virtue of being companion arts, they influenced each other in a meaningful way.

The *bīna*'s most glorious period was the reign of the Mogul Emperor, Akbar [sixteenth century]. Historian, Abul Fazal, mentions Shihab Khan and Purbin Khan as the pre-eminent *bīnakāra*s [exponents of the *bīna*] in Akbar's court. Other prominent *bīnakāra*s of the era were Bilas Khan and Imrat Sen, both sons of the legendary Tānsen, his daughter Sarasvati, and Misri Singh, his son-in-law. Of these four, Imrat Sen and Misri Singh perpetuated the art of the *bīna*, while the others developed the art of the *rabāba*, forerunner of the modern *saroda*. In later years, thus, the legacy of the *bīna* emerged as the foundation of the arts of all plucked lutes.

Dhrupad and the *bīna* started losing ground in the late eighteenth century when the decaying Mogul Empire prompted leading musicians to drift away from Delhi and its neighbourhood in search of alternative patronage. This exposed them to diverse stylistic environments, many of which were already being swept by the achievements of the rival *khayāla* genre.

Vocal music having been the traditional reference point for instrumental music, the *khayāla* wave began to make a different set of stylistic demands on the art of the plucked instruments. The *bīna* was unsuited for the melodic agility of post-*dhrupad* music. By this time, the *sitāra* was beginning to fill the vacuum, but was not yet acoustically sophisticated enough to challenge the *bīna*, especially in the leisurely rendition of the low-density melody, principally the *ālāpa*. To compete effectively with the *bīna*, sitārists devised the *surabahāra* [around 1825], an instrument which combined the acoustic richness of the *bīna* with the ergonomic features of the *sitāra*. This instrument could handle the *dhrupad*-style *ālāpa*, and also enable a transition from *dhrupad* to post-*dhrupad* stylistics. This led to the emergence of a multiple-instrument presentation format in the music of the fretted lutes — an elaborate *ālāpa* on the *surabahāra* followed by post-*dhrupad* compositions on the *sitāra*. As a solo instrument, the *bīna* ultimately succumbed to this challenge. Simultaneously, the decline of *dhrupad* vocalism was shrinking the *bīna*'s presence as an accompanist.

Around the same time, and responding to an urge similar to the development of the *surabahāra* by sitāraists, *rabāba* players developed the *surasiṅgāra*, a cumbersome hybrid between the *rabāba* and the *bīna*. In terms of physical construction, several variants are reported [Allyn Miner, 1997]. The most prominent amongst them was an instrument that had a lower gourd similar to the *surabahāra*, a finger-board like the *rabāba*, and an upper gourd similar to the *bīna*. But, unlike the *rabāba*, the *surasiṅgāra* had a metallic finger board, and used metallic strings. [Miner, *ibid*.]. By the early twentieth century, the *surasiṅgāra* had acquired an enviable following in terms of stature, though small in numbers. *Surasiṅgāra* recordings of

Alauddin Khan, Radhika Mohan Maitra, and B.K. Roychaudhury demonstrate the technical success at transferring the *bīna*'s acoustic richness and melodic potential to the *rabāba* family of instruments. But, once again, the ergonomic demands of post-*dhrupad* music triumphed. The *rabāba* quickly adopted the most promising features of the *surasiṅgāra* — the metallic fingerboard and metal strings — and re-engineered itself acoustically to transform itself into the *saroda*, driving the *surasiṅgāra* into history. The *bīna* thus became the grandfather of the *saroda*, yet another plucked lute to fill the vacuum it created.

Starting from the mid-nineteenth century, a majority of the lineages of *dhrupad* music diverted their energies to the *khayāla* genre. Simultaneously, there was a decline in the art of the *bīna*, as its practitioners bequeathed it to the emerging arts of the modern plucked lutes — the *sitāra*, the *surabahāra*, *surasiṅgāra*, and the *saroda*. The decline of the *bīna* was dramatic after Independence [1947] which dispossessed the feudal aristocracy, a part of which had continued to support *dhrupad* and the *bīna* in their sunset years.

In the early years after Independence, the *dhrupad* genre was frequently described as "a museum piece." This description was more appropriate to the *bīna*, than to the vocal art. For the *bīna* art, however, the transition from *dhrupad* to post-*dhrupad* music was unachievable, and *bīnakāras* were forced to make a living as vocalists or as performers and teachers of *sitāra*, *saroda* and *surabahāra*. This changed once Western Europe warmed up to *dhrupad* in the mid-1960s.

In the 1980s, after the vocal *dhrupad* genre had acquired an enthusiastic following abroad, the market for the *bīna* was cultivated by Asad Ali Khan, and Zia Mohiuddin Dagar, both scions of distinguished *dhrupad* lineages. Both performed extensively in the Europe and the US, and broke the traditional barrier to teaching the art beyond ties of kinship. Their acceptance of European and American students also laid the foundation of a self-propagating constituency for the *bīna* in the west. *Dhrupad* thus became a unique phenomenon in art music — losing ground in its home and flourishing amongst alien audiences.

At the moment of this writing, the vocal art of *dhrupad* boasts of a small group of vocalists who are credible musicians at home, but dependent largely on the Western market for their livelihood. Compared to *dhrupad* vocalists, the number of practitioners of the *bīna* is negligible. Asad Ali Khan, the seniormost contemporary *bīnakāra*, foresees extinction for the *bīna* art unless job opportunities are created in India for its practitioners [Interview with Utpal Bannerjee, *Sruti*, Issue 217, October 2002].

Design

The *bīna* is an instrument of simple construction with a tubular stem acting as the column resonator, and two large dried gourds attached towards its two ends functioning as chamber resonators.

Traditionally, the stem was made of bamboo. Asad Ali Khan reports that fastening the gourds to the bamboo stem was a highly skilled task because the two gourds had to bear the entire weight of the instrument, and withstand the tension of the musician virtually wrestling with it. The bamboo stem was originally polished with wax, and decorated with painted or inlay work in gold. Bamboo stems, however, had a limited life because they tended to split in a couple of years, thus weakening the acoustic output. [Interview with the author on 11 January 2000] Bamboo was later replaced with *śīśama* wood, which was light enough, but lasted only six to eight years. With stems currently made from teak wood, the instrument has a useful life of about twenty years. [Interview with Sunira

Kasliwal, Kala Varta, *Journal of the Madhya Pradesh Kala Parishad*, Bhopal, vol. 102, Year 19], Asad Ali Khan credits Zia Mohiuddin Dagar with design improvements, which made the instrument acoustically superior though heavier. He himself claims to have introduced changes, which have elongated the stem by about two inches, with similar objectives and results. The precise nature of these changes is not clear. However, the contemporary *bīna* certainly delivers a more pleasing acoustic output in the upper half of the melodic canvas than *bīna*s of the earlier generation did.

With a more durable stem, the gourds could be fixed to the stem. The contemporary design with detachable gourds is believed to have been developed by Z.M. Dagar, probably in response to transportation needs arising from frequent foreign tours. This belief is implicitly questioned by Hindaraj Diwekar, another contemporary *bīna* player [Diwekar, Hindaraj and Tribhuvan, Robin: *Rudra Vīṇā — an ancient musical instrument*] who claims to possess a 100 year old *bīna* with these features, purchased by his father in the 1930s.

The frets are made of wood, but have a metal cladding on top — either steel, copper, or brass. They were once attached to the stem with wax. However, over the last century, the frets are increasingly tied to the stem with cotton/nylon twines as on the *sitāra*, or affixed with screws, or kept partially moveable by mounting them on an aluminium channel. The instrument has seven strings. Four are used for executing the melody, the remaining three functioning as *cikarī*s [drones]. The twin-drone set on the inner side is tuned to the tonic of the middle and higher octaves, while the isolated drone on the outer side is tuned to the tonic of the lower octave. Z.M. Dagar, however, enlarged the drone set on the inner side to a triple-drone set, thus bringing the total number of strings to eight.

In the sunset years of *dhrupad* and the art of the *bīna*, its major centres were the Northern Provinces, Rajasthan, Bengal [including the present nation-state of Bangladesh], and Maharashtra in western India. Consistent with this geographical concentration, Varanasi, Kolkata, and Miraj emerged as the major manufacturing centres of quality instruments. Thanks to this legacy, the instrument makers of Kolkata and Miraj emerged, in later years, also as prime suppliers of the modern plucked lutes — *sitāra, saroda* and *tānapūrā*.

Ergonomics

The sound activation [plucking] of the *bīna* was traditionally done with the bare fingers, with the first three fingers deployed on the melodic strings, and the little finger being used for activating the *cikarī* [drone]. In recent years, the *miẓrāb* [wire plectrum] of the *sitāra* type has replaced the bare fingers for powering the strokes.

Bīna is unique amongst the major plucked instruments for the arrangement of its strings. The ultra-lower octave melody is played on the first/lowest/outermost string, rather than on the last/ highest/innermost string, as on the *sitāra, surabahāra* and the *saroda*. This is efficient because the first string is strung at the lowest level of tension, and used almost entirely in the *mīṇḍa*-based [string-deflection] execution of melody, which requires the maximum fret-space. The low-tension mounting in the fret-space available for the first string enables almost a complete octave to be covered by string-deflection from a single fret.

According to Asad Ali Khan [*ibid.*], the *bīna* is the only Indian instrument, which is tailor-made for the musician — like an upper garment. This is so because it is held across the breast, and must be mechanically efficient for the music making actions of both the hands, while also providing for the expansion and contraction of the rib cage in the process of breathing. For an instrument that is almost a millennium old, it is not surprising that a great deal of thought has gone into the ergonomics of music making.

The traditional posture for performing was *vajrāsana* [a demanding yogic posture], with the top gourd resting on the left shoulder, and right gourd tucked under the right armpit. The thumb of the right hand is used as the fulcrum, affixed at an appropriate distance from the bridge carrying the strings from the bottom end of the stem. Amongst contemporary *bīna* players, Asad Ali Khan and Shamsuddin Faridi still perform in the traditional posture, while Bahauddin Dagar, following his father, Z.M. Dagar, has adopted a posture akin to the *sarasvatī* [Carnatic] *vīṇā,* with both knees folded inwards, and the top gourd resting on the left knee, while the lower gourd rests on the ground in front of the right knee. According to Bahauddin Dagar [Interview with the author on 9 November, 2002], the ergonomics of the two postures are distinct, and either may be adopted depending on the musical style/bias of the *bīnakāra.* He argues that the traditional posture is more suitable for latter half of *dhrupad* presentation, requiring melodic agility and higher stroke density, while the lap-top posture is more suitable for *ālāpa* rendition, without compromising the efficacy of stroke-craft.

The ergonomics of music making on the *bīna* were a major factor contributing its decline, and replacement by the *sitāra.* In the right-hand [stroke-craft] department, the *bīna* could achieve neither the stroke density, the stroke complexity, nor the degree of control over the manipulation of acoustic output, which the *sitāra* achieved in shaping post-*dhrupad* music. In the left-hand [melodic execution] department, the *bīna* fell short of the melodic agility and complexity demanded by post-*dhrupad* music. However, the *bīna*'s weakness in relation to the *sitāra,* was an integral part of its design and function as accompaniment for *dhrupad* vocal music. Even during the Mogul period:

> a solo performance on the *Vīṇā* [*Bīna*] was frowned upon by the musicians — so much so, that it was called *śuṣka vādya* [dry instrument]. It is generally believed that the great *Vīṇā* player, Naubat Khan [Misri Singh] was seldom asked to give solo recitals in the court of Akbar. He usually accompanied Tānsen on the *Vīṇā*.
>
> — Sharmistha Sen,
> *String Instruments of North India*, vol. II

The *bīna* could develop an extremely sophisticated solo idiom because *bīnakāra*s tested the limits of the instrument's capabilities in their endeavour to liberate their art from its subordinate position relative to vocal music. With hindsight, we might argue that the role of an accompanist to vocal music was more inappropriate for a bowed and fretless instrument like the *sāraṅgī*. However, in the cultural and acoustic environment of the era in which their respective roles emerged, each was probably an appropriate choice.

Acoustics

Another anachronistic feature of the *bīna* is its acoustic output. The instrument was designed for an environment that relied on architecturally determined delivery of musical values. In the modern electronically engineered acoustic environment, the instrument requires extremely sensitive audio engineering. Musicologist, Ashok Ranade discusses these risks with respect to the ensemble for vocal *dhrupad* performance.

> The *bīna*'s acoustics are rich in sustain and the harmonics they deliver. Every time the string is struck, the resulting sound has a long shadow, which tends to drown out melodic subtleties in the vocal rendition. . . . The issue of accompanying instruments becomes

> even more critical in the contemporary environment of amplification electronics. Unless this is very astutely controlled, the rhythmic contours of the *pakhāwaja* [the barrel drum] and melodic contours of the *Rudra Vīṇā* can create a blurred, and even confusing aural experience.
>
> — "Perspectives on Dhrupad,"
> *Journal of the Indian Musicological Society*,
> Annual issue of 1999,
> ed. Deepak Raja & Suvarnalata Rao.

This issue now stands partly resolved by the lapse of the *bīna*'s role as an accompanying instrument, and its re-engineering to suit the requirements of amplification electronics. However, the music of some contemporary *bīna* players does occasionally appear insensitive to electronic amplification.

Stroke Craft

The inventory of *bīna* strokes is built on three basic components:

(a) *Da*: Downward/inward stroke of the index finger on the melodic string

(b) *Gā*: Downward/inward stroke of the middle finger on the melodic string

(c) *Rā*: Upward/outward stroke of the last finger on the *cikarī* drone

Based on these three building blocks, the *bīna* developed a complex stroke-craft, consisting of a large number of compound stroke-patterns corresponding to the patterns in the percussion idiom. Organologist, Sharamistha Ghosh lists 24 such patterns in her book on Hindustani string instruments. These patterns acquired special significance in the rendition of *tar-paraṇas*.

Techniques of Melodic Execution

The techniques deployed on the *bīna* are constrained by its ergonomics, but perhaps more by the melodic austerity of the *dhrupad* genre, thus ruling out the more agile and ornate techniques used on the plucked lutes that succeeded it. An important aspect of this distinction is the strong bias *dhrupad* has in favour of single intervallic transitions as the building blocks of melody characterized by its elephantine gait. This defines a more deliberate and leisurely approach to melody making, compared to the *sitāra* and the *saroda*, which habitually use a phrase consisting of two intervallic transitions as the basic unit of melody. The inventory of *bīna* techniques is large; however, four basic techniques may be mentioned here.

The left hand executes the melody on the *bīna* using two categories of techniques — [a] fretwork, which involves the movement of the fingers between the frets, and [b] string deflection, which involves the pulling of the string with one or more fingers static on a single fret.

Fretwork techniques: In addition to the straightforward melodic execution by movement of the fingers between frets, the *bīna* uses two types of fretwork technique: *ghasīṭa* [also called *sunṭa*], and *khaṭakā*.

Ghasīṭa [lit. dragging] does precisely that. It executes a phrase, usually flat-out and unidirectional, by dragging the left hand finger along the fret-board under the impact of a single stroke. This is accompanied by a light left-hand pressure over the string, so that the resultant glide delivers an aural impression of a fretless instrument. The *ghasīṭa* is deployed mainly for medium to long-span intervallic transitions.

Khaṭakā [lit. jerky motion] is also self-explanatory. It is deployed for short-span intervallic transitions, normally in descending melodic motion. It is also executed under a single stroke. The right-hand stroke is activated with the left-hand finger resting on one fret, while its follow-through in jerky motion implements the intervallic transition along the frets, using the residual power of the stroke, along with that of the jerky motion of the left-hand finger.

There are two principal deflection techniques [a] *mīṇḍa* and [b] *gamaka*.

The *mīṇḍa* is a simple execution of a phrase by pulling the string from a single fret, and executing a phrase under the impact of a single stroke. Three-*svara mīṇḍa*s were common in *bīna* music. Advanced musicianship can usually stretch this to four.

The *gamaka* creates a pulsating or quivering effect — a magnified *vibrato* — by repeatedly attacking a *svara* from a fret at a lower pitch. The *gamaka* is generally used for distances of upto two, and occasionally three *svara*s.

Recent Bīna Music

A brief survey of mid, and late twentieth century *bīna* music may serve as a useful backdrop to understanding its contemporary manifestation. For this purpose, I draw gratefully upon a small sample of recordings made available by the English *dhrupad* archivist, Vincent Naughton. The recordings are of Dabeer Khan [1902-72], Sadiq Ali Khan [1893-1964], and Abid Hussain Khan [early twentieth century]. In addition, I draw upon a few commercially available recordings of Zia Mohiuddin Dagar [died 1990]. This sample reflects merely the immediate availability of recordings.

Dabeer Khan was the grandson of Wazir Khan, a formidable *bīnakāra* employed by the Rampur court, and a descendent of the legendary Tānsen [by some accounts, a descendant of Faiyyaz Khan "Adarang," the nephew of Sadarang]. Dabeer Khan was, for many years, in the employ of the *sarodaist*, Radhika Mohan Maitra, who was the feudal chieftain of Rajshahi in present-day Bangladesh, and was also Maitra's tutor.

Available Dabeer Khan recordings are: Śuddha Sāraṅga [*ālāpa-joḍa-jhālā*], Śuddha Toḍī [*ālāpa-joḍa*], Lakṣmī Toḍī [*ālāpa-joḍa-jhālā*], and Bilaskhani Ṭoḍi [*ālāpa-joḍa-jhālā*]. None of the available recordings has a *pada* rendered to percussion accompaniment. It cannot be determined whether this is a peculiarity of the sample recordings, or integral to Dabeer Khan's concert strategy.

In the Dabeer Khan *ālāpa*, I find a considerable use of fretwork techniques, and a lesser use of the *mīṇḍa* and *khaṭakā* techniques than we would expect in the *dhrupad* genre. Compared to contemporary *sitāra ālāpa*s, the stroke-craft as well as the fretwork sound coarse. The fretwork is agile, and appears to mimic the *sitāra* style of rendition, with an effort to introduce tonal geometry into the phrasing. The steady and leisurely flow of improvizations typical of *dhrupad* is absent. Instead, we find frequent breaks of pace, with brisk passages punctuating the flow. The melodic approach of the Dabeer Khan *ālāpa* was flexible. One of the *ālāpa*s in the sample has no *antarā* at all, while another *ālāpa* is elaborate, with a *sthāyī*, *antarā*, and a brisk *sañcārī* movement.

In the Dabeer Khan *joḍa*, there were typically four levels of tempo. At the fourth level, there is a negligible use of the *cikarī*. In the *joḍa*, we come across a very demanding pattern of simultaneous striking on the melodic and *cikarī* strings — a feature later revived on the *sitāra* by Ustad Vilayat Khan. In an unorthodox departure from *dhrupad* tradition, the fourth level of the *joḍa*, and the *jhālā* are performed to *pakhāwaja* accompaniment. The Dabeer Khan *jhālā* deploys both patterns of interaction between the melodic strings and the *cikarī* currently played on the *sitāra* and the *saroda* — the first stroke on the melodic string followed by the *cikarī*, and its reverse.

The reverse pattern was revived by Ustad Vilayat Khan on the *sitāra*, and is played only in his lineage.

Sadiq Ali Khan belonged to a formidable lineage of *bīnakāra*s known as the Jaipur *bīnakāra*s. This lineage had, for a while, migrated to Golconda-Bijapur in the south, and also studied the art of the *vīṇā* from Carnatic musicians. The lineage later also adopted the *sitāra* as a vehicle for their art. Sadiq Ali studied the *bīna* with his father, Musharraf Khan, a formidable *bīnakāra*, in the lineage of the legendary Rajab Ali Khan of Jaipur. Despite the Jaipur background, anchored in the melodious Dagar Bani style of *dhrupad*, Sadiq Ali had spent many years in Rampur, a centre of the aggressive Khandhar Bāni style.

The available recordings of Sadiq Ali Khan are: *Darbārī* with *ālāpa* and a *dhrupad* composition in *cautāla*, *ālāpa-joḍa-jhālā* in *Jhinjhotī*, and *ālāpa* with *dhrupad* composition in *Bihāga*.

The Sadiq Ali *ālāpa* is steady-paced, with a highly refined left-hand technique sporting an adequate measure of *mīṇḍa*, fretwork, and *ghasīṭa* types of melodic execution. However, the pace of the *ālāpa* is less leisurely than the habitual pace of *dhrupad*. In some cases, the *ālāpa* is indistinguishable from an irregular *joḍa*. The use of the *cikarī* is irregular. The approach to phrasing, with attempts at symmetric and geometric phrasing suggests a melodic sophistication approaching that of the contemporary *sitāra* idiom. In the *joḍa* section, we observe the use of heavy *gamaka*s, and even *tāna*s approaching the agility achievable on the *surabahāra*. The *jhālā* incorporates complex stroke craft, in direct as well as reverse patterns. The stroke density in the *jhālā* compares favourably with that of contemporary *sitāra* music.

In the *pada* rendition, the relationship between the *bīnakāra* and his percussion accompanist corresponds to the "wrestling bout" description, with each of them taking off on his own trip immediately after the first iteration of the rhythmic cycle. In the improvizations around the *pada*, we observe the deployment of the *duguṇā/tiguṇā/cauguṇā* conventions of performing the *pada* at multiples of the base-tempo, as well as a generous use of *tar-paraṇas*. Interestingly, the *pada* rendition often ends with a *sitāra*-style *jhālā*.

Abid Hussain *bīnakāra* of Indore was the son of Jamaluddin bīnakāra, both descended from the same lineage of *bīna/sitāra* exponents from Jaipur, to which Sadiq Ali Khan belonged. This lineage also had a fruitful stylistic interaction with *Seniya* sitārists [descendents of the legendary Miyā Tānsen] who also served the Jaipur court. Abid Hussain's principal disciple, sitārist Bimal Mukherjee, described his *guru* as a versatile musician — a *bīna* player, sitārist, an accomplished *dhrupad* vocalist, and a veritable storehouse of compositions in the *dhrupad, khayāla, ṭhumarī*, Rajasthani folk, and *sitāra* styles. [Proceedings of the Seminar on Sitāra, ITC Sangeet Research Academy, 1992]

The only available recording of Abid Hussain's *bīna* performance is an *ālāpa-joḍa* and *cautāla* composition in Darabārī. The rendition is a thoroughbred *rāga* presentation in *dhrupad* style, albeit with a few post-*dhrupad* features. The solidity of his moorings in the *dhrupad* idiom might be attributed to his mastery over *khayāla, ṭhumarī* and folk genres, which would, expectedly, sharpen his faithfulness to the distinctive features of each genre.

The Darabārī *ālāpa* is an exquisite piece of leisurely *rāga* exposition, rendered at a steady pace, with graceful rounded melodic phrasing. The *ālāpa* has a *sthāyī, antarā* and a *sañcārī*. The *joḍa* is equally steady, with regular *cikarī* perforation. At a higher tempo, the *joḍa* escalates to *cikarī*-punctuated *tānas*, akin to the enhanced-*joḍa* movement of Ustad Vilayat Khan's *sitāra* idiom.

In the *cautāla pada* presentation, Abid Hussain uses *gata-toḍas* similar to the modern *sitāra* idiom, coupled with complex stroke craft, as well as *tar-paraṇas* typical of the *bīna* idiom. Rather unusually for the *bīna* of his era, we observe the use of clever *tihāyīs* to round off the improvisatory forays — a prominent feature of *dhrupad* vocalism of his time, and of later *sitāra/saroda* music. Like Sadiq Ali Khan, Abid Hussain also performed the *cautāla pada* in a progressive tempo, and ended it with a *sitāra*-style *jhālā* movement.

In a conversation with B.R. Deodhar, [1995], Prof. V.N. Bhatkhande [died 1936] disapproved of Murad Khan, who had started performing on the *bīna* with *tabalā* accompaniment, and had also adopted melodic ornamentations more suited to the *sitāra* idiom, but inappropriate for the *dhrupad* genre. Mid-twentieth century recordings, surveyed above, confirm that the *bīna* was fast becoming unsure of its moorings in the *dhrupad* genre. The ideation process of *bīnakāras* had substantially delinked itself from *dhrupad* vocalism, and linked itself to that of the *sitāra*, while their ability to translate it into the content and technique battled against the limitations of the instrument. Under these conditions, it is hardly surprising, that the *bīna* revival should have benefited from a *bīnakāra* who was sufficiently rooted in the *dhrupad* tradition, but free from the historical baggage of hereditary *bīnakāras*.

Zia Mohiuddin Dagar was a member of the Dagar family, deeply entrenched in *dhrupad* vocalism for several generations. He was an accomplished *dhrupad* vocalist and *sitārist* when he came to Bombay from his ancestral home in Udaipur in search of a career. As is to be expected of all *dhrupad* lineages, the Dagar clan had preserved the *bīna* as a part of a musician's training, although no one from it had yet chosen the *bīna* as a profession. Z.M. Dagar's father Ziauddin Dagar had studied the *bīna*, and played it in private. This background was evidently conducive for Z.M. Dagar's reinterpretation of the *bīna* art in the contemporary context.

According to his son, Bahauddin, Zia Mohiuddin hoped, initially, to make a living as a *sitārist* in Bombay. The *bīna* inspired style of the *sitāra*, however, failed to enthuse music lovers in the city. This obliged him to forsake the *sitāra* and switch to the *bīna*. Bahauddin reports that early *bīna* recordings of Z.M. Dagar demonstrate his excellent technical command over all departments of *bīna* music, including the percussion-accompanied *pada* presentation. In later years, however, he abandoned dazzling artistry in favour of the more soulful and serene facets of *bīna* music. This stage in his evolution coincides with his growth in stature and influence, thus providing clues to his success.

Z.M. Dagar developed the *ālāpa-joḍa-jhālā* as the primary vehicle of his performing presence, only rarely extending *rāga* presentation into the percussion-accompanied phase. This bias of later years turned out also to be strategically sound. It placed the *bīna* beyond the bounds of comparison with the *sitāra*, which had superior stroke-craft and melodic agility for percussion-accompanied music. Masit Khani and Raza Khani and other *gata*s composed for the *sitāra*, along with their compatible improvisatory patterns, had converted the rhythmic action of plucking into a sophisticated art of interaction with percussion. The *bīna*, on the other hand, had to perform *pada*s composed for vocal rendition, and was relatively handicapped by the *dhrupad* tradition and by its own ergonomics, in the handling of percussion-accompanied music. In an interview with the present author [9 November 2002], Bahauddin Dagar admitted these limitations of the *bīna* in the percussion-accompanied segment of *bīna* music.

Published recordings of Z.M. Dagar's *ālāpa-joḍa-jhālā* in Yaman and Śuddha Toḍī are representative of his music. His *ālāpa* has the leisurely, graceful, rounded melodic contours typical of *dhrupad* vocalism, totally devoid of angularities in the expression. It relies heavily on *mīṇḍa*, with very sparing use of fretwork techniques. The melodic movements are disciplined, though within the broad-span *ālāpa* strategy of the *dhrupad* genre. The movements consist of a *sthāyī, antarā* and a *sañcārī*. The *joḍa* — rendered at a steady tempo, without significant escalation — also relies heavily on *mīṇḍa*. It makes no demands of melodic agility on the instrument beyond what it can comfortably deliver. The *jhālā*, too, is delivered with the traditional *bīna* stroke patterns, with no attempt to compete with the artistry of the modern *sitāra* idiom. Throughout his presentation, there is virtually no trace of the *sitāra* idiom, of which he was an accomplished exponent.

In effect, Z.M. Dagar positioned the *bīna* in the small niche which his contemporary, Imrat Khan [Ustad Vilayat Khan's younger brother] had created for the *surabahāra* as a specialist instrument for the *ālāpa-joḍa-jhālā* movements. While Imrat Khan's *surabahāra* drifted towards the modern *khayāla*-inspired idiom, Z.M. Dagar provided an alternative, rooted in the medieval *dhrupad* genre. Like Imrat Khan, Z.M. Dagar exploited the acoustic richness of his instrument, and the special appeal of the *ālāpa-joḍa-jhālā* movements to give the *bīna* another lease of life.

The Disappearing Breed

The present author attempted a listing of significant *bīnakāras* in recent history from authoritative published sources. In such a compilation, it is inevitable that the issue of significance be blurred. A listed musician can either be a significant *bīnakāra*, or a significant musician who is also a *bīnakāra*. This distinction may not always be relevant because, in the *dhrupad* tradition, the art of the *bīna* was an important accomplishment of a musician, whether or not he performed on it professionally.

Paradoxically, after the progeny of the legendary Tānsen [sixteenth century], the next significant *bīnakāra* recorded in medieval history is the most luminous personage in the evolution of the *khayāla* genre of vocal music — Niamat Khan "Sadarang." Apparently, Sadarang, a distinguished *bīna* player at the Delhi court, was dismissed from the service of Emperor Mohammad Shah [reign 1719-48] for refusing to accompany a vocalist, considering it a "menial" task for so eminent a soloist. He decided to settle his score with his employer and all contemporary vocalists by creating a more charming style of singing that would replace *dhrupad*. The rest, as they say, is history.

The survey delivers only twenty-four significant *bīnakāra*s in the nineteenth century. This is more likely to reflect the poverty of documentation, than of the profession. The recorded history of the *bīna* in the twentieth century is probably more reliable. The first half of the century deprived the country of twenty-one significant *bīnakāra*s. In the latter half of the twentieth century, ten significant *bīnakāra*s departed from the scene. The survey reveals an amazing variety. For one, it includes Hindus and Moslems, each in substantial numbers. Secondly, it covers almost all parts of non-peninsular India. Thirdly, it includes professional musicians, priests, monks, aristocrats, royalty, and even courtesans. And, finally, it includes *bīnakāra*s who founded great lineages of *khayāla* vocalism, as also those who taught great *sitāra*, *surabahāra* and *saroda* players. This variety reflects the all-pervasive presence of the *bīna* in Hindustani music before it relinquished it in favour of instruments of superior ergonomics. In a sense, the decline of the *bīna* also paved the way for the divorce of instrumental music from vocal music, setting each on an independent, though partially interactive, path of evolution.

At the time of writing, and on reasonable reckoning, there are only six living *bīnakāra*s with training in a well established lineage of *bīna* music — Asad Ali Khan, the son of Sadiq Ali Khan; Shamsuddin Faridi, the son of Mohammad Khan Faridi Desai; Pandharinath Kolhapure, the son of Krishnarao Kolhapure; Bindumadhav Pathak, the son of Dattopant Pathak; Hindaraj Diwekar, the son of Shivrambuwa Diwekar; and Bahauddin Dagar, the son of Zia Mohiuddin Dagar. Only the last two named here belong the post-Independence generation. In the last quarter of the twentieth century, a few European students of the *bīna* have achieved a respectable level of competence. Amongst them is Philippe Bruguiere.

With respect to contemporary *bīnakāra*s, the issue of significance is trickier than for those of earlier generations, though for different reasons. An important reason is that they constitute a trans-cultural mix, with some of them having remained either largely, or wholly, aloof from a performing presence. Any attempt to impose a yardstick of musicianship on so small and mismatched a population can easily deliver absurd results.

5.2

THE SITĀRA*

THE *sitāra*, the most popular representative of Hindustani classical music, belongs to the long-necked, fretted lute family of instruments. Over just three centuries of evolution, the instrument has evolved from very limited melodic capability to a level of great sophistication. Most of this evolution has taken place during the twentieth century.

Initially, it is believed, the *sitāra* was used like a Banjo, as a rhythmic accompaniment to *qawwālī* performances, filling the pauses between verses. In due course, musicians of exceptional talent became aware of the *sitāra*'s melodic potential and developed it into a concert instrument.

The *sitāra* acquired its independent status on the concert platform towards the end of the eighteenth century. *Dhrupad* was the dominant mainstream genre at that time. The ancient *rudra vīṇā*, which had originally accompanied vocal *dhrupad* had by then laid the foundations of the *tantakāra aṅga* [literally, the style of plucked instruments]. In the early *tantakāra aṅga* phase, the *sitāra* adopted the *dhrupad*-based composition formats and instrumental techniques of the *rudra vīṇā*. Under *dhrupad* influence, *sitāra* music responded to the rhythmic patterns of the *pakhāwaja*.

By the end of the eighteenth century, musicians began to compose *gatas* [compositions] of different structures especially for the *sitāra*. The most significant amongst them were Masit Khan and Ghulam Raza Khan, both related by kinship to Niamat Khan Sadarang, the father of the modern *khayāla* style of singing, who served at the court of Emperor Mohammed Shah [1719-48].

Masit Khan's *gata* structure for *vilaṁbita* [slow tempo] *tīnatāla*, and the Raza Khani *gata* structure for *drut* [fast tempo] *tīnatāla*, began the process of giving *sitāra* music an identity distinct from the *dhrupad*-based music of the *rudra vīṇā*.

The *sitāra* technique uses four basic strokes of the plectrum:

Da: The inward stroke

Ra: The outward stroke

DiR: The inward followed by outward in quick succession

Rda: The outward followed by inward in quick succession

The Masit Khani and Raza Khani *gatas* used this raw material for building a distinctive pattern, with each stroke falling on a beat of the rhythmic cycle. Thus, in essence, these *gatas* constitute an interpretation of the rhythmic cycle which, naturally, influences the structure of melodic execution also. Their significance lies in freeing the language of the *sitāra* from the vocabulary of *dhrupad*. During the nineteenth century, the Masit Khani and Raza Khani *gatas*, together, became the basic framework of *rāga* presentation on the *sitāra*.

The Masit Khani Gata

The 4-beat subdivision of the 16-beat cycle of *tīnatāla* corresponds to the pattern of: *Da DiR Da Ra*, using only the first three strokes

The Masit Khani *gata* format																
Beat	12	13	14	15	16	1	2	3	4	5	6	7	8	9	10	11
Stroke	*Dir*	*Da*	*Dir*	*Da*	*Ra*	*Da*	*Da*	*Ra*	*Dir*	*Da*	*Dir*	*Da*	*Ra*	*Da*	*Da*	*Ra*

This 16-beat structure consists of one 8-beat structure rendered twice: *DiR Da DiR Da Ra Da Da Ra/DiR Da DiR Da Ra Da Da Ra*. When performed, this 8-beat element acquires a lilt which breaks down into a 5-3 subdivision as so: *DiR Da DiR Da Ra /Da Da Ra*. Thus, the Masit Khani *gata* superimposes a 5-3-5-3 asymmetry on the 4-4-4-4 symmetry of the cycle. This imposition of asymmetry over symmetry builds the tension; the tension creates the anticipation of its release; and the release creates the cathartic effect. Notice that every alternate 4-beat division contains the corresponding pattern *Da DiR Da Ra* strokes. And, yet, the totality of the stroke pattern creates a momentum quite distinct from that of the rhythmic cycle.

This partial liberation of melody from rhythm was a reflection of the same process that vocal music was undergoing with the ascendancy of the *khayāla* style over *dhrupad* music, and the emergence of the *ṭhumarī* style. Technically, of course, the *sitāra* was, at that time, a couple of centuries away from being able to execute a melodic mimesis of either the *khayāla* or the *ṭhumarī*.

The Raza Khani Gata

At about the same time, Ghulam Raza Khan, a sitāraist from Lucknow, the home of the *ṭhumarī*, developed *drut tīnatāla* composition patterns. Of the several structures developed by him, the most popular structure used all the four strokes of the *sitāra* for his crisp composition:

The Raza Khani *gata* format [simplified]																
Beat	5	6	7	8	9	10	11	12	13	14	15	16	1	2	3	4
Stroke	*Da*	*Ra*	*Dir*	*Dir*	*Da*	*Rda*	*Ra*	*Dir*	*Da*	*Dir*	*Da*	*Ra*	*Da*	-	*Da*	*Ra*

The Raza Khani *gata* distanced *sitāra* music further from its *rudra vīṇā* and *dhrupad* ancestry. For one, it was meant to be played at a pace faster than *dhrupad* music. And, secondly, these patterns drew their inspiration explicitly from post-*dhrupad* forms of vocalism. Because of the predominant *ṭhumarī* influence, many of the Raza Khani *gata*s were originally composed in the lighter *rāga*s such as Pilū, Kāfī, Khamāja, Zilā, Deśa, Bhairavī.

In the early twentieth century, the *khayāla* influence on the *sitāra* idiom became more pronounced as the instrument itself was modified to facilitate the stylistic drift towards vocalism. The pace of performing Masit Khani *gata*s slowed down to come closer to *khayāla* singing, and *rāga* elaboration techniques shifted away from the emphasis on rhythmic [right hand] dexterity, and towards melodic [left hand] refinement.

A further liberation of melody from rhythm followed, as a rich source of compositions from the various vocal styles [*dhrupad, khayāla, ṭhumarī* and *tarānā*] became accessible for adaptation to the *sitāra*.

Sitāra Styles

Today, it is possible to identify six distinct *gharānā*s of *sitāra* music. The best known amongst them are the Etawah/Imdad Khan *gharānā* represented by Ustad Vilayat Khan and the Maihar *gharānā* represented by Pt. Ravi Shankar. The influence of vocalism is evident in both the major *gharānā*s, though in very different ways. But, neither of these *gharānā*s has altogether abandoned either the Masit Khani and Raza Khani format of compositions or the distinctive techniques that exploit the character of the *sitāra* as an instrument of the fretted lute family. What they have, indeed, done is to re-invent *sitāra* music by transcending the instrument's technical limitations. As a result, contemporary *sitāra* music represents a blend of *tantakāra* and *gāyakī* elements in terms of the choice of compositions, as well as the style and technique of *rāga* elaboration.

Techniques of Melodic Execution

The techniques of melodic execution on the *sitāra* can be divided into two categories: [a] fretwork in which the fingers of the left hand move from fret to fret and [b] deflection, where the fingers are static on one fret, and tonal transition is achieved by pulling the string without movement between the frets.

Fretwork techniques belong to the traditional *sitāra* idiom, developed before the *sitāra* acquired sufficient strength to audibly deliver an array of *svara*s executed under a single stroke. The deflection techniques developed along with structural improvements in the *sitāra*, and their maturation enabled the evolution of the vocalized idiom.

Fretwork techniques: In addition to the straight forward execution, there are mainly two types of fretwork technique: *krintana* and *ghasīṭa*.

Krintana requires the dexterous movement of two fingers over the frets. The first *svara* executed with a right-hand stroke supporting one left-hand finger resting on the fret-board. The subsequent *svara*s of the phrase are executed with the second finger hitting the appropriate fret in a hammering motion, but without further right-hand stroke support. With this technique, a phrase of up to four *svara*s can be executed. This technique is unique to the *sitāra*, and originated even before the *sitāra* acquired sympathetic strings, and has remained an essential feature of *tantakāra ang* of the *sitāra*.

Ghasīṭa [lit. dragging] does precisely that. It executes a phrase, usually flat-out and unidirectional, by dragging the left hand finger along the fret-board over at least half an octave under the impact of a single stroke. This is accompanied by feather-touch left-hand pressure over the string, so that the resultant glide delivers an aural impression of a fretless instrument. It is not uncommon for the *ghasīṭa* to span a full octave unidirectionally, as it can do on the *rudra vīṇā*. The *ghasīṭa* on the *sitāra* is inspired by the *sūta* technique practised on the *rudra vīṇā* which, in turn, is inspired by the vocal idiom of *dhrupad* music.

There are three principal deflection techniques [a] *mīṇḍa* [b] *murkī* and [c] *gamaka*.

The *mīṇḍa* is a simple execution of a phrase by pulling the string from a single fret, and executing a phrase under the impact of a single stroke. Three-*svara mīṇḍa*s were common in *sitāra* music up to the 1930s. The contemporary *sitāra*, because of enhanced sustaining ability, can deliver a five-*svara mīṇḍa*.

The *murkī* is a special type of *mīṇḍa*, where the phrase involves a wrap-around execution with a jerky motion. The contemporary *sitāra* can support a *murkī* of up to eight *svara*s under a single stroke.

The *gamaka* creates a pulsating or quivering effect — a magnified *vibrato* — by repeatedly attacking a *svara* from a fret at a lower pitch. The *gamaka* is generally used for distances of upto two, occasionally three, *svara*s.

The Singing Sitāra

The supreme status of vocal music in the Indian performing arts tradition has made the lure of vocalism compelling for musicians performing on the various instruments. For the *sitāra*, the principal obstacle to vocalism arises from the technical limitation of the plucking technique of sound activation, and low acoustic sustain. Hence, the need to move the left hand from fret to fret in order to execute the melody, and the need for the intermittent priming of the sound by strokes of the plectrum worn on the right index finger. Both these actions are perceptible, and therefore militate against the melodic continuity required of vocalism.

In order to bring the *sitāra* close to vocal music, the design and construction of the instrument had to be modified, and the technique of playing the *sitāra* — the right hand as well as the left hand — had to be developed to exploit the melodic potential thus released. Although technical changes were evolutionary, it is twentieth century musicians and craftsmen who made the *sitāra* capable of singing.

By the late nineteenth century, the commonly used wooden chamber-resonators of the early *sitāra*s had been replaced by two dried pumpkins. In the early twentieth century, the basic 7-string *sitāra* acquired an additional 13 sympathetic strings tuned to the scale of the *rāga*. These changes gave a boost to amplification and sustenance.

In the 1950s, contemporary legends, Ustad Vilayat Khan, and Pt. Ravi Shankar worked closely with expert craftsmen to redesign the *sitāra* for delivering their own distinctive styles of music. Of the two, the Vilayat Khan design was more revolutionary in terms of sound production.

Vilayat Khan's solution to the sustenance problem was a more powerful right hand stroke. He designed a thicker *tabalī* [cover of the impact-receiving resonator], increased the height of the bridge that received the impact of the stroke, and introduced a metallic reinforcement of the joint between the chamber-resonator and the stem [column-resonator] to enable the instrument to withstand the power of his strokes.

By the late nineteenth century, the technique of producing melodic phrases by pulling the melodic string [called a *mīṇḍa*] from the same fret rather than moving the left palm between frets, had already been developed. But, up to the 1920s, the *sitāra* was technically unable to deliver more than three *svara*s from one fret.

Ustad Vilayat Khan made a 5-*svara mīṇḍa* possible by reinforcing the two bridges across which the wires are strung, altering the curvature of the frets and the stem, replacing the brass frets with frets from an alloy of superior malleability and acoustic quality, and introducing strings of a lower [thicker] gauge.

Because amplification electronics had, by now, reached a high level of sophistication, Vilayat Khan developed a method of directing the impact of his strokes towards achieving greater sustenance, rather than permit its dissipation on amplification. This was aided by a technique of fine-tuning the bridge that receives the impact of the stroke.

With these modifications and refinements, Ustad Vilayat Khan made it possible for both hands to move less frequently. Melodic expression could now be executed with a smoothness of flow approximating that of wind or bow instruments.

In order to simulate singing even more faithfully, Ustad Vilayat Khan introduced a method of tuning and strumming the strings to create an illusion of a continuous *tānapūrā* [a four/six stringed drone instrument] accompaniment. This obviated the need for *tānapūrā* support, and brought the melody and its harmonic ambience, both, under the *sitāraist*'s own control.

5.3

THE SURABAHĀRA*

THE *surabahāra* is to the *sitāra*, what the cello is to the violin. It is a large-size bass *sitāra*, with a flat rather than rounded gourd at the base, and a rounded *sitāra*-type, gourd-resonator at the top. In its contemporary form, the *surabahāra* has a string-count identical to the present-day *sitāra*, the difference being in the thickness of the strings, the pitch at which the instrument is tuned, and the tuning system covering four octaves.

Its construction gives the *surabahāra* a deep, sonorous, long-lasting sound. The extra width of its stem enables the execution of *mīṇḍa*s of up to a full octave. These features facilitate the parsimony of strokes as well as left-hand movement between frets, both these being fundamental to achieving a higher degree of melodic continuity.

The invention of the *surabahāra*, around AD 1825, is attributed, variously, to Ustad Vilayat Khan's great-grandfather, Ustad Sahebdad Khan, and to a lesser-known, Lucknow-based early nineteenth century sitārist, Ustad Ghulam Mohammed. The latest research favours the latter attribution.

The purpose of developing the instrument was to enable *sitāra*-players to present the elaborate *dhrupad*-style *ālāpa*

---

traditionally performed on the *rudra vīṇā*. They designed the *surabahāra* to combine the ergonomic facility of the *sitāra* with the melodic potential and acoustic richness of the *rudra vīṇā*. This combination looked attractive in an era in which the *sitāra* idiom was, by and large, a prisoner of the medieval *dhrupad* style, and struggling to match the *bīna* in terms of acoustic richness and melodic content. With *ālāpa* presentations on the *surabahāra*, *sitāra* players succeeded in overtaking *bīna* players in terms of popularity and stature.

The idiom of the *surabahāra* speedily achieved great sophistication. Initially, it was plucked, like the *bīna*, with bare fingers, but has been played, at different stages and by different musicians with one, two, and even three *mizrab*s [plectrums].

Until well into the twentieth century, sitārists presented the *dhrupad* style *ālāpa* on the *surabahāra*, followed by post-*dhrupad* styles of compositions on the *sitāra*. As the *sitāra* itself evolved technically and stylistically, it took over the elaborate *dhrupad*-format *ālāpa*, and added further sophistication to it. As a result, during the latter half of the twentieth century, the *surabahāra* suffered a steady depletion in the number of competent performers, although not in the size of audiences.

The contemporary *sitāra* of enhanced musical capability is now threatening the *surabahāra* with extinction. This is ironic considering that the *surabahāra* was originally developed by sitārists for their own musical needs. But, this is also inevitable because, the *surabahāra* remained relevant only as long as it could motivate sitārists to master two different instruments. Against this prospect, understandably, design improvements aimed at enhancing the acoustic capabilities of the *sitāra* looked like a more attractive proposition. Considering the success of these efforts, the *surabahāra* risks drifting into history, unless the community of musicians develops an independent role or idiom for the instrument.

The *surabahāra* remains, however, a major link of continuity between the *dhrupad* and post-*dhrupad* styles of instrumental music. Despite being rare, it remains an important part of the instrumental tradition of *dhrupad* music, and in the major *gharānā*s of *sitāra* music, which have helped the instrument make a transition into post-*dhrupad* stylistics. These traditions have not only preserved the art of the *surabahāra*, but are also searching for a legitimate, and hopefully unique, role for the *surabahāra* in the contemporary scenario of music on the long-necked fretted-lute family of instruments.

In the *dhrupad* stream, itself a greatly depleted segment of the music world, the *surabahāra* has started replacing the *bīna* as a presenter of comprehensive *dhrupad* performances, including the *ālāpa*, as well as *dhrupad* compositions. However, the *dhrupad* side of *surabahāra* music is still bereft of significant musicianship.

Surabahāra and the Imdad Khan Lineage

Amongst musicians of the post-*dhrupad* genres, the Etawah/Imdad Khan lineage has contributed most significantly to the development of the *surabahāra*. The *surabahāra* has hitherto been an essential part of the training of its members, irrespective of whether they performed on the *sitāra* or the *surabahāra*.

Ustad Sahebdad Khan, Vilayat Khan's great grandfather, was evidently competent enough on the *surabahāra* for him to have been considered, by some, to be its inventor. His son, Ustad Imdad Khan was a formidable *surabahāra* and *sitāra* player, as were his two sons, Ustad Enayet Khan [Ustad Vilayat Khan's father] and Ustad Waheed Khan [Ustad Vilayat Khan's uncle]. Starting from Ustad Imdad Khan, there exist 78-RPM recordings by way of evidence of the contribution of this lineage to the art of the *surabahāra*.

Ustad Vilayat Khan, and his brother, Ustad Imrat Khan, both received training on the *surabahāra* from their uncle, Ustad

Waheed Khan. At some stage, Vilayat Khan ceded the *surabahāra* territory to Imrat Khan, and decided to concentrate on the *sitāra*. The results of this bifurcation of territories have been most rewarding for the two brothers, and for the world of music in general.

In the hands of Ustad Vilayat Khan and his brother, Ustad Imrat Khan, the *surabahāra* technique has achieved a melodic continuity far beyond that of the *bīna* or the *sitāra*, and conceivable only on a fretless instrument. The three-tiered *ālāpa-joḍa-jhālā* format has remained the basic idiom of the *surabahāra*; but stylistically, the *dhrupad* idiom has receded, giving way to a marked influence of *khayāla*-oriented treatment of melody.

In the mid-1960s, came their first attempt at enlarging the canvas of *surabahāra* music, with the recording of a duet [A Night at the Taj: EMI:EALP:1323] with Ustad Vilayat Khan playing the *sitāra* and Ustad Imrat Khan, the *surabahāra*. On this landmark recording, they presented an *ālāpa* as well as a Masit Khani composition in *rāga* Candanī Kedāra with percussion accompaniment.

This recording encouraged the notion of the *surabahāra* as a male voice and the *sitāra* as a female voice. It also brought the *surabahāra*, for the first time in post-*dhrupad* music, out of its *ālāpa-joḍa-jhālā* territory, and into percussion-accompanied presentation of post-*dhrupad* compositions, including medium-paced *tāna*s utilizing the *gamaka* and *ghasīṭa* modes of execution.

This was followed by more duets of Ustad Vilayat Khan, not merely with Imrat Khan [Miya Ki Malhar: EMI: ASD:498:0], but also his son, Shujaat Khan on the *surabahāra* [Navras:NRCC:0533]. Shujaat Khan took the *surabahāra* deeper into *sitāra* territory by executing fast-paced *ekhara* [one *svara* per stroke] *tāna*s, almost matching his father's *tāna*s on the *sitāra*.

The success of this supporting, though enlarged, role for the *surabahāra* cannot be considered a final verdict on the unique potential of the instrument, because it merely represents the technical achievement of moving the *surabahāra* into *sitāra* territory. The present situation is not very different from that of the cello, whose musical value could not be unleashed by an intrusion into violin territory, but had to wait until composers like Bach and Boccherini started writing music specially for the cello.

5.4

THE SARODA*

IN TERMS of popularity and sophistication of its idiom, the *saroda* comes next only to the *sitāra*. Its present stature as a mainstream instrument conceals the fact that until the end of the nineteenth century, it was a fairly crude acoustic machine. Its transformation into a scintillating instrument has taken place entirely in the twentieth century.

History

The contemporary *saroda* is about 100 years old. It has three identifiable ancestors. Two of these were *rabāba*s, short-necked fretless lutes with wooden bodies, cat-gut strings, and a skin-covered chamber resonator. The Persian *rabāba*, later came to be known as the Indian *rabāba / dhrupad rabāba / seniya rabāba*. The Afghan or Ḳābulī *rabāba*, which came much later, provided a direct impetus for its own transformation into the *saroda*. The third ancestor was the *surasiṅgāra*, an indigenous adaptation of the Persian/*dhrupad rabāba*.

The Persian *rabāba* entered India in the eleventh century along with the Gazhnavid occupation of the Punjab. It became an important part of music in the early Mogul courts. During the mid-Mogul period, the legendary Miyā Tānsen at Emperor Akbar's court contributed substantially to performance on the *rabāba*. The Tānsen lineage, through his son Bilas Khan, perpetuated the *dhrupad rabāba* tradition. The *dhrupad rabāba* remained, along with the *rudra vīṇā*, a pervasive presence in the Hindustani mainstream for over two hundred years after Tānsen [Miner, 1997].

The Afghan *rabāba*, different in design from the Persian *rabāba*, entered India from Afghanistan with *paṭhāna* soldiers in the employ of the early-Moguls. Soldier-musicians played martial tunes on it, and prized it for the fervor and beat it created. This instrument retained its Afghan music and identity until the mid-eighteenth century, when a line of *rabābīya*s established a link with Hindustani musicians, and diverted its music towards the mainstream [*ibid.*].

There is no evidence about when the Afghan *rabāba* was renamed the *saroda*. The earliest significant *sarodīya* on record is Ghulam Ali Khan [early nineteenth century], who was the grandson of Ghulam Bandegi Khan Bangash, a *rabābīya* from Afghanistan, and lived in Rewa and Lucknow to finally settle down in Gwalior [*ibid.*].

Despite its considerable status as a mainstream instrument, the *saroda* was, until the late nineteenth century, an acoustically unstable instrument with gut strings, and a wooden fingerboard. It adopted the metallic fingerboard and metal strings probably from the *surasiṅgāra*.

After surrendering its most promising features to the *saroda*, the *surasiṅgāra* faded into history. Further re-engineering of the *saroda* took place during the 1930s to make it the sophisticated and versatile instrument we hear today. Most of this is credited to Ustad Alauddin Khan, and his brother, Ayet Ali Khan, who was also an expert craftsman.

After the short-lived *surasiṅgāra* experiment, the *rabāba*/*saroda gharānā*s have not been too enthusiastic about imposing melodic fluidity on the capabilities of the *saroda*, or to dilute the percussive element. Within limits, the instrument is being re-engineered to progressively offer a wider choice of idioms in terms of stroke-density relative to *svara*-density. The martial history of the *rabāba*, and the robust aural experience have begun to recede as dominant influences on contemporary *saroda* music. But, they remain firmly entrenched in the *saroda*'s musical personality.

Although the world of *saroda* recognizes several streams, its idiom is currently represented by three main lineages. The *rabāba*-inspired idiom of Ustad Hafiz Ali Khan, an early twentieth century maestro, was diverted towards a *khayāla* style vocalism by his son, Ustad Amjad Ali Khan. The Mohammed Ameer Khan/Radhika Mohan Maitra stream has reinforced its *rabāba*-oriented idiom in the music of its contemporary exponents, Buddhadev Dasgupta and Kalyan Mukherjea. The *rabāba* and *rudra vīṇā* based style of Ustad Alauddin Khan inspired the genius of his son, Ustad Ali Akbar Khan, to launch the most comprehensive exploitation yet of the distinctive acoustic features of the re-engineered *saroda*.

Organology

By modern organological classification, the *saroda* is a short-necked lute of the plucked variety. However, it also straddles the membranophone category by virtue of having a leather-bound cover for the chamber-resonator.

Although a monochord, the *saroda* has some features of a polychord. The melody is executed on four strings. The melodic execution also exposes the melodic strings to raw or unaided participation. In addition, the modern *saroda* has a three-string set mounted and tuned explicitly for harp-like strumming to deliver either a chord or a melodic phrase compatible with the *rāga*.

Because of the uniqueness of this instrument, the Indian organological classification is also relevant. Bharata's

Nāṭyaśāstra [200 BC-AD 200] classifies instruments into [a] *ghana* or solids, [b] *avanaddha* or covered with skin, [c] *suṣīra* or hollow and [d] *tata* or having strings. Using this classification as the basis, a seventeenth-century musicological text [*Saṇgītapārijāta* of Ahobala] mentions the *rabāba*, the ancestor of the *saroda*, below the drums, as a separate category called *tatāvanaddha* [*tat* + *avanaddha*] or a string instrument with a skin-cover. The creation of a special category, and its placement below the drums, recognizes not only its physical construction, but also acoustic character.

When the *saroda* discarded the wooden finger-board of its ancestor, the *rabāba* in the late nineteenth/early twentieth century, and adopted the metallic finger-board, it became the only lute still in the Indian mainstream to have a shell made of wood, and the upper made of skin and metal, thus defining its unique acoustics.

Design and Tuning

The shell of the *saroda* is carved, ideally, from a single block of teak [*Tectona Grandis*] wood. The carved shell is about 32 inches, end-to-end. At the bottom, is a skin-covered elliptical or spheroid chamber resonator, which extends into a tapering stem [column resonator] covered with a stainless steel finger-board. A second, but smaller, chamber resonator mounted at the end of the finger-board, on the rear side, is optional. The finger-board extends into a bar, 10/14 inches in length, which holds eight pegs for the primary strings, for which two different tuning systems are in vogue.

The traditional tuning system, practised by the lineage of Pt. Radhika Mohan Maitra, uses five strings for melodic execution. They are tuned to Middle-octave *mā*, the tonic [*sā*], lower-octave *pā*, lower-octave *sā*, and ultra-lower *pā*, thus providing a melodic canvas of virtually four octaves. The last three constitute a *cikarī* [drone] set, with the innermost tuned to the tonic, and the outermost two tuned to the higher-octave *Sa*. In the modern system, practised by Ustad Ali Akbar Khan, and his disciples, the first four strings are tuned exactly as in the traditional system, thus limiting the melodic canvas to three-and-half octaves. In addition to the conventional *cikarī* set, this system, however, includes a set of three strings, mounted at a lower level, and tuned either to a chord or a melodic phrase compatible with the scale of the *rāga*. The contemporary *saroda* has 15 sympathetic strings [sometimes fewer] mounted below the primary strings. They are tuned to the scale of the *rāga*.

Acoustics

The acoustics of an instrument depend on the materials from which it is made, as also its shape. In the *saroda*, the skin-cladding over the chamber-resonator primarily enhances percussive sustain. The metallic finger-board, devoid of a fibre-structure, deprives it of melodic sustain, even though it contributes to the instrument's timbre. Thus, despite substantial acoustic re-engineering over the last 50 years and its enhanced sustain, the *saroda* remains inferior on sustain, and superior on percussive potential, compared to the *sitāra*, the other prominent lute in the Indian mainstream.

These features demand, from the *saroda*, a higher frequency of sound-priming than a *sitāra* and impose, on the musical idiom of the *saroda*, a high stroke-density relative to the *svara*-density. A rhythmic bias is thus inherent in the design of the instrument. The enhanced melodic potential of the contemporary *saroda*, still inferior to that of the *sitāra* or *surabahāra*, has enabled it to shape a satisfying slow *ālāpa* of reasonable *svara*-density relative to stroke-density.

Ergonomics

The performer normally sits with his right knee folded over

his left knee. The left foot, folded to the right, supports the bulbous chamber resonator. The centre of the stem is supported on the right thigh at an incline of 15/20 degrees. The instrument is stable in this posture, leaving the left hand free to move at will for melodic execution. The instrument is plucked with a triangular plectrum cut out of coconut shell and laminated with shellac. Most sarodists hold the plectrum between the thumb and first and second fingers of the right hand. Sarodists of Pt. Radhika Mohan's *gharānā* use a two-finger grip. They believe that this produces a better percussive punch, and provides superior bi-directional mechanical efficiency.

The right arm wraps around the base of the chamber resonator, the fore-arm rests at the root of the base, and uses wrist-movements for stroke-play, almost equally in both directions. The posture and the manner of handling the instrument results in the strokes being near-vertical. The downward is aided by gravity, while the upward is weakened by having to work against it. Because of multiple-string melodic execution, the span of movement in each direction is about 3.5 inches, the maximum rotation the wrist can manage with the fore-arm firm at the base.

The ergonomics of music-making on the *saroda* militate against strokes requiring the simultaneous execution of string-shifts and direction-reversal. Hence, the traditional idiom of the *saroda* has come to be dominated by multiple strokes supporting each *svara*, especially at medium-to-higher tempi. Although the more demanding *ekhara* treatment [one stroke per *svara*] is in greater evidence over the last three decades, a higher stroke density remains the distinguishing feature of the *saroda* idiom. In totality, the design of the instrument, and the ergonomics of music making together make the *saroda* a percussive-melodic instrument, and bias its musical idiom towards the rhythmic exploitation of its percussive character.

The Saroda Idiom

The contemporary *saroda* idiom is a blend of three principal stylistic influences, broadly represented by the three leading exponents of the instrument. The traditional *rabāba*-influenced idiom dominates the music of the *rabābīya* tradition of Pt. Radhika Mohan Maitra. The *rudra vīṇā*-influenced idiom, following the medieval *dhrupad-dhamāra* genre of music, dominates the music of the Maihar-Seniya *gharānā* of Ustad Alauddin Khan. The influence of the post-*dhrupad* genres, mainly *khayāla* vocalism and contemporary *sitāra* music of the Imdad Khan/Etawah *gharānā*, dominates the music of the next generation of maestros, especially Ustad Amjad Ali Khan.

Running through all the contemporary manifestations of the *saroda* idiom lies an undercurrent that the *saroda* shares with the *sitāra* idiom. Like the *saroda*, the *sitāra* is a plucked lute, which developed its independent idiom as a solo concert instrument almost a century before the *saroda* did. This made a certain degree of borrowing inevitable. The sharing of idioms was facilitated by the sharing of a common home — pre-Partition Bengal of the nineteenth and early twentieth centuries.

Techniques of Melodic Execution

Melodic execution techniques on the *saroda* can be divided into three different types. [a] sliding of the finger along the finger board without lifting the fingers from the melodic string [b] execution by the alternative/successive use of two fingers on the same melodic string [c] multiple-string execution inevitably requiring the alternative/successive use of two fingers.

Type [*a*] ***techniques***: The design and the ergonomics of manipulation of the instrument make this the basic technique of executing any melodic phrase in the slow-to-medium tempi, unless it requires the use of more than one melodic string. Thus, the fundamental melodic character of the instrument is conjunct rather than disjunct. It is the limited sustain of the instrument and the necessity for higher stroke frequency, which tilts the bias of the aural experience in favour of the rhythmic element and melodic discontinuity.

Mīṇḍa: The *mīṇḍa* is a unidirectional glissando of short-melodic span executed under a single stroke.

Murkī: The *murkī* is phrase executed by a bi-directional glissando under the power of a single stroke, and involving a wrap-around movement around one *svara* with jerky motion mostly at the point of direction-reversal.

Gamaka: A *gamaka* is a magnified *vibrato* created by repeatedly attacking a target *svara* from an adjacent *svara*, under multiple stroke activation.

Ghasīṭa: A *ghasīṭa* is a *mīṇḍa* of broad melodic span, generally a full octave or more. The technique is borrowed from the *sūta* technique of the *rudra vīṇā*.

Type [b] techniques: Being a fretless instrument, finger-work belongs to the special effects department of the *saroda* idiom.

Sparśa: The *sparśa* involves the lifting of one finger from the string almost immediately after the stroke, and allowing the other finger to execute the adjacent *svara*. The two near-simultaneous *svara*s can be activated either under a single stroke or even two or more strokes.

Krintana: This technique, a specialty of the *sitāra*, involves the execution of a phrase of four or more *svara*s under the power of a single stroke. The first *svara* of the phrase receives stroke power, while the subsequent *svara*s are powered by the action of the middle finger being lifted from one *svara*, and the index finger attacking an adjacent *svara* in hammer-like vertical impact.

Type [c] techniques: This facet of the *saroda* technique, possessing elements of the polychord, dominates the aural experience in the medium-to-faster tempi, especially in broad-span melodic phrasing. This facet is emphasized by regarding the multiplicity of melodic strings as a distinctive musical element rather than unavoidable. *Saroda* players revel in opportunities for a harp-like activation of the melodic strings, and compose symmetric, geometric, and kaleidoscopic patterns to maximise such exposure.

Since multiple-string execution requires lifting of at least one finger from any particular melodic string, the Type [c] special effects are a subset of the type [b] technique. Multiple-string execution of both, *sparśa* and *krintana*, is possible.

New Path to Sculpting of Melody

The search of the *saroda* for an idiom uniquely suited to its ergonomic and acoustic character, has contributed significantly to the melodic richness of Hindustani instrumental music. Because of its short stem, the *saroda* became the first plucked instrument in classical music to require multiple-string melodic execution for even a single full octave. It is therefore described as a semi-polychord. Because of its design, it delivers distinctively different timbres on each string. Thus, the instrument became not only a canvas of pitch-frequencies, but also a canvas rich in multiple timbres. This combination inspired the development of a new approach to the melodic interpretation of *rāgas*.

Conventional wisdom regarding Hindustani music says that the basic building-block of its melody is a phrase of two or more *svaras*, characterized by at least two melodic transitions to define three points in conjunct — rather than disjunct — intervallic transition.

This description, arising from the vocal music model, implicitly recognizes three kinds of melodic path:

[a] the melodic or *rāga* driven, which composes and arranges phrases with the purpose of exploring the melodic character of the *rāga*,

[b] the symmetric, which composes and arranges phrases in order to exploit the symmetry of the *rāga*'s permissible phraseology without the existence of any correspondence between the *svara*s and the transitions, and

[c] the geometric, which composes and arranges phrases in order to emphasize the congruence between permissible phrases as defined by the first-fourth or first-fifth correspondence between the *svara*s and the transitions within each phrase.

In the latter half of the twentieth century, the *saroda*, and later the *santūra*, a classic polychord, obliged us to recognize a fourth path to melodic development, arising from their highly evolved contemporary idioms.

The technique of sound-activation on these instruments [plucking or striking] imposes a discontinuity on the melodic flow. This has encouraged musicians to develop a path of disjunct rather than conjunct melodic development. This path dispenses with the phrase as the basic building-block of melodic development, and utilises permissible *svara*s either in isolation, or in groups of two, in interesting juxtaposition.

The tonal patterns so developed — if they can be called patterns — can often be non-descript in terms of its *rāga* connotation, though not inimical to the *rāga* being performed. By suppressing the listener's consciousness of the specific *rāga*, these patterns divert the attention of the listener from the melodic component, towards the manipulation of timbres, volume, and rhythmic patterns, these being the primary territory of the sound-priming action [strokes].

This path to melodic development enables the *saroda* to fully exploit its distinctive acoustic character — by highlighting the manipulation of timbres and time-intervals through high-frequency, variable-frequency, and multiple-string stroke craft. The primary musical purpose of this path is non-melodic. Yet, these expressions have to be described as melodic because they are not harmonic. But, to the extent that they do not have a well-defined melodic contour, they can be described as kaleidoscopic.

5.5

THE SANTŪRA

The *santūra* is a unique instrument in Hindustani music. It has risen from virtual oblivion to the peak of popularity in an unusually short time — less than three decades. It is the only string instrument subjected to percussive sound activation. All others are either plucked or bowed. The *santūra* is also the sole survivor in its organological classification of struck polychords. Three instruments in this grouping have vanished in recent times — the *jala taraṅga,* a set of china clay cups of different sizes tuned to scale by filling them with water, the *kāṣṭa taraṅga,* an Indian version of the xylophone, and the *tabalā taraṅga,* a set of treble drums tuned to different pitches to produce melody. The acceptance of the *santūra,* after the failure of the other three, is explained by its ergonomic and acoustic superiority, and the contribution of Pt. Shivkumar Sharma.

Sharma started performing classical music on the *santūra* in 1952, but attracted national attention only after his concert at the Sur Singara Samsad festival at Bombay in 1955. The instrument's acceptance on the art-music platform took years of struggle. But, Shivkumar and his instrument became an instant rage with composers of music for the movies. The *santūra* soon penetrated the public mind as the musical signature of the Kashmir valley where many of India's films were shot in the 1960s. That phase of the *santūra*'s glory receded in the 1980s when Kashmir became unsafe as a location, and film music started going electronic. By this time, Sharma and the *santūra* were firmly entrenched on the classical platform.

Sharma's ascendancy on the art music horizon attracted a large number of musicians to take to the *santūra*. As a result, the instrument and its idiom are now in a state of flux, with every *santūra* player attempting to explore new musical directions, and redesigning the instrument to suit his own musical vision.

Organology

The *santūra* belongs to the box polychord variety of struck instruments. Until recently, it was virtually unknown to Indians outside the Kashmir valley, where it was common as an accompaniment for vocal renditions of *sūfīānā mauṣiqī* (chants of the Sūfī sects). Shivkumar Sharma [in a private interview on 02/12/03] questions the popular notion of *sūfīānā mauṣiqī* as folk music. He prefers to describe it as Kashmiri classical music. It uses melodic structures [called *maqāms*, as in Persian classical music], and rhythmic cycles (*tāla*s) of four or eight beats derived from Hindustani as well Persian traditions, requires considerable training, and acknowledges different levels of musicianship. It is performed at a slow, deliberate tempo, and is accompanied by the tabalā.

The instrument is related to similar instruments in the neighbouring regions of the Middle East and Central Asia. According to Shivkumar Sharma, similar instruments [the hammered dulcimer/cimbalom family] exist in Persia, Iraq, China, Tibet, Hungary, Kazakhstan, Uzbekistan, Greece, Ireland, Italy, and even in the foothills of the Alps. There exists one platform-mounted variant in central Europe, which is played in a standing position, and has foot-pedals for acoustic manipulation. That is probably the father of the piano. Some authors have linked the name to the *Psantir*, a similar instrument known to Mesopotamians since the pre-Christian era. The name is, however, in all likelihood of Sanskrit, or Persian origin. The original Sanskrit name for it is *śatatantrī* [*śata* = 100 + *tantrī* = stringed instrument], and the Persian name, now popular, is *santūra* [*sad* or *san* = 100 + *tūra* = strings].

The Persians believe that the instrument originated in their land, and travelled from there to other parts of the world. The theory of Indian origin is also plausible considering that polychords of various types have been a part of the Indian musical tradition from ancient times. This family faded away after the tenth century AD, leaving only two significant survivors, both of the box polychord variety — the *svaramaṇḍala* and the *santūra*. The descriptions of *śatatantrī vīṇā* and the *vāna vīṇā* in ancient Indian literature closely approximate the *santūra*. However, organologists have been unable to establish the evolutionary connection between them and the present-day instrument. [Deva, B.C. *Musical Instruments of India*, 2nd edn., Munshiram Manoharlal Publishers Pvt. Ltd., New Delhi, 2000].

After studying this dulcimer/cimbalom family of instruments in several parts of the world, Sharma [*ibid.*] discovered that the Indian [Kashmiri] *santūra* is the only one with exactly hundred strings. According to him, contemporary Persian experts are unable to explain the 100-stringed name for the Persian instrument, which has only 72 strings. Sharma also finds it interesting that ancient Indian texts have referred to the *śatatantrī* and the *vāna* as being used for accompaniment to the chanting of *mantras* [religious chants/hymns], this being also the purpose for which the instrument is used in the Kashmir valley.

Construction and Tuning

The contemporary *santūra* used in classical music consists of a trapezoid box, which acts as a rest for the strings stretched across it, as well as the resonator. The box is 60 cm long, 60 cm wide at one end, tapering to 30 cm width at the other. The tapering width has 30 bridges for strings, 15 on each side, over each of which passes a set of three/four strings. The strings are fixed to iron pegs, which are turned for tuning. Sound activation is done by the hammering action of two sticks of walnut wood [mallets], curved at the striking end. The grip of the sticks is shaped for optimal impact control under manipulation by the thumbs and the index fingers [Deva, 2000].

There are two tuning systems in practice. The traditional system tunes the string-sets to the scale of the *rāga* to be performed. This poses a problem of retuning the instrument for each *rāga*. This problem is compounded by the fact that the *santūra* has four strings for every pitch. Retuning even three *svara*s across three octaves implies retuning thirty-six strings. As a solution to this problem, chromatic tuning has now gained popularity. This solution limits the use of abrasion as a technique of melodic execution, but is otherwise efficient.

Being a polychord, the *santūra* activates the sound and executes the melody simultaneously. The three categories of mallet impact in use are: [a] primary impact, [b] secondary impact, and [c] abrasive action.

The dominant technique consists of staccato melodic execution, using the primary impact of a vertical or near-vertical hammering action of the mallet on the desired string-set. The secondary impact of the mallet stroke is used to prolong the activation of a particular pitch in a progressive fade-out. In this kind of action, the musician allows the mallet to bounce on the particular string-set until it has lost momentum. When the musician desires a continuity of sound activation across different pitches in order to shape a melodic contour, he uses abrasive action similar to the bowing action on a bowed instrument.

As an acoustic machine, the *santūra* permits a partial manipulation of volume and timbre, and a reasonable approximation to the melodic continuity characteristic of Indian music. At the present stage in the evolution of its idiom, the *santūra* is therefore best understood as a melodic instrument performed percussively, and whose melodic potential is still in a state of evolution.

Evolutionary Perspectives

Pt. Shivkumar Sharma was ideally suited for his pioneering role because he had received early training in vocal music, and had established himself as a *tabalā* player of eminence before deserting it for the *santūra*. His mastery over melody and rhythm enabled him to develop a balanced melodic-rhythmic idiom, which astutely exploits the essential rhythmicality of the instrument, while also neutralizing it.

Sharma took up the *santūra* upon the insistence of his father, Pt. Umadatta Sharma, a *tabalā* exponent of the Punjab *gharānā* and a vocalist trained in the Benares tradition under the celebrated Guru, Bade Ramdasji. During his tenure as Chief Producer of music on Kashmir Radio, Pt. Umadatta heard the *santūra* and saw in it a challenge worthy of his son. The instrument Shivkumar inherited from the *sūfiānā* tradition was incapable of delivering contemporary *rāga*-based music in an electronically engineered acoustic environment. However, that was the very instrument on which Shivkumar practiced, and made his debut as a *santūra* exponent. While the popular music industry was swept off its feet by the novelty and charm of the sound, the world of classical music was unenthusiastic about its future because of its obvious limitations in the handling of continuous melody and microtonal nuances. This triggered off Sharma's efforts at re-engineering the instrument and developing an idiom aimed at exploiting its unique character, while also enhancing its melodic capabilities.

Sharma first altered the tuning system. The *santūra* of *sūfīānā mauṣiqī* was tuned to Bilāwal scale of Hindustani music, with only *śuddha svara*s. The steel string-set raised to the right delivered the middle octave, while the brass string-set raised to the left delivered the lower octave. On both octaves, two additional *svara*s were available on each side of the octave. This system was adequate for *sūfīānā mauṣiqī* but lamentably wanting against the demands of *rāga*-based music. Shivkumar replaced this system with chromatic tuning similar to the *harmonium* with *śuddha svara*s on the right side, and the *komala/tīvra svara*s on the left side. He adopted this as the stable system, to resort occasionally to *rāga*-scale tuning.

The second major effort was the re-engineering of its acoustic output. He experimented briefly with mallet design, but decided finally to leave it alone, and concentrate on the ergonomics of the *santūra* art. The traditional [*sūfīānā*] method of handling the instrument was to place it on a triangular wooden platform in front of the musician without direct contact between the instrument and either the musician's body or the floor. This was efficient for slow melody typical of *sūfīānā mauṣiqī*, rendered before intimate gatherings and without electronic amplification. Sharma found that, in high-density melody [*tāna*s] delivered through microphones, this created a blurred melodic contour. Shivkumar placed the instrument on his lap so that half of the instrument was in contact with his thighs, while the other half was suspended in midair. This provided an "earthing" to the acoustic output without muffling it. Incidentally, this also allowed the musician an upright posture, enhancing the overall ergonomic efficiency of performance. For ideal results, this solution required the *santūra* performer to be — like Sharma — at least six feet tall.

But, at that stage, Sharma did not need to think beyond his own needs.

The placement and posture solution did not entirely work out the acoustic problem. So, he reviewed the standard 4-string set for each *svara*. After some experimentation, he settled down to a 3-string set for the middle and higher octaves and a 2-string set for the lower octave. In addition, he devised an original *cikarī* set — conceptually distinct from the conventional *cikarī* [drone] set used on the *sitāra* and the *saroda*. His *cikarī* is modelled after the extra set Ustad Ali Akbar Khan uses on the *saroda*, which is tuned to the dominant *svara*s of the *rāga*. With these changes, the instrument acquired a satisfactory output for the contemporary acoustic environment, while also reinforcing its distinctive acoustic character.

The desire for superior control of timbre and volume led him next to standardizing the ergonomics of performance. Drawing on the principles of stroke classification [*da/ra*] on the *sitāra* and *saroda*, Sharma standardized the impact protocol for different categories of phrases. The combination of mallet-choice and impact-points became the basis for a notation system uniquely designed for the instrument. Sharma perfected this combination in his performance, and adopted it as the basic pedagogical tool for his disciples.

These developments in the design and technique of the *santūra* were inspired by, and synchronous with, the growth of Sharma's musical vision, and the content of music he wished to execute. Beyond the purely ergonomic and the acoustic, his primary concern has been to enhance the capability of the *santūra* for melodic continuity, without denying its essentially percussive character. The issue of melodic continuity pertains to two melodic effects — the elongation of intonation on a single *svara*, and a smooth melodic transition from one *svara* to another — both challenges on an instrument designed for staccato melodic execution.

To the basic technique of using the primary impact for melodic execution, Shivkumar made an early addition of secondary impact. In his early recordings, we hear the use of this secondary impact technique for a *tremolo* effect caused by the bouncing of the mallet on the same string-set for elongated intonation. According to Sharma, he found the results of this technique limited in usefulness, and also "alien" to Hindustani music. He therefore drifted towards the abrasion technique. With this simulation of bowing, which also required a modification of the mallet-grip, he could obtain continuous melody for unlimited durations. This development not only helped the refinement of the melodic facet of his music, but became especially important for executing the delicate ornamentation typical of his renditions in the semi-classical and folk genres. This was a breakthrough because a non-impact technique for a mallet-driven instrument amounted to transcending the intrinsic character of the instrument, without denying it. Because abrasion was possible only within a narrow physical space, Sharma increased the frequency with which he resorted to the *rāga*-scale tuning of the instrument, abandoning the chromatic tuning.

Shivkumar Sharma's Music

Sharma's approach to music can be analysed in four facets — *rāga* grammar, architecture [*rāga* presentation protocol], sculpture [tonal patterning], and the balance between melodic and rhythmic elements of his music.

Sharma's stature has been substantially determined by his unimpeachable *rāga* grammar. Without doubt, this has also contributed significantly to the stature of his instrument. The present author has had several occasions to compare the rendition of the same *rāga* by the most respected names in contemporary music with the documented forms of the mature *rāga*s. With respect to seemingly non-controversial *rāga*s like

Ahīra Bhairava, as well as the rare *rāga*s like Gorakh Kalyāṇa, Shivkumar Sharma's renderings are amongst the very few which fastidiously follow documented *rāga*-grammar. Shivkumar's recording of Sohinī, another classic, is rigorous enough on grammar to embarrass a few *paṇḍit*s. He treats the middle-octave *gā* as the scale-base, and his rendition of this *uttarāṅga-pradhāna rāga*, almost ignores the region below the notional scale-base throughout the rendition, except as a reference point for tonality.

Sharma modeled the architecture of his music after the dominant idiom of the *sitāra* and *saroda* in the 1950s with a substantial dependence on *tīnatāla bandiśa*s. He adapted the stroke-craft component of *sitāra/saroda* music to suit the technique and acoustic capabilities of his instrument. In his early music, he also relied heavily on *tihāī*s and *cakradāras*, as was commonly done in *sitāra/saroda* music. However, he soon realized that the *santūra* idiom would find respectability in the Hindustani mainstream only if he could save the melodic element from being swamped by the rhythmic element, which was magnified by the intrinsic rhythmicality of his instrument. By his own admission [Interview of 21/06/04], he adopted the philosophy of "melody not at the cost of rhythm, and rhythm not at the cost of melody."

In his search for a distinctive as well as balanced idiom, Shivkumar later banked increasingly on *jhaptāla* and *rūpaka*. Both *tāla*s have asymmetrical beat structures and, therefore, an explicit rhythmicality. With this level of basic rhythmicality, Sharma could concentrate on melody. Progressively, he reduced his reliance on *tihāī*s and *cakradāra*s and began replacing them with *gāyakī*-style *āmada*s.

In the sculpture department, Sharma veered more towards the language of the *saroda* than the *sitāra*. This was natural because the *saroda* is a semi-polychord of percussive-melodic character, whose immediate ancestor was the Afghan *rabāba*, an instrument meant for playing martial music. *Saroda* music of the 1950s and 1960s provided an appropriate backdrop to the emergence of the *santūra*'s melodic evolution. In its search for a distinctive language, the *saroda* had broken through the traditional barrier of melodic [*calana*/*rāga* phraseology], geometric and symmetric tonal patterning. Ali Akbar Khan introduced the dazzling kaleidoscopic approach to tonal patterning to exploit the semi-polychord character of his instrument. At the same time, Radhika Mohan Maitra, was adapting the *rabāba*'s percussive-melodic idiom to the *saroda*, permitting the rhythmic element to drive the melodic. Though without conscious adoption, both these tendencies are reflected in Sharma's *santūra* idiom. This combination of musical elements is consistent with the unique character of his instrument.

The role of kaleidoscopic patterning in the *santūra* idiom, highlighted in Sharma's music, deserves special attention because it has accelerated the process of instrumental music seeking a distinctive language of expression, liberated from its traditional reference point in the vocal expression. The *santūra*'s evolutionary achievement in the hands of Sharma, a highly trained *tabalā* exponent, is magnified by the fact that it has also resisted the lure of the percussion idiom.

Shivkumar Sharma's contribution has woven the music of the instrument intimately into the fabric of modern Hindustani music, while also shaping an independent genre for it. This genre has clear reference points in the music of the plucked lutes. With Shivkumar's refinement of the instrument's melodic capabilities, the genre can also claim reference points in the modern vocal genres — Khayal and *ṭhumarī*. These reference points not withstanding, it is a genre arising uniquely from the character of the instrument, and comparable to none other.

The Santūra after Shivkumar Sharma

Sharma's rise to the peak of the profession attracted a sizeable inflow of fresh talent to the instrument. The first generation of converts was obviously self-taught, and came from amongst struggling *tabalā* players, and performers on the near-extinct instruments like the *jalataraṅga* and *vicitra vīṇā*. The physically undemanding character of the instrument, and the misconception about the instrument being easy to master, attracted the second generation. The booming demand for *santūra* training led the second generation of aspirants to a large number of teachers who probably qualified as musicians, but not as *santūra* players. Shivkumar Sharma denies having formally initiated or accepted a single disciple. This leaves his son, Rahul, as the only *santūra* player with known access to his *santūra* expertise and musical wisdom.

Not surprisingly, therefore, the *santūra* has yet to witness the emergence of a significant successor to Sharma. Significance, in this context, can only mean an acknowledged contribution to evolution, which is rooted in the present, but also reveals a clear vision of the instrument's unique destiny as defined by its distinctive acoustic and ergonomic character, though not without regard to its limitations.

Sharma's approach to music represents a fine balance between the melodic and rhythmic elements. He has exploited the rhythmic potential of the instrument astutely, without allowing it to interfere with his parallel refinement of its melodic capabilities and expressions. The rhythmicality of his music is intrinsic to the character of the instrument, and validates its claim to a unique place on the contemporary music-scape. His approach to melodic patterning has stayed within the traditional Indian concept of melody and the exploration of tonal geometry within its confines. At any given time, both his mallets are engaged in executing the same, single, melodic idea. His mallets are, almost always, operating either individually, or in alternating action. Rarely, if ever, are they engaged in simultaneous impact on different string-sets.

The succeeding generation of *santūra* players has, interestingly, developed a special fondness either for semi-classical/*ṭhumarī rāga*s, and for *rāga*s imported recently from the Carnatic tradition into Hindustani music. The semi-classical *rāga*s, in their very nature, permit a libertarian interpretation of grammar, while most Carnatic *rāga*s have yet to acquire a stable melodic personality in Hindustani music, and therefore are not accountable to any yardstick of grammatical propriety. This freedom from accountability towards the legitimacy of the melodic experience allows the younger *santūra* players to undertake their daring explorations into the instrument's extra-melodic potential. Their basic architecture remains rooted to modern *sitāra/saroda* music. Beyond this, the music is obsessed with the percussive-rhythmic possibilities of the *santūra*, and an exploration of the acoustic experience beyond melody. The next generation has begun flirting with pitch-activation routines hitherto alien to Hindustani music, such as harmony, heterophony, and polyphony. As a minor element, younger *santūra* players even interrupt mallet-based music to strum or pluck the strings as on a harp, or to execute short melodic passages on a bass string as on a slide-Guitar. The epidemic combination of audacity and technical virtuosity has resulted in some young *santūra* players — with only two mallets in their grips — harbouring delusions of competing with a piano.

These directions have implications for the integrity of the *rāga* experience, which may yet be difficult to assess. They also appear to imply a view of the melodic canvas as a set of unconnected acoustic variables, rather than a frequency-calibrated continuum. Such a view implicitly isolates the acoustic meaning of *svaras* from their cultural meaning rooted in the principle of tonality. Although these directions do not explicitly defy the principle of tonality fundamental to Indian music, they certainly suppress the listener's awareness of melodic progression as practiced in Hindustani music. This combination of a splintered melodic experience, and an enlarged acoustic experience, defines a new, perhaps alien, musical culture. Not surprisingly, the second generation of competent *santūra* players is far busier on the international concert circuit than the Indian.

Essentially, Sharma's successors are exploring two principal directions for the instrument — the percussive-rhythmic direction derived from percussion/the *tabalā* and the harmony-polyphony-heterophony direction inspired by keyboard-based polychords/the piano. The *tabalā* direction grossly underutilizes the melodic potential of the *santūra* while the piano direction demands far more from the *santūra* than it can ever deliver. Viewed from where the *santūra* is today, the former direction seems like a regression, while the latter, a dead-end street. The *santūra*'s attempts at mimicking either of these instruments amounts to a denial of its own distinctive character as hitherto revealed. In addition to issues of aesthetics and cultural meaning, neither of them can, therefore, be said to constitute an evolution in consonance with contextual relevance and specificity.

An evolutionary vacuum, or worse, experimental chaos, following on the heels of a pioneering contribution, is a familiar pattern. It is, for instance, also evident in respect of the Hawaiian Guitar, introduced to Hindustani music by Brijbhushan Kabra around the same time as Shivkumar's launch of the *santūra*. Any instrument acquires a propensity for self-generating evolution after several generations of musicians, of different backgrounds, have contributed to the development of its technique and idiom. Shivkumar Sharma picked up an obscure regional instrument, and gave it stature on par with more mature instruments in Hindustani art music. Even if the immediate post-Sharma directions appear bewildering, the *santūra* is now firmly established in Hindustani music.

5.6

THE ŚEHNĀYĪ*

THE *śehnāyī* could qualify as the single most widely heard instrument in India, having become an integral part of the tribal, folk, ceremonial and religious traditions of the sub-continent [India/Pakistan/Bangladesh/Sri Lanka]. In India, it is proclaimed the *maṅgala vādya*, the auspicious instrument. *Śehnāyī* music leads religious processions, sanctifies marriages, announces the opening of temple doors to the public every morning, inaugurates major cultural events and welcomes dignitaries to public functions. It is only in the latter half of the twentieth century that the instrument was elevated to the art-music platform, singular credit for which goes to the formidable musicianship of Ustad Bismillah Khan of Varanasi.

Organology

The instrument belongs to the Oboe family of beating-reed aerophones. Instruments answering to this description, and of near-identical construction, are found in all parts of India, though known by different names. This fact makes the *śehnāyī* yet another unresolved mystery in Indian organology. Many of its names are of Sanskrit derivation suggesting ancient Indian origins. Others indicate Perso-Arabic etymology, suggesting Middle-Eastern or Central Asian origins. Some names allude to processions, assemblies and courts, thus referring to their ceremonial function under feudal patronage. And, still others are merely descriptive of either its physical form, or its piercing sound, pointing towards untraceable folk and tribal origins. Organologist, B.C. Deva [2nd edn., 1987,] appears to favour the theory of indigenous origin and evolution of the instrument.

Design

The main body of the instrument is a conical bore of wood, ideally Teak [*Tectona Grandis*]. *Śehnāyīs* made of gold, silver, and even soapstone are known to exist. The body has four to seven holes punched into it. The musician covers and uncovers these holes to manipulate the melody. The narrow end of the bore is fitted with a mouthpiece [staple], to which are affixed two winnow-shaped reeds, about a centimeter in length. The reeds are made either of marsh-grass or special leaves. The reeds merely regulate the flow of air into the body by beating against the wall of the mouthpiece, but play no role in the manipulation of the pitch. The broad end of the bore, the output end, is fitted with a metallic cup, made usually of brass, but occasionally also of other metals [*ibid.*].

Śehnāyīs are made to a specific pitch in terms of tonality. An average *śehnāyī* player manages a melodic canvas of an octave and a half on the instrument. A maestro can, however, coax two octaves out of it, without producing unmusical sounds. Varanasi and Lucknow have been the principal centres of *śehnāyī* manufacture. In recent years, however, research oriented enthusiasts in Nashik, about 150 km from Mumbai, have made the city another major supplier of quality *śehnāyīs* [Shailesh Bhagwat, *Saaz-e-śehnāyī: Nāda-bramha Marathi Quarterly*, Bombay, Issue of January 1996].

Idiom and Repertoire

Being a breath-driven instrument, its natural musical output is continuous melody. The intermittent or rhythmic stopping of the airflow by the action of the tongue is, however, used for creating melodic discontinuities of the staccato variety. Logically, therefore, the *śehnāyī* has adopted the idiom of the vocal genres. In the art-music segment, *śehnāyī* music borrows its *rāga* presentation protocol from the *khayāla* genre, while in the semi-classical and light segments, it borrows its melodic-rhythmic material from the *ṭhumarī*, *kajarī*, *caitī*, and similar regional genres. Within the predominantly vocalized expression of these genres, however, *śehnāyī* music increasingly incorporates staccato expressions simulating the music of the plucked lute family, principally, the *sitāra*.

The repertoire of the *śehnāyī* acknowledges the fact that its performers make their livelihood primarily in the ceremonial and religious segment of the music market. In this segment, the repertoire must assume that its audience is involuntary and inattentive. It must also assume that the vast majority of the audience is uncultivated in art music. The *śehnāyī* player's repertoire is, therefore, dominated by popular, folk and regional music. This dominance also influences the idiom of the *śehnāyī* player in his handling of art-music. Even in the idiom of the most acclaimed *śehnāyī* players on the art-music stage, the connoisseur will observes the breaching of the boundaries of art music with a drift into folk and popular elements. This tendency has allowed the *śehnāyī* to achieve immense popularity on the concert platform, while straddling several other categories of music within Indian musical culture.

Probably for the same reason, the *śehnāyī* has been the most successful instrument in the *jugalabandī* [duets] segment of the art-music market. Ustad Bismillah Khan's duets with *sitāra* maestro, Ustad Vilayat Khan, have become the stuff of legend. But, even moderately accomplished *śehnāyī* players have been able to produce eminently charming, and even saleable, music in collaboration with partners of compatible stature.

Since the elevation of the instrument to the concert platform by Ustad Bismillah Khan, the *śehnāyī* has contributed several maestros to the art-music world. Notable amongst them are Ali Ahmed Hussain of Calcutta, Baburao Khaladkar and Shankar Rao Gakewad, both deceased, of Pune, and Anant Lal of Delhi. Amongst the younger generation of musicians, Shailesh Bhagvat of Bombay has recently acquired some stature.

Genres in Śehnāyī Music

On the concert platform, the repertoire and the idiom of the *śehnāyī* have been influenced almost entirely by the towering presence of Ustad Bismillah Khan, spanning over six decades. If, therefore, one has to refer to *gharānā*s of the *śehnāyī*, there is probably only one *gharānā* on the art-music scene — the Bismillah Khan *gharānā*. He has adopted the *khayāla* genre as his principal inspiration for the presentation of *rāga*-based music, and the regional melodies popular in his home in Varanasi, and its environs as the source for his semi-classical and popular repertoire. The most important amongst these are the *bola-banāo ṭhumarī*, and seasonal songs such as the *kajarī*, *caitī*, *phāguna* and *sāvana*.

Śehnāyī players from other regions have tended to follow this pattern, although *śehnāyī* players from the western state of Maharashtra [Bombay/Pune] do include local folk and regional music, such as *lavaṇīs* and *nāṭya-saṅgīta* in their presentations. These are also poetry-dominant forms, and are subjected to the same kind of transformation in their *śehnāyī* presentation as the *kajarī*/*caitī* category of north Indian genres do.

The Ensemble for Śehnāyī Performances

The traditional ensemble for *śehnāyī* performance has been determined by its role as an outdoor instrument, played in public virtually as background music, and without amplification. In this role, the supporting ensemble was a *sura-śehnāyī*, and a pair of *tāśā/nagārā* drums. The *sura-śehnāyī* is a single-pitch drone, on which no melody can be played. The *sura-śehnāyī* performed a role comparable to a *tānapūrā* in vocal music, filling the silences. The *tāśā* or *nagārā* are pairs of kettledrums, played with sticks, and commanding an idiom of their own, though less sophisticated than that of the *pakhāwaja* or the *tabalā*.

In the concert context, the *śehnāyī* ensemble has become more elaborate. Lead *śehnāyī* players are now frequently accompanied by a supporting *śehnāyī* player, who allows them periodic respite. For a drone, they frequently replace the *sura-śehnāyī* with a *tānapūrā*. And, the traditional *tāśā* is frequently replaced by the *tabalā*. These deviations from the traditional ensemble recognize the existence of a superior acoustic environment, and the availability of electronic amplification.

The Disappearing Śehnāyī

The meagre supply of *śehnāyī* musicianship to the art music stage is explained by the socio-cultural reality. Very few *śehnāyī* players have either the motivation or the training in art-music to qualify for the concert platform. Even fewer can hope to make a living exclusively as art musicians. More fundamentally, however, the supply of talent to the *śehnāyī* profession itself is dwindling because of shifting preferences in its mainstay market segments. The ceremonial and religious market in the cities is shifting to pre-recorded music, electronic synthesisers, and brass bands. The film-music industry, once a significant user of the *śehnāyī*, has gone almost entirely electronic. On the concert platform, therefore, the art of the *śehnāyī* could risk a growing shortage of quality musicianship in the future.

Interestingly, a similar fate confronts the *sāraṅgī*, yet another instrument believed to be of entirely indigenous origin and evolution, and enjoying a similar presence across the art, tribal, popular, and folk traditions. The *śehnāyī* and the *sāraṅgī* appear to be victims of a larger phenomenon in Hindustani music, which is phasing out some indigenous instruments, and enthusiastically adopting instruments of foreign origin, such as the *santūra* and *saroda*. Implicit in these trends is the decline of the music of melodic continuity, and its substitution by the music of melodic discontinuity.

5.7

THE SĀRAṄGĪ*

The *sāraṅgī* belongs to the bowed chordophone family of short-necked fretless lutes. It is found in various forms all over the Indian subcontinent. The *sāraṅgī* family originated as folk instruments, and now include the sophisticated acoustic machine used in classical music. Instruments of this family represent a wide range of design, from the single-string tribal instrument called *dhodro banam* to the classical *sāraṅgī*. Throughout its history, the *sāraṅgī* has been used for accompanying vocal music. It made its debut as a solo instrument on the art music scene in the early twentieth century and has, since then, enlarged this presence considerably, though only sporadically.

Unlike several other popular instruments in Hindustani music today, the *sāraṅgī* family is believed to be entirely of Indian origin and evolution, with virtually no trace of foreign influence or inspiration. It is related to the *pinākī vīṇā* and the *rāvaṇahasta*, two instruments encountered in Hindu mythology. There is evidence, though not conclusive, of their use for accompanying folk and religious music during the eleventh and twelfth centuries. Clearer evidence exists, from the early seventeenth century, of its use as a classical instrument. The classical *sāraṅgī*, as we know it today, evidently evolved around 1850, with Meerut, in the vicinity of Delhi, as the principal centre of manufacturing.

Construction, Design, and Tuning

The classical *sāraṅgī* is carved from a single block of wood, ideally Tun [*Tuna Ciliata Roem*], which has been seasoned for a year, and treated with *geru* [Red Ochre] dissolved in water in order to restore its natural colour and sheen.

The instrument is 64-67 cm long with a belly hollowed out in front. The head consists of two peg-boxes, hollowed out from behind. Thus, the instrument consists of four separate chambers. In the partition between the belly and the neck, there is a large hole at the back, which is often used for keeping the bow during transportation. The walls of the *sāraṅgī* shell have to be 7-10 mm thick in order to withstand the tension of 35 sympathetic strings and three heavy gut strings for melodic execution.

The instrument is tuned in the pitch range of C sharp to F sharp. The best acoustic output is obtained by tuning the first string to D sharp or E. Unless the *sāraṅgī* player decides to use separate instruments for accompanying male and female vocalists, the tuning of the pitch needs to be varied as required by the vocalist. However, there have been *sāraṅgī* players, like Abdul Lateef Khan [1928-2003] who kept the instrument tuned to the same pitch, irrespective of the fundamental at which the vocalist was singing. His logic, as reported to the present author, was that the instrument sounds best at a certain pitch, and he preferred to vary his playing to maintain the quality of the acoustic output. The three melodic strings are tuned to *sā-pā-sā* or *sā-mā-sā*. Of the two sets of sympathetic strings, the main set is tuned chromatically starting with *komala dhā* or *komala nī* in the lower octave, while the subordinate set is tuned to the scale of the *rāga* for solo playing, and chromatically for accompaniment to obviate retuning for change of *rāga*s.

Playing Technique

Melodic execution is done by the left hand. Pressing the fingernails sideways against the melodic strings activates the desired *svara*s. Some *sāraṅgī* players use the skin above the cuticles for this purpose, with the fingertip touching the fingerboard. Talcum powder is used as a lubricant. The technique of melodic execution involves sliding or articulating separate *svara*s using a systematic fingering technique. The traditional fingering technique uses all the four fingers. Increasingly, however, musicians now use only three fingers, with a selective use of the fourth finger for special effects. There are four distinct schools of fingering.

The sound activation is done with the bow held in the right hand. The shaft of the bow is a straight length of a hard wood, preferably ebony. The shaft is 70 cm long, round in section, which bends when strung with a hank of horse hair from the tail of a stallion. Resin is applied periodically to the playing surface for retaining its abrasive action for sound-activation.

The bow is held in an underhand grip. The first two fingers positioned on the shaft regulate the pressure, while the other two, or three, embrace the nut. In order to elicit the desired acoustic response from the instrument, the bow needs to engage the melodic strings close to the bridge.

The Role of the Sāraṅgī in Music

Throughout history, the *sāraṅgī* has been the instrument on which wandering bards and minstrels in India accompany themselves. At some stage, the more talented and ambitious amongst them were attracted by the glamour of city life, and drifted towards the feudal courts to make a living as accompanists to courtesans. In this role, the *sāraṅgī* emerged as a significant instrument in art music, enlarging it in later years to become the preferred melodic accompaniment for female as well as male singers.

As accompanists to female vocalists, *sāraṅgī* players were involved with the entire range of music performed in the salons of the courtesans, which catered to the needs of genteel society until the end of the nineteenth century in northern India. The instrument soon became an integral part of the vocalist's ensemble — from the lowbrow music performed in establishments verging on the flesh trade, to the middlebrow *ṭhumarī* and *ghazal*, the devotional *qawwālī*, to the highbrow *khayāla* form. Performers of the *dhrupad* genre, however, have kept away from any form of melodic accompaniment, preferring to sing accompanied only by the *tānapūrā*.

By the early nineteenth century, *sāraṅgī* players had become formidable repositories of *rāga* knowledge and compositions, and were recognized as maestros in their own right. Their art had become a part of the system of hereditary musicianship, giving rise to several distinguished families of *sāraṅgī* players. In the salons of the courtesans, *sāraṅgī* players became tutors of female singers and custodians of the vocalist arts, with a share in its revenues. This institution of courtesans operated, understandably, on the fringes of genteel society. An association with it gave *sāraṅgī* players, and the instrument, a stigma that it could not shed until it was too late.

In the early twentieth century, Victorian morals imposed by India's colonial rulers, and social reformist movements launched by the Indian bourgeoisie, pushed the institution of courtesans to the brink. Although art music was not their target, their impact severely dented the future of the *sāraṅgī*, which serviced all genres of vocal music, but depended largely for its sustenance on the world of courtesans. The deathblow, however, came from the *harmonium*, invented in Paris [1840], which caught on speedily as a replacement for the *sāraṅgī*.

The Harmonium Challenge and the Response

The *harmonium*'s tempered scale made it singularly unsuitable for Hindustani music. However, it was untainted by social stigma, and had several practical advantages. Being a keyboard instrument, the mastery of intonation on it did not require as arduous a training as it did on the bowed and fretless *sāraṅgī*. A *harmonium* accompanist was also far less likely to bruise a vocalist's ego by challenging his musicianship on the concert platform. Being an easier instrument to master than the *sāraṅgī*, the *harmonium* also created an ample supply of accompanists, who were cheaper to hire. For performers in the lighter genres, the *harmonium* was an even greater boon because the vocalist could herself master the instrument, thus dispensing with the accompanist altogether.

Towards the end of the nineteenth century, the declining fortunes of the *sāraṅgī* gave rise to two significant developments. Some exceptional *sāraṅgī* players abandoned the *sāraṅgī* in favour of a career as vocalists. Legendary twentieth century vocalists — Ustad Abdul Kareem Khan, Ustad Abdul Waheed Khan, Ustad Bade Ghulam Ali Khan — had all begun their careers as *sāraṅgī* players. Another landmark vocalist, Ustad Ameer Khan, belonged to a distinguished family of *sāraṅgī* players and, according to some historians, had also started life as a *sāraṅgī* player. The other significant development was the emergence of the *sāraṅgī* soloist. In the 1920s, spurred by the emerging gramophone record industry, Ustad Bundu Khan [died 1955], the greatest *sāraṅgī* player of the period, started recording 78 RPM discs of solo performances. In later years, several other *sāraṅgī* players also published solo recordings.

In the post-Independence period, Pt. Ramnarain [born 1927] has been the most significant *sāraṅgī* player to bid farewell to accompaniment, and to perform exclusively as a soloist. Interestingly, the maestro has received as many years of training from vocalists, as from *sāraṅgī* players. He is largely responsible for creating an international constituency for the *sāraṅgī*, and reviving interest in the art amongst scions of the *sāraṅgī* playing families. At the time of writing, however, the ageing wizard of the Indian fiddle is still the only member of his tribe with an economically viable career as a soloist.

Pt. Ramnarain's individual achievement does not, evidently, symbolize anything like a revival in the fortunes of the *sāraṅgī*. The population of competent *sāraṅgī* players, estimated currently at about 250, is shrinking along with the demand for their art. The accompaniment market has been lost to the *harmonium*. The government-owned broadcast media, which helped the *sāraṅgī*'s survival for several decades by banning the *harmonium*, have now lifted the ban. The popular music industry, once a significant user of *sāraṅgī* talent, has shifted almost totally to electronic music.

By way of alternative career models, Pt. Ramnarain has demonstrated the viability of a soloist career. In the succeeding generation, Sultan Khan, a distinguished accompanist and soloist, is attempting a revival of the original model of the bards and minstrels on the art music platform, by turning vocalist and accompanying himself on the *sāraṅgī*. The Sultan Khan model is open only to the rare musician endowed with a trained voice along with formidable talent as an instrumentalist. The soloist model of Pt. Ramnarain might hold greater promise for the *sāraṅgī*, provided the art can attract talent with the required training, innovativeness, and tenacity.

The most significant accomplishment of the few eminent soloists has been the sculpting of a distinctive musical experience, which exploits the soloist's freedom from the vocalist vision, while exploiting the basic acoustic character of the instrument within the broad framework of the *khayāla* and *ṭhumarī* genres. Paradoxically, therefore, the emergence of great *sāraṅgī* soloists could depend on the revival of the demand generated by the accompaniment market. Such a scenario is no longer conceivable.

Quality solos available to contemporary audiences are, therefore, predominantly of *sāraṅgī* players who have distinguished themselves as accompanists. Their calibre as soloists rests on the soundness of their basic training in music, and a musical vision that is not constrained by subordination to a diversity of vocalists performing different styles and genres.

The Sāraṅgī — As the Second Fiddle and the First

The role of the *sāraṅgī* [or *harmonium*] as an accompanist to vocal music has been amongst the more intractable documentation problems in Indian musicology. This is primarily because, beyond its basic functionality, the role depends on the level of musicianship represented by the two partners in music making, and the chemistry between them. Since there is no clear tradition of stable partnerships or of prior rehearsals, the chemistry itself is volatile.

The basic contribution of the *sāraṅgī* is to enhance the average acoustic density [sound bytes delivered per unit of time] of the aural experience in a vocal performance. The function has value because the human voice, driven by the breathing cycle and subject to its limitations, is susceptible to involuntary discontinuities in voice production. The melodic accompaniment [*sāraṅgī* or *harmonium*] is intended to fill up the silences that a vocal rendition creates. Beyond this, the function is aesthetic and, therefore, amenable to a bewildering variety of descriptions. Mature *sāraṅgī* players most frequently describe their accompaniment role as that of "following" or "supporting" the vocalist. Central to these descriptions is the primacy of the vocalist as the architect of the concert, and the subordination of the accompanist to the vocalist's musicianship.

As a solo artist, the *sāraṅgī* player has no vocalist to follow or support. Despite this, he is obliged to work within the framework of vocalism because his instrument is designed explicitly as an acoustic match for the human voice, and as a worthy vehicle for the modern genres of vocal music. These realities impose handicaps, and also offer some advantages.

The handicap lies in having to render a genre of vocal music without the spoken word. In their vocal manifestation, the *khayāla* and the *ṭhumarī* forms use three different categories of articulation — literary verse, *saragama* [enunciation of solfa symbols], and *ākāra* [the *ā* vowel]. Collectively, these articulations permit a vocalist to [a] cement the structure of the melodic and rhythmic elements [b] reinforce/enhance the communication of the *rāga*'s emotional content, [c] impart a phonetic and textural richness to the aural experience. Performing a vocal genre of music without the articulations poses a challenge to the attention-holding power of a *sāraṅgī* solo.

As a soloist, the *sāraṅgī* player compensates for the handicap by focusing his musical energies on exploiting the technical capabilities of his instrument. Contemporary *sāraṅgī* solos appear to follow a combination of two approaches for this purpose. One approach is to stretch the melodic complexity and *svara* densities of typically vocal movements to a level which a vocalist is either unable to match, or will not attempt out of fear of becoming un-musical. The other approach is to incorporate musical ideas and movements borrowed and adapted from the plucked instruments [*sitāra/saroda/rudra vīṇā*], guided by the limitations of musicality. This latter approach is evident in the solo *sāraṅgī* renditions of the young maestro, Dhruva Ghosh.

With its continued anchoring in the *khayāla* and *ṭhumarī* genres of vocal music, the *sāraṅgī* cannot be said, yet, to have evolved a distinctive language for solo performance. However, even at the present stage of its evolution, a solo by a mature *sāraṅgī* player can be a memorable musical experience.

Acknowledgement: The perspective on the historical, technical, and sociological facets of the *sāraṅgī*, draws generously upon the pioneering work of Prof. Joep Bor of the Rotterdam Conservatorium, Netherlands, published under the title "The Voice of the Sāraṅgī" in the *Journal of the National Centre for the Performing Arts*, Bombay [vol. XV and XVI, nos. 3, 4, 1, Sept-Dec. 1986 and March 1987].

5.8

THE INDIAN CLASSICAL GUITAR*

THE Indian classical guitar is an adaptation of the Hawaiian Slide guitar, one of the several foreign instruments that the assimilative Indian mind has incorporated into its musical traditions. In most cases, the shell of the instrument is an F-hole guitar, acoustically and structurally enhanced to support the multitude of strings.

The design of the instrument is far from standard yet, with several variants in vogue. The commonest variant has a total of twenty-one strings. The melody is executed on five melodic strings. The five strings are tuned, respectively, to the tonic [Base *sa=D*], the lower octave *pa*, the lower-octave *sa*, the ultra-lower *pa*, and the ultra-lower *sa*. This provides a melodic canvas of four complete octaves. At the same level as the melodic strings, are strung four supporting strings. Two of these are *cikarī* drones, tuned to the upper-*sa*, while the other two are tuned to the dominant *svara*s of the *rāga* to provide an ambient reinforcement of the *rāga*'s tonal geometry. Running parallel to the melodic strings, and at a lower level, are twelve sympathetic strings tuned to the scale of the *rāga*.

The sound activation is done by the thumb, forefinger, and the middle finger of the right hand, all equipped with

---

metal or plastic picks. The forearm of the right hand rests at the base of the chamber resonator, with the forearm and palm muscles providing the motive power for the strokes. The melody is executed by a cylindrical or semi-cylindrical metal bar, held in the left hand, either stopping or sliding over the strings along the stem of the instrument. The playing technique is identical to the Hawaiian slide guitar.

The Hawaiian slide-guitar entered Hindustani music about four decades ago. As such, the instrument is still the subject of considerable experimentation and divergence in terms of acoustic design, technique and, indeed, musical idiom and style.

Evolutionary Perspectives

The slide-guitar came to India before Second World War through the recordings of Sol Hoopii, and Joe Kaipo, with Jimmie Rodgers and others. Touring Hawaiian troupes inspired local imitators. Calcutta's Aloha Boys band, formed in 1938, was often heard on All India Radio. Within a generation, the Hawaiian guitar had become an integral part of Indian film scores. The sound of the slide-guitar penetrated India's musical consciousness with the prelude to the epoch-making semi-classical song [a *bandiśa ṭhumarī*] *bāṭa calat nāyī cunarī raṅga ḍārī* in the film "Ladki" in 1953. [Mark Humphrey, *The Hindustani Slide*, www.IndusLive.com]

By the early 1960s, the Hawaiian guitar had found a secure home in the musical culture of Calcutta, and the state of Bengal, the most prolific nursery of instrumental music talent in the country, and also home to the leading composers of film music until late into the twentieth century. Within Bengal, the instrument became immensely popular for solo renderings of classico-modern genres such as *Rabindra Sangeet* [the compositions of Nobel Laureate Rabindranath Tagore], and folk genres such as *baul* and *plligīti*. The melodic intricacy of these genres produced a vast and mature resource of musicianship on the instrument, and paved the way for its acceptance by the broadcast media, and finally, for its entry into classical music.

Although the immediate inspiration for an Indianized slide-guitar came from North America, the instrument is the heir to an Indian technique of melodic execution. There is, in fact, some basis for speculation that the ancient Indian slide technique for the plucked lute family of instruments may have played a role in the early development of the Hawaiian instrument. There exist accounts of one Gabriel Davion, born in India, and kidnapped by a sea captain to Honolulu in the late nineteenth century, as being the first guitarist to use the slide technique to execute melody on a single string. It is conceivable that this Davion brought the technique of Indian slide-activated melody to Hawaii.

The *ghoṣaka* described in Bharata's *Nāṭyaśāstra* [200 BC-AD 200], and the *ekatantrī vīṇā* repeatedly referred to in musicological texts from the eleventh century AD, are both plucked instruments, on which melody was executed by sliding a hard and smooth mechanical device along the strings, rather than by stopping the strings as on a fretted instrument. In more recent times, the slide principle of melodic execution was represented, in the Hindustani tradition, by the *vicitra vīṇā*, a fretless zither and, in the Carnatic tradition, by the *goṭṭu vādyam*, a fretless lute — both instruments of considerable antiquity. [B.C. Deva, 2nd edn., 2000]. Despite their current rarity on the concert platform, both these instruments have resisted total extinction.

It is significant that the *vicitra vīṇā* and the *goṭṭu vādyam* are, in their respective traditions, near-identical in construction and design to their fretted counterparts. It may therefore be surmised that the slide-principle of melodic execution on these fretless *vīṇā*s defined a distinctive musical capability and role. It is interesting that, while the fretted *vīṇā*s in both the traditions are present as accompanists to vocal music and also as solo concert instruments, the fretless slide *vīṇā*s are more predominantly encountered in solo performance. In a tradition that considers the vocal expression as the validatory model even for instrumental music, it is reasonable to surmise that the fretless slide-*vīṇā* was allowed a more predominant solo role because of its closer-to-vocalism capability.

The Vicitra Vīṇā Legacy

In the Hindustani tradition, the decline of the fretless *vicitra vīṇā* has been virtually simultaneous with that of the fretted *rudra vīṇā*. Their decline is only partially explained by the decline of the medieval *dhrupad/dhamāra* genre of mainstream music, of which the two instruments were an integral part. The major reason for their decline would appear to be their cumbersome ergonomics, and an acoustic quality unsuited for the contemporary environment, governed by electronic amplification and manipulation of musical output.

The Hawaiian slide-guitar appeared to solve both these problems simultaneously while offering the distinctive quality of the fretless slide-*vīṇā* — the ability to reproduce every nuance of Indian classical vocalism with minimum interference from the sound-priming [plucking] activity. Admittedly, the slide-guitar was inferior in this role to the *sāraṅgī*, a bowed instrument. But, within the plucked lute family, it could have no peer as a mimic of the vocal expression. Because of this advantage, the Hawaiian slide-guitar offered a much wider range of stylistic options than the *sitāra* and *saroda*, both of which required a much higher frequency of plucking.

The only trigger the Hawaiian slide-guitar required for slipping into the *vicitra vīṇā*'s role in Hindustani music was towering musicianship, which could demonstrate its musical potential, especially relative to the *sitāra* and *saroda*. The instrument found its pioneering champion in Brijbhushan Kabra [born 1937].

Kabra's Guitar

Brijbhushan came from a business family with a deep involvement in music. His father had studied the *sitāra* under the legendary Ustad Enayet Khan, the father of Ustad Vilayat Khan. Brijbhushan's elder brother, Damodarlal, had studied under the celebrated Ustad Ali Akbar Khan, and was a distinguished *saroda* player. In defiance of acute cynicism within the family, Brijbhushan said "no" to the *sitāra* as well as the *saroda*, and accepted the challenge of elevating the slide-guitar to a level of parity with them under the tutelage of Ustad Ali Akbar Khan.

There was a historical as well organological inevitability about Kabra going along with the established musical approach, and the *rāga* presentation protocol of the major plucked lutes, the *sitāra* and *saroda*. The first step in this direction was the introduction of *cikarī* [drone] strings. As on the *sitāra* and the *saroda*, his *cikarī* set is mounted on a post midway up the stem of the guitar on the bass [inward] side. His repertoire includes a three/four tiered *ālāpa-joḍa-jhālā* movement, slow tempo compositions primarily of Masit Khani format in *tīnatāla*, medium tempo compositions in *rūpaka* and *jhapatāla*, and fast tempo compositions in *tīnatāla* followed by a *jhālā*. As with the *sitāra* and *saroda*, light and semi-classical compositions in a variety of *tāla*s became an important part of a comprehensive repertoire to satisfy contemporary audiences.

Despite the benefit of guidance from a giant amongst musicians, Kabra had to rely on his own resourcefulness for technique. Kabra's musical vision is deeply entrenched in vocalism. It might even be said that, in the melodic content of his music, he has pitted his instrument against the *sāraṅgī*, rather than the *sitāra* or *saroda*. He places the highest premium on the capabilities of the slide-guitar for delivering the melodic continuity and microtonal subtleties of Hindustani vocalism. This logically meant the development of an idiom and technique that would minimize the frequency of strokes, and maximize the melodic density achievable under the impact of each stroke. These became the guiding principles of Kabra's musical endeavours.

Within the *rāga* presentation format of the plucked lutes, Kabra's musical vision, and the instrument's capabilities, led Kabra to develop the anarhythmic and melodically rich *ālāpa* form as his forte. In order to pack the maximum power into each stroke, Kabra dispensed with the picks conventionally used by slide-guitarists, and opted to play with wire plectra [*miẓrab*s] used by sitārists.

Once he had harnessed additional stroke power with *sitāra* plectra, he could achieve the desired manipulation of timbre, volume, and sustain without the addition of sympathetic strings. In a private interview with the present author, Kabra expressed the view that the slide-guitar is so rich in the delivery of microtonal values and melodic continuity, that the *sitāra/saroda* model of acoustic design is irrelevant for the instrument. Kabra also argued that the sympathetic strings, which support only the discrete *svara*s in the *rāga* scale, have the effect of drowning out microtonal subtleties. As a result, the delivery of melodic value is limited, rather than enhanced, by the sympathetic strings.

In order to minimise the melodic discontinuity in his music, Kabra reduced the role of multiple-string execution by opting, once again, for a *sitāra*-style solution — of using the first string as the main melodic string, and tuning the second and third strings also in the *sitāra* style [lower-octave *pa* and lower-octave *sa*]. This enabled him to execute melody across two full octaves on the main string, requiring the second and third strings only for the lower octave. In his interviews to the American press, he has argued that Hindustani music, with its vocalist model, does not require a melodic canvas larger than three octaves.

Kabra established himself and the slide-guitar in Hindustani music at a time when three giants — Ustad Vilayat Khan, Pt. Ravi Shankar, and Ustad Ali Akbar Khan — were in the prime of their trailblazing careers. In such an environment, the mere novelty of the slide-guitar could not have assured the instrument a future in Hindustani music. His success was a victory of his perception, and exploitation, of the distinctive musical value that the Hawaiian slide-guitar had to offer.

After Kabra

In response to the changes in the environment of Hindustani music, Kabra's successors on the slide-guitar scene, including his own disciples, have drifted away from the technical and stylistic choices he made. Most of them have chosen a stylistic direction with a much higher stroke density than Kabra's, and an extensive use of multiple-string execution as an important element in their music. The slide-guitar idiom is now drifting closer to the semi-polychord idiom of the *saroda*, but surpassing it in dazzling potential, thanks to the slide-guitar's superior ergonomics. The technical decisions of the younger guitarists are consistent with these directions.

A melodic canvas spanning four octaves, and across five strings, is now in favour. Sympathetic strings have now become a stable feature of the Indian classical guitar. The emphasis is now on kaleidoscopic tonal patterning and dazzling virtuosity, rather than elaborate *rāga* presentation and melodic richness. Strokes therefore need ergonomic facility more than depth or power. To this end, guitar-style picks have replaced Kabra's *miẓrab*. Some guitarists have also found it efficient to shift the *cikarī* drones to the treble [outward] side of the instrument.

Whether as an acoustic machine, or as the presenter of a well-defined style of instrumental music, the Indian classical guitar is still in a state of dynamic evolution. With the enthusiastic response the instrument has evoked amongst audiences in North America and Europe, its future could well be shaped as much by the global music market as by the Indian mainstream.

GLOSSARY

Abhaṅga : *Abhaṅga* is a Sanskrit adjective meaning "indestructible." The word defines a specific genre of devotional folk poetry written in Marāṭhī, the principal language of the western state of Maharashtra. The term gained currency after Chundarasa, the thirteenth-century Kannaḍa poet [Kannaḍa is the principal language of the neighbouring southern state of Karnataka] described his deity, Viṭṭhala, a manifestation of Lord Viṣṇu, as "Abhaṅga Viṭṭhala." The verse of the *abhaṅga* genre is written in the metre of "Ovi," an older poetic format in Marāṭhī literature, encompassing three different sub-formats within the genre.

The term *abhaṅga* is used specifically to describe poetry written by the poet-saints of the *bhakti* movement in Maharashtra during the mediaeval period — mainly Sant Nāmadev, Sant Tukārāma and the solitary lady saint, Bahinā Bāī. The genre is of high literary merit and also enjoys great popularity. The poetry is generally encased in simple folk-based melody, often corresponding to popular *rāga*s, and set to Kehervā, the ubiquitous eight-beat rhythmic cycle in all of non-art music. Its rendition on the art music platform as the tailpiece of a *khayāla* concert is of recent origin. In this context, the renditions remain anchored to the poetic and emotional content of the poetry, with a negligible role for improvisations. [Also see: **Maharashtra, Bhakti**] See Chapter 4.3.

Abhinaya : The word is Sanskrit for the act of artistic communication with the aid of bodily movements. The language of dance consists of three vehicles for non-verbal communication — the language of the eyes and the facial muscles, the language of the torso, and the language of footwork. The term *abhinaya* refers specifically to the language of the eyes and the facial muscles — the element of mime in dance, with a negligible role for the torso and footwork.

Ābhoga : The term derives from the Sanskrit *bhoga* = satiation/ contentment. The *ā* vowel prefix in Sanskrit connotes "in the direction of/towards." The *ābhoga* is the fourth and valedictory phase of *rāga* exposition in any movement. Like the *sañcārī*, it has now been dropped from *dhrupad* and post-*dhrupad bandiśas*. Its relevance is now limited to the prefatory *ālāpa* and the improvisatory movements of *bandiśa* rendition. The melodic-aesthetic function of this phase is to fold back the melodic canvas which was fully unfolded in the first two phases, and on which, in the third phase, the *rāga*'s distinctive melodic personality is detailed. Though a few musicians do still render a distinct *ābhoga*, especially in the *ālāpa*, each musician has his own approach to winding up an improvisatory movement with a distinct valedictory phase of exposition. [Also see: **Dhrupad, Bandiśa, Sthāyī, Antarā, Sañcārī**]. Refer Chapter 2.1.

Adbhut : See **Rasa/Navarasa**.

Addhā Ṭhekā : See **Tīnatāla/Tritāla, Ṭhekā**.

Āḍā Cautāla : *Āḍā cautāla* is a *tāla* [rhythmic cycle] of fourteen beats in seven equal sub-divisions of two beats each. Though not very popular in contemporary music, it is amenable to rendering across a wide range of tempi — from slow to moderately fast. It is encountered more frequently in vocal music of the *khayāla* genre than in any other vocal genre or in instrumental music.

Ākāra : *Ākāra* is derived from *ā* = the uttered vowel *ā* + *kāra* = process. It is an important articulatory device deployed in *khayāla* performance. It is found most suited for the delivery of low-density and high or even ultra-high density melody. Of the three articulatory devices used in Hindustani [north Indian] art music, the full-throated *ākāra*, arising from the navel, is regarded as having the greatest psycho-phonetic impact, and also the greatest self-illuminating and personality-transforming potential. These qualities relate to the neuro-acoustic triggers of this form of vocalization, and the demands this form of articulation makes on the deployment of lung-power. These facets of vocalization are well understood in the Indian mystical tradition, and *yogic* practice of *prāṇāyāma*. [Also see: **Khayāla, Yogic, Prāṇāyāma**]

Alaṅkāra : The strictest meaning of the Sanskrit *alaṅkāra*, derived from its semantic meaning, is adornment, embellishment, decoration. In this sense, all modes of intonation and intervallic transition in Hindustani music, other than staccato, would fall under the category of *alaṅkāra*. In contemporary usage, however, the term has emerged as a generic description of the host of symmetric practice exercises that are given to music students with the aim of cultivating their technical excellence in the handling of melody. [Also see: **Alaṅkāra Tānas**]

Alaṅkāra Tānas : The word *alaṅkāra* stands for the perfectly symmetrical practice exercises that are given to students of music for cultivating their technical competence in handling melody. These patterns, when deployed as *tāna*s — an improvisatory movement — require little melodic imagination. They do, however, appear conspicuously, and often unimaginatively, in contemporary music because of their ability to dazzle with their speed and clarity. [Also see: **Tānas**] Refer Chapter 4.2.

Alpatva/Bahutva : *Alpatva* is an abstract noun [Sanskrit] for the quality of brevity. Bahutva is its antonym. The *alpatva*/*bahutva* parameter in *rāga* grammar deals with the explicitness with which each of the permitted tones/*svara*s of the *rāga* can be intoned, relative to others. Most tones/*svara*s in a *rāga* will receive "normal" weightage. A few may, however, be prescribed either for subliminal or imperceptible intonation, or for prolonged intonation. This is a special and selective dimension of *rāga* grammar, not universally relevant to all *rāga*s. [Also see: **Rāga**] Refer Chapter 3.1.

Ālāpa : The word derives from Sanskrit *ālāpa* = dialogue/conversation. The aesthetic implications of this word are appropriately translated in the *ālāpa* movement in Hindustani [north Indian] art music. The *ālāpa* is a leisurely, deliberate, almost conversational, exposition of the *rāga*'s melodic form aimed at achieving, for it, the highest possible level of intelligibility. This intelligibility is achieved by conformity with traditional principles of melodic progression. Within this general definition, the word describes different categories of movements in different genres of vocal music, and on the different instruments.

Ālāpa/Joḍa/Jhālā : See *ālāpa* on the plucked instruments and the *santūra*.

Ālāpa in Dhrupad : In the *dhrupad* genre of art music, the word *ālāpa* describes a three-tiered prefatory movement rendered without percussion accompaniment. The first tier of the movement, called "*vilaṁbita* [slow tempo] *ālāpa*," consists of anarhythmic melody presented in the prescribed progression. The second tier called "*madhya laya* [medium tempo] *ālāpa*," presents melody with a pulsation at about two beats per second, once again in the prescribed progression. The third tier called "*drut* [fast tempo] *ālāpa*" raises the rate of melodic pulsation to four beats per second or higher. In the third tier, however, melody adopts a broad-span approach, with the laws of progression being considered less binding than in the first two phases of the *ālāpa*. [Also see: **ālāpa**].

Ālāpa on the plucked instruments and the Santūra : In terms of melodic-rhythmic structuring, the major plucked instruments of Hindustani music — the *rudra vīṇā, sitāra* and the *saroda* — and the struck polychord, the *santūra*, all follow the three-tiered *dhrupad* protocol for the prefatory *rāga* exposition, and present it without percussion accompaniment. They differ only in name. The first stage of anarythmic melody is called the *ālāpa*. The second stage of mild pulsation of melody is called *joḍa*. The third stage of accelerated pulsation of melody is called the *jhālā*. The differing nomenclature is also explained by the fact that these instruments use *cikarī* [drone] strings for achieving the pulsation, and perforating the flow of melody, thus adding an acoustic element to the treatment of the three tiers. [Also see: **Ālāpa, Ālāpa in Dhrupad**]

Ālāpa in khayāla and on wind and bow instruments : The prefatory low-density *ālāpa* movement is identical in *khayāla* vocalism and on the wind and bow instruments because, being instruments capable of melodic continuity, these instruments have traditionally presented music in the *khayāla* format. The *khayāla* format presents the *ālāpa* as a percussion-accompanied movement. It is the first improvisatory movement in the *vilaṁbita* [slow-tempo] *khayāla* rendition. The *ālāpa* in the *khayāla* format consists of rounds of low-density anarhythmic melodic improvization, in the prescribed progression, woven around intermittent returns to the pre-composed form of the *Bandiśa*. In the vocal manifestation, the *ālāpa* of the *khayāla* format may deploy either the poetic form, or vowel forms as articulatory devices.

Note: In recent years, some performers on the wind and bow instruments have adopted the *dhrupad* format for presenting the *ālāpa*. [Also see: **Ālāpa, Bandiśa, Khayāla, Ālāpa in Dhrupad**]

Āmada : The word is probably colloquial for the Sanskrit verb *āgamana* = to arrive. The *āmada* in a *bandiśa* is the last phase of either the *sthāyī* or the *antarā*, which terminates just before the rendition can return to a rendition of the *mukhaḍā* of the *sthāyī*. [Also see: **Bandiśa, Mukhaḍā, Antarā, Sthāyī**]

Antarā : The term is an abbreviation of the Sanskrit *antara-dhātu* = "Intermediate material." In the *bandiśa*, *antarā* is centred in the upper half of the melodic canvas. It ascends categorically from the mid-octave region of the middle octave to the upper-tonic, provides a climactic and reposeful pause at the upper-tonic, ascends into the higher octave, and then descends in deliberate steps to base-*sa* [the tonic/fundamental]. The *antarā* of the improvisatory movements is identical in its progression logic to the pre-composed *antarā* of a *bandiśa*. Collectively, the *sthāyī* and the *antarā* provide a complete coverage of the melodic canvas. [Also see: **Bandiśa, Sthāyī, Sañcārī, Ābhoga**]. Refer Chapter 2.1.

Aṅga : See **Aṅga/Apāṅga.**

Aṅga/Apāṅga : *Aṅga* is Sanskrit for limbs. A limb being a facet of the human body, the term is also used metaphorically to describe a facet of an aesthetic endeavour. *Apāṅga* [common noun] is Sanskrit for a cripple, and derives its meaning from *aṅga*, denoting a compromised/defective/missing limb. In aesthetics, *apāṅga* is used metaphorically to describe the unintended and displeasing results of creating or emphasizing a particular facet of an aesthetic endeavour. A cripple, being an object of derision or pity, there is a satirical pun implicit in such usage, as its implications tread the borderline between its literal and metaphorical meaning. Refer Chapter 2.2.

Aṅga [Gāyakī, Tālavādya, Tāntakāra/Tata] : *Aṅga* is Sanskrit for limbs. A limb being a facet of the human body, the term is also used metaphorically to describe a facet of an aesthetic endeavour. In such metaphorical use of the term, the idiom of each category of musical endeavour is metaphorically described as a facet of the totality of musical experience. The Hindustani tradition recognizes three primary *aṅga*s of musical expression — *gāyakī* [vocalism or the idiom of melodic continuity], *tāntakāra/tāta* [plucked instruments, or the idiom of melodic discontinuity], and *tālavādya* [percussion instruments or the atonal idiom of rhythm]. These idioms are derived from the design, ergonomic and acoustic features of the respective sound producing mechanisms. The human voice is regarded as the most authentic exponent of the musical idea. For this reason, the *gāyakī aṅga* is traditionally recognized as the reference point, and ideal of all musical expression.

Aṅga Prādhānya : The term derives its meaning from Sanskrit *aṅga* = limb/facet + *prādhānya* = dominance. This term refers to classification of *rāga*s on the basis of the region of the melodic canvas in which their centre of gravity falls. In this context, the octave is divided into three overlapping regions [*aṅga*s or limbs]. The lower tetrachord [*sā, re, gā, mā*] is called the *pūrvāṅga* [*pūrva* = early + *aṅga* = limb/region]. The mid-octave region [*gā, mā, pā, dh*] is called the *madhyāṅga* [*madhya* = middle + *aṅga* = limb/region]. The upper tetrachord [*pā, dh, nī, sā*] is called *uttarāṅga* [*uttara* = north = *aṅga* = limb/region]. The awareness and observance of this parameter of *rāga* grammar ensures that the musician invests a substantial part of his musical energies in the appropriate region of the melodic canvas, and thus maximizes the probability of achieving the psycho-acoustic goals of *rāga* exposition.

Anucita : See **Aucitya/Ucita/Anucita.**

Anuraṇan : See **Svara/Tone.**

Aprasiddha: The word is Sanskrit for "not famous." In music, it is used primarily for classifying *rāga*s into *aparasiddha* = rare/not widely recognized, or *prasiddha* = common/popular/widely recognized. These classifications are dynamic, as *rāga*s move freely between popularity and rarity from generation to generation.

Artha-Bhāva : The term derives from Sanskrit *artha* = semantic meaning + *bhāva* = emotional meaning. The *bola-banāo ṭhumarī* is also called the *artha-bhāva ṭhumarī*, because it uses song-texts as a platform for luxuriant and leisurely melodic ornamentation, with the purpose of making the words come to life. [Also see: **Ṭhumarī, Bola-banāo Ṭhumarī, Nāyikā Bheda**] Refer Chapter 4.3.

Āroha : Ascending melodic motion.

Āroha pradhāna: See **Diśā prādhānya**.

Aucara : The term refers to an anarhythmic prelude, rendered without percussion accompaniment, preceding a *khayāla* presentation. The *aucara* has no clearly defined melodic movements, though it does follow an ascending-descending progression. It remains generally in the lower half of the melodic canvas, does considerably more than merely identifying the *rāga* and aims at creating its atmosphere. [Also see: **Rāga vākya**]

Aucitya/Ucita/Anucita : *Aucitya* is an abstract noun, derived from the Sanskrit adjective *ucita* = proper, the antonym for which is *anucita* = improper. *Aucitya* is Sanskrit for the sense of propriety. In its very nature, the meaning and significance of the term relates to history, geography and specificity, and is, therefore, contextual. In the present context, it is an important yardstick by which oriental societies judge the conduct of individuals, especially those in positions of power and influence. *Aucitya* is, admittedly and explicitly, an elitist criterion of conduct. In each field of human activity, the yardstick is applied by, and from the perspective of, peers and others qualified to sit in judgement over those being judged. For passing muster on this criterion, individual conduct requires social acceptability. But, *aucitya* neither begins nor ends with such acceptability. In the field of culture, the application of the *aucitya* yardstick functions as a mechanism for preventing art from drifting towards populist titillation. Refer Chapter 2.2.

Aucitya bhaṅga : The term is derived from Sanskrit *aucitya* = propriety + *bhaṅga* = breach. *Aucitya bhaṅga* is the act or process which breaches the limits of propriety. [Also see: **Aucitya/Ucita/Anucita**]

Auḍava : The word describes pentatonic *rāga*s [those that deploy five tones/*svara*s]. The description does not double-count a tone/*svara* if the *rāga* uses the natural as well as its suppressed or enhanced microtones. In this classification, the ascent and the descent are considered together. However, *rāga*s may be described by dual classifications such as *auḍava-sampūrṇa* if, for instance, they are pentatonic in the ascent and heptatonic in the descent. [Also see: **Catusvara, Ṣaḍava, Sampūrṇa**]

Aurangzeb : Aurangzeb was a Mogul emperor of ascetic temperament [seventeenth century] and the only one in the lineage who disapproved of the performing arts as immoral and incompatible with the tenets of Islam. Since then, the term "Aurangzeb" has come to symbolize individuals in positions of power and influence conspicuously lacking in interest in, or affinity to, the performing or fine arts.

Avanaddha : *Avanaddha* is one of the five primary classifications of musical instruments in Indian organology. It represents instruments, which are covered with membranes, mainly animal skin. This category describes percussion instruments such as the *pakhāwaja*, *tabalā*, and other drums.

Avaroha pradhāna : See **Diśā prādhānya.**

Avaroha : Descending melodic motion.

Avatāra : Common noun derived from the Sanskrit verb *avataraṇa* = to manifest/to incarnate. The allusion is to the Hindu belief in reincarnation. It hypothesizes that individual souls manifest themselves repeatedly in different bodies, and in different eras, while maintaining a continuity of relationships and unfinished tasks through their eternal journey. The journey is believed to end when an individual dies without any emotional attachments and unfinished tasks. The word *avatāra* is used more specially to signify manifestations/reincarnations of Lord Viṣṇu or Lord Maheśa/Śiva, in either human or alternate divine form, appearing with the purpose of relieving humanity of the tyranny of evil forces. [Also see: **Bramhā, Viṣṇu, Maheśa**]

Baḍā Khayāla : The word derives its meaning from the Hindī *baḍā* = major/big/large/expansive + *khayāla* = vision/imagination. The term denotes the slow-tempo rendition of vocal music in the *khayāla* genre of Hindustani [north Indian] art music. In such meaning, it represents the pre-composed element [the poetic-melodic-rhythmic shell of the rendition] along with prescribed improvisatory movements. [Also see: **Khayāla**] Refer Chapter 4.2.

Baḍhata : The word is Hindī for evolution/progression/growth, and is derived from the Sanskrit *vṛddhi*, an abstract noun of identical meaning. In Hindustani [north Indian] music, it refers to the melodic progression prescribed for the improvisatory movements. The prescription is relevant only for the first two phases of *rāga* exposition protocol — *sthāyī* and *antarā* — and not to the remaining two phases — *sañcārī* and *ābhoga*, which are free from the progressive logic, and whose rendition varies considerably. [Also see: **Sthāyī, Antarā**]

Baḍhata Tānas : The word *baḍhata* stands for a sense of melodic progression. *Baḍhata tāna*s are clusters of high-density melodic runs, which correspond to a notion of deliberateness and disciplined sequencing of ascending and descending melody in the coverage of the melodic canvas. [Also see: **Baḍhata, tānas**] Refer Chapter 4.2.

Bandiśa [also called Cīẓa or Gata] : The word derives from the Sanskrit verb *bandhana* = to bind. A *bandiśa* is that which is bound, encased, pre-composed. The word refers to the pre-composed element in Hindustani [north Indian] vocal or instrumental music. In vocal music, it refers to the pre-composed poetic-melodic-rhythmic shell, which constitutes the nucleus around which the improvizations revolve. In instrumental music, it refers only to the melodic-rhythmic shell. In art music, a *bandiśa* is composed in a specific *rāga*, is set to a specific *tāla*, and conforms to traditional rules of composition. [Also see: **Rāga, Tāla**]

Bandiśa Ṭhumarī : The *bandiśa ṭhumarī* is the older of the two sub-genres of the *ṭhumarī* genre of semi-classical vocal music. The word *bandiśa* in this context signifies its reliance on the pre-composed poetic-melodic-rhythmic form. The word *ṭhumarī* signifies its origins as accompaniment to *Kathaka* dance, and its continued association with it. Having evolved from older traditions of dance-related musical forms, the *bandiśa ṭhumarī* achieved a mature form by the eighteenth century, touched its zenith by mid-nineteenth century, and had become near-extinct as an independent musical genre by late twentieth century. Its evolution into a sophisticated genre was synchronous with the emergence of the princely state of Awadh [Lucknow] as the cultural capital of northern India. Stylistically, the *bandiśa ṭhumarī* is a lively piece of music, performed primarily in medium tempo, and composed in the popular *tīnatāla/tritāla*, along with its stylized variants. The *bandiśa ṭhumarī* exerted considerable influence over the evolution of the idiom of the modern plucked-lute family of musical instruments — principally, the *sitāra* and the *saroda*. [Also see: **Bandiśa, Ṭhumarī, Bola-banāo Ṭhumarī**] Refer Chapter 4.3.

Bānī : *Bānī* is colloquial for Sanskrit *vāṇī* = speech/language. The reference is to the various styles of performing *dhrupad* that existed in mediaeval times, which were originally also associated with the different dialects in which their lyrics were written. During the period of Miyā Tānsen's influence over *dhrupad* vocalism [sixteenth century], the different *bānī*s merged their identities into the Seniya tradition. Though this merger did not eliminate the stylistic diversity immediately, the subsequent decline of the *dhrupad* genre has had this consequence. [Also see: **Dhrupad, Miyā Tānsen, Seniya**]

Behlāvā : The word is Hindī, and has connotations of a leisurely quality, informality and indulgence. It is used to describe the anarhythmic *ālāpa* of certain stylistic lineages of *khayāla* vocalism. The *behlāvā* form is characterized by the use of the poetic form as the articulatory device, and its relative informality of progression. The *behlāvā* approach in *khayāla* vocalism has inspired a similar movement in the rendition of slow-tempo *bandiśa*s on the *sitāra* and *saroda*. [Also see: **Khayāla, Ālāpa in Khayāla, Bandiśa**]

Beṅgālī/Bengal : Adjective derived from "Bengal," a region of undivided India on the east coast, now bifurcated into the nation-state of Bangladesh and the Indian state of West Bengal. Beṅgālīs are residents of either part of undivided Bengal, whose mother tongue is Beṅgālī [also called Banglā], written in the Beṅgālī script. In the latter half of the twentieth century, the Indian state of West Bengal emerged as the primary resource of instrumental musicianship simultaneously with the western Indian state of Maharashtra emerging as the most prolific nursery of talent in *khayāla* vocalism.

Bhajana : The word derives from the Sanskrit verb *bhaja* = to serve/ to worship. A *bhajana* is a song based on devotional poetry, and owes its influence to the literary flowering triggered off by the *bhakti* movement. These songs were originally performed in the temples, and moved from there into people's homes as solo or choral expressions. They are composed typically in folk tunes, or based on a handful of classical *rāga*s. The advent of the gramophone record gave a tremendous boost to their popularity and standardization in rendering. The infusion of classicism into their rendition, and their adoption as repertoire for the concert platform is a twentieth-century phenomenon. In the latter context, the *bhajana* has steadily replaced, and displaced, the *ṭhumarī* and *ṭappā* genres. [Also see: **Bhakti, Ṭhumarī, Ṭappā**] Refer Chapters 4.3 and 4.4.

Bhakti : The word is Sanskrit for "devotion/surrender," and derives from the verb *bhaja* = to serve/to worship. As a backdrop to the literary and musical culture, the term refers to the movement [the *bhakti* movement] in Hindu society starting from around the eighth century. The movement revolted against the power of the clergy over the spiritual lives of the laity, and espoused a direct emotional relationship between the devotee and God. The movement found its most potent symbol in the legend of Lord Kṛṣṇa, an incarnation of Lord Viṣṇu, the preserver of the universe in Hindu mythology. The mischief of the infant Kṛṣṇa became a stimulus for the maternal/parental instinct, while his dalliances with his paramour, Rādhā, became a powerful trigger for the romantic sentiment. By imagining himself/herself as Kṛṣṇa's mother or paramour, the human devotee could establish an emotional bond with Lord Kṛṣṇa. Depicted in mythology as a Machiavellian warrior, a worldly philosopher, and a Casanova, Kṛṣṇa is "human," while also being divine. This combination of accessibility and inaccessibility has provided infinite momentum to the cult of Kṛṣṇa, and dominated the literary, musical, and choreographic culture of northern India during the second millennium. All the major genres of Hindustani [north Indian] art music — *dhrupad, khayāla,* and *ṭhumarī* — and the *Kathaka* genre of classical dance, are imbued with the thematic content of the *bhakti* cult.

Bhaya : See **Rasa/Navarasa.**

Bībhatsa : See **Rasa/Navarasa.**

Bīna : See **Rudra Vīṇā.** Refer Chapter 5.1.

Bīnakāra : A musician who performs on the *rudra vīṇā/bīna* [Also see: **Rudra Vīṇā**]

Bola : The word is Hindī for "articulated sound/speech." In the context of Hindustani [north Indian] art music, it refers to the use of the poetic form as the vehicle for the delivery of music. As a vehicle for the communication of musical meaning, the poetic form enjoys the highest premium in the *bola-banāo ṭhumarī* genre, followed by *dhrupad*, and finally by *khayāla*. Being a device equipped with vowels, consonants, as well as semantic and syntactical meaning, the poetic form lends itself to any combination of poetic, melodic and rhythmic manipulation. As such, it is the most versatile articulatory device across a wide range of tone densities. Moreover, it is far less demanding than pure vowel devices, to which the vocalist perforce resorts for delivery of ultra-high density melody. These considerations make the poetic form [*bola*] the most popular articulatory device in contemporary art music. [Also see: **Khayāla, Dhrupad, Bola-banāo Ṭhumarī, Ākāra, Saragama**]

Bola-ālāpa : When the *ālāpa* of the *khayāla* genre is presented using the poetic form as the articulatory material, it is called *bola-ālāpa*. [Also see: Bola, **Ālāpa, Rūpakālapti, Ālāpa** in **Khayāla** and on wind and bow instruments]

Bola-banāo : *Bola-banāo* is the leisurely process of using musical expression to convert the semantic meaning of a song-text into emotional meaning. This mode of musical communication is considered appropriate only in the romanticist *ṭhumarī* genre of semi-classical music. The aesthetics of *bola-banāo* aided the erotic allurement of a courtesan. The process is artistic, takes place in public and fulfils the requirements of decorum worthy of genteel society. Within these constraints, it has to achieve an intimacy not available to the classicist genres, because it is aimed at obtaining the highest price for the courtesan's favours. *Bola-banāo* represents vocal expression of explicitly manipulative intent, traditionally rendered to the accompaniment of mime and gesture. The mode of musical communication relies heavily on ornate melodic embellishments and seductive manipulations of volume and timbre considered inappropriate in the classicist genres — *dhrupad* and *khayāla*. [Also see: **Ṭhumarī, Bola-banāo Ṭhumarī, Dhrupad, Khayāla**] Refer Chapter 4.3.

Bola-banāo Ṭhumarī : The *bola-banāo ṭhumarī* is the more recent of the two sub-genres of the *ṭhumarī* genre of semi-classical vocal music. The prefix *bola-banāo* describes the leisurely process by which the sub-genre uses musical expression to convert semantic meaning into emotional meaning. The suffix *ṭhumarī* refers to its origins as accompaniment to *Kathaka* dance, and its continued association with it. The *bola-banāo ṭhumarī* evolved and flourished primarily in the city of Benares, and reflects a considerable influence of folk traditions of the neighbouring districts. This *ṭhumarī* sub-genre reached its zenith during the nineteenth century, and began to loose ground in the early twentieth century when it moved out of the salons of the courtesans and into the concert halls. At the time of writing [December 2003], the genre claims only a handful of significant performers. Besides the *khayāla* vocalists who perform the *bola-banāo ṭhumarī*, only two specialist performers of the genre remain — Girijadevi and Shobha Gurtu. The genre now faces extinction as an independent musical genre. [Also see: **Bola-banāo Ṭhumarī, Bandiśa Ṭhumarī**]. Refer Chapter 4.3.

Bola-bāṇṭa/Laya-bāṇṭa : The terms are derived from *bola* = poetic form [or *laya* = tempo] + *bāṇṭa* = distribution. They are forms of improvization in the vocal genres of Hindustani music, the distinctions between them being ill-defined with respect to vocal renditions. *Bola-bāṇṭa* alters the relationship between the poetic and rhythmic elements in the pre-composed form of the *bandiśa* without substantially disturbing the melodic element. *Laya-bāṇṭa* [temporal redistribution] is a similar improvization, but may also encompass the melodic component. The term *laya-bāṇṭa* may also be used for comparable improvizations in instrumental music, which do not have the poetic form for manipulation. Both forms are generally practiced in medium melodic density. [Also see: **Bola, Laya, Bola-laya**]

Bola-laya : The term is derived from *bola* = the poetic form + *laya* = tempo. *Bola-laya* is the name given to the medium density movement, sequentially the second improvisatory movement, in contemporary *khayāla* rendition. It involves improvizations utilizing the poetic form as the articulatory device, with melody adopting an explicit rhythmicality in the rendition. This movement may include elements of *bola-bāṇṭa / laya-bāṇṭa*. Some musicians may, however, choose to replace — either partially or entirely — the poetic form with the *saragama* [solfa symbols] as the articulatory material for this second, medium-density movement. This represents a "logical" progression from the preceding *ālāpa* movement, which involves only an anarhythmic treatment of low-density melody. [Also see: **Ālāpa, Ālāpa in Khayāla, Bola-banta, Bola, Bola-ālāpa**]

Bola-tāna : The term derives from *bola* = the poetic form + *tāna* = high-density melodic runs. When *tāna*s are rendered in *khayāla* vocalism with words and phrases from the song-text as the primary articulatory device, rather than the alternatives available, the *tāna* form is called a *bola-tāna*. This form of *tāna* may also be occasionally encountered in *bandiśa ṭhumarī* rendition, and is routinely adopted in *ṭappā* singing. [Also see: **Tāna, Bola, Ṭappā**].

Brahmā : The Creator of the Universe in Hindu mythology. [Also see: **Trimūrti**]

Bṛhat Kinnarī : See **Kinnarī/Kinnarī Vīṇā.**

Cañcara : See **Dīpacaṇḍī, Carcarī.**

Caitī : The word is derived from the name of the Caitra month of the Hindu calendar [spring]. The *caitī* is a genre of folk songs from the eastern part Uttara Pradesh [northern Provinces] and its adjacent districts. Its signatory feature is verse in which poetic lines end with *ho rāma*. The songs are generally of two stanzas each, and of standard melodic construction, which does not correspond to the art music definition of *sthāyī-antarā* progression. The thematic content of the poetry is primarily romantic, and deals with the pangs of separation from the beloved, as narrated by a female protagonist. It is a poetry-dominant genre, possessing limited scope for melodic elaboration and improvization, and set to a 7-beat or 14-beat rhythmic cycle common in *ṭhumarī*-related folk genres. The courtesans of Benares and neighbouring Gayā elevated the *caitī* songs to the status of a semi-classical art form. The genre is regarded as one of the allied genres of the *bola-banāo ṭhumarī*. [Also see: **Bola-banāo Ṭhumarī**] Refer Chapter 4.3.

Cakradāra : The word derives from Sanskrit *cakra* = circle, and is Hindī for a circular pattern. The *cakradāra* is an expanded version of a *tihāyī*. There are many patterns available for expanding a *tihāyī* into a *cakradāra*. However, the most common is one that renders the same *tihāyī* three times to culminate at the *sama*. [Also see: **Tihāyī, Sama**] Refer Chapter 2.4.

Calana : The word derives from the Sanskrit *cala* = to walk or Hindī *cāla* = gait/demeanour. A *rāga*'s distinctive melodic personality is outlined by a set of characteristic phrases, which incorporate a substantial part of its grammar. This set of phrases — generally not more than eight or ten in number — are collectively called the *calana* of the *rāga*. [Also see: **Rāga**] Refer Chapter 3.1.

Carcarī : *Carcarī* is the name of a north Indian dance form of folk origin. It is an erotic dance, accompanied by song and instrumental music. *Carcarī* is also the name of a *tāla* [rhythmic cycle] to which the accompanying music of the dance form is composed. The *carcarī* dance form, along with the associated musical content, has been identified as an important source for the modern *ṭhumarī* genre of semi-classical music. The beat-pattern of *carcarī tāla* is also called *cañcara* or *dīpacaṇḍī*. This *tāla* is used exclusively in the *bola-banāo ṭhumarī* genre, and may be considered its most important *tāla*. [Also see: **Cañcara, Dīpacaṇḍī, Ṭhumarī**] Refer Chapter 4.3.

Carnatic/Hindustani music : The word derives from the name of the "Karnāṭ" region of India, approximately covering all of peninsular India south of the Vindhyachal range of mountains. A unified Indian tradition of art music underwent a bifurcation starting in the early part of the second millennium. The north of the country came under increasing middle eastern [mainly Perso-Arabic] cultural influence consequent to a series of invasions, while south India remained relatively insulated from such influences. This bifurcation was probably magnified by art-music responding more explicitly to the regional musical cultures of the north and south, and to the differing predilections of its patrons. These forces gave rise to two parallel art music traditions — the north Indian tradition, called Hindustani music, and the south Indian tradition, called Carnatic music. The two systems have similarities as well as dissimilarities, and follow their independent evolutionary paths. However, there is evidence of growing cross-fertilization of musical ideas and practices between the two traditions after Independence [1947].

Catusvara : The word is derived from the Sanskrit *catur* = four + *svara* = tone. The term describes a *rāga*, which utilizes only four tones/*svara*s. In this classification, the ascent and the descent are considered together. Quadratonic *rāga*s are very few in Hindustani [north Indian] music, five tones/*svara*s being considered the minimum required to form the basis of an aesthetically satisfying musical rendition. However, *rāga*s may be described by dual classifications such as *catusvara-sampūrṇa* if, for instance, they are quadratonic in the ascent and heptatonic in the descent. [Also see: **Auḍava, Saḍava, Sampūrṇa**]

Cauguṇa/Caturguṇa : The word derives from *cau* = four + *guṇa* = multiple. When any melody is performed at a melodic [tone] density four times the beat density [tempo] of accompanying percussion or the base-tempo of the *bandiśa*, the expression is called *cauguṇa*/*caturguṇa*. The highest ratio of tone-density to beat-density practiced in Hindustani music is eight times. [Also see: **Bandiśa**]

Cautāla [loosely also called Dhrupad] : *Cautāla* is a *tāla* [rhythmic cycle] of twelve beats in six equal sub-divisions of two beats each. It is the primary *tāla* of the *dhrupad* genre of mediaeval art music, and is generally performed in medium tempo.

Chūṭa Tānas : The word derives probably from *chūṭa* in Hindī = "abandon/release." When a melodic motif, once defined, is abandoned or released, it escapes/flees/leaps. The *chūṭa tāna* conveys such an impression by leaping to different regions of the melodic canvas, while retaining the tonal geometry of the basic motif. The totality of the aural image is a collage of similar patterns strewn across the melodic canvas, generally in ascending and/or descending sequence, though not necessarily so. [Also see: **Tānas**] Refer Chapter 4.2.

Choṭā Khayāla : The word derives from the Hindī *choṭā* = minor/small + *khayāla* = vision/imagination. The term denotes the fast-tempo rendition of vocal music in the *khayāla* genre of Hindustani [north Indian] art music. In such meaning, it encompasses the pre-composed element [the poetic-melodic-rhythmic shell of the rendition] as well as the conventional architecture of the rendition with respect to the improvisatory movements. Compared to the *baḍā khayāla*, the architecture of a *choṭā khayāla* presentation is informal. [Also see: **Khayāla**] Refer Chapter 4.2.

Cīẓa : See **Bandiśa.**

Dādarā : *Dādarā* is a *tāla* [rhythmic cycle] of six beats in 3+3 sub-division. The *tāla* is generally used in medium and fast tempi. However, the term also refers to a genre of folk-based semi-classical genre of vocal music allied to the *bola-banāo ṭhumarī*. This genre, originating in the musical traditions of the districts around the city of Benares, is performed not only in the *dādarā tāla*, but also in a couple of other *tāla*s. The dividing line between the *dādarā* and *bola-banāo ṭhumarī* is blurred. The significant feature of the *dādarā* vocal genre is the heightened rhythmicality of rendition, relative to the subdued rhythmicality of the *bola-banāo ṭhumarī*.

Dhamāra : *Dhamāra* is a *tāla* [rhythmic cycle] of fourteen beats with an irregular/asymmetrical 5+2+3+4 sub-division. It is an integral part of the repertoire of the *dhrupad/dhamāra* genre of art music, and is ideally suited for medium tempo rendition. *Dhamāra* is one of the very few *tāla*s, which does not begin on an accentuated beat. For this reason, and also because of its irregular sub-division of beats, *dhamāra* is considered an enigmatic *tāla* of reluctant rhythmicality.

In the *dhrupad/dhamāra* genre, poetry composed to the *dhamāra tāla*, irrespective of the *rāga* in which it is composed, is related predominantly to the *Holī* [also called *Horī*] the spring festival of colours. This makes the *dhamāra tāla*, along with its associated poetic element connected with *Holī/Horī*, a distinct sub-genre of the *dhrupad* genre. Subsequent to the *dhrupad* revival in the last quarter of the twentieth century, many instrumentalists, especially *saroda* players, have begun to occasionally perform post-*dhrupad* music in the *dhamāra tāla*.

Dhrupad : [Also called *dhrupad-dhamāra*] : The word derives from sanskrit *dhruva* = fixed/immutable + *pada* = verse. It refers to a genre of *rāga*-based music, which dominated the Hindustani [north Indian] tradition between the fifteenth and eighteenth centuries. The genre evolved as an art form consequent to the transportation of the devotional music of the Vaiṣṇava temples to the secular environment of feudal courts. The genre places a high premium on the integrity of its poetic element in rendition and is, therefore, predominantly a genre of vocal music. Its primary instrumental manifestation is the *rudra vīṇā* [also called *bīna*]. After the decline of its strongest patron, the Mogul Empire, in the early nineteenth century, *dhrupad* progressively surrendered the mainstream platform to the modern *khayāla* genre, taking the *rudra vīṇā* along with it on the downhill path. *Dhrupad* was near extinct by mid-twentieth century, but experienced a minor revival in the last quarter of the century, primarily supported by audiences and scholars in Europe and the US. [Also see: **Vaiṣṇava, Rudra Vīṇā, Khayāla**] Ref. Chapter 4.1.

Dīpti : See **Svara/Tone.**

Dīpacaṇḍī : *Dīpacaṇḍī* is a *tāla* [rhythmic cycle] of fourteen beats in 3+4+3+4 sub-division. It is related genealogically to *cañcara/carcarī tāla*s associated with the *ṭhumarī* genre of semi-classical vocal music, and is virtually indistinguishable from them. *Dīpacaṇḍī* itself is also encountered exclusively in the *bola-banāo ṭhumarī* genre. Like the *dhamāra tāla* [also of 14 beats] the *dīpacaṇḍī tāla* is also associated with songs celebrating the spirit of *Holī/Horī*, the spring festival of colours. This sub-genre of the *bola-banāo ṭhumarī* is occasionally referred to as *horī-dīpacaṇḍī*. [Also see: **Ṭhumarī**]

Diśā Prādhānya : The term derives its meaning from Sanskrit *diśā* = direction + *prādhānya* = dominance. This term refers to a classification of *rāga*s on the basis of the direction of melodic motion in which the *rāga*'s distinctive melodic personality is most significantly expressed. *Rāga*s are classified as either *āroha pradhāna* [*āroha* = ascending melodic motion + *pradhāna* = dominant] or *avaroha pradhāna* [*avaroha* descending melodic motion + *pradhāna* = dominant]. Awareness and observance of this parameter of *rāga* grammar encourages the musician to invest a substantial part of musical energy in melodic thrusts in the appropriate direction, thus maximizing the probability of achieving the psycho-acoustic goals of *rāga* exposition.

Doguṇa/Dviguṇa : The word derives from *dvi* or *do* = two + *guṇa* = multiple. When any melody is performed at a melodic [tone] density twice the beat density [tempo] of accompanying percussion, or the base-tempo of the *bandiśa*, the expression is called *doguṇa*. The highest ratio of tone-density to beat-density practised in Hindustani music is eight times. [Also see: **Bandiśa**]

Drut [or Drut laya] : An adjectival phrase derived from the Sanskrit *drut* = running/galloping + *laya* = tempo. It describes a rendition in fast tempo. The notion of tempo [slow/medium/fast] is relative and dynamic. It differs between generations, between stylistic lineages, between different genres of vocal music, and between vocal and instrumental music.

Ekatantrī Vīṇā : The word derives from the Sanskrit *eka* = one/single + *tantrī* = string + *vīṇā* = stringed instrument. The *ekatantrī vīṇā* is described in musicological texts from the eleventh century AD. Evidently, it was a long-necked fretless lute with a single string, on which melody was executed by sliding a hard and smooth mechanical device along the strings, rather than by stopping the strings with the bare fingers. This instrument may also be regarded as an ancestor of the *vicitra vīṇā* and the slide-guitar. [Also see: **Ghoṣaka, Vicitra Vīṇā, Indian Classical Guitar**]. Refer Chapter 5.1.

Ekatāla : *Ekatāla* is a *tāla* [rhythmic cycle] of twelve beats in six equal sub-divisions of two beats each. The *tāla* is immensely popular for slow as well as fast tempo renditions in the *khayāla* genre of vocal music. It is amenable to rendition in a wide range of tempi, from below 20 beats per minute to over 240 beats per minute. Its use in medium tempo *khayāla* rendition is rare. The use of this *tāla* in instrumental music is restricted to performers on the wind and bow instruments, who generally render *khayāla* genre compositions.

Fāguna : *Fāguna* is a genre of folk songs, which derives its name from the month of *Fālguna* in the Hindu calendar [early spring]. The genre belongs to the eastern districts of Uttar Pradesh [Northern Provinces], and evolved as an ally of the *bola-banāo ṭhumarī* performed by courtesans of Benares. In the Indian literary and musical tradition, spring is most clearly associated with man's romantic urges. Hence, the lyrics of *fāguna* songs are dominated by romance. The explicit reference to the month of *Fālguna* is generally found in *fāguna* songs. The songs are normally rendered with emotive embellishment of the poetic element, but without substantive melodic improvization. [Also see: **Bola-banāo Ṭhumarī**] Refer Chapter 4.3.

Gamaka : The term derives from the Sanskrit verb: *gama* = to go. In the strictest musicological sense, the word is generic to all intervallic transitions in Indian music, classified according to the melodic contours they respectively define. In contemporary Hindustani usage, however, the word has come to denote one specific category of *gamaka* — the *tribhinna gamaka* — which creates a vibratory melodic contour. It is a contextual intonation of a tone/ *svara*, conveying the impression of being repeatedly attacked from an adjacent tone/*svara*. The effect may be compared with a magnified *vibrato* in Western music. The *gamaka* is practised in vocal as well as instrumental music.

Gata : See **Bandiśa.**

Gata-toḍa : The term derives from *gata* = composition/*bandiśa* performed on the plucked lute family of instruments + *toḍa* = complex rhythmic patterns. The *gata-toḍa* is a medium density improvizational movement in the traditional idiom of the *sītāra* and the *saroda*. It involves the rhythmic manipulation of melody, accompanied by complex bi-directional stroke patterns mimicking the idiom of percussion. This form is akin to, and a modern successor of, the *tara-paraṇa* form of improvization practised on the *rudra vīṇā* in *dhrupad* music. [Also see: **Bandiśa, Tara-paraṇa, Paraṇa, Dhrupad**]

Gāyakī Aṅga : See **Aṅga [Gāyaki, Tālvādya, Tantakāra/Tata].**

Ghana : *Ghana* is one of the five basic classifications of musical instruments in Indian organology. These classifications are independent of the technique of sound activation and technique of melodic execution.

Ghana, in Sanskrit, means solids. Such instruments are mainly percussive or percussive-melodic in character. The *kāṣṭha taraṅga*, [the Indian xylophone] now extinct, was the last instrument in this category to be performed in Indian art music. [Also see: **Kāṣṭha Taraṅga**]

Gharānā : The word derives its meaning from the Hindī *ghara* [Sanskrit *gṛha* = house]. *Gharānā* is a collective noun meaning a group, which shares the same homestead. In the era of hereditary musicianship, the term came to represent a lineage, which cultivated a distinctive style of rendering music over successive generations. Once kinship ceased to be the primary criterion for entry into the music profession, the term was redefined to denote a stylistic lineage. As a stylistic lineage, a *gharānā* is characterized by three critical features — [a] a long period of rigorous training and aesthetic indoctrination of each aspirant under an authorized *guru* of the lineage [b] acquisition of the art through aural transmission [c] a sworn loyalty of each member to the music making philosophy and style of his mentor/lineage. The decay of the *gharānā* phenomenon began in the second quarter of twentieth century and is now almost complete. The *gharānā* model of continuity and change has been replaced by alternative models, yet to be conceptualized. Refer Chapter 1.6.

Ghasīṭa/Sūta : The word derives from the Hindī *ghasīṭa* = to drag, and Sanskrit *ghriṣṭa* = abrasion. The explicit reference here is to an intervallic transition achieved on the plucked string instruments, by dragging a finger of the left hand over a large melodic span under the impact of a single right hand stroke. This process defines a linear, rather than curvilinear melodic contour. Such a transition, when executed in vocal music, is called a *sūta* or *syūnta*.

Ghaẓal : The word is Persian for "addressing a lover in poetic form." The term defines a poetry dominant genre of music imbued with the romantic sentiment. Its poetic structure derives probably from the *kasīdā* form in Persian literature. The Islamic Sūfī sects adopted the *ghaẓal* form early during their presence in India, making the love of God an important thematic element. *Ghaẓal*s were originally written in Persian. When the form was adopted in Urdu literature, its thematic content was substantially enlarged, to encompass *ishq* [love], *ashq* [tears] and *maut* [death]. *Ghaẓal*s were originally sung in a very simple, repetitive, melodic structure, with no improvization. In the nineteenth and twentieth centuries, its melodic approach began to drift towards that of the *bola-banāo ṭhumarī*. The genre, however, continues to accord an autonomous status to the poetic element, far more categorically than the *ṭhumarī* genre does. [Also see: **Urdu, Bola-banāo Ṭhumarī**] Refer Chapter 4.3.

Ghoṣaka : The word is derived from the Sanskrit verb *ghoṣaṇa*, meaning announcement. In the present context, the term refers to a fretless stick-zither of the plucked variety, described in the ancient text on dramaturgy, Bharata's *Nāṭyaśāstra* [200 BC - AD 200], on which melody was executed by sliding a hard and smooth mechanical device along the strings, rather than by stopping the strings with the bare fingers. This instrument, along with the *ekatantrī vīṇā*, is considered the ancestor of the *vicitra vīṇā*, and the Hawaiian slide- guitar. [Also see: **Ekatantrī Vīṇā, Vicitra Vīṇā**]. Refer Chapter 5.1.

Gītakīrī : The word is colloquial and partially onomatopoetic. There is no consensus on its definition. It is frequently used to signify a short, crisp, brisk melodic passage, across adjacent tones/*svaras*, without loops or angularities. It warrants a nomenclature when inserted, for dramatic effect, into either low-density or convoluted/zigzag melodic movements. The presence of this expression is most prominent in the *ṭappā* genre of semi-classical music, though it is also deployed by some lineages of *khayāla* vocalism. [Also see: **Ṭappā, Khayāla**].

Gopāla : The word is derived from Sanskrit *go* = cows + *pāla* = one who breeds/nurtures/protects. The word "*gopāla*," though defensible as a generic description of all cowherds, is normally mentioned reverentially as a name for Lord Kr̥ṣṇa, the Divine Cowherd. This facet of his persona is especially important because of his popularity with *gopīs*, the women of the cowherd community in which he grew up. This nexus with the community constitutes the thematic material for the cultural manifestations of the *bhakti* movement in non-peninsular India. [Also see: **Bhakti**]

Guru : See **Guru-śiṣya Paramparā.**

Guru-śiṣya Paramparā : The term derives from Sanskrit *guru* = teacher/mentor/guide + *śiṣya* = disciple/ward/student/aspirant + *paramparā* = tradition. The term refers to the traditional relationship between a teacher and his students, which forms the basis of the transmission of all forms of knowledge, including musical knowledge. The salient features of this relationship are total subordination of the personality of the student to that of his teacher, in return for which the teacher accepts total responsibility for the grooming of the disciple in the chosen field of education. The two-way unconditionality and totality of commitment characteristic of this relationship is critical to its success because of the aural mode of transmission and the personality-transforming goal of education. In this tradition, therefore, the *guru* is accorded a status on par with God. [Also see: **Gharānā**]

Harmonium : A member of the keyboard based family of free-reed aerophones. Although such instruments have existed in India and other parts of Asia for centuries, Christian missionaries probably introduced the *Harmonium* to India from Britain in the eighteenth century, as accompaniment for choirs in Churches. The original import was a platform mounted pedal-primed version, which was later replaced with a portable hand-pumped variant with 37 keys. Despite the incompatibility of its tempered scale with Indian intonation practices, the instrument is now the most widely used melodic accompaniment to all genres of vocal music — other than *dhrupad/dhamāra* — and has replaced the *sāraṅgī* in this role. Attempts to establish it as a solo instrument have met with only limited success. [***Also see Sāraṅgī***].

Hāsya : See **Rasa/Navrasa.**

Hindustani music : See **Carnatic/Hindustani music.**

Hindustani slide-guitar : See **Indian Classical Guitar.**

Holī/Horī : Semi-classical genres of vocal music associated with *Holī*, the spring festival of colours, but more particularly with poetry describing the mischief the infant or adolescent Lord Kṛṣṇa played on the occasion with the womenfolk of his village. They are set primarily to the *dīpacaṇḍī* and *dhamāra tāla*s. [Also see: **Dīpcaṇḍī, Dhamāra**]

Hopping Tānas : These are, as the name suggests, melodic patterns that hop across alternating tones/*svara*s, often repeating each hop, and most commonly in ascending formation. Only a few stylistic lineages of *khayāla* vocalism practice this form of *tāna*s. [Also see: **Tānas**] Refer Chapter 4.2.

Horī-Dīpacaṇḍī : See **Dīpacaṇḍī, Holī/Horī.**

Indian classical guitar/Hindustani slide guitar : The Indian classical guitar/Hindustani slide guitar is an adaptation of the Western F-Hole Hawaiian slide guitar, modified to meet the requirements of Hindustani [north Indian] art music. The instrument was introduced to Hindustani music in the 1960s by Brijbhushan Kabra, a disciple of the *saroda* maestro, Ustad Ali Akbar Khan. In terms of technique of melodic execution, the Indian classical guitar and the Hawaiian guitar are both heirs to the ancient Indian fretless stick-zithers, the *ekatantrī vīṇā*, the *ghoṣaka*, and the *vicitra vīṇā*. The technique of these ancient instruments evidently travelled to Hawaii with one Gabriel Davion, kidnapped from India to Honolulu by a sea captain in the nineteenth century. The technique gave birth to the Hawaiian guitar, and returned to India before Second World War through the recordings of American guitarists, Sol Hoopii and Joe Kaipo. [Also see: **Ekatantrī Vīṇā, Ghoṣaka, Vicitra Vīṇā**]. Refer Chapter 5.8.

Jala Taraṅga : The word is derived from Sanskrit *jala* = water + *taraṅga* = waves. The term describes an ancient Indian polychord of the struck variety, consisting of 12/15 china-clay bowls of different sizes, which are tuned to a *rāga*-scale by filling them with appropriate quantities of water. Sound activation is done by beating the cups with sticks akin to sticks used for drums used in popular Western music. The instrument receives mention in musicological texts only from the late seventeenth century and is now nearly extinct, appearing occasionally in orchestral ensembles. Refer Chapter 5.5.

Jamajama/Zamzama : The word is colloquial and partially onomatopoetic. There is no consensus on its definition. It appears to signify a repetitive and deliberate intonation of pairs of tones/*svara*s in quick succession. Though used in the context of instrumental as well as vocal music, it appears to be more applicable to the idiom of the plucked instruments.

Jhālā : See **Ālāpa/Joḍa/Jhālā.**

Jhapatāla : *Jhapatāla* is a *tāla* [rhythmic cycle] of ten beats in 2+3+2+3 sub-division. This *tāla* is suited for slow to medium tempo rendition.

Jhūmrā : Jhūmrā is a *tāla* [rhythmic cycle] of fourteen beats in 3+4+3+4 sub-division. It is ideally suited for slow and ultra-slow rendition in the *khayāla* genre of vocal music. The *jhumrā* tempo rarely exceeds 20 beats per minute.

Joḍa : See **Ālāpa/Joḍa/Jhālā.**

Jugalabandī : The term derives its meaning from Sanskrit *jugala/yugala* = a couple + *bandī* = linked/tied/locked. The term describes duet performances of music by two lead musicians in collaborative effort. The total ensemble for a *jugalabandī*, including supporting musicians, can go up to six people. Being an improvization-dominant art form, Hindustani music is not particularly amenable to collaborative efforts, except under rare conditions conducive to compatibility. *Jugalabandīs* [duets] are, however, a popular format. Refer Chapter 2.3.

Kajarī/Kajalī : The word is derived from Hindī *kājala* = kohl, representing the black colour, darkness. The name of this genre of poetry-dominant vocal music probably alludes to the cloudy skies, and the ambient darkness associated with the rainy season [July to September] in which this genre is performed. It is performed by women, and accompanied by circular dance. Like the *caitī* genre of seasonal songs, this genre belongs to the folk tradition of Uttar Pradesh [Northern Provinces] and was elevated to the status of a semi-classical art form by the courtesans of Benares. The genre is regarded as one of the allied genres of the *bola-banāo ṭhumarī*. [Also see: **Caitī, Bola-banāo ṭhumarī**] Refer Chapter 4.3.

Kalāwanta/Kalāwantī Khayāla : The word derives from Sanskrit *kalā* = art + *wanta* = owner. Literally, the word denotes the practitioner of any art. In the present context, the term refers to a mediaeval community of *dhrupad* vocalists. *Kalāwantī* is an adjective derived from *kalāwanta*. The *kalāwantī khayāla* was presumably distinguished from its other variants by virtue of its practitioners having been groomed in the stylistics of the *dhrupad* genre. [Also see: **Dhrupad, Khayāla**]

Kaṇa/Sparśa : The word is Sanskrit for "grain/microscopic particle." When a tone/*svara* is intoned after — but almost simultaneously with — the fractional intonation of an adjacent tone/*svara*, the incidental tone/*svara* is called a *kaṇa svara*. This embellishment of intonation is used in vocal as well as instrumental music. In instrumental music, this form of embellishment is executed by the consecutive — though near simultaneous — use of two fingers. It involves no more than a summary touch of the incidental tone/*svara*. This is why, it is also called *sparśa*, Sanskrit for "touch."

Karuṇa : See **Rasa/Navarasa.**

Kāṣṭha Taraṅga : The word is derived from Sanskrit *kāṣṭa* = wood + *taraṅga* = waves. The term describes an ancient polychord of the struck variety, an Indian version of a xylophone. Sound activation is done by impacting wooden strips of different sizes with sticks with rounded heads. The instrument is nearly extinct, now encountered occasionally in orchestral ensembles. Refer Chapter 5.5.

Kathaka : *Kathaka* is the name of the principal genre of classical dance in the north Indian performing arts tradition, closely linked to its musical and poetic traditions. The word derives from Sanskrit *kathā* = story + *kāra* = narrator. *Kathaka* is also the name of an ancient community of story-tellers, who specialized in the narration of episodes from the major Hindu epics through mime and vocal-instrumental accompaniment. By religious orientation, the *Kathaka*s were devotees of Lord Kṛṣṇa, an incarnation of Lord Viṣṇu. Members of this community, and their religious and artistic traditions, have shaped the modern *Kathaka* genre of dance, as well as the modern *ṭhumarī* genre of semi-classical music, both of which revolve around the legend of Lord Kṛṣṇa. [Also see: **Ṭhumarī, Viṣṇu**] Refer Chapter 4.3.

Kehervā : *Kehervā* is a rhythmic cycle of eight beats in 4+4 sub-division. It is generally performed in medium tempo.

Khayāla : The term derives its meaning from the Perso-Arabic word *khayāla*, meaning idea, imagination, subjectivity, individuality, or impression. It represents a confluence of *rūpakālapti*, an ancient genre of Indian art music [eighth/ninth centuries], and Perso-Arabic music, encouraged by the landmark poet-musician, Ameer Khusro [thirteenth century]. *Khayāla* is the modern genre of vocal music, which replaced *dhrupad* as the mainstream genre starting in the early nineteenth century. *Khayāla* is an improvization-dominant genre, compared to its predecessor, *dhrupad*, which had a strong tendency towards being a pre-composed genre. The *khayāla* is characterized by its linear architecture, involving a progressive intensification of melodic and rhythmic density and complexity. A *khayāla* rendition generally consists of two parts — a slow tempo rendition called the *baḍā* [major] *khayāla* and a medium-to-fast tempo rendition called *choṭā* [minor] *khayāla*. [Also see: **Rūpakālapti, Dhrupad, Baḍā Khayāla, Choṭā Khayāla**] Refer Chapters 4.2 and 2.1.

Khaṭakā : The word is colloquial and partially onomatopoetic. Its definitions vary considerably. The word has two connotations — of a jolting quality, and of a forceful, audible impact. A generally acceptable definition would be the intonation of two neighbouring, though not necessarily adjacent, tones/*svara*s in quick succession, generally staccato, in which the first tone/*svara* is intoned with considerably greater force and impact than the second. The *khaṭakā* description is also appropriate for melodic expressions involving sudden drops across a distance of three or four tones/*svara*s specifically required by the grammar of some *rāga*s.

Kinnarī/Kinnarī Vīṇā : The word *kinnarī* is an adjective derived from the Sanskrit *kinnara*, meaning a category of celestial being. *Kinnara* also denotes a community of professional musicians. The word *kinnarī* may be construed either as an adjective derived from *kinnara*, or translated as as "female *kinnara*." In the present context, it refers to an ancient instrument, a member of the fretted stick-zither family, which is considered the ancestor of the *rudra vīṇā*. *Kinnarī vīṇā*s were of two varieties: the *bṛhat* [great/major] *kinnarī*, and the *laghu* [small/minor] *kinnarī*. The *laghu kinnarī* is believed to be the direct parent of the *rudra vīṇā*. [Also see: **Rudra Vīṇā**] Refer Chapter 5.1.

Kīrtana : *Kīrtana* is the verb associated with the Sanskrit abstract noun *kīrti* = glory/praise. A *kīrtana* is a song sung in praise of, or dedicated to the glory of someone, principally God. In thematic content, the *kīrtana* is similar to the *bhajana*, the distinction between them often being no more than semantic. *Kīrtana*s are, generally, shorter forms of poetry than *bhajana*s. *Kīrtana*s are written in all Indian languages and in every dialect of them. Its poetic form varies from region to region, as does its mode of rendition. As a piece of devotional music often sung in a choral modality, it is poetry-dominated, makes modest demands on musicianship and has no role for deliberate improvisation. In the Carnatic [south Indian] art music tradition, the *kīrtana* is a very definite compositional form, and is rendered in accordance with prescribed rules. [Also see: **Bhajana, Carnatic**].

Komala [with respect to svara/tone] : The word derives from Sanskrit *komala* = soft. The Hindustani scale consists of seven natural tones, plus mutations representing either suppressed or enhanced frequencies of five of the seven tones. The seven natural tones are called *śuddha*, the suppressed tones are called *komala*, Sanskrit for "Soft," while the solitary enhanced tone is called *tīvra*, Sanskrit for "Sharp." The Hindustani scale deploys *komala*/suppressed mutations/frequencies of the 2nd, 3rd, 6th, and 7th degrees [*re, gā, dhā, nī*] and a *tīvra*/sharp mutation of the 4th [*mā*]. [Also see: **Śuddha, Tīvra**].

Kṛti : The word is used generally as a common noun, meaning "artefact" [the product of a creative endeavour], though derived from the Sanskrit *kriyā* = action. In the context of art-music, the term refers to a specific category of songs performed in the Carnatic [south Indian] art music tradition, which follow certain rules of composition. [Also see: **Carnatic/Hindustani music**].

Kṛntan : The term is colloquial and partially onomatopoetic. It is especially suited to the technique of the *sitāra*. *Kṛntan* requires the dexterous movement of two fingers over the frets. The first *svara* executed with a right-hand stroke supporting one left-hand finger resting on the fret-board. The subsequent *svara*s of the phrase are executed with the second finger hitting the appropriate fret in a hammering motion, but without further right-hand stroke support. With this technique, a phrase of up to four *svara*s can be executed.

Laḍīguthāva Tānas : The term is a compound of two words: *laḍī* = chain + *guthāva* = knitting. This pattern progressively weaves an intricate web of interlocked patterns along its melodic path. [Also see: **Tānas**] Refer Chapter 4.2.

Laggī : *Laggī* is a lively *tabalā* solo which, in most cases, heralds the end of a *bola-banāo ṭhumarī* rendition. This form appears to be an early twentieth century innovation. The *laggī* is always performed in an eight-beat or sixteen-beat rhythmic cycle, irrespective of the *tāla* [rhythmic cycle] in which the *bola-banāo ṭhumarī* is rendered. The beat-density of the *laggī* rendition is normally twice that of the preceding *bola-banāo ṭhumarī* rendition. [Also see: **Bola-banāo Ṭhumarī**] Refer Chapter 4.3.

Laghu Kinnarī : See **Kinnarī/Kinnarī Vīṇā.**

Lāsya : *Lāsya* is an interpretative dance form described in Indian texts dating back to the pre-Christian era. It is a solo female dance form, accompanied by female singers and an orchestra. In the dance, the dancer utilizes mime to interpret the accompanying song, which describes her lover, and complains about his conduct. The musical content and context of this ancient dance form makes *lāsya* the earliest identified ancestor of the modern *ṭhumarī* genre of semi-classical vocal music. [Also see: **Ṭhumarī**] Refer Chapter 4.3.

Lāvaṇī : The word derives from Sanskrit *lāvaṇya* = seductive grace/ charm of a woman. *Lāvaṇī* is the name of a titillating folk dance form popular in the rural areas of southern Maharashtra. The songs that accompany the dance enjoy immense popularity independently of the dance form. Mirroring the emergence of the *bola-banāo ṭhumarī* from a decelerated version of the *bandiśa ṭhumarī* in northern India, the *lāvaṇī* form also evolved *baiṭhakī-cī-lāvaṇī* — literally, the sitting *lāvaṇī*. This is presented with the musician seated on the floor. In this format, music is presented at a slower tempo, and the dance element is restricted to mime and gesture. In this variant of the *lāvaṇī*, the emphasis is on emotive poetic-melodic communication. This is a sophisticated romanticist genre which has remained a regional genre, primarily because of lyrics written in a regional language. [Also see: **Maharashtra, Bandiśa Ṭhumarī, Bola-banāo Ṭhumarī**].

Laya : *Laya*, Sanskrit for tempo, is the time interval between the equidistant beats of a *tāla*, when rendered. It represents a linear calibration of the flow of time, while the *tāla* is a cyclical calibration of it. *Laya* may be expressed as a number of beats per minute, while the *tāla* is defined, amongst other criteria, by the number of beats within a cycle. In performance, a *tāla*, rendered in a particular *laya*, may be defined by number of seconds per cycle. [Also see: **Tāla**].

Laya-bāṇṭa : See **Bola-bāṇṭa/Laya-bāṇṭa.**

Layakārī : The word derives from Sanskrit *laya* = tempo + *kārī* = expertise/craftsmanship. When a musician, either a percussionist or a lead-musician, indulges in a display of rhythmic craftsmanship or artistry, deviating from the standard or pre-composed melodic, rhythmic, or melodic-rhythmic form, the resultant musical experience is called *layakārī*. [Also see: **Laya, Tāla**].

Madhya Laya : An adjective derived from the Sanskrit *madhya* = medium + *laya* = tempo. The notion of tempo [slow/medium/fast] is relative and dynamic. It differs between generations, between stylistic lineages, between different genres of vocal music, and between vocal and instrumental music.

Madhya Saptaka : The term derives from Sanskrit *madhya* = middle + *saptaka* = a group of seven tones/*svaras*. The term describes the middle octave of the melodic canvas. While the Western tradition considers the scale as consisting of eight points, the Indian system treats the same distance as consisting of seven frequency intervals. Hence, the reference to the scale as seven, rather than eight. This highlights a fundamental cultural difference. The act of music making in Indian music is focused on the handling of tonal intervals and transitions rather than the tonal point themselves.

Madhyāṅga pradhāna : See **Aṅga prādhānya.**

Mādhurya Rasa : See **Viraha Rasa/Mādhurya Rasa/Vātsalya Rasa.**

Mahārājā/Nawāb/Zamīndār/Sultan : Mahārājā [*mahā* = Great + *rājā* = King], Nawāb [Feudal Lord or Nobleman, generally Moslem], and *zamīndār* [*zamīn* = land + *dār* = owner of], Sultan [Persian for Mahārājā]. These terms denote different levels/categories of power and influence in feudal-agrarian India. Under colonial rule, the *Mahārājā*s, *Nawāb*s, *Zamīndār*s, *Sultān*s were guaranteed military protection of British armies in return for a share of land revenue. This aristocracy became a significant patron of the fine and performing arts. Its support was largely responsible for the emergence of the *gharānā*s in Hindustani [north Indian] art music, and for ushering in the Golden Age of Hindustani music. [Also see: **Gharānā**]

Maharashtrian/Maharashtra : Adjective derived from "Maharashtra," the name of the Indian state on the west coast. Maharashtrians are residents of Maharashtra, whose mother tongue is Marāṭhī, a Sanskrit-based language, written in Devanāgarī [Sanskrit] script. In the latter half of the twentieth century, Maharashtra emerged as the most prolific nursery of talent in *khayāla* vocalism, simultaneously with the emergence of the eastern Indian state of West Bengal as the primary resource of instrumental musicianship.

Maheśa/Śiva : The destroyer of the universe in Hindu mythology. [Also see: **Trimūrti**].

Mandra Saptaka : The term derives from Sanskrit *mandra* = lower + *saptaka* = a group of seven tones/*svara*s. The term describes the lower octave of the melodic canvas. The octave below the lower octave is frequently described as the *ati-mandra* [the ultra-lower] *saptaka*. While the Western tradition considers the scale as consisting of eight tonal points, the Indian system treats the same distance as consisting of seven intervals. Hence, the reference to the scale as seven, rather than eight. This highlights a fundamental cultural difference. The act of music making in Indian music is focused on the handling of tonal intervals and transitions rather than the tonal point themselves.

Maṅgala Vādya : The term derives its meaning from Sanskrit *maṅgala* = auspicious + *vādya* = musical instrument. It is an epithet accorded, amongst Hindustani [north Indian] instruments, only to the *śehnāī*. [Also see: **Śehnāī**].

Mañjha : The term is colloquial for Sanskrit *madhya* = middle. The term refers to a section of the *bandiśa*, not necessarily found in all *bandiśa*s, and often also indistinct — between the *sthāyī* and the *antarā*. Although its melodic structure is not standardized, it always fails to qualify as an *antarā*. It may therefore be viewed as the composer's attempt at an unusually comprehensive mapping of the *rāga*'s melodic personality within the confines of the pre-composed element. [Also see: **Bandiśa, Sthāyī, Antarā**].

Mata : *Mata* is Sanskrit for opinion/ideology/doctrine. At different stages in the history of Indian musicology, different schools of thought have emerged, called *mata*s, each with its own classification and codifications of *rāga*s. These classifications ostensibly reflected a diversity in the melodic entities they handled, and in the manner of their treatment in performance. *Mata*s are now only of academic/historical significance. This evidence is cited in support of the view that the Indian musical tradition has always been replete with, and tolerant of, diversity. This diversity was, in later years, reflected in the *gharānā*s of Hindustani music. Refer Chapter 1.5.

Matta Tāla : *Matta tāla* is a *tāla* [rhythmic cycle] of eighteen beats, in nine subdivisions of two beats each. It is a minor *tāla* of the *dhrupad/ dhamāra* genre. When performed, it is generally performed in medium to fast tempo.

Mīṇḍa : *Mīṇḍa* is the primary mode of intervallic transition in Hindustani music — vocal as well as instrumental. It describes a transition, akin to a traction, which literally "stretches" a tone/ *svara* in order to reach another tone/*svara*, defining a curvilinear path. It is the opposite of a staccato transition.

Mirāsī : *Mirāsī* is the name of a community of Moslem musicians who accompany courtesans on various musical instruments, mainly the *sāraṅgī* or *tabalā*, and teach them music. Being a professional classification, the term also came to be used, though rarely, for Hindu musicians in similar professions. Hereditary musicians residing in Punjab have also been called *mirāsī*s. Traditionally, members of this profession claimed a share of the income of the salons to which they were attached. The profession has been viewed with some reservations in art music circles. A career in the courtesan districts had "second grade" connotations in an era when feudal patronage was the most coveted certification of musicianship. Secondly, accompaniment is/was seen as a compromise forced upon those who are/were not good enough to become lead performers. Thirdly, accompanists are/were not expected to be able to retain/cultivate a clear musical vision. And, finally, the music of the courtesan districts is/was not viewed as "pure" art music. These factors led to an image of *mirāsī*s as unreliable teachers for "pure" music. On the other hand, it cannot be denied that some very respected names in twentieth-century *khayāla* vocalism came from *mirāsī* backgrounds. Most of these issues have lost their relevance in contemporary music.

Miyā Tānsen : The word derives from Persian "Miyā" = Honourable/Lord + "Tānsen" = the sixteenth-century musician who served the court of the third Mogul emperor, Jalaluddin Mohammad Akbar. He was invited to the Mogul court after he had acquired a formidable reputation as a musician in the court of *mahārājā* of Rewā in the Central Provinces. A Hindu brāhmaṇa by birth, his original name was Ramtanu Mishra, which became Tānsen upon his conversion to Islam and entry into Mogul service. In addition to his legendary musicianship, Tānsen's significance to music also rests on his contribution as manager of the patronage function at the imperial court, and perpetuation of vocal as well as instrumental musical traditions through his direct descendants. [Also see: **Senīya**].

Mukhaḍā : The word derives its meaning from Sanskrit *mukha* = face. The word describes the first phrase [but, occasionally a string of phrases] of the *sthāyī* in a *bandiśa* — literally its face — which culminates at the *sama*, the first beat of the rhythmic cycle. By implication, the term is not relevant for *bandiśa*s which commence on the first beat of the rhythmic cycle. By virtue of being the launch phrase of the *bandiśa*, and by also being its most frequently iterated phrase right through the rendition, it qualifies for its nomenclature. The *mukhaḍā* is the signature of the *bandiśa*, and often contains the *pakaḍa* [the catch-phrase or signature] of the *rāga*. The best-composed *mukhaḍā*s are able to build and release aesthetic tension within a very short span of time. For this reason, the composition and rendition of the *mukhaḍā*s is accorded great importance in the musical arts. [Also see: **Bandiśa, Sthāyī, Pakaḍa, Rāga**]

Murkī : The term is colloquial, though probably related to the Hindī verb *maroḍanā* = to twist. The *murkī* is a special type of *mīṇḍa*, where the phrase involves a twisted/wrap-around execution with a jerky motion. This melodic expression is encountered in vocal music as well as instrumental music. [Also see: **Mīṇḍa**]

Nagārā/Nakkārā : See **Tāśā/Nagārā.**

Nāṭya Saṅgīta : The term derives from Sanskrit *nāṭya* = theatre + *saṅgīta* = music. The term refers to a modern genre of *rāga*-based music from regional theatre, which dominated the entertainment of bourgeois society in the western state of Maharashtra during the nineteenth and early twentieth centuries. The Marāṭhī theatre movement was an important manifestation of the nationalist renaissance in both respects — culturally as well as politically. Its leaders had close links with nationalist leaders like Balgangadhar Tilak and Savarkar, and deployed drama astutely to provoke public sentiment against India's colonial rulers. Marāṭhī theatre participated in the nationalist movement as a covert insurgency, utilizing historical and mythological themes as metaphors for the prevailing socio-political reality. The musical and choreographic component of the productions perhaps helped camouflage the insurgent undercurrents, while also providing entertainment through an additional expression of "Indian-ness" at a time when it was severely threatened.

The music in Marāṭhī theatre was presented in monologue, conversational as well as choreographic contexts, and was almost always based on classical *rāga*s, though also occasionally on folk melodies. In its balance between poetic, melodic and rhythmic elements, and in the relative weightage to pre-composed and improvized elements, the predominant *rāga*-based segment of *nāṭya saṅgīta* falls between the *choṭā khayāla* and *bandiśa ṭhumarī* genres of art music. It therefore demands a high level of musicianship.

The theatre movement maintained close links with the stalwarts of the Hindustani art music tradition, enlisting many of them as composers, teachers, singer-actors, and accompanists on the instruments. Very successful and prosperous theatrical companies toured the length and breadth of the large Marāṭhī-speaking region of India. Their activity created the most solid regional constituency for the modern *khayāla* genre of Hindustani [north Indian] vocal music, and supported the cultivation of a massive resource-base of musicianship. Since Independence, the touring theatre company, and the musical theatrical production have both succumbed to the onslaught of the feature film and television as the dominant entertainment media. The accumulated asset of *nāṭya saṅgīta* is, however, still a formidable force in the musical culture of Maharashtra. [Also see: **Maharashtra, Choṭā Khayāla, Bandiśa Ṭhumarī**] Refer Chapter 4.3.

Nawāb : See **Mahārājā/Nawāb/Zamīndār/Sultān.**

Nāyikā Bheda : The term derives from Sanskrit *nāyikā* = female protagonist + *bheda* = classification. The lyrics of the modern *ṭhumarī* genre of semi-classical vocal music are dominated by the erotic/romantic sentiment. Even within this broad theme, they portray primarily the agony of a female protagonist separated from her beloved. *Nāyikā bheda* is an eight-way classification of such situations in the amorous relationship [ten, according to some aestheticians]. These are not merely academic constructs for the thematic classification of poetry. They aid contextual visualization and guide the auto-suggestive and communicative processes of the performer. These concepts are crucial to the aesthetics of the *bola-banāo ṭhumarī* genre, which uses song-texts as a platform for a luxuriant and leisurely melodic ornamentation, with the purpose of making the words come to life. [Also see: **Ṭhumarī, Bola-banāo Ṭhumarī**] Refer Chapter 4.3.

Nom Tom : The term refers to the meaningless consonants used as articulatory material in the *ālāpa* of the *dhrupad* genre of art music. The practice has its origins in the chanting of the names of Lord Viṣṇu — Oṁ, Hari, Ananta, Nārāyaṇa etc., which later gave way to meaningless consonants [*nom, tom, ta, na, ri,* etc.] encouraged partially by a religious barrier when performed by Moslem musicians, and guided partially by greater articulatory convenience in high-density melody. As a result, the *dhrupad ālāpa* is often also referred to as *nom tom ālāpa*. [Also see: **Dhrupad**]

NRI : An abbreviation for "Non-resident Indians." Members of the Indian diaspora, residing primarily in the USA, Europe and the Middle East, but increasingly, also in Australia and New Zealand.

Nyāsa : *Nyāsa* is Sanskrit for "pause/rest/stabilise." *Rāga* grammar allows only some, and not all, of its permissible tones/*svara*s as termination points for melodic phrasing. These are called *nyāsa svaras*. [Also see: **Rāga**] Refer Chapter 3.1.

Pada : The word derives its meaning from Sanskrit *padya* = verse/poetic form as distinct from *gadya* = prose. The word has, however, come to be more closely associated with devotional poetry. In contemporary music, the term is used to denote, not merely the poetic element, but the entire poetic-melodic-rhythmic shell of compositions in the *dhrupad* genre of art music. A substantial proportion of *dhrupad* verse is no longer of devotional character. However, because of the origins of the *dhrupad* genre in the music of the Vaiṣṇavite temples, the word *pada* has been retained. In the *dhrupad* genre, the word *pada* has the same meaning as *bandiśa* in the post-*dhrupad* genres. [Also see: **Bandiśa, Dhrupad**]

Padāśrita : The word derives its meaning from Sanskrit *pada* [*padya*] = verse/poetry + *āśrita* = dependent on. The term describes a genre of music dominated by the poetic element. *Dhrupad* and *ṭhumarī* may both be described as *padāśrita* genres. [Also see: **Dhrupad, Ṭhumarī**]

Pakaḍa : The word is Hindī for "grip." In Hindustani music, it refers to the signatory phrase or phrases of a *rāga*, which identify it beyond reasonable doubt. [Also see: **Calana, Rāga**]

Pakhāwaj : [loosely, also called Mṛdaṅga].

The name derives from the Sanskrit : *pakṣa* = sides + *vādya* = instrument for sound production. It dates back to the pre-Christian era, with its origins shrouded in mythology. The *pakhāwaj*, a horizontal two-faced tapering cylindrical drum, was the principal percussion instrument of the Hindustani [north Indian] art music tradition, until the advent of the *tabalā*. Both sides are covered with goat-skin and tuned, at each performance, by laying, in the centre of each face, a fresh paste of wheat-flour. This coating enhances the sustain of its acoustic output. The instrument emits an atonal, bass sound. It remains, to this day, the standard rhythmic accompaniment to performances of the *dhrupad / dhamāra* genre, but has no presence in the modern genres of art music. Other two-faced barrel drums descended from the *pakhāwaj* are, however, still used in popular and folk music. The *pakhāwaj* of the Hindustani [north Indian] tradition corresponds to the *mṛdaṅgam* in the Carnatic [south Indian] tradition, though the two differ marginally in construction and design, and substantially in idiom. [Also see: **Tabalā, Dhrupad**].

Paṇḍit : The word is Sanskrit for a person who commands respect in society by virtue of his knowledge of theory in his chosen field. In the music world, however, the honorific is accorded to any Hindu musician of exceptional attainments as a performer, the knowledge of theory being implicit in his musicianship. A Moslem of comparable attainments is called an *ustād*. In print journalism, it is common to represent the word *paṇḍit* in its abbreviated form "*Pt.*" and *ustād* in its abbreviated form as "Ust." No formalized framework exists for conferring such honorifics to musicians. They emerge through an informal process of consensus building within the community of musicians.

Paraṇ/Sur Paraṇ/Tāra Paraṇ : The *paraṇ* [etymology speculative] is the major compositional form typical of the *pakhāwaj*, the prime percussion instrument of the *dhrupad* genre. A *paraṇ* usually spans across at least two cycles of the *tāla*, and may, or may not, end in a *tihāyī*. Unlike post-*dhrupad* music, the *dhrupad* genre allows the principal musician and his percussion accompanist to take-off simultaneously into improvizations/variations on the pre-composed form. The percussionist's primary deviations from the *ṭhekā* are pre-composed *paraṇs*. They are mirrored/mimicked by the principal musician [vocalist/instrumentalist], who matches them with his own improvizations to ensure that melody and rhythm arrive synchronously at the *sama*. The matching *paraṇ* pattern performed by a vocalist is called a *sur* [melodic] *paraṇ*, while the one performed on the *rudra vīṇā*, or any other plucked instrument is called a *tāra* [string] *paraṇ*. [Also see: **Ṭhekā, Sama, Tihāyī, Rudra Vīṇā, Dhrupad**] Refer Chapter 4.1.

Paṭhān : A tribe of Moslem warriors hailing from Afghanistan and the north-western districts of Pakistan.

Peśakāra : The word derives from the Persian/Urdu *peśa* = to present respectfully. The *peśakāra* is the opening movement of a *tabalā* solo recital, played in a perceptibly slow tempo. For this reason, it is often called the *ālāpa* of the *tabalā* idiom. It is characterized by a balanced distribution of sound symbols between the bass and the treble drums. It is based on a stylized rendition of the *ṭhekā* of the *tāla*, which is elaborated through various permutations and combinations of sound syllables and beat-densities within the same tempo. Although the basic pattern of the *peśakāra* is pre-composed, the musician has considerable scope for improvized variants on the basic pattern. [Also see: **Tabalā, Ṭhekā**]

Prāṇa/Prāṇāyāma : *Prāṇa* is Sanskrit for "the life force." *Āyāma* is Sanskrit for "control/discipline." In Hindu philosophy, the involuntary process of breathing represents the life force. The Hindu mystical tradition prescribes complex breathing exercises, called *prāṇāyāma*, as a means of acquiring control over the life force. Submitting an involuntary act — breathing — to the human will is one of processes prescribed in the practice of *yoga*. Its perfection leads ultimately to salvation, defined as a release from the cycle of death and rebirth. This science is intimately related to the technique of vocalization and intonation in art-music, evolved as a self-illuminating and personality transforming pursuit.

Prabandha gāna : The term derives from Sanskrit *prabandha* = organization/structure/format + *gāna* = singing/song. The reference is to the genre of vocal music which dominated Hindustani art music between the eleventh and thirteenth centuries. The nomenclature suggests that it was a highly disciplined, probably entirely pre-composed, genre of music. One of the streams of *prabandha gāna* is believed to have evolved into the mediaeval *dhrupad* genre, which dominated the mainstream from the fifteenth to the eighteenth centuries. [Also see: **Dhrupad**] Refer Chapter 4.1.

Prasiddha : The word is Sanskrit for "famous." In music, it is used primarily as a means of classifying *rāgas* into *prasiddha* = common/popular/widely recognized, or *aprasiddha* = rare/not widely recognized. These classifications are dynamic, as *rāgas* move freely between popularity and rarity from generation to generation.

Pukāra : The word is Hindī for "calling out." It describes a cry, an appeal, a calling for attention. As a musical expression, it is ill-defined, but is generally used to described an exclamatory expression, which leaps upwards briskly, and across a substantial tonal distance, from a lower tone/*svara* to one much higher and then returns to the starting tone/*svara*. The expression is dramatic, and therefore found more often in the romanticist *ṭhumarī* genre than in the classicist *khayāla* genre. Its use would be frowned upon in the ultra-formal *dhrupad* genre.

Punjābī Ṭhekā : See **Tīnatāla/Tritāla, Ṭhekā.**

Pūrvāṅga pradhāna : See **Aṅga prādhānya.**

Qawwālī : *Qawwālī* is a poetry-dominant genre of music, with lyrics originally in Persian, and later in Urdu. A controversial theory regards the *qawwālī* as an important influence on the evolution of the modern *khayāla* genre. The Islamic Sūfī sects adopted this as a major vehicle for the propagation of their philosophy. Ameer Khusro, the legendary thieteenth-century poet-musician and a Sūfī, contributed substantially to its evolution and stature. In recent times, however, its thematic content has been enlarged substantially. In its contemporary form, a great deal of *qawwālī* is, in fact, *ghaẓal* in a different mode of rendition. Another distinguishing feature of the contemporary *qawwālī* is a combination of alternating solo and choral modalities of presentation, and a large ensemble, often including multiple melodic and percussion accompaniments. [Also see: **Khayāla, Urdu, Ghaẓal**].

Qawwālī Ṭhekā : See **Tīnatāla/Tritāla, Ṭhekā.**

Quaidā : The word is Persian/Urdu for "the law/the principle." The *quaidā* is normally the second movement in a *tabalā* solo performance. The *quaidā* is more structured than its preceding movement, the *peśakāra*, and has negligible scope for improvization. The *quaidā* is presented in four well-defined phases, in proper sequence. In the first phase, the unadorned basic motif [the *quaidā* / the law / the principle] of the movement is presented in its unadorned form. In the second phase, the basic motif is broken down into smaller units to facilitate elaboration. In the third phase, the basic motif is interpreted in close adherence to the structure of the *tāla* in which the *quaidā* is composed. In the fourth and final phase, the particular *quaidā* is rounded off with a *tihāyī*. [Also see: **Peśakāra, Tihāyī**]

Rabāba : The *rabāba* is an instrument of the short-necked fretless lute family, played by plucking. It has a carved wooden body, with the lower half covered by goat-skin, and the upper half with a wooden finger board. It uses catgut strings and, like a mandolin, is plucked with a triangular plectrum. The *rabāba* came to India from two sources. The first *rabāba*, a larger instrument, came from Persia with conquering armies around the eleventh century. The second, a smaller instrument of similar construction, came from Afghanistan with soldiers in the employ of early Moguls. The Persian *rabāba* became a significant performer of the *dhrupad* genre during the Mogul period, while the Afghan *rabāba* participated in the evolution of post-*dhrupad* genres during the nineteenth century. Though extinct now, the two *rabāba*s are significant because they are the ancestors of the contemporary *saroda*. [Also see: **Saroda**] Refer Chapter 5.4.

Rabābīya : A musician who performs on the *rabāba* [Also see: **Rabāba**] Refer Chapter 5.4.

Rabindra Sangeet : This is a modern [twentieth century] genre of vocal music named after the Nobel laureate poet-composer, Rabindranath Tagore. His poetry was written in his mother tongue, Beṅgālī. Because of his calibre as a composer, his songs have attained autonomous stature independently of their poetry, and are prized also as pieces for rendition on the instruments. Tagore was well versed in *dhrupad*, *ṭhumarī* and *ṭappā* genres, had studied the art music tradition of south India, as also the music of the Vaiṣṇava temples. He was conversant with the folk music of his native Bengal, several parts of India, and of many Asian and European countries. His compositions represent a mix of melodic and rhythmic ideas from Indian art music traditions, along with all genres of music from various parts of the world. A lot of his music is *rāga*-based, though not categorically bound by *rāga* grammar. Despite the catholicity of his approach to composition, Tagore's compositions bear the unmistakable and inimitable imprint of his musical vision. In its vocal as well instrumental manifestations, Rabindra Sangeet is performed strictly in its pre-composed form, without any melodic or rhythmic improvization. Although Rabindra Sangeet enjoys a substantial following outside Bengal, it is primarily a regional genre of modern music. [Also see: **Sangīta, Dhrupad, Ṭappā**]

Rāga : The word, generally used as a suffix, is Sanskrit for "attitude/ quality of response/emotional content of a relationship." In music, it has come to denote a melodic idea or framework, associated with a specific quality of emotional response. The notion of *rāga*-ness is, therefore, inseparable from the concept of *rasa* in Indian aesthetics. A *rāga* is a psycho-acoustic hypothesis, which states that melody, created and rendered in accordance with a certain set of rules, has a high probability of eliciting a certain quality of emotional response. The set of rules for the creation and rendition of the melody constitute the grammar of a *rāga*. An awareness of the target response enables a musician to transcend grammar and enter the realm of literature.

As a melodic entity, a *rāga* is neither a pre-composed melody nor a mode or scale. It is represented by a set of rules governing the selection, sequencing and treatment of tones/*svara*s. These rules define a framework, which is tight enough to ensure aesthetic coherence, while also providing sufficient freedom for individual creativity. This approach to guiding the melodic content of music was necessary for a tradition, which combines the role of the composer and performer in the same individual. As a cultural choice, this approach harmonizes the competing demands of continuity within change, and unity within diversity. This enables each performed piece of music to retain a familiarity while giving audiences a substantial access to a novelty and freshness of the musical experience. Every *rāga* is a plausible psycho-acoustic hypothesis because of the accumulated experience of society, and continues to remain plausible by every musician being allowed to test it, and even revise it, at every performance. The hypothesis is perennial and ever-changing, never intending to attain the finality of a theory.

Each *rāga* is shaped and re-shaped by each performance, and has no existence exogenous to this context. The achievement of its emotional goals is accepted as a random event because it is susceptible to a host of variables, many of which may be un-controllable and even unrelated to the music itself. The names of *rāga*s, and their grammar, are only the starting point of familiarity for contemporary audiences. The music itself is bound by neither names nor grammar, beyond the willingness of musicians and their audiences to accept such a binding. Their interaction has the sole purpose of sharing the experience of literature — a happening — while grammarians struggle to relate the happening to a name, and to document what made it happen. [Also see: **Rasa/Navarasa**] Refer Chapters 3.1 to 3.4.

Rāga-mālikā : The term is derived from Sanskrit *rāga* = melodic framework + *mālikā* = garland. A *rāga-mālikā* is a presentation format which strings together — mechanistically and sequentially — several *rāga*s for the purpose of telescoped/abbreviated presentation. In such a presentation, each *rāga* retains its melodic identity, without forging either a compound or emulsion of the component *rāga*s. The *rāga-mālikā* format delights primarily by the cleverness with which the musician makes the transitions between sequentially rendered *rāga*s. Refer Chapter 3.2.

Rāga svarūpa : The term derives from *rāga* = melodic framework + *svarūpa* = form/image. *Rāga svarūpa* is a notion of a *rāga*'s distinctive melodic personality enshrined in pre-composed strings of melodic phrases — virtually melodic sentences. This approach, espoused primarily by certain lineages of *dhrupad* vocalism, is more rigid than the *calana* approach, which permits the musician greater freedom in the sequencing of phrases. [Also see: **Rāga, Calana**] Refer Chapter 3.5.

Rāga vākya : The term derives its meaning from Sanskrit *rāga* = melodic framework + *vākya* = sentence. The term describes a string of two or three prefatory phrases — a sentence — rendered before the commencement of a *khayāla* presentation, with no objective beyond identifying the *rāga*. The *rāga vākya* is, in a sense, a cryptic/telegraphic/abbreviated version of an *aucar*. [Also see: **Aucar**].

Rāsak/Rāsa Līlā : *Rāsak* is the name of an erotic fertility dance of folk origin, accompanied by song and instrumental music. The music is set to *rāsa tāla*, corresponding to the modern *kehervā tāla*. The *rāsak* is closely associated with *rāsa līlā*, a ballet form celebrating the legend of Lord Kṛṣṇa, which shaped the modern *Kathaka* genre of classical dance. The choreographic, thematic and musical content of the *rāsak* and the *rāsa līlā* has been identified as an important source for the modern *Kathaka* genre of dance and the modern *ṭhumarī* genre of a semi-classical music. [Also see: **Kathaka, Ṭhumarī, Kehervā**] Refer Chapter 4.3.

Rāsa Līlā : See **Rāsak/Rāsa Līlā.**

Rasa/Navarasa : The Indian aesthetic tradition views the sensory experience as a pathway to the emotional, and the emotional as a pathway to the spiritual. This reflects the fundamental transcendentalism of Hindu thought. All art is, therefore, validated by a single dominant criterion — its ability to elicit an emotional response. This criterion acknowledges that, at its most intense, the experience of beauty evokes a response that transcends its qualitative aspect, and acquires a mystical quality. This defines the potential of the artistic endeavour, and its reception, for personality transformation and spiritual evolution. At the intermediate aesthetic level, however, the tradition allows for the classification of works of art on the basis of the quality of the emotional response. The name given to these qualities is *rasa*, a metaphorical expression derived from the Sanskrit *rasa* = extract/essence/juice.

Orthodox aesthetic theory, annunciated in pre-Christian texts, recognizes nine basic emotions/sentiments, called *navarasa*, Sanskrit for *nava* = nine + *rasa* = qualities of sentiment/emotional experience. The nine are: [a] *śṛṅgāra*, the romantic sentiment, [b] *Karuṇa*, the sentiment of pathos, [c] *Hāsya*, the sentiment of mirth, [d] *Raudra*, the sentiment of wrath, [e] *Vīra*, the sentiment of valour, [f] *Bhaya*, the sentiment of fear, [g] *Bībhatsa*, the sentiment of disgust, [h] *Adbhut*, the sentiment of surprise/marvel, [i] *Śānta*, the sentiment of peace. Over the two millennia since this enumeration, critical literature has added several other sentiments, and combinations of orthodox sentiments, to the interpretation of the emotional content of artistic endeavours. [Also see: **Rāga**]

Rasika : The word is a common noun derived from the Sanskrit *rasa* = the target emotional response of a work/piece of art. The word is loosely translated as "connoisseur," but is unique in its cultural meaning. A *rasika* is a person who is equipped with the knowledge, beliefs and emotional receptivity required to partake of *rasa*.

Classical musicological texts have enumerated the qualifications of a *rasika* in considerable detail. In the Hindustani tradition, the listener is not the passive recipient of a unidirectional musical communication. The *rasika* — individually as well collectively — is an active participant in the process that constantly shapes and re-shapes *rāgas* and every other aspect of the musical tradition. By virtue of his connoisseurship, he constitutes one of the pillars of the quality control mechanism in the musical culture, and is as responsible for the trends in the musical tradition, as are the musicians themselves. [Also see: **Rāga, Rasa/Navarasa**].

Raudra : See **Rasa/Navarasa.**

Rūpaka Tāla : *Rūpaka* is a *tāla* [rhythmic cycle] of seven beats in 3+2+2 subdivision. Like the *dhamāra tāla, rūpaka* also begins on a subdued beat, and has an irregular cadential structure. For this reason, it is considered ideal for slow and medium tempo rendition in art music. Folk traditions do, however, deploy variants of the *tāla*, which are performed at a brisk tempo, though with a dented beat pattern. *Rūpaka* is generally encountered in the *khayāla* genre of vocal music and in instrumental music. A few *ṭhumarī* compositions are also composed in this *tāla*. Contemporary musicians have frequently rendered traditional compositions set to *dhamāra* of 14 beats in *rūpaka* of 7 beats. [Also see: **Dhamāra**].

Rūpakālapti : The term derives from Sanskrit *rūpaka* = definitive form + *ālapti* = conversation/dialogue. As a musical expression, *ālapti* has the same connotation as *ālāpa*. An *ālāpa* is a leisurely, deliberate, even conversational, exposition of the *rāga*-form. The Indian musical tradition recognizes two categories of *ālāpa/ālapti*. [a] *rāga-ālapti*, which uses only vowel form as articulatory device, and [b] *rūpaka-ālapti*, which uses the poetic form as the articulatory device. This latter form, dating back to the eighth/ninth centuries, is believed to have been the precursor of the modern *khayāla* genre. Interestingly, the *bola-ālāpa* in the contemporary slow-tempo *khayāla* corresponds to the definition of *rūpakālapti*. [Also see: **Ālāpa, Khayāla, Qawwālī**] Refer Chapter 4.2.

Rudra Vīṇā : [*Also called Bīna*]. A member of the fretted stick-zither family of plucked instruments. A revered instrument with strong mythological and mystical associations. Evolved around the thirteenth century when frets were added to a fretless predecessor. The instrument is associated with the mediaeval *dhrupad/dhamāra* genre of music. It was originally used as accompaniment to vocal performances, but later acquired its independent performing domain. The *rudra vīṇā* is the principal inspiration — acoustic as well as stylistic — for the plucked instruments in contemporary Hindustani [north Indian] art music. As *dhrupad* receded from centre-stage of art music, the *rudra vīṇā* surrendered its place to later instruments which were ergonomically more efficient, and could adapt themselves to the contemporary environment — acoustic and stylistic. At the time of writing, only five competent performers on the *rudra vīṇā* are known to exist (December, 2003). They are — in descending order of age — Pandharinath Kolhapure, Asad Ali Khan, Shamsuddin Faridi Desai, Hindaraj Diwekar, and Bahauddin Dagar. Only the last two are below 50. [Also see: **Dhrupad**] Refer Chapter 5.1.

Sacivālaya : The word derives from Sanskrit *saciva* = Secretary + *ālaya* = a building. In India, a *saciva* [Secretary] is the seniormost bureaucrat in a government department. *Sacivālaya* is the common noun for the various seats of the state governments and of the central government. The bureaucrat is a symbol of immense power over all aspects of public life — including the cultural — without any accountability either for the *bona fides* of his decisions, or for the results they deliver.

Sadra : A genre of vocal music composed exclusively in the *jhapatāla* rhythmic cycle of ten beats. It is believed to derive its name from the village of Shahadra near Delhi. The village was home to two brothers, Shivnath and Shivmohan [sixteenth century], disciples of the legendary Nayak Baiju, credited with having developed this genre. Like *dhrupad* and *khayāla* lyrics, *sadra* lyrics are written in *brajabhāṣā*, the dialect spoken in and around the city of Mathurā. The *sadra* genre, now almost extinct, is regarded as a transitional genre heralding the decline of *dhrupad* supremacy in art music. [Also see: **Jhapatāla, Dhrupad, Khayāla**].

Sādhāraṇī Śailī : The term derives from Sanskrit *sādhāraṇī* = common/ordinary + *śailī* = style. The reference here is to a style of presenting *rāga*-based vocal music, presumably widely practised during the last centuries of the first millennium. One of the presentation formats within this style was the *rūpakālapti* form, which is regarded as the precursor of the modern *khayāla* genre of vocal music. [Also see: **Rūpakālapti, Khayāla**] Refer Chapter 4.2.

Sama : The word is an abbreviation of the Sanskrit *samāvasthā*, a compound of two words *sama* = equilibrium + *avasthā* = state. It defines the first beat of the rhythmic cycle, at which it releases the aesthetic tension built up by its internal arrangement of beat sub-divisions and cadences. The *sama* is also the point at which the *mukhaḍā* of the *bandiśa* culminates, releasing the aesthetic tension built by its melodic design, and its interaction with the rhythmic cycle. Because it is the focal point for the synchronous release of aesthetic tension by the rhythmic as well as the melodic elements, the *sama* has a magnified cathartic value, and is critical to the aesthetics of Hindustani [north Indian] art music. [Also see: **Mukhaḍā, Bandiśa Tāla**].

Sampūrṇa : The word is Sanskrit for complete/comprehensive, and describes heptatonic *rāga*s [those that deploy seven tones/*svara*s]. The description does not double-count a tone/*svara* if the *rāga* uses the natural as well as its suppressed or enhanced microtones. In this classification, the ascent and the descent are considered together. However, *rāga*s may be described by dual classifications such as *ṣaḍava-sampūrṇa* if, for instance, they are hexatonic in the ascent and heptatonic in the descent. [Also see: **Catusvara, Auḍava, Ṣāḍava**].

Saṁvādī : See **Vādī/Saṁvādī.**

Sañcārī : The term derives its meaning from Sanskrit *sañcāra* = dispersion/diffusion. This is the third and penultimate phase in the *rāga* presentation protocol. This segment of pre-composed *bandiśa*s is frequently dropped in the contemporary rendition of *dhrupad* compositions [*pada*s], and not found in *bandiśa*s of the post-*dhrupad* genres. This phase of *rāga* exposition protocol therefore pertains only to the improvisatory movements. As the term suggests, the logic of this phase is freed from ascending-descending progression of the *sthāyī-antarā* phases of *rāga* exposition, which are designed to jointly and systematically unfold the *rāga* across the entire melodic canvas. The melodic-aesthetic function of the *sañcārī* is, instead, to summarize the first two phases, while emphasizing those facets of the *rāga*'s melodic personality, which are insufficiently expressed by the progressive logic of preceding phases. It is, in its very character, a free-flowing phase of improvisation. [Also see: **Dhrupad, Bandiśa, Sthāyī, Antarā, Ābhoga**]. Refer Chapter 2.1.

Sangīta : The word derives its meaning from Sanskrit *sam* = company + *gīta* = song. The term originally referred to the totality of a song, accompanied by instrumental music as well as dance. Gradually, dance was separated from the meaning of the term, which now describes, collectively or individually, the vocal and the instrumental musical arts.

Santūra : A member of the box-polychord family of struck instruments, and related to the hammered dulcimer/cimbalom family of instruments found in several parts of Asia and Europe. Origin most likely in India as *śatatantrī vīṇā* [*śatatantrī* = 100 strings + *vīṇā* = a stringed instrument] or in Persia as *santūra* [*san/sad* = 100 + *tūra*-strings]. It was traditionally performed only in the Kashmir valley in India as accompaniment for religious chants of the Islamic Sūfī sects. In the latter half of the twentieth century, it was re-engineered and elevated to the concert platform as a solo instrument by Paṇḍit Shivkumar Sharma, who remains its most significant exponent. Refer Chapter 5.5.

Sapāṭa Tānas : *Sapāṭa* is Hindī for "flat-out," a straight melodic run pattern with no loops or angularities. *Sapāṭa tāna*s can be descending or ascending, and of varying melodic spans. [Also see: **Tānas**] Refer Chapter 4.2.

Saptaka : See **Mandra Saptaka, Madhya Saptaka, Tāra Saptaka.**

Sāraṅgī : A member of the short-necked lute family of bowed instruments. An instrument of considerable antiquity and almost certainly of Indian origin. For centuries, the instrument — known by several names, and in several forms — has been used by bards and roving minstrels for accompanying themselves. It entered art music around the seventeenth century, and has been an accompaniment to the modern genres of vocal music — *ṭhumarī, ṭappā* and *khayāla*. In recent years, it has begun to emerge also as a solo instrument. It is, however, threatened with extinction since the emergence of the *harmonium* as the more popular accompaniment to vocal music. In the latter half of the twentieth century, the most distinguished exponent of the instrument has been Pandit Ramnarain, the only exponent to carve out a viable career as a soloist. Refer Chapter 5.7.

Sarasvatī Vīṇā : The name derives from Sarasvatī, the Hindu goddess of learning and the fine arts, whose iconographic representation invariably shows her holding a long-necked fretted lute. The term *sarasvatī vīṇā* refers to the fretted lute popular in Carnatic [south Indian] tradition of art music. Though, at one stage, the Hindustani [north Indian] *rudra vīṇā* — organologically, a stick-zither — was also occasionally called a *sarasvatī vīṇā*, the two instruments are now clearly associated with their independent respective names. The instruments have near-identical histories, and are of comparable antiquity. Both started as accompaniment to vocal music, and later also acquired solo performance status.

Saragama : The *saragama* derives its name from the first four solmnization/solfa symbols [*sā, re, gā, mā*] of the Hindustani scale. The use of solfa symbols as an articulatory device in vocal performance is called *saragama*. Such use is well established in the Carnatic [south Indian] tradition. Ustad Abdul Kareem Khan is credited with initiating its use in *khayāla* performance in the early twentieth century. Having been only a pedagogical device until recently, it was frowned upon, by some stylistic lineages of *khayāla* vocalism, as childish. The other major genres of vocal art music — *dhrupad* and *ṭhumarī* — do not deploy this device at all. The *saragama* has proven its aesthetic potential primarily as a vehicle for medium-density melody in the *baḍā* [slow-tempo] *khayāla*. Its use in low-density and high-density melody is limited and acceptable. Its occasional use in ultra-high density melody is pregnant with unmusical results. [Also see: **Khayāla, Baḍā Khayāla, Dhrupad, Ṭhumarī**].

Saroda : A member of the short-necked fretless lute family of plucked instruments. The *saroda* has two identifiable ancestors — a Persian instrument called *rabāba* which came to India around the eleventh century, and the Kābulī [Afghan] *rabāba,* which came to India around the thirteenth century. The art of the *rabāba* received great support from the Mogul court [fifteenth-eighteenth centuries]. The present physical form of the *saroda* evolved from the *rabāba* and the *surasiṅgāra* in the early part of the twentieth century. In the latter half of the twentieth century, the most eminent exponents of the instrument have beena Ustad Ali Akbar Khan and Pandit Radhika Mohan Maitra. [Also see: **Surasiṅgāra, Rabāba**] Refer Chapter 5.4.

Sarodīya : A musician who performs on the *saroda* [Also see: **Saroda**] Refer Chapter 5.4.

Ṣaḍava : The word describes hexatonic *rāga*s [those that deploy six tones/*svara*s]. The description does not double-count a tone/*svara* if the *rāga* uses the natural as well as its suppressed or enhanced microtones. In this classification, the ascent and the descent are considered together. However, *rāga*s may be described by dual classifications such as *ṣaḍava-sampūrṇa* if, for instance, they are hexatonic in the ascent and heptatonic in the descent. [Also see: **Catusvara, Auḍava, Sampūrṇa**].

Śānta : See **Rasa/Navarasa**.

Senīya : Seniya is an adjective derived from the name of the legendary sixteenth century musician, Miyā Tānsen. It is used to describe his genealogical as well as stylistic heirs. The Senīya lineage is represented in vocal music, music of the *rudra vīṇā,* and also its successors amongst the plucked lutes, the *saroda* and the *sitāra.* There are occasional references to a *Senīya gharānā* as a distinctive lineage with identifiable stylistic features preserved through several generations of musicians. In the contemporary environment, however, these claims appear untenable. [Also see: **Miyā Tānsen, Gharānā**].

Śehnāī : The word probably derives from Persian *śāha* = king + *nāī* = pipe. The instrument played in India is, however, almost certainly of Indian origin. The instrument belongs to the oboe family of beating-reed aerophones. It has the status of the most preferred instrument at religious ceremonies and public functions. As such, it could be the single most widely heard instrument in India. In this traditional role, the *śehnāī* addresses involuntary audiences of indeterminate profile in terms of aesthetic cultivation. Consequently, its traditional repertoire has been dominated by regional and folk genres of music. In the latter half of the twentieth century, Ustad Bismillah Khan, who remains its tallest exponent, elevated the instrument to the art music platform. The instrument is heading for extinction, as the ceremonial market moves towards pre-recorded music, brass-bands and orchestral ensembles, and the film/popular music industry — once its major client — goes electronic. Refer Chapter 5.6.

Śiṣya : See **Guru-Śiṣya Paramparā.**

Sitāra : A member of the long-necked fretted lute family of plucked instruments. Theory crediting its origins to a Persian instrument called "Sehtār" [lit: three strings] and its adaptation in the thirteenth century by Ameer Khusro, are no longer tenable. Instruments of this variety have existed all over India for centuries before Ameer Khusro. Latest research attributes the systematic development of the instrument to Fakir Khusro Khan [eighteenth century], the brother of Niamat Khan Sadarang, a landmark figure in the evolution of the *khayāla* genre of vocalism. In the second half of the twentieth century, the most distinguished exponents of the *sitāra* are: Ustad Vilayat Khan, Pandit Ravi Shankar, Pandit Nikhil Bannerjee, and Ustad Abdul Haleem Jaffar Khan. Refer Chapter 5.2.

Śiva/Maheśa : The destroyer of the universe in Hindu mythology. [Also see: **Trimūrti**]

Sparśa : See **Kaṇa/Sparśa.**

Śṛṅgāra : See **Rasa/Navarasa.**

Sthāyī : The word is Sanskrit for "stable/immoveable." The *sthāyī* in a *bandiśa* functions as the core of the *bandiśa* as well as the entire rendition, including the improvisatory movements. It is the nucleus around which the presentation revolves, and is the refrain to which the musician returns intermittently between rounds of improvization. The *sthāyī* is generally anchored either in the lower half of the melodic canvas, or in that region of it, in which falls the *rāga*'s melodic centre of gravity. As the core of the pre-composed *bandiśa*, the *sthāyī* generally identifies the *rāga* beyond reasonable doubt, though some *sthāyī*s are deliberately oblique in this respect.

Improvisatory movements also have their *sthāyī* and *antarā* sections. In this context, the *sthāyī* performs a similar, though not identical, melodic-aesthetic function, as in the *bandiśa*. The improvisatory movements follow a linear rather than cyclical logic. Therefore, the *sthāyī* does not function as a refrain for intermittent repetition. The improvisatory movements are, instead, subjected to a discipline of progression. The *sthāyī* of an improvisatory movement is centred categorically in the lower half of the melodic canvas. It is required to commence with improvisations around base-*sa* [the tonic/fundamental], to descend first into the lower octave, and then ascend to the scalar midpoint in deliberate steps. [Also see: **Bandiśa, Antarā, Sañcārī, Ābhoga**]. Refer Chapter 2.1.

Sthāyī, Antarā, Sañcārī, Ābhoga : These are names of distinct phases in the *rāga* exposition protocol prescribed for sequential rendition aimed at the satisfactory communication of a *rāga*'s melodic and emotional personality in Hindustani music. In the sixteenth century, the legendary Miyā Tānsen enunciated them as rules of composition for *dhrupad padas* [*bandiśas*] consisting of four stanzas of verse each. The soundness of their aesthetic logic caused them to be accepted as guiding principles also for the melodic structuring and sequencing of the improvisatory component of art music. These principles are respected, to this day, in the *dhrupad* as well as post-*dhrupad* genres, though with some telescoping of protocol. The last two movements — the *sañcārī* and *ābhoga* — have been dropped from music in the post-*dhrupad* genres. In the *ālāpa* movement in vocal as well as instrumental music, the four-part protocol is still respected. [Also see: **Miyā Tānsen, Pada, Bandiśa, Sthāyī, Antarā, Sañcārī, Ābhoga, Ālāpa**]. Refer Chapter 2.1.

Śuddha [with reference to *svara*/tone] : The word derives from Sanskrit *śuddha* = pure. The Hindustani scale consists of seven natural tones/*svaras*, plus mutations representing either suppressed or enhanced frequencies of five of them. The seven natural tones are called *śuddha* [pure], the suppressed tones are called *komala*, Sanskrit for "soft," while the solitary enhanced tone is called *tīvra*, Sanskrit for "sharp." The Hindustani scale deploys *komala*/suppressed mutations/frequencies of the 2nd, 3rd, 6th, and 7th degrees [*re, gā, dhā, nī*] and a *tīvra*/sharp mutation of the 4th [*mā*]. [Also see: **Komala, Tīvra**]

Śuddha [with respect to rāgas] : The word is Sanskrit for the adjective "pure/unalloyed." The word is used to describe a *rāga*, when performed in consonance with its melodic grammar as currently recognized, without making any deliberate attempt at either its tonal/melodic enhancement, or at introducing melodic features of other *rāgas* into it. A *śuddha rāga* is definitely not either an allotrope of a *rāga*, or a compound or emulsion of more than two or more *rāgas*. Allotropes, compounds, and emulsions have no accepted *rāga* grammar, and provide considerable creative freedom to the musician. This is the context and rigorous adjectival meaning in which this book has used the term, except when naming *rāgas* with the word *śuddha* prefixed to them. When used as a prefix to a proper-noun, the prefix *śuddha* can have a variety of connotations other than the lexicographic adjectival sense. Refer Chapter 3.2.

Śuṣka Vādya : The term derives from Sanskrit *śuṣka* = dry/lifeless + *vādya* = musical instrument. This epithet is used to describe instruments which are considered incapable of solo performance, and are permitted a role only either as accompaniments to vocal music, or in orchestral ensembles. This classification is not organological, but arbitrary, and valid only in the historical context in which it is given. At one stage [around the sixteenth century], even the venerable *rudra vīṇā*, the precursor and stylistic parent of the contemporary plucked lutes, was considered a *śuṣka vādya*. Today, in view of the sophistication of the solo idiom of the *rudra vīṇā*, it is impossible to sympathize with this description. [Also see: **Rudra Vīṇā**].

Sūta : See **Ghasīṭa/Sūtā.**

Sūfīānā Mauṣiqī : The term derives its meaning from Persian *sufiānā* = of the Sūfī sects + *maushiqui* = music. It defines a genre of music practiced in the Persia/Kashmir/Afghanistan region, is based on the poetry of the Islamic Sūfī sects, and is rendered in consonance with the principles enshrined in their philosophy. These renderings are accompanied either by the *rabāba* or by the *Santūra*, both instruments of percussive-melodic character. [Also see: **Rabāba, Santūra**]

Sulatāla: *Sulatāla* is a *tāla* of ten beats with five equal sub-divisions of two beats each. It is ideally suited for fast-tempo rendition. It is an integral part of the repertoire of the *dhrupad/dhamāra* genre of art music. It is rarely, if ever, heard in other vocal genres or in instrumental music.

Sultān : See **Mahārājā/Nawāb/Zamīndār/Sultān.**

Sur Paraṇ : See **Paraṇ/Sur Paraṇ/Tāra Paraṇ.**

Sur Śehnāī : A member of the beating-reed Oboe family of instruments. It is used as a drone accompaniment to a *śehnāī* recital, either along with a *tānapūrā* or even exclusively. In design and construction, it is identical to the *śehnāī*, the only difference being it has only one hole punched into its stem for delivering a single *svara*/tone/pitch, which is the tonic to which the lead-*śehnāī* player's *śehnāī* is tuned.

Surabahāra : A member of the long-necked fretted lute family of plucked instruments. The *surabahāra* is a bass-*sitāra*, near-identical in construction to the *sitāra*, though enlarged to scale. The invention of the *surabahāra*, around 1825, is attributed variously to Ustad Sahebdad Khan, great grandfather of the contemporary *sitāra* maestro, Ustad Vilayat Khan, and to a lesser-known *sitārist*, Ustad Ghulam Mohammed. The latest research favours the latter attribution. *Sitārist*s conceived the instrument for presenting the prefatory *ālāpa-joḍa-jhālā* movements, derived from the idiom of the *rudra vīṇā* [*bīna*]. With recent developments in the acoustic capabilities of the *sitāra*, the *surabahāra* is heading for extinction. The most distinguished exponents of the instrument in the latter half of the twentieth century have been Ustad Mushtaque Ali Khan and Ustad Imrat Khan. [Also see: **Sitāra, Ālāpa, Joḍa, Jhālā**] Refer Chapter 5.3.

Sursiṅgāra : *Sursiṅgāra* is a member of the short-necked fretless lute family of plucked instruments. It represents a short-lived late-nineteenth century attempt at driving the acoustic and melodic capabilities of the Afghan *rabāba* closer to that of the *rudra vīṇā*. The most significant version grafted a *surabahāra*-style chamber-resonator at the bottom, to a *rabāba*-style fingerboard, along with a *rudra vīṇā* type chamber-resonator at the top. It was a cumbersome instrument to play and was suited, like the *surabahāra*, only for prefatory movements. After surrendering its most promising design features to the *saroda*, the instrument faded into history. [Also see: **Rudra Vīṇā, Saroda, Rabāba, Surbahāra**] Refer Chapter 5.1.

Suṣīra : *Suṣīra* is one of the five primary classifications of musical instruments in Indian organology. It represents instruments with holes in them. These classifications are independent of the technique of sound activation and technique of melodic execution. The *suṣīra* category corresponds to aerophones in Western organology.

Svara/Tone : The word derives from Sanskrit *sva* = self + *ra* = illumination. *Svara* is, therefore, an utterance expressing the entirety of the practitioner's being, and has the potential for personality transformation. Though an avowedly subjective expression, it necessarily has certain known and measurable acoustic features. However, the Indian musical tradition also identifies two features, which pose conceptual problems. The Sanskrit texts do not define the terms for them, which are almost impossible to translate. The qualities are *dīpti*, loosely translated as luminosity, and *anūraṇan*, loosely translated as a haunting quality. Clarity on these dimensions may have to await either an acoustically meaningful translation of these terms, or their recognition as hitherto unknown/unmeasured acoustic dimensions. This brief etymological-acoustic discussion supports the growing realization that, *svara* in Hindustani music does not correspond efficiently to the Western notion of tone or a pitch-ratio relative to the tonic.

The Hindustani scale has twelve *svara*s, all of which acquire musical meaning only with reference to the tonic, arbitrarily chosen by the musician. These twelve *svara*s have names. But, the existence of standard frequency ratios for eleven of them, relative to the tonic, is debatable. Nor is it clear that their musical values depends upon the existence of such standardized acoustic relationships. There could, in reality, be stronger evidence to support the opposite argument — that their musical value depends precisely on the freedom the musician has to intone them in accordance with aesthetic, rather than acoustic, principles. This is particularly so since, as a rule, Hindustani music eschews staccato intonation.

This is consistent with the crucial difference between the Hindustani and the Western scales The Western scale is an octave with eight fixed points, while the Hindustani scale is a *saptaka* with seven intervals covering the same tonal distance. Music making activity in Hindustani music is focused on the handling of intervals, while Western tradition focuses its attention on handling the tonal points.

The issue here is, in fact, philosophical and cultural more than acoustic. Any cultural manifestation can be held accountable only to its own goals and values. The primary values of the Indian musical tradition are spiritual, with the aesthetic and the sensory being subservient to it. In the hierarchy of music-making goals, the primary place belongs to the generation of *rasa* at the highest possible level of intensity. A musician shapes and re-shapes *rāga*s in order to achieve the *rasa* goal. In the process, he also arranges and re-arranges relationships between the individual units of melodic expression, the *svara*s. The amorphous character of *rāga*s and the floating pitch values in Hindustani music are an essential part of a tradition that gives the musician the combined role of a composer-performer, requiring both these processes to be performed simultaneously. The *rāga* and the *svara* both have only ephemeral validity as the stimuli of an interactive process validated solely by its generation of the target emotional response, the *rasa*. [Also see: **Saptaka, Rāga**]

Svarāśrita : The term derives its meaning from Sanskrit *svara* = tone/ melody + *āśrita* = dependent on. The term describes a genre of music dominated by the melodic element. To a lesser or greater extent, every musical genre is *svarāśrita*. The term acquires greater meaning when in conjunction with other dimensions. The *dhrupad* genre is, for instance, *padāśrita* and *svarāśrita*, while the *tarānā* genre may be considered *svarāśritā* and *layāśrita* [*laya* = tempo + *āśrita* = dependent upon]. [Also see: **Dhrupad, Padāśrita, Tarānā**]

Svaramaṇḍala : The instrument is a member of the harp family and belongs to the box-polychord variety of plucked instruments. It is used as an accompaniment to vocal renditions of the *khayāla* and *ṭhumarī* genres. Unlike the *sāraṅgī* or the *harmonium*, on which melody is executed, the *svaramaṇḍala* is only strummed intermittently as a filler of silences. The strumming is done bi-directionally with grown finger nails, or guitar-style metallic or plastic picks. The instrument is not a replacement for a *tānapūrā*, and may be used either in addition to a melodic accompaniment, or exclusively. In the 1950s, the towering vocalist, Ustad Bade Ghulam Ali Khan popularized its use, to be followed on a substantial scale by vocalists of the succeeding generations. The *svaramaṇḍala* is, however, not as universally used for vocal accompaniment as is the *tānapūrā*. Attempts at establishing it as a solo instrument for playing melody have been isolated and futile. [Also see: **Tānapūrā**].

Tabalā : Though the name resembles a middle eastern drum called *tabalā*, the *tabalā* is a uniquely Indian instrument. The *tabalā* came into being when the *pakhāwaj/mr̥daṅga*, the ancient tapering barrel drum, was split half-way in order to make the instrument easier to play. Historicity of event remains vague. The bass drum is played by the left hand, while the treble, by the right. Both drums are covered with goat-skin membranes. Both drums have a coating of iron-filings and carbon permanently affixed on the membranes. This coating is affixed in the center of the treble drum and off-centre on the bass drum. The bass drum is made of metal, while the treble drum is made of wood. The *tabalā* is now standard percussion accompaniment to all vocal and instrumental genres of Hindustani [north Indian] music, other than *dhrupad*, folk and some popular genres. [Also see: **Pakhāwaj**]

Tabalā Taraṅga : The term is derived by linking two words : *tabalā* = the treble drum of the *tabalā* = pair + *taraṅga* = waves. It describes a polychord of the struck variety, consisting of 12-15 treble drums, each tuned to a different tone/*svara* of the *rāga* scale. It is the only Indian instrument to deploy a percussion instrument, or a part of it, to produce melody. Unlike other struck polychords, the *tabalā taraṅga* is struck with the bare hands rather than mallets or sticks. The instrument has survived primarily on its rare use in film and orchestral music. Only one living exponent of competence is known to exist [in December 2003].

Tāla : The word derives from the Hindī *tāla* = sound of clapping with the hands. It originated in the ancient practice of keeping time with the clapping of hands, or tapping on the thighs to the accompaniment of recitations of Sanskrit hymns. Such a practice was necessary because the hymns were composed to standard metres prescribed by the literary tradition, and their poetic integrity could be preserved only by recitation at a specific tempo. In musical usage, the same function is performed by a rhythmic cycle performed on percussion instruments. Each *tāla* is a rhythmic cycle defined by its distinctive number of beats, sound symbols for percussion impact and beat-subdivisions representing its cadence. Each *tāla* also has a tempo — or a range of tempi — at which it is appropriately deployed. The *tāla* also defines the metric structure of the *bandiśa*, and regulates the cyclical component of the improvisatory movements woven around it. [Also see: **Bandiśa**].

Tālavādya Aṅga : See **Aṅga [Gāyakī, Tālavādya, Tantakāra/Tata]**.

Tānas : In contemporary usage, *tāna* refers to high-density melodic patterns in the *khayāla* genre and post-*dhrupad* instrumental music. A melodic passage may be described as a *tāna* only if its *svara*/ tone density is at least twice the beat-density [tempo] of the rendition at that particular stage in the presentation of percussion-accompanied music. As a general principle, a melodic run exceeding a *svara*/tone density of four intonations per second can be called a *tāna*. In consonance with the prescribed architecture of the modern genres, *tāna*s are rendered after the rendition has passed through the presentation of low-density and medium-density improvisatory movements. Even within the high-density *tāna*s phase of the rendition, it is considered proper for the musician to observe certain principles of logical sequencing.

Though *tāna*s are essentially a display of technical virtuosity, their melodic construction is subject to the constraints of *rāga*-grammar, and their *svara*/tone density is constrained by the requirements of musicality. It is finally the melodic imagination that goes into the construction of *tāna*s, rather than their speed, that distinguishes the truly great musician from the merely competent. The imagination works — though with varying degrees of success, no doubt — with a few basic melodic patterns which constitute the raw material of *tāna*s. Some frequently recurring patterns in *tāna*s are: [a] *baḍhata*, [b] *laḍīguthāva*, [c] *sapāṭa*, [d] *chūṭa*, [e] *alaṅkāra*, [f] hopping. [Also see: **Khayāla, Baḍhata Tānas, Laḍīguthāva Tānas, Sapāṭa Tānas, Chūṭa Tānas, Alaṅkāra Tānas**] Refer Chapter 4.2.

Tānapūrā : The word derives from Hindī *tāna* = a musical phrase/ melodic line + Sanskrit *pūraka* = filler/supplement. This etymology defines its function in Hindustani music. It supplements the aural experience and supports the musician's creative effort. It performs primarily a drone function as an accompaniment to music of all genres of vocal as well instrumental Hindustani art music. The instrument is standard accompaniment to vocal music, but optional in instrumental music. The instrument is a member of the long-necked family of fretless plucked lutes. In musicological texts, oblique references to it are available from the thirteenth century, while unambiguous references exist from the seventeenth century. The instrument has four, five, or six strings tuned to the middle octave and lower-octave tonic chosen by the musician, along with supplementary strings tuned to corresponding/ dominant pitches as permitted by *rāga* grammar. Unlike the *svaramaṇḍala*, which is strummed only intermittently, the *tānapūrā* is plucked continuously during a performance. However, like the *svaramaṇḍala*, the *tānapūrā* does not execute melody. Both are designed for a tonally blurred acoustic output, which shapes the acoustic ambience. The *tānapūrā* is, however, valued more for its psycho-acoustic influence on the auto-suggestive and creative processes of the musician, than for the enrichment of the aural experience for listeners. [Also see: **Svararamaṇḍala**]

Tantakāra/Tata Aṅga : See **Aṅga [Gāyakī, Tālavādya, Tantakāra/ Tata].**

Ṭappā : The *ṭappā* is a modern semi-classical genre of vocal music. It owes its inspiration to the songs of the camel-drivers of Punjab and India's north-western frontiers. Originally a folk form, later adopted by courtesans, it was accepted in genteel society by the late seventeenth century. The pioneering role in the refinement of the genre is attributed to Ghulam Nabi, a late eighteenth-century vocalist from Lucknow, who composed under the pseudonym "Shorie Miya." The genre was enthusiastically adopted thereafter by *khayāla* as well as *ṭhumarī* singers. The identifying feature of the *ṭappā* is a vivacious, even mischievous, treatment of melody. The treatment is not only naughty within itself, but also in relation to the beat patterns of the rhythmic cycle. Like the semi-classical *ṭhumarī* genre, the *ṭappā* is also heading for extinction, though it has a better chance of a revival than the former. [Also see: **Ṭhumarī**] Refer Chapter 4.4.

Ṭap-Khayāla : The *ṭap-khayāla* is a sub-genre of the *khayāla* genre vocal music. It superimposes the mischievous treatment of melody characteristic of the *ṭappā* genre on to *khayāla* compositions, guiding the improvisatory movements towards a similar direction. [Also see: **Khayāla, Ṭappā**]

Tāra Paraṇ : See **Paraṇ/Sur Paraṇ/Tāra Paraṇ.**

Tāra Saptaka : The term derives from Sanskrit *tāra* = higher frequencies + *saptaka* = a group of seven tones/*svaras*. The term describes the higher octave of the melodic canvas. The octave above the higher octave [the ultra-higher] is frequently described as the *ati-tāra* [ultra-high] *saptaka*. While the Western tradition considers the scale as consisting of eight tonaı points, the Indian system treats the same distance as consisting of seven frequency intervals. Hence, the reference to the scale as seven, rather than eight. This highlights a fundamental cultural difference. The act of music-making in Indian music is focused on the handling of tonal intervals and transitions rather than the tonal point themselves.

Tarānā : The *tarānā* [etymology speculative] is a genre of vocal music, which uses meaningless consonants as articulatory material, instead of the poetic form. Though the contemporary *tarānā* falls broadly within the *khayāla* genre, the use of meaningless consonants is much older than the *khayāla* genre. These consonants are drawn primarily from the sound symbols used in the "language" of percussion [*dha, dhin, tirkit*, etc.] and the plucked lute family of instruments [*da, ra, dir*, etc.]. The occasional use of *nom-tom* phonemes used in *dhrupad* is also encountered in *tarānā* compositions. *Tarānā*s are composed in all *rāga*s and all *tāla*s, and generally performed in medium and fast tempi. The rendition of *tarānā*s is much like the *choṭā khayāla*, though usually without virtuoso *tāna*s. [Also see: **Khayāla, Choṭā Khayāla, Nom Tom, Dhrupad, Tānas**]

Tāśā/Nagārā : The *tāśā* and the *nagārā* belong to the family of indigenous kettle-drums used as rhythmic accompaniment to the *śehnāī*. The shell of these drums was originally formed on a potter's wheel, but later cast in metal — mainly copper or a copper alloy. The drums come in pairs of pan-like vessels, covered with a membrane of goat skin. Though their sound is atonal, one is a bass drum, while the other — the smaller — is a treble drum. They are struck with sticks. In addition to their role as accompaniment to the *śehnāī*, they have also enjoyed an independent adrenalin-pumping and heralding function in military ceremonies of the feudal era, either on their own, or in conjunction with other ceremonial instruments such as the Indian bugles and trumpets. Though played with sticks, the *tāśā* and *nagārā* have evolved a sophisticated idiom, which has also influenced the idiom of the *tabalā*, an instrument of far superior musical capability played with bare hands. [Also see: **Śehnāī, Tabalā**]

Tata : *Tata* is one of the classifications of musical instruments in Indian organology. The word represents all instruments with strings, irrespective of technique of sound activation and technique of melodic execution.

Tatāvanaddha [*also called Vitata*]: *Tatāvanaddha* is one of the five primary classifications of musical instruments in Indian organology. The term is derived from the Sanskrit *tata* = stringed + *avanaddha* = covered with a membrane. This category covers a small group of instruments, mainly short-necked lutes of the plucked variety such as *rabāba* and *saroda*, and of the bowed variety, such as the *sāraṅgī*. [Also see: **Tata, Rabāba, Saroda, Sāraṅgī**]

Ṭhekā : Every *tāla* [rhythmic cycle] played on the *tabalā* or *pakhāwaj* is defined by sound syllables representing the strokes on the two surfaces of the drums. These sound syllables and corresponding stroke patterns represent the internal arrangement of sub-divisions and cadences characteristic of the *tāla*. This standard form of the *tāla*, without any improvization or stylization, is called the *ṭhekā*. Several *tāla*s have *ṭhekā* variants. The immensely popular *tīnatāla*/*tritāla*, for instance, has stylized variants variously called *addhā ṭhekā*, *Punjābī ṭhekā* and *qawwālī ṭhekā*. [Also see: **Tāla, Tīnatāla/Tritāla**].

Ṭhumarī : The word derives from an onomatopoetic expression *ṭhumakā*, signifying the sound of anklet bells of a dancer. The *ṭhumarī* is a modern genre of semi-classical music, which originated as an accompaniment to the *Kathaka* genre of north Indian dance, and evolved into an independent art form. The genre subsumes two sub-genres — a brisk and lively form called *bandiśa ṭhumarī*, and a leisurely sentimental form called *bola-banāo ṭhumarī*. The thematic content of the genre revolves around the mythical romance between Lord Kṛṣṇa, an incarnation of Lord Viṣṇu, and his paramour, Rādhā. In the cult of Rādhā and Kṛṣṇa, the romance is viewed as a metaphor for the intimate relationship between God, representing the male/active principle, and man representing the female/passive principle. The *bandiśa ṭhumarī* reached its zenith in the mid-nineteenth century and was nearly extinct by the early twentieth century. The *bola-banāo ṭhumarī* acquired the status of a mainstream genre in the early twentieth century, and is now headed for extinction. [Also see: **Bandiśa Ṭhumarī, Bola-banāo Ṭhumarī**]. Refer Chapter 4.3.

Tigun/Triguṇa : The word derives its meaning from *tri* or *ti* = three + *guṇa* = multiple. When any melody is performed at a melodic [tone] density three times the beat density [tempo] of accompanying percussion, or the base tempo of the *bandiśa*, the expression is called *triguṇa/tigun*. The highest ratio of tone-density to beat-density practiced in Hindustani music is eight times. [Also see: **Bandiśa**].

Tihāyī : The word derives from the Hindī *tīna* = three. The repetitive iteration of any melodic, rhythmic melodic-rhythmic, or choreographic pattern exactly three times is called a *tihāyī*. Its purpose is to create rhythmic interest by building up and releasing aesthetic tension within a very short period of time, normally less than a minute. The triplet form which probably originated in the choreographic art, was mimicked by the percussion art which accompanied it and finally found its way into melodic expression. The *tihāyī* is a rhythmic expression which may be interpreted choreographically, rhythmically, or melodically. The number of iterations in a *tihāyī* [three] has a very definite aesthetic significance, which cannot be fulfilled by any other number of iterations of the pattern. [Also see: **Sama**] Refer Chapter 2.4.

Tilwāḍā : *Tilwāḍā* is a *tāla* [rhythmic cycle] of sixteen beats in four equal sub-divisions. It is suited for slow and ultra slow rendition in the *khayāla* genre of vocal music. The *tilwāḍā* tempo rarely exceeds 20 beats per minute.

Tīnatāla [also called Tritāla] : *Tīnatāla* is a *tāla* [rhythmic cycle] of sixteen beats in four equal subdivisions. It is the single most popular *tāla* of Hindustani [north Indian] art music, more particularly in instrumental music. The primary reason for its popularity is its tested amenability to rendition at virtually any tempo — from 30 beats per minute to over 500 beats per minute. Stylized or dented versions of the *tīnatāla* — *addhā ṭhekā, qawwālī ṭhekā* and *Punjābī ṭhekā* — are used in the *ṭhumarī* genre.

Tīvra [with respect to svara/tone] : The word derives from Sanskrit *tīvra* = sharp/strident. The Hindustani scale consists of seven natural tones, plus mutations representing either suppressed or enhanced frequencies of five of the seven tones. The seven natural tones are called *śuddha*, the suppressed tones are called *komala*, Sanskrit for "Soft," while the solitary enhanced tone is called *tīvra*, Sanskrit for "Sharp." The Hindustani scale deploys *komala*/ suppressed mutations/frequencies of the 2nd, 3rd, 6th, and 7th degrees [*re, gā, dhā, nī*] and a *tīvra*/sharp mutation of the 4th [*mā*]. [Also see: **Śuddha, Komala**]

Trimūrti : The word derives its meaning from Sanskrit *tri* = three + *mūrti* = manifestation. It refers to the Holy Trinity of Hindu mythology — Brahmā Viṣṇu and Maheśa/Śiva. They are conceived as a collective entity because they are regarded as manifestations of the Divine Power. Of the three, Viṣṇu enjoys the most frequent and intimate involvement with human affairs, followed by Maheśa, and Brahmā, in that order. [Also see: **Brahmā, Viṣṇu, Maheśa**].

Ucita : See **Aucitya/Ucita/Anucita.**

Urdu : A dialect of Hindī, the mainstream north Indian language, with a substantial presence of Persian and Arabic vocabulary, but only minor syntactical influence. The dialect is written in the Persian script. The name derives from the Turkish word "Urd" = the market in a military camp. This suggests its origins amongst settling soldiers from conquering Middle Eastern armies. Unlike Persian, Urdu never became a language of the feudal courts in India. However, the dialect did trigger off a major literary flowering during the colonial era [nineteenth and early twentieth centuries] primarily through the *ghazal* genre. [Also see: **Ghazal**]

Ustād : The word is Persian for a teacher. In the music world, it signifies a Moslem musician of sufficient attainments to qualify as a teacher. A Hindu of comparable attainments is called a *paṇḍit*. In print journalism, it is common to represent the word *paṇḍit* in its abbreviated form *"Pt."* and *ustād* in its abbreviated form as *"Ust."*. No formalized framework exists for conferring such honorifics to musicians. They emerge through an informal process of consensus building within the community of musicians.

Uttarāṅga prādhānya : See **Aṅga prādhānya.**

Vādī/Saṁvādī : *Vādī* is derived from the Sanskrit verb *vada* = to speak. Contextually, *vādī* may be translated as "proponent/ protagonist." *Saṁvādī* derives from *saṁvāda* = dialogue. The *vādī* and *saṁvādī* are the two dominant tones/*svaras* in a *rāga*. The *vādī* is the primary dominant, while the *saṁvādī*, generally in the alternate tetrachord of the scale and in acoustic correspondence with the *vādī*, is the secondary dominant tone/*svara* of the *rāga*. The two, together, form the foci around which the *rāga* exposition revolves. [Also see: **Rāga**] Refer Chapter 3.1.

Vādya : A common noun derived from the Sanskrit verb *vada* = to speak. *Vādya* = that which can speak/can emit a sound. The term is descriptive of all musical instruments.

Vaiṣṇava/Vaiṣṇavite : Adjective derived from the name of Viṣṇu, the Preserver of the universe in Hindu mythology. It is used primarily to describe the code of conduct and ecclesiastical culture associated with the sects devoted to Lord Kr̥ṣṇa, one of the ten incarnations of Viṣṇu. Similarly, cults devoted to Maheśa/Śiva are described as Śaiva or Śaivite. [Also see: **Maheśa, Brahmā**]

Vajrāsana : The word refers to a posture, practised in the science of *yoga*. The word is of Sanskrit derivation. Of its several meanings, the most appropriate in the present context is *vajra* = severe/ hard/demanding + *āsana* = posture. The posture involves sitting on the floor with both knees folded tightly together in front, with the soles of the feet facing in the opposite direction, and buttocks resting on the heels. For its ergonomic efficiency, this was — until recently — the prescribed posture for *rudra vīṇā* players. The posture was probably also considered appropriately reverent for laity in the presence of royalty or in the temples. [Also see: **Yogic**]

Vāna Vīṇā : A member of the box-polychord variety of struck instruments. It is an ancient Indian instrument with a hundred strings, whose description matches the ancient *śatatantrī vīṇā* and the contemporary *santūra*. [Also see: **Santūra, Śatatantrī Vīṇā**]

Vātsalya Rasa : See **Viraha Rasa/Mādhurya Rasa/Vātsalya Rasa.**

Vicitra Vīṇā : A member of the fretless stick-zither family, on which melody is executed by sliding a piece of rounded glass, akin to a paper-weight, along the strings. This instrument is a successor to the ancient *ekatantrī vīṇā*, and a precursor of the Hawaiian slide-guitar. The *vicitra vīṇā* of the Hindustani [north Indian] tradition is identical to the *goṭṭuvādyam* of the Carnatic [south Indian] tradition, now renamed *citra vīṇā*. [Also see: **Ekatantrī Vīṇā, Indian classical guitar**]

Vilaṁbita [or Vilaṁbita laya] : Adjective derived from Sanskrit *vilamba* = delay. In music, it is used to describe slow-tempo rendition. For ultra-slow tempo renditions, the term used is *ati-vilaṁbita* [*ati* = extreme]. The notion of slowness, or briskness, is relative and dynamic. It differs between generations, between stylistic lineages, between different genres of vocal music, and between vocal and instrumental music.

Vīra : See **Rasa/Navarasa.**

Viraha Rasa/Mādhurya Rasa/Vātsalya Rasa : *Viraha* and *mādhurya* are two *rasa*s — outside of the nine *rasa*s in orthodox aesthetic theory — relevant to the lyrics of all the major genres of Hindustani music. *Viraha* is Sanskrit for absence/separation. *Mādhurya* is Sanskrit for the quality of sweetness/tenderness in a human relationship. *Vātsalya* is Sanskrit for maternal/parental sentiment. Conceptually, the three are connected in Indian aesthetic theory.

Viraha rasa is regarded as a compound of *śṛṅgāra rasa* = the romantic sentiment and *karuṇa rasa* = the sentiment of pathos. Poetry of the *viraha rasa* deals with the agony experienced by a woman separated from her beloved. *Mādhurya rasa* = the sweetness/tenderness of feeling, is viewed as a component of *śṛṅgāra rasa*. *Śṛṅgāra* is a compound of *mādhurya* [tenderness] and *kāma* [physical/erotic desire]. Once *mādhurya* has been isolated as an independent emotion, it can be seen as a participant in other compound emotions/sentiments. One such compound is *vātsalya*, the maternal sentiment, of which *mādhurya* is the dominant component. [Also see: **Nāyikā Bheda, Rasa/Navarasa**].

Viṣṇu : The Preserver of the universe in Hindu mythology. [Also see: **Trimūrti**]

Yogic : An adjective derived from the Sanskrit *yoga* = union, representing the ancient Indian science of attaining a state of harmony between the body, mind, and soul.

Zamīndār : See : **Mahārājā/Nawāb/Zamīndāra/Sultān.**

Zamzama : See : **Jamajama/Zamzama.**

SUGGESTED BIBLIOGRAPHY

Musical Aesthetics

Eisenberg, Evan, 1988, *The Recording Angel — the experience of music: From Aristotle to Zappa*, New York: Viking Penguin Inc.

Hanslick, Eduard, 1974, *The Beautiful in Music*, London, New York, Novello, Ewer & Co.

Mathieu, W.A., 1994, *The Musical Life*, Boston : Shambhala Publications.

Meleish, Kenneth [ed.], 1993, *Key Ideas in Human Thought* — Facts on File Inc., New York.

Rao, Suvarnalata, 2000, *Acoustical Perspectives on Raga-Rasa Theory*, Delhi: Munshiram Manoharlal.

Saxena, Sushil Kumar, 2001, *Hindustani Sangeet and a Philosopher of Art Music, Rhythm and Kathaka Dance vis-à-vis Aesthetics of Susanne K Langer*, Delhi, D.K. Printworld.

Seashore, Carl, 1967, *Psychology of Music*, Mineola, NY: Dover Publications.

Stockhausen Karlheinz, 1989, *Towards a Cosmic Music*, Shaftesbury, Dorset, UK: Element Books.

General [Hindustani Music]

Bhatkhande, Vishnu Narayan [Hindi] *Bhatkhande Sangeet Shastra*, vol. I to IV, Hathras, Sangeet Karyalaya.

Garg, Lakshmi Narayan [ed.], 1989, Hindi, *Nibandha Sangeet*, Sangeet Karyalaya, Hathras, UP.

Jaidev Singh, Thakur, 1995, *Indian Music*, Calcutta: Sangeet Research Academy.

Mehta, R.C. [ed.], 1993, *Composition in Hindustani Music*, Baroda: Indian Musicological Society.

Ranade, Ashok D., 1984, *On the music and musicians of Hindoostaan*, Delhi, Promilla & Co.

Ranade, Ashok D., 1993, *Hindustani Music*, Delhi, National Book Trust of India.

Dhrupad/Dhamāra

Raja, Deepak & Rao, Suvarnalata [ed.], 1999, *Perspectives on Dhrupad*, Baroda: Indian Musicological Society.

Srivastava, Indurama, 1980, *Dhrupada — a study of its origin, historical development, structure and present state*, Delhi: Motilal Banarsidass.

Khayāla

Deshpande, Vamanrao H., 1973, *Indian Musical Traditions — An aesthetic study of Gharānās in Hindustani music*, Bombay: Popular Prakashan, 2nd edn. 1987.

Deshpande, Vamanrao H., 1989, *Between Two Tanpuras*, Bombay: Popular Prakashan.

Deodhar, B.R., 1993, *Pillars of Hindustani Music*, Bombay: Popular Prakashan.

Nadkarni, Mohan, 1999, *The great masters — Profiles in Hindustani classical vocal music*, Delhi: Harper Collins.

Wade, Bonnie C., 1984, *Khayāla — creativity within North India's classical music traditions*, London, New York: Cambridge University Press.

Ṭhumarī

Manuel, Peter, 1989, *Ṭhumarī in Historical and Stylistic Perspectives*, Delhi: Motilal Banarasidass.

Sinha, Shatrughna, 1983, *Hindi Ṭhumarī ki utpatti, vikās aur sahiliyan*, Delhi: University of Delhi.

Organology and Instrumental Music

Bor, Joep, 1987, "The Voice of the Sarangi," Bombay: *Journal of the National Centre for the Performing Arts* [vol. XV and XVI, Nos. 3,4,1. Sept-Dec. 1986 and March 1987].

Deva B.C., 1977, *Musical Instruments*, Delhi: National Book Trust of India.

Miner, Allyn, 1997, *Sitar and Sarod in the 18th and 19th centuries*, Delhi: Motilal Banarsidass.

Journals

Journal of the Indian Musicological Society (English Annual), Ambegaokar Building, Jambu Bet, Vadodara 390 001, India.

Sangeet Natak (English quarterly), Sangeet Natak Akademi, Rabindra Bhavan, New Delhi, 110 001, India.

Sruti (English monthly), 10, Kasturi Ranga Road, Chennai, 600 018, India.

INDEX